EMORY UNIVERSITY STUDIES IN LAW AND RELIGION

John Witte Jr., General Editor

BOOKS IN THE SERIES

Faith and Order: The Reconciliation of Law and Religion
Harold J. Berman

Rediscovering the Natural Law in Reformed Theological Ethics
Stephen J. Grabill

The Ten Commandments in History:
Mosaic Paradigms for a Well-Ordered Society
Paul Grimley Kuntz

Theology of Law and Authority in the English Reformation
Joan Lockwood O'Donovan

Suing for America's Soul: John Whitehead, The Rutherford Institute,
and Conservative Christians in the Courts
R. Jonathan Moore

Political Order and the Plural Structure of Society
James W. Skillen and Rockne M. McCarthy

The Idea of Natural Rights:
Studies on Natural Rights, Natural Law, and Church Law, 1150-1625
Brian Tierney

The Fabric of Hope: An Essay
Glenn Tinder

Liberty: Rethinking an Imperiled Ideal
Glenn Tinder

Religious Human Rights in Global Perspective: Legal Perspectives
Johan D. van der Vyver and John Witte Jr.

Early New England: A Covenanted Society
David A. Weir

God's Joust, God's Justice
John Witte Jr.

Religious Human Rights in Global Perspective: Religious Perspectives
John Witte Jr. and Johan D. van der Vyver

LIBERTY

Rethinking an Imperiled Ideal

Glenn Tinder

WILLIAM B. EERDMANS PUBLISHING COMPANY

GRAND RAPIDS, MICHIGAN / CAMBRIDGE, U.K.

Published 2007 by

Wm. B. Eerdmans Publishing Co.

2140 Oak Industrial Drive N.E., Grand Rapids, Michigan 49505 /

P.O. Box 163, Cambridge CB3 9PU U.K.

Printed in the United States of America

12 11 10 09 08 07   7 6 5 4 3 2 1

Library of Congress Cataloging-in-Publication Data

Tinder, Glenn

Liberty: rethinking an imperiled ideal / Glenn Tinder.

p.   cm.   — (Emory University studies in law and religion)

ISBN 978-0-8028-0392-4 (cloth: alk. paper)

1. Liberty — Religious aspects — Christianity.   I. Title.

BT810.3.T56   2007

261.7 — dc22

2007019899

www.eerdmans.com

To my sons,

Evan and Galen

Contents

————◉————

CONTENTS

Contents

CONTENTS

Prologue

———◈———

This is a different kind of book from most that are written today on the subject of liberty. To begin with, it is not scholarly. There is not a single footnote in it, nor do I append a bibliography at the end. It is not that I am lacking in respect for scholarship or for books on liberty, a great many of which I have read repeatedly and studied. It has been my intention, however, to write a book of ideas. This is a work of reflection. As such, it has another characteristic (aside from lack of scholarly apparatus) for which I want to prepare readers. It contains a great many broad generalizations. I try to look at liberty in its entirety, a vast subject, although designated with a small and familiar word. For this I ask the reader's indulgence. I submit that we need to look not only at the trees (which scholars examine) but also at the forest (which is the province of philosophers), and to do that we need to run the heavy risk of generalizing broadly. Finally, I might say that my manner of presentation is conversational rather than systematic. I try to make clear, in the course of the conversation, that there is a coherent structure of ideas taking shape. But I also try to follow the leadings of thought rather than conforming with a prior plan.

The present book is distinctive in content as well as in style, and it may help those who read it for me to remark briefly on its distinguishing themes. One of these is that it combines a rather strong pessimism with an equally strong optimism. I am convinced that what Kant called "radical evil" — a human disposition to do the wrong thing — is a fact.

PROLOGUE

While there have been pessimistic liberals, such as Alexis de Tocqueville, most liberals have been optimists. They have anticipated more or less unambiguous benefits from liberty. I depart emphatically from this tendency. Nonetheless, those who read the book to the end will find arguments to the effect that some of the highest values, such as community, can be pursued and in some measure realized in spite of the radical evil that threatens them. My sense is that simplistic pessimism or optimism, that is, either characteristic in the absence of the other, is shallow.

Another distinguishing theme of the book is associated with its pessimism. If human beings often behave badly, liberty must often have unhappy consequences. Social relations will be more or less deranged. This means in turn that people who withstand the force of radical evil will often find themselves more or less alone, perhaps even hated. Those who, while far from saints, are merely strong protagonists of liberty and practitioners of the communality that is the whole point of liberty, may have few companions. Society as a whole, even if structured by a liberal constitution, may follow practices and indulge in emotions unfavorable to liberty and to the communicative life to which liberty opens the way. Hence a serious liberal must be prepared to stand alone, doing everything possible to safeguard general liberty and live the life proper to liberty, while granting others the attention without which liberty merely brings social disintegration. Accordingly, the axis of the book is chapter 6, entitled "The Liberal Stance." This chapter is about the political art and the moral posture inherent in standing fast on the side of liberty. This is individualism of a kind. But it is a communal individualism. The only proper way of standing fast is through fidelity to one's fellow human beings, to values such as truth, and perhaps to transcendence, or God.

A final distinctive characteristic of the book I mention with fear and trembling. I write from a Christian point of view, and I argue and assume at various points that Christianity contains truths — for example, about human nature — that everyone, regardless of religious or irreligious orientation, should seriously consider. I mention this fact with apprehension because I know that a religious commitment arouses profound suspicions in many minds — among these the minds of people I respect and with whom I would like to converse. Hence I am fearful of obscuring the fact that I strongly believe in reason, as well as in the major tenets of traditional Christian faith. I consider myself a Socratic and Kantian Christian. Further, I believe that we reason well, and allow reason to fulfill its part in our common lives, only when we reason together. Truth is not something we create, nor do we simply summon it when we wish to do so. It is given to us, perhaps as an idea that unexpectedly strikes us, perhaps as one of the paradigms through which science progresses, perhaps through an artist's vision, or perhaps through the transporting insight usually called "revelation" by those who accept it. This implies that we normally learn the truth by hearing it from one another. So we must pay attention and must speak. Communication is a primary human work and is a work of reason. This all makes it clear, I hope, that my Christian orientation is far from the bigotry that many fear when any particular religious persuasion is represented in the realm of public communication.

It may be in order, finally, to alert readers to the central dilemma in the book and, I believe, the central dilemma in any philosophy of liberty. Is liberty to be understood as simply not being interfered with, or as being free of the inner entanglements and iniquities that make us miserable? Is a liberal society mainly one that removes unnecessary restrictions or one that guides people into a fulfilling life? I argue emphatically on the former side — in favor of what is often called "negative liberty." But positive liberty will not allow itself to be entirely shut out of reflections on liberty. If our inner demons could never be cast out and happiness were absolutely unattainable, liberty would be purposeless. Major efforts have thus been directed toward opening the door a crack without allowing the idea of positive liberty to enter the room and, as it is wont to do, lay waste to everything most of us mean by liberty.

These comments may not cohere very readily in the mind of the reader. I hope they do by the end of the book. There is an image drawn from the Bible, however, that nicely symbolizes my sense of the state of human beings possessed of liberty. It is that of the Israelites in the wilderness. The early Jewish tribes were a liberated people, having been freed from the tyranny of the Egyptian pharaoh. On gaining their liberty, however, they did not enter directly into the Promised Land. Rather they embarked on a long and harsh sojourn in the wilderness. During their decades in the wilderness their lives were torn by human evil and natural hardships. They were not, of course, simply overwhelmed with misery and hopelessness. Good things happened, such as the bestowal of the law. Above all other good things, however, was this: they were guided at night by a pillar of fire. Their lives — the lives of a liberated people — were not pleasurable or righteous, but they were nevertheless guided by light, or truth. Liberty brought them into a wilderness but it also set before them the pillar of fire. This vision is carried into Christian scripture. Jesus, at the end of his forty days in the wilderness, is tempted by the devil to offer his followers bread, or perfect material security; miracles, or public spectacles calculated to paralyze their minds; and the bliss, through submission to an absolute authority, of relief from all moral responsibility. Had Jesus acquiesced in these temptations, he would have banished the wilderness — by depriving the Israelites of their liberty. But he refused the temptations. He left men and women with their liberty and, according to the Gospel of John, himself became the light shining in the darkness. This story tells us a great deal, I think, both about Christianity and about liberty.

CHAPTER 1

Liberty, Faith, and Reason

Liberty: The Ideal and the Reality

The great issue of the twentieth century was liberty. This was the issue that made the conflict between totalitarianism and constitutional democracy, in World War II and the Cold War, a moral drama. It made an era of savage conflict among nations something more than a mere struggle for power. As we contemplate the turmoil of the world at the outset of the third millennium, the fate of liberty is the foremost concern of many minds. Can liberty be preserved in a spiritual setting being steadily transformed by the interpenetration of diverse civilizations? Can it be preserved amid conditions, both spiritual and physical, that are changing ceaselessly under the impact of technological development? Is popular culture undermining the spiritual resources on which liberty depends? Such questions occur to all serious people.

It is not only the present age, however, that derives its meaning from the standard of liberty. Past ages as well are apt to be read in the light of that standard. Ancient Athens stands out not only because philosophy and literature flourished there, but also because it was a free society. The political philosophy of Aristotle attracts us partly because it seems to sketch the kind of institutional order required by liberty. Rome commands interest for numerous reasons, but none is more compelling than the law, which was to play so vital a role in the development of liberty in later ages. When we look at the Middle Ages, we par-

1

ticularly notice universities, parliaments, courts, and other institutions that in coming centuries were to buttress the structures of liberty. And we readily conceive of the history of the modern period, stretching from the Renaissance and Reformation to the Enlightenment, in terms of the unfoldment of liberty.

Why all this is so, however, why liberty occupies so central a place in our minds, is not very clear. It is fair to say that liberty has not been a manifest success, even though it emerged victorious from some signal international conflicts. In the latter part of the twentieth century it gave rise to widespread conditions, like use of drugs, breakdown of families, a degraded popular culture, preoccupation with money, and drastic economic and social inequalities, that call into question the very worth of our civilization. An observant and reasonable person might well ask why we should greatly care about liberty. Hasn't it proven to be, at very best, merely one among several competing preferences and values? Why accentuate liberty rather than authority, or wisdom, or justice, or some other time-honored concept of the good?

It can be argued with great plausibility that liberty leads inevitably toward a degraded society. Left free to shape their own lives, people are sure to choose pleasure rather than virtue, entertainment rather than beauty, and sentimentality rather than wisdom. The spectacular and melodramatic will be preferred to the subtle and sublime. Talk of true value and the moral law will be regarded suspiciously, as threatening every person's right to live as he pleases. Intellect, even among writers and university professors, will be unable to stand against the doubts occurring to the best minds and cultivated and proclaimed by the worst.

And not only will culture decline. So will justice. It was common in the nineteenth century to assume that once liberty became general, maintaining a reasonable degree of equality would be easy. Wealth, privilege, and power would be equalized spontaneously. Indeed, leveling would almost inevitably be carried so far that adequate recognition of superior performance, and political and economic efficiency, would be undermined. But this expectation, for better or for worse, has proven to be groundless. Under the conditions of advanced industrialism, moneyed minorities easily induce free people, through proffered pleasures, recreation, and other diversions, to acquiesce in drastic economic, social, and political inequalities. A free society, it has become apparent, is apt to take the form of a moneyed oligarchy.

Why, then, should liberty be so highly esteemed? Is guarding liberty really the chief task before us? These questions have no obvious answer. Liberty surely is not more important than serious art and literature, or than highly developed philosophy and religion, or than rectitude of life and conduct. If in accordance with the classical triad we take the highest values to be truth, beauty, and goodness, we must ask whether liberty that strays from these ends — as it does continually in a free society — has any value at all. Or if, to follow an ancient formulation, we assume that the standards reflected in the life of a good man or woman are temperance, justice, courage, and wisdom, and if we note that in a free society temperance is ceaselessly assaulted by advertising, justice corroded by the influence of money, courage undermined by abundant comforts and pleasures, and wisdom neglected even in universities, we have to ask why liberty should be our highest political ideal.

We may begin to notice, in spite of our tendency to recount history as the story of liberty, how little enthusiasm there has been in the past for liberty. We look back on Athens as resplendent with liberty. But Athens was not the most admired polity among the ancient Greeks. It was Sparta, a decidedly illiberal polity, that was most widely honored. If we consider the opinions of those presumably best able to judge, it is striking how few of the great philosophers gave their allegiance above all to liberty. Locke and Mill are exceptions. And of the great religious writers and thinkers, such as Augustine, Aquinas, and Luther, not many cared greatly for liberty. Liberty has been a relatively recent enthusiasm, exhibited mainly by Enlightenment figures, many of them inexperienced in liberty and naively overconfident in the power of reason to understand human needs and control human actions. The banner of liberty has been held aloft mainly by unrealistic optimists.

Some basic thinking is apparently needed. It would be reckless to cast liberty aside, yet we can hardly embrace it without qualms. So we have to inquire yet again into its grounds. Are there any that are solid? Or could it be that liberty endures mainly because of people who care little for values or for righteousness but simply do not want to be interfered with? Is liberty anything more than a current and casual preference? Before asking questions of this sort, however, we must ask questions even more basic. How do we approach an inquiry into the grounds of liberty? Where do we look for our standards of truth?

3

The Issue of Faith and Reason

It may seem that we should start by establishing a philosophical basis, that is, by casting about among alternative philosophies, such as Platonism, Kantianism, and pragmatism, hoping to identify one that would help us understand liberty and assess its value. I suggest, however, that there is a more fundamental issue than any posed by competing philosophies. This is an issue that has to be decided by will, as well as by reason. The issue is that of reason *versus* faith. In exploring reality and in organizing our lives, can we rely entirely on reason? Or must our minds make room — do they even have a profound need? — for faith and for its ostensible ground, revelation?

It is an arresting fact that neither reason nor faith has come close to conquering the human spirit. There was a time (in the age of Augustine, for example) when faith was expected by many to spread inexorably; there was also a time (the Enlightenment) when the gradual and inevitable triumph of reason was anticipated. Both expectations have been disappointed. At the beginning of the third millennium, there is no prospect that faith will at some time recover its dominance over reason, or that reason will ever extinguish faith.

This, I submit, is the context in which we must situate ourselves to think fundamentally about liberty. Where do protagonists of liberty find firm ground under their feet: Where ultimate authority is granted to supposed revelation or where all reliance is placed on reason? Openness to this question distinguishes the present essay from almost all other discussions of liberty. It is everywhere assumed, when a matter of concern to people both in the camp of faith and in the camp of reason is under consideration, that any reference to revelation — the ostensible ground on which all faith is based — is out of place. This I believe to be a crippling assumption and by no means required by the imperative (which I do not contest) that protagonists of faith seek grounds of discourse where protagonists of reason can freely meet them. And it is a crippling assumption in more ways than one. I will try to show why in the course of this essay.

First of all, key terms must be clarified. The issue is not simply faith against reason. A respectable religious faith is never wholly divested of reason, but rather is permeated and fortified by reason. Scholasticism, often thought of as the hypertrophy of reason, is only a conspicuous ex-

4

ample of the rationality always inherent in faith. The very word "theology," deriving from *theos* and *logos,* points to the interpenetration of faith and reason. Conversely, the worldviews constructed by reason are never wholly independent of faith of some sort, such as faith in the orderly character of the universe, or faith simply in reason. Many rationalists would like to think that every assumption without exception is subject to rational examination. While that may be so in principle, it is not, and cannot be, so in practice. Granted, any particular assumption, once identified, can be critically examined. But not every assumption made by a reasoning person can be identified and examined, nor can every assumption thus examined be placed on rational grounds. Reason is always situated, and to be situated is to depend on premises that are never fully recognized, examined, or proven. In this sense, reason is never pure.

The issue, rather than faith against reason, is *religious* faith against *humanist* reason. Religious faith rests primarily on ostensible revelation, that is, on intuitions of ultimate reality that are accorded the authority of being disclosures by God of his ways in the world. The role of reason is to clarify, organize, and supplement these disclosures. Humanist reason, in contrast, rests primarily on deductive operations of the human intellect and on common human experience, on experience that is or can be public, like that of a color or a visible form. Revelation is not allowed any role. It is important to note that the two approaches are differentiated not by mutual exclusion but by primary reliance. Humanist reason does not lose its character by examining claims of faith with a readiness to accept them should they show themselves to be reasonable. Correspondingly, religious faith may be quite open to results from secular research — widespread interest among Christians in psychoanalysis is an example — but need only take care that revelation retain supreme authority. In short, faith and reason overlap. This, as I will try to show, is a fact of fundamental importance for understanding liberty and the kind of life it entails.

Ready examples of the dichotomy of faith and reason, so defined, are Thomas Aquinas and Sigmund Freud, one a rationalistic man of faith, the other a relentlessly reasoning man who found the idea of God "infantile" and impossible. As soon as one observes these examples, however, one may see a possibility apparently at neither extreme — that represented by thinkers such as Plato and Spinoza. Both, although

5

committed to the sovereignty of reason, were in some sense religious. For Plato the idea of the good, and for Spinoza the whole order of the cosmos, was effectively divine. Here, however, I will take "religious" to denote reliance on purported revelation rather than on reason alone. Plato and Spinoza, while entertaining conceptions of a divine reality, were humanist in looking primarily to reason for elucidation of the divine. The divine did not disclose its own nature to humankind but awaited human discovery. It did not, so to speak, take an epistemological initiative. This means that humanist reason is not necessarily atheistic. It is humanist, not because of any antireligious conclusions, but because of its reliance on a human faculty, that of reason.

I grant that I am subjecting the words "religious" and "humanist" to some strain with these definitions. I hope I am justified in doing that, however, by the advantage gained in focusing on a sharp division running through intellectual history — the division between those who trust primarily in reason and those who trust primarily in what they take to be an act of self-disclosure on the part of God.

A final point of clarification needs to be made. I shall employ Christian faith as a stand-in for religious faith generally. It goes without saying that there are vital faiths other than Christianity. No disrespect for these is intended by my focus on Christianity. The great non-Christian religions have distinctive and worthwhile features not found in Christianity. Nonetheless, much that is true of Christianity is true of other religions as well. And trying to take into account the deep and numerous differences among religious faiths would make our task of reflection hopelessly complicated. Oversimplification is thus a necessity. Through such oversimplification I hope to cut one pathway through a thicket of complexities and in that way help readers, not only to follow the pathway I cut, but also to cut other pathways of their own.

I must give some indication, at the outset, of the pathway I shall follow.

Rational Universalism

My point of view in this essay is that of a Christian. Of course, Christians do sometimes conceal their faith, when addressing the general public, and write from the standpoint of humanist reason. This is presumably so they can be heard by everyone, including the numerous intellectuals unwilling to listen to anyone who speaks openly as a Christian. I too would like to be heard by everyone. To conceal my faith, however, would be to conceal a significant part of my mind and of my understanding of liberty. Hence I can only ask those reluctant to listen to religious voices whether it isn't incumbent on us, in the common humanity that remains even in the absence of a common faith, to listen to anyone who is seriously searching for the truth. Shouldn't representatives of humanist reason, in the openness connoted by the word "reasonable," listen to representatives of religious faith when they speak reasonably concerning the truth as they understand it? Can reason close its ears to faith without betraying its primary principles?

I suggest that there is such a thing as Christian wisdom (and, I have no doubt, Jewish wisdom, Islamic wisdom, and Buddhist wisdom). I mean by this a body of valid insights that are derived from the fundamental articles of faith — insights taken on the side of faith as revealed, yet having rational or empirical grounds that render them comprehensible, and even acceptable, to humanist reason. A familiar example is a principle that comes to the fore in any discussion of liberty, "the dignity of the individual." For religious faith every individual is sacred, and this, above all, is because every individual is of concern to a God who is not indifferent to the fall of a sparrow. Proponents of humanist reason will not agree that the dignity of an individual reflects the holiness and mercy of God. Nor will they grant that our knowledge of human dignity comes mainly from revelation. Most of them, however, will concede that "the dignity of the individual" is a phrase with some meaning and truth. Might not they, accordingly, explore with proponents of faith its rational grounds and its worldly consequences?

Good and serious conversation is rare, and willing interlocutors should not be casually spurned. Christian wisdom is ground on which such conversation can occur. Christians have often refused to meet non-Christians on that ground, and in doing that have made their own wisdom poorer, a situation I shall discuss below. But more often, in late modern times, it is humanists who refuse any meeting. It would be hard to find a Christian theologian who has not paid serious attention to Freud, Marx, and Darwin. It would be equally hard to find a secular philosopher who has paid serious attention to Barth, Bonhoeffer, and Bultmann.

7

From the humanist side the complaint will be raised that Christian theology is a labyrinth of cryptic and mystifying propositions. There is a measure of truth in this complaint. No one can claim that the great Christian writers such as Augustine and Aquinas, or Calvin and Luther, are easy reading. Those who make the complaint need to recognize, however, that something similar can be said of the great philosophers of reason. The writings of Kant, of Hegel, of Wittgenstein are notoriously difficult. And there is another response that faith might make — a response with some bearing on whether reason needs to listen to revelation.

Reasoning divested of all that comes from faith, hence based exclusively on clear deliverances of ordinary experience, tells us surprisingly little. At least it tells us little that is objectively certain. This is shown by the fact that every carefully written statement — every essay, every book, every address — can be plausibly "deconstructed," that is, traced back largely to subjective sources. The very subjectivity of such sources signifies their dependence on faith. We need not appeal to current intellectual fashion, however, to realize how confusing and uncertain a ground experience provides for us to stand on. We can see this in the work of great empiricists such as Locke, Hume, and James. Substance, essence, causal necessity, and most other structural elements of the commonsense universe and the commonsense order of experience have fallen as empiricism has developed. As we all know, the greatest of modern philosophers, Immanuel Kant, denied that experience alone provides any of the structural elements essential to its own existence. Although reason may open itself to every kind of insight, it has tended in recent centuries to restrict itself to "facts," to things everyone can see. Thus restricted, it is a remarkably inadequate tool. It is far better at overturning ostensible but uncertain truths, and at defining its own limits, than at bringing large truths to light.

Reason cannot go very far except by means of unproven premises used to guide and shape its work. Some of these premises may be of a kind that seems obvious to many people, such as the "law of cause and effect." Some may be intuitions of the sort that originates in genius, as in Darwin's development of the principle of natural selection. And some, like the sacredness of every person, may arise from what faith regards as revelation. One of the most powerful works of reason in our time, Marx's, could not have been carried out if its author had not had a vision of historical conflict and unfoldment that comes mainly from

Hebrew and Christian scripture. For Freud and Darwin, one major and indispensable premise was simply that of universal determinism. Even the seemingly most strange and wayward acts of consciousness, Freud believed, must be explicable in terms of mechanical causation. And Darwin could not have done the work he is remembered for had he shared Kant's conviction, expressed only a few decades before his time, that there would never be a Newton to explain the origins of even a single blade of grass.

As another example of the vital role of these undemonstrable premises, consider their role in estimating the historical consequences and the philosophical implications of Darwin's discoveries. Does the law of natural selection rule out altruism? Is the struggle for survival a proper model for the economic order? If the origin of the species is natural, does it follow that it is not supernatural too? Questions of this kind can be satisfactorily dealt with — even within the camp of humanist reason — only by thought and argumentation of a kind that would stall and come to a stop without the fuel of irrational insight. Outside the bounds of the physical sciences, and perhaps within those bounds as well, rational discourse cleansed of all ideas and conjectures drawn from irrational sources could lead only onto a moonscape littered with trivia.

All of this bears on the relations of reason, relying as far as possible on what can be rationally defended, and faith, appealing to revelation. If champions of reason faced fully the extent of their dependence on premises without rational grounds, they might be less inclined than they usually are to deny revelation any sort of hearing. Revelation, after all, is no more than a set of basic intuitions having an authority and significance indicative, in the eyes of faith, of a supernatural source. I am not suggesting that unbelievers should become believers but only that they might find conversation with believers sometimes provocative and profitable. Take the myth of the last judgment as an example. For unbelievers it is one of the eschatological fantasies all too characteristic of faith; for believers it is a solemn truth. For both alike, however, it can be a symbol of personal accountability as one of the first truths of human existence. Every person's life as a whole is subject to moral appraisal, if only by the person whose life it is, and the significance of such an appraisal is not nullified by death. These are not controversial assertions. Yet they are important and are enigmatic, hence they call for thought on the part of everyone. Given our ignorance and our sociability, we should look for the truth together. Our lives should be conversational, with none excluded. What grounds can proponents of humanist reason possibly have for spurning such lives?

When I speak of the universalism of reason, I mean to say only that rejecting unexamined any serious claims to truth is unreasonable. This is particularly the case when such claims are made by successive generations of sane and thinking people and have come in this way to constitute a traditional body of beliefs, matured by long experience. Yet when it comes to religious traditions, apostles of reason almost uniformly adopt a posture of unreasoning rejection. They often assert, of course, that it is those on the other side of the divide, the Christians, who have rejected reason. Sometimes this is true, and I will discuss this fact in the following section. My point here is simply that humanist reason and religious faith are by no means mutually exclusive and that dividing them into two noncommunicating universes of discourse is false to the human mind. In particular, it is false to reason, and this should be recognized by reason's most outspoken and uncompromising defenders.

The ears of humanist reason, then, should listen — however critically — to the voices of religious faith. Surely, however, the converse relationship should also hold. Christian ears should be open to humanist voices.

Christian Universalism

Christians cannot ignore this challenge. It is necessary to take issue not only with protagonists of humanist reason who scorn Christian voices, but also with Christians who cannot envisage speaking and listening seriously to non-Christians. There are many such. From the time of Paul to that of Karl Barth, great Christians, as well as lesser ones, have dramatized the chasm separating faith from reason. No doubt such a chasm exists. There are fundamental Christian doctrines, such as the incarnation, that are foolishness to the Greeks. To ignore that fact puts the integrity of Christian faith at risk. Yet readers of Paul and Barth should bear in mind that the universalism inherent in the gospel is no less emphatic than that inherent in reason. Christ addresses all humankind. The Christian message thus involves a tacit claim to unrestricted comprehensibility and relevance. This fact is vital, as I will try to show, to the understanding of liberty.

A useful starting point for understanding Christian universalism is the simple proposition that Christianity is a joyful faith. This may seem uncontroversial, given the gospel's traditional characterization as "good news." The angel that visited the shepherds in the field on the night of Jesus' birth brought glad tidings, the coming of a Savior. It has proven strangely difficult, however, for Christian leaders to maintain the spirit of this proclamation. They have cultivated among their followers a mood less of joy than of anxiety and terror. They have impressed on their minds the awful question of whether the Savior might, when the time comes, find them unworthy of salvation. Some of the greatest Christians — Augustine, Dante, Michelangelo, and Calvin, for example — have engaged in this strange and seemingly subversive work. The principle of justification by faith primarily rather than by works, common in a general way to both Protestants and Catholics, and suggesting that salvation is within the grasp of everyone, has not greatly helped. Although apparently seen by Paul as liberation from anxiety about the adequacy of one's works, and thus as a source of reassurance and peace, it was used by many succeeding Christians in a different way. Faith was tied indissolubly to stern doctrinal and behavioral standards. In this way it was tacitly turned into the hardest of all works, with Christians left to wonder whether an implacable God would find their faith sufficient. Christian life lost its joy and peace. This is clearly apparent in Augustine, and again in Calvin and his followers. Kierkegaard, a Lutheran, wrote powerfully of how harrowing the life of a true Christian was bound to be. This development, to be sure, is not purely adventitious. The Savior does call for a response, and humans may fail to provide it. Nonetheless, a grim and harrowing Christianity has somehow gone awry. It has lost the exultant spirit that pervades the Psalms and emerges repeatedly in Paul. It has become incapable of heeding Paul's injunction to "rejoice in the Lord always" (Phil. 4:4). The good news has become alarming. What does all this have to do with the loss of Christian universalism? The answer emerges as soon as you ask what went wrong.

The core Christian idea, that God is love — an idea forcefully expressed many places in the Old Testament, and given dramatic force by the crucifixion — somehow lost authority in the minds of many Christians. God came to be thought of as exceedingly angry. No longer could one be sure that in the final judgment love would reign over wrath. God could no longer be trusted. Fear of God, properly understood as awe before the divine mystery, turned into fright. Again, such a development was not purely adventitious. The biblical understanding of God is inseparable from the sense that God is sometimes wrathful and is never fully calculable. But in true Christianity these qualities are subordinate to divine love. Wrath works toward salvation, and God's incalculability is the face of a fathomless mercy. God is not merely patient and kind; he bound himself to a perverse and frivolous human race by the unconditional commitment expressed in Christ's death on the cross. When that commitment is forgotten, however, God's frightening attributes begin to break free from their subordinate theological position. What came originally as good news has become an alarm bell.

Thus it was that Christianity lost the universality that belongs to its essence. This universality is anchored in the concept of God's love. But when Christians began to think that divine anger held equal sway with divine love, universality disappeared. Just as divine anger took a place alongside divine love, the terrifying concept of hell took a place alongside the vision of eternal life. The human race fell apart. It was now composed of two camps, the beneficiaries of God's love and the victims of his wrath. Augustine's concept of the two cities consolidated this outlook. Calvinist sermons on the terrors of hell expressed its upshot. The natural consequence has been not only that the peace and good spirits that ought to inhabit Christian hearts gave way to fear. Love for a human race befriended by God was replaced by animosity toward those presumably damned — a large category, including not only all non-Christians but also a great many Christians.

But why did an idea so deeply appealing, and so dramatically presented in the New Testament, as that of divine compassion for a race immersed in the misery and darkness caused by its own perversity lose its authority? In trying to answer this question it is hard to distinguish assuredly between cause and consequence. It is also hard, however, not to think that a primary part was played by human pride and malice. We are talking about a growing insistence on the exclusiveness of God's love. It was bestowed on some but not on others. Indeed, it may have been bestowed only on a small, mysteriously select minority, and withheld from the human race at large. How else to explain so drastic a revision of the gospel without reference to the human failings from which it is obvious that professions of Christian faith do not deliver us? Pride and malice typically lead us to exculpate ourselves and despise others. The concepts of divine election and divine reprobation provided incomparably invidious means for doing this. Thus Augustine, at the end of his life, was apparently convinced that most of the human race was damned. One of his late pieces of writing, in *The City of God,* was a painstaking effort to demonstrate that bodies might burn forever and the suffering of the damned thus be literally everlasting. Unsurprisingly, Augustine's habitual tone in speaking of pagans and heretics was one of scorn and loathing. And one finds in Calvin's *Institutes* the same pervasive rancor in speaking of theological opponents. The universalism of the gospel has largely disappeared from sight.

I hasten to grant that I am passing over serious theological complexities. For one thing, conspicuously present on the world scene are numerous people who provide every sign of being atrociously and unrepentantly evil. Can we think of heaven as a place where Hitler or Goebbels might be encountered? Also, there are a great many who regard with indifference or disdain the divine offer of mercy. Must not one accept God's mercy in order to receive it? Equally serious is a theological consideration. The concept of original sin, which holds in substance that all of us are in our hearts rebels against God, cannot be lightly dismissed. Indeed, it can be supported by compelling psychological analyses (these to be discussed at a later point in the essay). The upshot of the concept is that we are a great deal more sinful than the record of our lives may show or than we ourselves may realize. God's anger may be more justified than human beings in their self-satisfaction and superficiality can appreciate.

Still, surely the "good news" should have remained just that. It became, however, a source of terror, and numerous Christian leaders and theologians, at best in well-meaning efforts to spur conversions, at worst in what look like expressions of profound personal resentments, incited the terror. Men and women were induced to envision their lives as potentially only a brief passage to everlasting physical and emotional torment. Worse, perhaps, they were induced to envision the lives of many others in this way. In consequence, any idea such as a universal conversation in search of the truth became unthinkable. As Berdyaev somewhere ironically observed, he could not sit down pleasantly at tea with someone who would, he was sure, soon be in hell. People divided from one another by an irrevocable divine judgment and the eternal chasm thus created are unlikely to live together in peaceful fidelity to authentic values. They are unlikely to join in a common quest for truth. This is particularly the case when the dichotomy of saved and damned is assumed — as is common among Christians — to coincide with that of believer and unbeliever. Believers tend to take the truth as already known on their side, and spurned and irrecoverable on the other side.

It goes without saying that Christians cannot regard the distinction between believers and unbelievers as unimportant. But they will hesitate to pronounce on the eternal significance of the distinction if they take seriously the scriptural dictum that God is love. They will, for example, examine critically the relationship between the profession and the actuality of belief. They will wonder whether there are believers whose professed belief is shallow and thoughtless and therefore tantamount to unbelief. They will ask themselves if there are unbelievers who, by virtue perhaps of an unspoken, even unconscious wisdom, are anonymous believers. Such reflections have not played a large part in the history of Christian thought, however, and we must therefore admit that the narrow-mindedness of many humanists has been matched by that of many Christians.

In a particularly notable New Testament passage, Jesus names as the one unforgivable sin speaking, *not against the Son,* but against the Holy Spirit (Matt. 12:31-32). The implications of this passage for Christian relations with the world surely are profound. Rejecting Christ, it seems, is not necessarily a damning act. It would be a damning act only for those given, *by the Holy Spirit,* the power of recognizing Christ. This implies that unbelievers as such, even those who have heard the gospel, are not necessarily lost. Only those unbelievers are lost who have heard the gospel and by the grace of God have understood it, yet defiantly remain in unbelief. The damned, it may be said, are only those who knowingly will to be damned. Divine love is not forced on anyone.

The doctrine of universal salvation cannot, for various reasons, be taken as definitive truth. Yet the biblical principle that God is "the Savior of all men" (1 Tim. 4:10), that divine compassion extends to all persons without exception, is indispensable to the Christian spirit. Christians are bound, *in fidelity to their God,* to contend against the pride and malice that gladly imagine the unending tortures to be inflicted on their enemies. And they ought to entertain with interest hypotheses like that offered by C. S. Lewis in *The Great Divorce:* that hell is not necessarily a permanent habitation, and that those who dwell there forever do so because they would rather be there than in heaven.

The inalterable assumption that many — or even any — members of the human race are eternally lost undermines the core principle of the Christian ethic: love of neighbor. This principle requires that I regard everyone I encounter, every "neighbor," as one on whom God has mercy and who therefore may be saved. I must think that if some are not saved, that may be because in their freedom they do not want to be saved. And I must therefore struggle in every situation and relationship to envision those I am dealing with as potential beneficiaries of a divine commitment to the salvation of the whole human race. However, if I am convinced that God has rejected many or most people, I cannot help suspecting that those I dislike or find morally flawed or intellectually perverse are doomed. Love for neighbor becomes a meaningless sentiment, unrelated to daily life. Augustine was a very great mind, and played a vital role in the development of Christian faith, but his acquiescence — if not exultation — in the damnation of most human beings set an example Christians surely should not follow.

Christian universalism has important implications for the relations of religious faith and humanist reason. These do not define altogether separate communities, as Christians have so often supposed that they do. Christians cannot regard those who rely on reason rather than on revelation as definitely and finally outside the circle of truth and of possible communication. The concept of revelation does not require such an attitude. In the course of this essay I shall try to show that the supreme standard of human relations is properly defined in terms of serious speaking and listening. We are authentically together only in truth-seeking dialogue. Many activities, like sports and sex, and politics and physical labor, link us with one another. But they are truly communal only if they are taken up in reflective conversation. This implies that Christians should address, *and also accord attention to,* fellow humans on the other side of the great divide between reason and revelation. Love of neighbor should be manifested in availability for conversation that is serious (not mere "idle talk") and is unbounded in either subject matter or participants. They can do this, however, only if they are free of condescension, which means treating each of their fel-

15

low humans as a neighbor, one deserving not only to be addressed but also to be heard.

Listening is a practice Christians are particularly in need of learning. They have often, of course, been willing to *preach* to those not sharing their faith. They have, so to speak, assumed the *evangelical* unity of the human race. This, however, is not enough. Anything deserving the name "community" must involve a common aspiration to the truth. No such aspiration can exist where members of one party assume that they already know all or most of the truth worth knowing, and that other parties have nothing they could teach them. Listening in that case is pointless. Community is common inquiry and is possible only among people with the humility to learn from one another. Christians have often, even normally, been without very much of that humility.

Looking at things from a Christian standpoint, however, what might Christians learn from non-Christians? It is difficult to say precisely what they might *not* learn — with one exception. They will not learn, presumably, that Jesus is the Christ. That they already know, *in some fashion,* and it is unknown to anyone who can be accurately called a non-Christian. But the proposition that Jesus is the Christ is not a piece of information that is either totally known or totally unknown. It is the center point of a body of wisdom, much of which, while related to the center point, may be more or less independently viable. Socrates and Plato, for example, realized that a good person does no evil to anyone — *not even to his enemies.* They gained a piece of moral wisdom, highly flavored with Christianity, and perhaps in the final analysis defensible only on Christian grounds, four centuries before Christ lived. A fact of this sort should give pause to condescending Christians. It is, of course, not the only such fact. Not only Socrates and Plato, but also figures like Aristotle and Plotinus, and Buddha and Lao-tzu, show unmistakably that the wisdom centered in Christ overflows Christian chalices. Even atheistic reason, as some Christians have recognized, reaches insights that are valuable to Christians. So notorious and intransigent an enemy of Christianity as Nietzsche, for example, can teach a great deal to Christians with the breadth of spirit to listen to him.

For what good reason should Christians be reluctant to acknowledge a divine generosity that pours possibilities of understanding over the whole human race? If God is love, is it logical to think he would leave a great many human beings forever in darkness? Who are Christians, in the poverty of spirit blessed by Jesus in the Beatitudes, to insist that the divine wisdom they believe God bestowed in its fullness in the life and death of Jesus, be withheld totally from all but themselves? The attitude I am expressing is not new among Christians. Paul, in the first two chapters of his epistle to the Romans, explicitly acknowledged that non-Christians can have a general knowledge both of God and of the moral law. And Christians have often affirmed the religious and moral range of the reason that all humans have in common. They have also granted the reality of "common grace," grace that is heedless of religious and ecclesiastical boundaries. But the history of Christianity shows a strong tendency, particularly among the most ardent Christians, to liken the contrast between themselves and the world to that between day and night. Christianity is light (which all Christians do and must believe); the world and its creeds are darkness (which they can believe only by placing in jeopardy their faith in the power and mercy of God). This radical dichotomy has no doubt heightened their spirits. To feel embattled against the forces of darkness is to feel your own faith strengthened. This feeling, however, is illusory, as preceding arguments show. Falsifying the relations between faith and reason means falsifying God, and that means losing the happiness offered by the "good news." The light is turned into darkness.

To look at the matter from a different angle, if there is a divine generosity that pours possibilities of understanding over the whole human race, might not that same generosity pour out for everyone possibilities of righteousness? Let me put the question in very simple terms. Can non-Christians be good people? Augustine was unwilling to say that they can. He acknowledged that a great deal of discipline and courage was required for building up and defending the Roman Empire. But these he considered merely "splendid vices" — an attitude no doubt unattractive but not indefensible. Augustine reasoned (speaking very broadly) that righteousness arose from faith and that those without faith therefore could not be genuinely righteous. Lack of true faith implied lack of true virtue. But such reasoning can be reversed. Christians must accept the postulate that righteousness is based on faith. If that were not so, then, since faith (as Christians see it) is our primary link with God and creation, righteousness separate from faith would be, as it were, suspended in the air, accidental and ungrounded. If we find

17

nevertheless that people apparently lacking in faith exhibit righteousness, can't we infer that their righteousness — rather than being false — testifies to a temper of mind that is tantamount to faith? Can't we conjecture the presence of *virtual* faith? This we might define as an attitude — not embodied in any formal religious commitment — of trust in the ultimate ground of things, and of consequent responsibility toward others and toward the course of common affairs. When Jesus said, "you will know them by their fruits" (Matt. 7:20), he may have been allowing for something like virtual faith, a faith manifest in manner of life rather than in formal profession.

For Americans, an example of such faith is at hand. Abraham Lincoln was by every appearance a man of uncommon discernment and goodness; yet he was not formally a Christian. Doesn't the general character of Lincoln's life — his profound disapproval of slavery, his unwavering fidelity to his responsibilities as president, his refusal to despair even in desperate circumstances, his charity toward his and his country's enemies — reflect a frame of mind so much like faith that the lack of any formal profession of faith seems almost insignificant?

The idea of virtual faith suggests that the line between believers and unbelievers is not nearly as sharp as Christians have often tried to make it. It invites a rethinking of the significance of the line. It may be asked, for example, not only whether in the camp of formal unbelievers there are not numerous tacit believers, but also whether the mantle of formal belief — particularly in societies where being a respectable member of the established order and being a Christian are tacitly equated — is not often worn by unbelievers. Jesus tells of a man with two sons whom he told to go work in the vineyard. One answered, "I will not," but later thought better of his answer and did as his father had directed. The other responded to his father more obediently, saying, "I go, sir." Nevertheless, he did not go. "Which of the two," Jesus asks, "did the will of his father?" (Matt. 21:28-31). This parable surely has profound implications for Christian ecclesiology. Not that it denies the significance of faith. This has been stressed in Christianity from the time of Jesus on. But it does raise the question of who the faithful and the unfaithful — the true believers and the true unbelievers — really are. It undercuts Christian condescension toward non-Christians. It suggests that the range of authentic community, which is realized in the common search for and enjoyment of truth, does not coincide with the range of the church.

There is at least one weighty objection to my whole argument here. The God depicted in the Bible is a "jealous" God. His attitude toward those who invent their own gods, or in any way turn aside from the one true God, is far from indulgent. God does not direct the children of Israel to talk with inhabitants of the land promised them, but rather to kill them. And Paul writes powerfully of the unavoidable "folly," in the eyes of the world, of Christian truth. "Since, in the wisdom of God, the world did not know God through wisdom, it pleased God through the folly of what we preach to save those who believe" (1 Cor. 1:21). Those are not words that encourage dialogue. On the contrary, they suggest that the preceding argument is too simple if not wholly wrong. Account must be taken of the fact that Christians (that is, true Christians, true believers) see things, or believe they see things, that are unbelievable to the non-Christian world. And account must be taken of the corresponding fact that reason unswayed by faith sometimes reaches conclusions that Christians regard as not merely mistaken but calamitous. We must ask whether Christian speech and listening can be as unreserved as I have suggested. To address this question suggests a concept of the character and mission of Christianity that departs considerably from traditional views.

Christianity as an Inquiring Faith

The issue is idolatry. What is demanded of the Israelites and Christians is that they worship God and not something that is ostensibly divine but in fact is finite and man-made, such as "images resembling mortal man or birds or animals or reptiles" (Rom. 1:23). The ruthlessness commanded relative to natives of the land destined for the Jewish people reflected not so much divine animosity toward the natives themselves as divine determination that the Jews not be lured into idolatry. The issue is not out-of-date. Through the centuries idols have changed their shape, but they have not disappeared or lost their seductiveness. It seems manifest from the perspective provided by the tyrannies and wars of the twentieth century that idols need not be physical things. States and parties, money and material possessions, are finite and man-made and are far more alluring objects of worship, at least for modern peoples, than are images of animals and other creatures.

19

How can Christians justify not only talking with non-Christians — many of them, judged by the standards of Jewish scripture, probably idolatrous — but also listening respectfully to them, and doing this, moreover, as a regular practice? Isn't this like the ancient Israelites settling down with the Gentiles and deliberately exposing themselves to the allure of their idols? Doesn't it mean opening Christian minds to the meretricious wisdom of those who put all their trust in nations, leaders, and parties, but are ignorant of God? All these questions may be brought to a focus in a single question: How should Christians stand in relation to the world around them?

Let me put the question in the most challenging possible way, which is, I believe, in terms of the doctrine of election. According to the great Karl Barth, the doctrine of election is at the very center of Christian faith. This is because it recognizes the absolute sovereignty of God. And it does this in relation to the overriding concern of every individual, that is, salvation. According to this doctrine in its traditional form, those who affirm Christianity do so primarily, not by their own powers of discernment, but rather because they have been chosen by God to glimpse the light present in Christ. They are chosen without regard to any virtues or powers of their own. Only as a result of divine initiative will they come to understand the truth of Christianity. On the other side, those who find Christianity incredible are not necessarily deficient in intellect or judgment. It is rather that their hearts have, at least for a time, been hardened. The relationship of a person to God is decided by God.

It is easy to read into this doctrine an ethic of passivity. Everything depends on God, nothing on man. As everyone knows, however, the most famous expression of the doctrine of election in modern times, that of Calvin, typically was an incitement to a life of intense activity. And this makes sense. Divine election presumably demands a human response. And an adequate response presumably involves, along with the passivity inherent in attending to the initiative of God, the activity that would come from employing in response the full range of human powers, such as those of reason and persuasion. Obviously this might be done in business or in government. I suggest, however, that the primary element in such a response must be the effort to understand what the act of election means and who the God is who has carried out this act. This is not to say that a true Christian would devote his life to academic, rather than business or political, activity, but only that every activity would be a way of inquiring into God and his ways. To be called by God to the Christian faith is to become, not a possessor of the truth, but a seeker of the truth.

This has implications for the relationship of the Christian to the world. Any inquirer, whether Christian or not, knows that inquiry is a collective as well as a personal activity. One seeks insight from others; and one tests one's insights by offering them to the scrutiny of others. This applies to Christians. In seeking the truth they must of course converse as much as possible with fellow Christians. But they must also heed the manifest fact that many people who are not Christians nevertheless inquire earnestly into the truth and gain some knowledge of the truth. Intellectual history places this assertion beyond need of argument. The consequences are plain to be seen. Christians who ignore truth-seeking or truth-bearing unbelievers violate their own principles — that faith seek understanding and that respect be paid all neighbors.

The idea of Christianity as an inquiring faith does not involve any disavowal of the claim that the ultimate truth is revealed in Christ. Skillful searchers must in some sense know what they are searching for. Effective inquirers must have a kind of understanding already of the truth they are inquiring into. But they know the truth in a way that makes them conscious of not knowing it. They come as close as possible to knowing it when they persist in looking for it. This is the paradox dramatized in the life of Socrates, the wisest man in Greece according to the Delphic oracle, who knew at the end of his life only that his wisdom lay in ignorance. It is the paradox expressed by Lessing when he said that if God held before him all truth in one hand and the endless search for truth in the other, and asked him to choose, he would choose the endless search. Christians in some sense know, or believe they know, certain truths such as the incarnation, the Trinity, and the expiation of human sins accomplished on the cross. But Christians who really know these truths know that they do not know them. They know that they have to spend a lifetime inquiring into them. They know too that light may come from surprising places.

In living as inquirers, Christians may bring truth into the world — but as something possessed only by being sought. They may, for example, help to keep alive the idea of the dignity of the individual. This is an idea essential to the justice of society and to the humanity of civilization, yet it is not a plain, empirical fact. Hence the state of mind of anyone knowing this truth will be like Socrates' wisdom. It will be, so to speak, an inquiring ignorance. The idea of personal dignity will live not in being plainly stated and surely comprehended but in being sought. It will not be a piece of knowledge they bestow on those wholly ignorant of it, but rather a truth of which they have an inkling, through the divine mercy expressed in the life and death of Christ, and are driven to inquire into with others, not all of them necessarily Christians.

This is obviously far from the usual way that Christians have thought of their role in the world. But humans are inveterate oversimplifiers. The motive is often pride. By oversimplifying they can exaggerate the iniquity and folly of others and thereby exalt themselves. Christians are not immune to this temptation. The assertion that the division between believers and unbelievers is equivalent to the division between those who know the truth and those who do not is one of the most stunning acts of oversimplification in Western history. By indulging in it, Christians have often cut their connections — connections of love, respect, and discourse — with much of the human race. Anti-Semitism is one of its most notorious consequences.

Doesn't the doctrine of election, however, indicate that the outcome of all inquiry has already been settled and that many of those who inquire are predestined to end in a prison of lies and delusions? Paul suggests an approach to this question in his discussion of the eternal destiny of the Jewish people (Rom. 9–11). The redemption of humanity does not occur in a moment but comes about in time. It is the work of God's prolonged and profoundly mysterious strategy of salvation — a matter on which Paul was followed by Barth. The election of some does not imply the irreversible rejection of others. Those cast down may later be lifted up. They may even be lifted up after death; that such a thought is not unthinkable is indicated by the concept of purgatory. It is even conceivable that eventually all who have ever lived will be lifted up. Those who ignore possibilities like these, or repudiate them as heretical, attenuate their relations with God because they try, so to speak, to put God in a box — to constrict the range and mastery of his love. It might behoove Christians to consider the possibility that divine election does not undergird the barriers proud Christians erect between themselves and their non-Christian neighbors, but deranges and breaches them. Perhaps the glory of God does not lie in the elevation of a few human beings into the light and the consignment of multitudes to final darkness, but rather in the ingenuity and the power of a love that eventually lifts incalculable numbers, even all, into the light.

The idea that God has from all eternity damned a certain part of the human race, and that there are therefore many with whom communal and inquiring relations are impossible, has the look of an imposition of mere human conceptions on the unfathomable designs of God. It strongly suggests not only spiritual pride but also obliviousness of the truth Paul expressed when he exclaimed, concerning the strategies by which God effects the salvation of both Jews and Gentiles, "How unsearchable are his judgments and how inscrutable his ways!" (Rom. 11:33).

It may seem, however, that this whole discussion does not quite meet the issue of idolatry. One may grant that the doctrine of election does not imply hard-and-fast lines between the saved and the damned, that it does not mandate a closed mind or a passive life, and even that it allows for the possibility of more dialogic relations between believers and unbelievers than Christians have traditionally admitted. Still, how does all of this bear on the issue presented when God commanded the Israelites to shun all association with the idolatrous natives of the land they were destined to inhabit? Don't Christians who cross the boundary line separating them from non-Christians contravene a clear divine command? And don't they put themselves in jeopardy of falling under the spell of one kind or another of idolatry? We have, I believe, been indirectly addressing the subject of idolatry all along.

In the first place, non-Christians are not necessarily idolaters. The line between true believers and idolaters is not coincident with the line between Christians and non-Christians. This is not to minimize the danger of idolatry. Humans are strongly inclined, if not bound by an inner necessity of their nature, to treat one reality or another as a god — as a fully reliable guide and refuge, beyond every doubt and misgiving. And the consequences of idolatry, it is safe to say, are invariably harmful, and sometimes disastrous, for idolatry falsifies reality by treating what is finite as infinite, and what is imperfect as perfect. Idolatry is truly something to fear. Moreover, those who reject Christianity may fall under unusually subtle and powerful temptations to idolatry. Rejecting the true God, they may be drawn more powerfully than are Christians toward false gods. Yet they may — Christians might say through the

23

grace of God — perceive the falsity of these gods and hunger for the truth. This is shown by the innumerable instances in which agnostics and atheists have acted with fortitude and courage in behalf of the truth. Surely anyone sincerely devoted to the truth and to the search for the truth is something other than a full-scale idolater. Christians believe that truth, ultimate truth, is God. If this is so, then anyone concerned with the truth is concerned with God — even when the Christian concept of God is denied. Christians might therefore see even a man like Freud, explicitly an atheist and contemptuous of believers, as ennobled by his dedication to finding the truth.

As I have suggested, moreover, professed Christians are not usually free of idolatry themselves. This is not to speak only of the idolatry inherent in devotion to making money (as applies to innumerable Christians) or in maintaining a worshipful and uncritical attitude toward one nation or another (which Christians have done with embarrassing regularity). It is to speak also of the idolatry implicit in assuming that God has been captured and is held in certain human doctrines, never to be questioned or revised. It is to speak of the idolatry implicit in thinking that God can act on human beings only through one particular ecclesiastical organization. Authentic Christians should, as is often said in the churches, be joyful and confident in their faith. That is one thing. But to be proud in their faith, and disdainful of those outside the faith, is to imperil the faith.

Finally and above all there is the point already made about the divine attitude toward the human race. Granted, God in his jealousy condemns idolatry, the worship of false gods. But God is not only jealous, in the sense of condemning the deification of the nondivine. He is also a God of love. The supreme sign of this, Christians believe, is the life and death of Christ. As the God of love, he commands that we love one another. And only so far as we love one another do we love and know God. "No man has ever seen God; if we love one another, God abides in us and his love is perfected in us" (1 John 4:12). This proposition lends itself to an arresting inference. Only by loving our neighbor, who may be an idolater, do we come to know God and thus avoid idolatry. Even in the case of non-Christians who succumb to the temptation to idolatry, we cannot help them by spurning or injuring them. Here it may be that a decisive difference between the Old and New Testaments appears. The imperative of neighborly love requires different — less violent, more communicative — strategies for dealing with idolatry than those employed by the ancient Israelites. Paul said very plainly that the faith of Christians who lack charity is worth nothing at all (1 Cor. 13:2). Don't Christians who proudly and contemptuously look down on non-Christians lack charity?

Nothing I have said is intended to deny that Christians are obliged to make known to the world the truth — the Word of God — as they comprehend it. But they should do this as inquirers. They are trying to see more deeply into the truth they now only "see in a mirror dimly" and only know "in part" (1 Cor. 13:12). This suggests that Christian evangelism should be dialogic. The terrible fault of traditional evangelism has been the pride of those who presumed to see themselves as possessors of, not inquirers into, the truth. As such, they tried, with visions of unending torture in hell, to terrify those they aspired to convert. In doing this they sought to control and magnify their emotions and silence their reason. They sought, in other words, to deprive them of the freedom inherent in thought and deliberation. And in thus falsifying their neighbors, they falsified God, who was transformed, in their imagination, from a God of love into a God of wrath. A dialogic evangelism would be very different — marked by humility in spite of a certain assurance of having glimpsed the truth, by respect for neighbors as capable of thinking and of choosing, and by faith in a God who cannot be assumed, as a matter of dogma and beyond all doubt, to have destined anyone irrevocably to eternal darkness.

In the idea of an inquiring Christianity and a dialogic evangelism we can see the answer to the challenge of idolatry. True Christians would respond to idolaters not by killing them but by trying to engage them in truth-seeking — which for Christians is God-seeking — conversation.

The Present Essay

At the center of this essay, of course, is the subject of liberty. As we have seen, even though liberty has been courageously defended during most of the twentieth century, it is not perfectly clear that it deserves the esteem it has enjoyed in the modern mind. Liberty is a very clouded value. It is vulnerable outwardly to serious dangers, inwardly to conscientious doubts. The preceding pages have been an effort to lay the groundwork for understanding the value of liberty — a value great enough, I believe, to surmount the challenge of the misuses to which liberty is subject.

This effort accorded with my assertion, at the outset of the chapter, that in trying to understand liberty one must first of all decide where to stand, and that the fundamental issue one faces in doing this is that of humanist reason *versus* religious faith. While I believe that these two positions overlap to an indefinite degree and that communication between them is therefore possible, it can make a profound difference which position one adopts. A humanist who relies primarily on reason, and is clear concerning the meaning of this reliance, will ordinarily have a different way of looking at reality and will live a different kind of life than a Christian who is similarly clear about the meaning of Christianity. Hence one will use liberty in a different way, and have a different understanding of liberty, than the other.

Some of the conflicts that arise between faith and reason will of course prove irresolvable. Without such conflicts, neither side could preserve its integrity. Christianity, in spite of the universal wisdom it incorporates, has characteristics that are offensive to humanist reason; this is why Paul spoke ironically of the "folly" of what he preached. A Christian who is determined not to offend anyone on the side of humanist reason will almost certainly sometimes betray his faith. On the other side, the soul of reason is independence. Those who rely primarily on reason, refusing to believe anything about which reason has reservations, will sometimes diverge fundamentally from what believers regard as revelation. Their honor, and even their value in common discourse, depends on their willingness to do this. Realistically, then, the communal ideal — and the aim of liberty — is not complete and unvarying agreement. Rather, it is what might be called "discordant dialogue."

One of the main premises of this essay is that such dialogue is possible and is essential to the life of liberty. Thus, although I write as a Christian, I do this in the belief that Christianity contains insights that can be of use to the whole society but lie at depths that reason alone cannot reach easily, if at all. Christianity can help people of all persuasions, even people completely out of sympathy with religion, to gain a better understanding of reality in general and of liberty in particular. While it is vital to liberty that church and state be separate, it is dangerous to liberty for Christians and non-Christians to be separate. Both sides then suffer the intellectual impoverishment that is incurred through enmity and estrangement.

It will be apparent that I am committed not only to Christianity but also to reason and to the boundless communication to which reason naturally leads. For one thing, it is through communication, both as argumentation and as mutual reinforcement, that the struggle for truth occurs. Furthermore, as earlier remarks have suggested, only in the context of communication, and of the uncertainties that necessarily attend all serious communication, is the truth properly known. Only in that context can one possess the truth as something that is not possessed but is sought. Finally, I stress communication not only for the sake of advantages thus to be gained but also for its own sake. Community is good in itself. Indeed, if fully understood, it is the final and only good. At least I will so argue. Liberty, above all else, is a communal opportunity, and the highest achievement of liberty in the public world would be a dialogic realm encompassing both faith and reason. These pages accordingly may be seen as the first steps in an argument culminating in chapter 9, which concerns public dialogue.

These matters have implications for the method I shall follow in the course of the essay. Writing as a Christian, I shall always try to see whether Christianity sheds light on the questions that arise. But I shall also try to see what reason says. Since the clashes between faith and reason arise spontaneously, however, I shall not emphasize the differences between them, although I shall try not to obscure them. Rather I shall continually look for common ground. I shall cast Christian truth in humanist terms whenever I can without compromising it. And I shall bring out possible agreements between faith and reason whenever this is possible. I hope in this way to point out possibilities of dialogue as well as to bring out the truth of the matters under consideration.

Finally, a note concerning terminology. The words "liberty" and "freedom" are often used interchangeably. Doing this, however, risks confusing two different realities that inevitably enter into any discussion of liberty. The term "liberty," as used in the following pages, refers to the social and political arrangements that protect individuals against undue interference by other individuals or by private groups or governmental agencies. Anyone so protected possesses liberty. Such a person can live — always, of course, within limits — as he pleases. The term "freedom," in contrast, refers not to external arrangements but to the internal nature of the person on whom those arrangements impinge. Freedom is the power to choose. Every person possesses freedom by virtue simply of human nature, although not every person possesses liberty. People ought to have liberty because they are free. Deprived of liberty, with their power of choice denied, they are not recognized as persons. A great deal more will be said about all of this in the following pages.

CHAPTER 2

Liberty and Human Evil

The Christian View of Human Nature

Christians cannot claim, as they might like to in a liberal era, that Christianity is staunchly on the side of liberty. It is true that most Christians in the twentieth century supported liberty in one form or another. But this is not the normal state of affairs. Looking back, we see that faith has usually been wary of liberty if not actively opposed to it. Paul was not a friend of liberty — if we understand liberty in terms of outward arrangements safeguarding opportunities for personal choice — nor was Augustine. Both affirmed the importance of authority and of undeviating obedience. It is striking that even the Reformation, although in various ways a movement toward religious liberty, carried forward the emphasis on obedience that is so prominent in Paul and Augustine. Not that liberty necessarily involves disobedience. But it does involve a centering on personal responsibility that would, in some circumstances, involve disobedience. Thus, while any full history of liberty would note the primary significance of certain Christian attitudes, like the sharp awareness that not everything belongs to Caesar, still it must be said that the kind of glowing appreciation of liberty that one sees in John Stuart Mill's essay *On Liberty* is a product more of the Enlightenment than of Christianity. It is humanist reason, not religious faith, that has found in liberty a stirring cause.

The explanation for this appears to be quite simple. Liberty is obviously desirable if human beings are good. Orthodox Christianity, however, holds that they are thoroughly evil. I say "evil" rather than "sinful" in order not to obscure the force of the Christian claim with a theological term that for many is either suspect or not very meaningful. I will sometimes speak of "sin," however, for the word is irreplaceable. It indicates not evil alone, but evil that is freely willed and embraced, and moreover, that consists in the intentional rejection of an absolute good. Human beings are not evil in their God-created nature, of course. But they have made themselves evil by repudiating the very source and essence of all good, that is, God. This is not to say that they are altogether depraved, although some Christians have held that they are. It is rather to say that they have a powerful, and humanly ineradicable, tendency to devote themselves to something other than God, the one unqualified good. The result is emotional derangement and an incapacity for discerning authentic values. Liberty is unlikely to be beneficial to either such marred beings or their society. This, at any rate, is the Christian view.

Such an appraisal of man is not of course a casual thought, easily dropped. It derives from a structural requirement of Christian belief. To affirm the goodness and omnipotence of God, in a universe containing much evil, it is necessary to attribute the evil to human beings. What other source could it have? Not God, since God is sovereign in power and perfect in nature. And not a flaw in the design of the universe, for the universe is created by God. Evil can be due only to human beings. This is not, of course, because God created them evil. It is because he created them free. He gave them the power of choosing evil and thereby mutilating their created nature. Humans used this power. The very idea, so fundamental in Christian faith, that Christ is a savior presupposes sin. Those who need to be saved must be gravely flawed. Otherwise they would save themselves.

Moreover, the evil in man is not a mere weakness, which might with effort be overcome. A mere weakness would be an implausible explanation for the terrible deeds done by humans in all periods of history and all regions of the earth. Nor is it the kind of derangement that is susceptible to human therapy. Successful therapy requires a healthy therapist, or at least a healthy therapeutic faculty, such as reason was thought to be in the ancient world and in the era of the Enlightenment. The disorder, to be healed, must be bounded. It must be a condition that can be set apart and objectively analyzed and acted upon. But sin is not a condition of this sort. It affects the therapist, or the therapeutic faculty, no less than all else. There is no sinless vantage point from which sin can be comprehended and attacked.

This is one way of pointing toward what Christians mean when they speak not just of sin but of *original* sin. Sin is primary and all-pervasive in human nature. The story of Adam's sin — which few modern Christians take as literal truth — is a way of describing mythically a human rebellion against God. The notion that the stain of sin has been inherited by all of Adam's descendants is in substance a characterization of human beings as rebels against God. In less mythical terms, humans persistently deny their connection with the source and essence of good. In this way they are disabled in every part of their created nature. They have largely lost their ability to discern and choose things of true value.

Kierkegaard somewhere states that sin presupposes sin. Beneath every particular sinful deed lies a freely affirmed predisposition toward sin. We sin because of a prior and completely uncoerced willingness to sin. Hence it is, as we all know, that someone may carry on a life free of evil deeds yet still be evil, or at least not very good. Hence, too, inexplicable feelings of guilt. It is a commonplace of psychology that people sometimes have a sense of ineradicable guilt without being able to name anything they are guilty of. The presdisposition toward evil may not be literally inherited from Adam, but it is present from birth. Babies, as Augustine notes, are harmless because they are helpless, not because they are good. Who but children would, as children often do, taunt the disabled and disfigured?

There are two major kinds of sin. One is commonly regarded, both in the Bible and by Christians generally, as more basic than the other. This is pride, the fundamental form of human moral disorientation. Pride, in very broad terms, is giving priority to oneself — relying absolutely on one's own intelligence and power, privileging oneself over all others in the distribution of good things, finding complete satisfaction in the company of the self alone. For Christians it is putting the self in place of God, that is, self-deification. Pride issues naturally in the quest for fame, high office, and wealth, and these conditions in turn encourage pride.

A secondary form of sin is often called "sensuality," but is better termed "distraction" since it is more broad and various than indulgence in sensual appetites. Distraction is the very opposite of pride. Rather than the whole of life being centered on the self, the self is abandoned. This can come about through immersion in sensual pleasures, such as eating, drinking, and sex. But it takes other than sensual forms. To devote all of one's time and energies to a set of routines, without ever pausing to think; to follow unhesitatingly every command of a despot and accept without question every tenet of a ruling creed; invariably to behave as those around you are behaving — these are all forms of distraction. The self and its freedom are forgotten. This is deliberate. Distraction is a product of despair. It is secondary to pride in that it comes out of pride that has failed to fulfill its ambitions. Everyone would like to be a god. But when efforts to be godlike collapse, many resort, not to God, but to something in the world, like a routine, or a crowd, or a despot, in which the self can be drowned and forgotten.

In addition to pride and distraction, there is a widespread moral derangement usually called "idolatry." This is not, I think, a third form of sin, but rather a variation on pride. Idolatry consists in trusting and serving unreservedly something finite and imperfect and therefore unworthy of trust. The idol is an entity, such as a nation, treated as though it is free of limits and flaws. The self is identified with this entity, as in fervent patriotism, and in this way pride is served indirectly. It might seem that idolatry could serve distraction equally well, by allowing the self to be wholly immersed and lost in the idolized entity. Idolatry, however, involves an act of self-consecration not found in distraction. The self is not abandoned but is devoted unconditionally to something that is not God. Nazis did not abandon, but rather disfigured, themselves by their dedication to Hitler and the Nazi cause. It may be that pride usually involves idolatry. Only the most egregious egoists can make a god of the self alone.

Sin, then, is misusing the self — making too much of it or obliterating it. It is raising the self into the heavens or casting it into nothingness. The doctrine of original sin, at its core, holds first of all that every person is deeply inclined to do these things. It holds in addition that this inclination does not come from mere personal weakness or the allure of the evil that is chosen. It comes from a free but perverse commitment to a counterfeit god. The inclination is itself chosen. That choice is the sin presupposed by sin. It is the Christian idea that only by trusting absolutely in God can the self in its true proportions, and stationed in its proper place, emerge. Hence, by rejecting God we have mutilated and dislocated ourselves. A rebellion against God turned out to be a rebellion against the self.

The impact such a view of human nature has on the ideal of liberty is readily apparent. Humans are a dangerous species. Possessing liberty, they naturally create disorder and work destruction. The multitudinous ills of American society today cannot surprise any Christian with a grasp of Christian fundamentals. Nor is it surprising that one of the first and greatest diagnosticians of the ills inherent in liberty was a Christian, Alexis de Tocqueville. If modern Christians have gradually lost their fear of liberty, this may be due to their having lost sight of some of their Christian principles. Perhaps they have forgotten the somber lessons Christianity teaches about human nature. The traditional Christian emphasis on the sanctity of established powers and the duty of obeying them was not a passing preference, a product of a particular historical time and place. It was a reasonable — although not inevitable — inference from the Christian view of human nature.

Disciples of the Enlightenment are apt to feel little inclination to question or rebut any argument that puts Christians at odds with liberty. Christians have long been suspect to lovers of liberty. But does humanist reason provide better foundations for liberty? It may seem that some humanists have, mainly by entertaining optimistic views of human nature. But does reason, soberly applied, support those views? Does it say anything different about human nature than Christianity does? The greatest of Enlightenment figures, Immanuel Kant, thought not.

Sin as Seen by Reason

Kant wrote of the "radical evil" in man. This characteristic was for Kant empirically manifest. It "need not be proved," he declared, "in view of the multitude of crying examples which experience *of the actions* of men puts before our eyes" (*Religion within the Limits of Reason Alone*, p. 28, emphasis Kant's). Kant's appeal to empirical evidence is particularly noteworthy. The concept of original sin may seem festooned in theological cobwebs. It has been massively confirmed, however, by the horrors of twentieth-century history — by the Soviet gulags and the killing fields of Cambodia, the Nazi death camps and the Rwanda massacres, and the unbounded brutalities of leaders like Mao Tse-tung, Pol Pot, and Saddam Hussein. It is remarkable that so many people who appeal to empirical evidence as the highest standard of truth find the Christian stress on sin unacceptable.

Kant did not appeal to empirical evidence alone, however. He worked out a concept of radical evil that was virtually equivalent to the Christian concept of original sin. It was based, not on the allurements of sensual enjoyment that figured so largely in the classical Greek concept of sin, but rather, like the Christian concept, on a perverse choice. The choice, in Kant's case, was to obey the moral law only conditionally. The categorical imperative was made hypothetical. One might adhere to the imperative most of the time, yet would do so with the inner proviso that in some circumstances it might be suspended. The proviso would allow sensuous impulses occasionally to be indulged. When indulged, however, this would not be because they were too powerful to be resisted. They did not, in Kant's mind, have in themselves that kind of power. They were indulged because of the primal perverse choice — the original sin — that granted them such power. For Kant, as for Kierkegaard, sin presupposed sin. This was the radical evil Kant believed innate in every human being, even though it did not belong to the human essence. Kant was not a Christian, but he explicitly recognized the kinship between the Christian concept of original sin and his own view of human nature.

Yet most people, someone might claim, are quite decent. You can't judge the human race as a whole by monstrous exceptions like the dictators of the twentieth century. This may seem at first glance to be a valid objection to the Christian and Kantian strictures on human nature. Surely the monsters of recent history are aberrations from the human norm. We should note, however, that monsters have been able to rule nations only because populations at large have more or less willingly supported them. Terror alone cannot keep large masses in subjection. Moreover, the totalitarian dictators have been able to commit mountainous atrocities only with the assistance of tens of thousands of willing allies — the police, the spies, the camp guards, and so forth. Neither Stalin nor Hitler ruled alone, nor did Mao Tse-tung and Pol Pot murder millions with their own hands. Judged by what they did with their own hands, the mass killers of our time were innocent of human blood.

Still, someone might assert, the vast majority of people under modern dictators have not been oppressors, but only oppressed. The majority of people under Hitler were not Nazis and did not commit any crimes. They suffered in silence. But in many cases there was sin in silence itself, as when ordinary Germans unprotestingly allowed their Jewish neighbors and fellow citizens to be stripped of their possessions and killed. Moreover, the populations over whom the dictators ruled were not really oppressed. Terror wielded by a small minority cannot, over a period of years, subdue a large majority. The majority must acquiesce. Thus a well-known German political scientist estimated that considerably over half the German people were more or less favorably disposed toward Hitler during the Nazi era and that only a small minority were adamantly opposed.

And finally, in evaluating the proposition that most people are quite decent, it ought to be noted that decency is not a very demanding standard. Most of those who are decent have probably never been very severely tempted to be indecent. Crime, after all, is ordinarily attended by numerous dangers and inconveniences. Ordinary decency may in most cases be a manifestation less of virtue than of prudence and timidity. It is not only Christianity that tells us this, but also modern psychology. Psychoanalysis, of course, is a highly developed technique for looking below the surface of everyday decencies. When that is done, according to the founder of psychoanalysis — an atheist — we find impulses so horrifying to those moved by them that they can't acknowledge them in their own minds but repress them, creating profound disorders in the psyche.

Of course, there are not only multitudes of "decent" people but also saints and heroes, a few of whom stand out for exceptional courage and goodness. The twentieth century was distinguished by the presence not only of Hitler and Stalin, but also of Andrei Sakharov and Dietrich Bonhoeffer. Such people undeniably testify in behalf of human nature. Still, they are exceptional. Their lives entail dangers and sacrifices of a sort most of us strive assiduously to avoid. Also, it is noteworthy that people of this kind rarely if ever seem to feel that they are very good. On the contrary, they are typically humble and apparently lacking in much assurance of their own virtue. One hesitates to charge people apparently so wise with misunderstanding their own nature.

It has been claimed by some of the most powerful minds of the past, such as Jean-Jacques Rousseau and Karl Marx, that while human beings are deformed by evil, and deformed in a way that affects the few and the many alike, they are nonetheless not intrinsically evil. They are made evil by historical circumstances, such as the institution of private property or the capitalist system of production. If such circumstances were changed, their native goodness would emerge. This is one of the most alluring hypotheses ever conceived, and there is no way of definitively disproving it. Neither, however, is there any way of rendering it plausible. To begin with, it cannot be convincingly shown how human beings, if good, could become entangled in circumstances destructive of their goodness. Nor can it be shown plausibly — as distinguished from seductively — how they might extricate themselves from such circumstances if everyone has been corrupted. The most serious efforts to act on the hypothesis of human goodness are represented by the various communist revolutions that began in 1917. As everyone knows, rather than confirming the hypothesis, they brought forth startling manifestations of the callousness and cruelty they set out to erase from the earth.

The very conditions constituting what is often called "the human condition" reinforce the Christian and Kantian view. They do this by exhibiting the dynamic and the source of sin. Finite personhood, unconnected with anything eternal or divine, is a tormenting state if fully faced. It is a state of radical ignorance — of our ultimate origin and our final end, and of all the forces, inward and outward, that determine the shape of our lives. It is therefore a state of intrinsic insecurity. At the same time, since choices have to be made (if only by refusing to make them), and in everyone there is a conscience that may unpredictably set off moral alarms, it is apt to be a state of moral uneasiness and spiritual anguish. The temptation to distract ourselves with pleasures, thrills, and thoughtless activities of various sorts, or else to indulge in illusions of practical sovereignty and moral infallibility, is overwhelming. In this way people are drawn toward lives that are either trivial and wasted or pretentious and destructive. In a word, they are drawn toward sin.

In the light of reason, we see again that sin is self-falsification. Either the self is treated as a mere thing, without freedom, hence without moral responsibility, or it is tacitly deified, thought of as immune to physical danger and moral error alike. Under one misrepresentation difficult choices are evaded and the moral dimensions of selfhood are

36

forgotten. Life is based on anything that allows time to pass agreeably — on physical pleasure, perhaps, or on mindless devotion to organizational functions. Under the other misrepresentation it is not selfhood that is forgotten but rather the self's finitude and moral fallibility. Other persons cease to be persons and become things to be ignored or managed as convenience requires. One is either solitary and self-absorbed or preoccupied with power, perhaps over many people, but usually over only an unfortunate mate, or an animal, or casual acquaintances and contacts. The former sin is distraction, the latter pride. Both are ways of withholding love.

Sin is dreaming. Distraction is indulgence in a dream of being no longer free, no longer under moral constraint or judgment, merely a thing among other things in the world. Pride is dreaming that one entirely transcends and controls the world of things and therefore has nothing to fear. The great crimes of history occur when a people falls fully under the spell of such dreams. Masses hungry for distraction become willing slaves, and a few who are bold enough to deify themselves become their masters. However, no one, in any historical situation, entirely evades the influence of such dreams. As responses to the universal conditions of human existence, they are natural and in some degree unavoidable. They indicate how solidly grounded the concept of original sin is. It does not depend mainly on theological considerations, compelling perhaps for believers but meaningless for others. Nor does it depend among unbelievers altogether on empirical evidence, as abundant and dramatic as that is. It is demonstrated by analysis of the structure of human existence on earth. In short, it makes historical and psychological sense.

The question, Why liberty? is obviously much harder to answer than either most philosophers of liberty or most people in possession of liberty have realized. The old liberal answer — that liberty leads to harmony and happiness — is nearly impossible. It rests on an untenable optimism about human nature. Would-be defenders of liberty must find a way of reconciling liberty with the fallenness perceived by people of faith and with the harsh realities evident to those relying on experience and reason. They must show why liberty is good even though its results, in many ways, are evil. To grapple with this problem is the main purpose of the present essay.

Before setting out to do this, however, we need to take more careful measure of the problem itself. We will be concerned in the pages imme-diately following with some of the characteristic forms that evil as-sumes under the conditions of liberty.

The Naked Human Soul

One of the most common charges against liberty and liberalism is that it dissolves human relationships, particularly the kinds of warm, unques-tioned relationships that rest on custom and tradition. The charge is quite valid. Liberty in the hands of creatures, each strongly inclined to exaggerate the value and power of the self, is corrosive. It disconnects in-dividuals from one another and sets them adrift. It turns society from a more or less coherent hierarchical structure into an array of dissociated human particles. This is one of the most prominent themes in Tocqueville (who was basically on the side of liberty, even though acutely conscious of its drawbacks). Living through the aftermath of the French Revolution, Tocqueville observed the decomposition of feudal order. He witnessed the great historical transition effected by the power of liberty to dissolve long-standing traditions, customs, and authorities. In Amer-ica he saw that even in a society largely free of feudal structures, liberty was an atomizing force. It was a source of radical individualism.

The upshot was precisely characterized by a poet and novelist living in Russia but sensitive to global conditions. Boris Pasternak wrote in *Doctor Zhivago* that "all that's left is the naked human soul stripped to its last shred" (pp. 402-3). These words are far from covering the whole state of the individual in liberal society or all the possibilities before that individual. But they characterize quite exactly an experience every mature and sensitive person in liberal societies goes through repeat-edly. Nothing in the world can be altogether relied upon. No human au-thorities, living or dead, no books, no standards or principles, are un-questioned or unshaken. All is in doubt. Pasternak was particularly attuned to lives under a despot. That he saw something that applies to lives under the conditions of liberty is not surprising. The similarity of these two lives was explicitly and dramatically noted by Tocqueville. Despotism, like liberty, dissolves relationships.

To understand this aspect of liberty, one must realize that we are speaking of the liberty of all, not just of a few. We are speaking of what is sometimes loosely called "democracy." Strictly defined, liberty and democracy are not the same, one denoting absence of constraint, the other equality, carrying with it the implication of popular rule. Since the time of the American and French Revolutions, however, the cry of liberty has meant *equal* liberty. It has meant democracy. And the cry of democracy has meant that everyone, equally, ought to be *free.* In writing *Democracy in America,* Tocqueville was concerned with the consequences of applying the principle classically stated in the Declaration of Independence, a statement fusing in one key proposition the ideals of both equality and liberty, namely, that "all men are created equal, that they are endowed, by their Creator, with certain unalienable Rights." The corrosive impact of liberty on society is explained by its fusion with equality.

At the beginning of the third millennium the dissolution of human relationships seems to be continuing in spite of spontaneous restorative responses such as the proliferation of private groups. We can see this in the uneasy and sometimes tumultuous relations between onetime superiors and their onetime subordinates — between men and women, parents and children, teachers and students, governments and citizens, and priests and laity. One of the most fiercely defended convictions of most individuals in most Western nations, at the outset of the twenty-first century, is that no one else can rightfully tell them what to think or how to live. These, it must be admitted, are merely empirical observations. They point, however, toward enduring human characteristics and toward forces liberty will tend to generate throughout history.

The reason why liberty is a dissolvent of human relations is so apparent that it scarcely needs explaining. The liberal injunction is "Go your own way." Properly understood, this is not an invitation to impetuosity or frivolity. It is a summons to everyone to find and follow his or her own particular vocation. It is a recognition of the responsibility, bearing on every person, not only to follow the moral law but to do this in a way that constitutes a distinctive realization of one's own personal being. Nor is the injunction to go your own way a permit to offend or forget about others. Among morally unimpaired beings, going your own way would mean making a unique contribution to common enterprises like discovering new truths or creating things of beauty. It would mean — and at times does mean — participation in the ongoing task of creating community. Among sinful creatures, however, it also means disagreement and contention, callousness and self-seclusion. Society tends to fall into as many little pieces as there are individuals within it.

Closely connected with this social atomism is the moral and cultural relativism that liberalism has had a hand in producing. It is an easy — although invalid — inference from the standard of liberty that individuals should be unrestricted by moral norms. They should respond in any way they please to their own particular impulses and should pursue uninhibitedly their own personal ambitions. The fulfillment of their desires should not be frustrated by moral norms and rules. The result has been a popular tendency to call even the most scandalous conduct, provided no one is killed or grievously harmed by it, a private matter, of no proper concern to society. Liberty best flourishes, it is assumed, in an atmosphere of amorality.

Cultural standards have been eroded in like fashion. Free individuals should be as unconstrained by cultural norms as they are by moral norms. The supreme criterion of artistic and literary excellence comes to be mere personal preference. To suggest that someone ought to learn to appreciate Rembrandt or Beethoven is taken as an intrusion into a sphere of purely private taste and pleasure — a sphere sanctified by the axiom of liberty. Granted, the result may be not so much a diversity of cultural works and opportunities as the uniform degradation apparent in modern popular culture. Even so, individuals maintain a rebellious posture in relation to any suggestion that excellence lies anywhere but in the things they immediately and spontaneously like.

In sum, the upshot of liberty is moral and cultural relativism. Both undergird the dissolution of human relationships. Individuals no longer inhabit a social universe bound together by established standards of goodness and beauty. Liberty is construed in a way that sanctions social decomposition and even idealizes moral and cultural anarchy. Although these centrifugal forces are apt to be curbed by group activity and social conformity, people live in what they conceive to be, even if it is not in fact, a moral and cultural area entirely their own. Every person is ruler and legislator of a private moral world and a private culture. David Riesman wrote of "the lonely crowd." The phrase points tellingly toward the persistence of a kind of personal, inward dissociation in the midst of outward social unities.

Endeavoring to explain one of the many school shootings occurring in America near the turn of the millennium, a school official spontaneously hit on the condition underlying much of the moral and cultural decay of the time. He noted that the students had only tenuous connections with parents and older relatives and concluded by observing that "they're all on their own." This is true, in various ways and to various degrees, of almost everyone in modern liberal societies. They are all on their own. That can be seen, of course, as fulfilling the very idea of liberty, namely, that final authority in every life belongs in the hands of the one whose life it is. Properly construed, this principle is a way of accentuating the responsibility bearing on each one, a responsibility with moral, cultural, and various other dimensions. Construed by self-assertive and self-magnifying creatures, however, it comes to authorize doing anything one feels like doing.

The dissolution of human relations has not, of course, been caused solely by the ideal of liberty. Fragmentation, produced by multiple causes, has been a major phenomenon in modern history. Luther's revolt against the Roman Catholic Church did as much to reduce society to personal atoms as anything that has happened in Western history. Rationalism and science, by encouraging individuals to think critically about the norms and authorities over them, have worked in the same general direction as the Reformation. And technology and industry have ceaselessly unsettled social patterns, and by producing material abundance have in countless instances and ways released individuals from social constraints. The idea of liberty has perhaps done less to cause than to legitimize such forces. It has told the human race that following your own religious impulses is your right, that thinking for yourself testifies to your humanity, and that inventiveness and acquisitiveness are worthy qualities. It has thus made religious tolerance, freedom of thought and speech, and capitalist enterprise into the main premises of modern social order. I believe that in themselves these premises are fully valid. As employed by a fallen, that is, proud and self-assertive, race, however, they have called forth and buttressed the disconnected individual — the naked human soul.

Eloquent expressions of the individualism comprised in the liberal cause are found in John Stuart Mill's great essay *On Liberty*. Individualism is by no means the only sentiment animating Mill's essay. Mill's discussion of free speech, for example, displays a profound appreciation of intellectual community. One of Mill's most heartfelt chapters, however, is an encomium on individuality — on personal originality and distinctiveness. It has been said with some justice that what Mill celebrates in this chapter is eccentricity. Sheer energetic uniqueness, with little regard to standards of any kind, comes close to being equated with excellence. Yet the chapter is far from flimsy. It has a cogency and eloquence that carry along most readers. This indicates that the stripping of the individual (to use Pasternak's terms) is not merely incidental to the liberal movement. It is close to its heart and soul.

It may seem that in most of this discussion we have not been speaking of evil. We began with the concept of original sin and the apparent incongruity between the reality of human evil and the ideal of liberty. In seeing how liberty has eventuated in social disintegration, however, we have been observing things most people feel to be either neutral or positively good. Individuality is generally admired, at least in principle, and even eccentricity is not usually censured. As for the Reformation, the Enlightenment, and industrial capitalism, these can be criticized on various grounds, but they can hardly be treated simply as manifestations of original sin.

It is not my claim that these things are evil in themselves, but only that they are readily used in evil ways and inevitably are where liberty is possessed by evil men. Individuality can be glorious, as it was in the instance of Socrates or Jesus. Mill's error was in failing to note that it can also be sinister and diabolic. Rasputin displayed individuality in a striking fashion, as did Hitler. Something comparable can be said about the historical movements we have discussed. There is nothing intrinsic to the impulse toward religious purification that renders the fragmentation of the church, or the spiritual isolation of the individual, inevitable. Further, the inclination to work toward rational human relationships, and to attack major human problems with the weapons of reason, did not have to bring on war between faith and reason, nor did it of necessity culminate in the nihilism of academic postmodernism. And finally, industrial capitalism, contrary to Marx, was not bound by any historical destiny to produce poverty, class conflict, and ruthless business competition. Such consequences arose from human pride and irresponsibility, in a word, from sin. It is not liberty in itself that has dissolved human relations, but the liberty of creatures who are, except when captivated by a despair that causes them to flee from selfhood and responsibility, ingenious and persevering in pursuing their own aims at the cost of others.

Fundamentally it is pride that has brought into existence the naked human soul. I use the word "pride" to denote all kinds of self-assertion — the quest for social eminence, for political power, for commercial dominance, and for personal luxury and pleasure. Given the opportunity, individuals are inclined to devote themselves to the self and its private ends. Liberty gives them the opportunity, and the avidity with which individuals seize the opportunity manifests what Christians mean by "original sin" and what Kant meant by "radical evil." In a word, pride, liberated, causes individuals to pay little heed to values such as justice, truth, and beauty. Hence the stark inequalities and the desolate scenes associated with the rise of industrialism. Hence the development of refined techniques for inducing others to think and behave according to the desires of capitalists and political managers. It is not, of course, liberalism that has created such tendencies. They are universal, and were therefore visible to Pasternak, a Russian. But liberalism sets these prideful energies free. Liberating the individual, it liberates all that is worst — as well as all that is best, as we shall see — in the human race.

Liberal atomism is an ambiguous phenomenon in more ways than one. It is the work of self-assertive individuals and in this sense represents a triumph of personal power and initiative. At the same time, the individual is a victim, one who is trampled on in the course of this triumph. And this is true not only of those trampled on by the triumphant, but also of the triumphant themselves. It was not, for example, only the workers whose lives were rendered desolate by industrial capitalists in the nineteenth century. The capitalists themselves were disfigured in their humanity. Souls on both sides were stripped. Another ambiguity lies particularly close to the main themes of this essay. For human relationships to be dissolved is manifestly evil. The naked self is alone, vulnerable, fearful. All truths are in doubt, all expectations uncertain. ("Anything can happen — anything," someone remarks in Sartre's *Nausea*.) Pasternak speaks of the individual as "cold and shivering." Yet for everything to be cast into question creates possibilities of limitless personal freedom and responsibility, and that cannot be unequivocally condemned. As free (ontologically, whether or not politically), man is responsible for every aspect of his life. This, to use a common phrase, is the human condition. This is why, in the same set of remarks from which I have been quoting, Pasternak says of "the naked human soul" that "nothing has changed because it was always cold and shivering and reaching out to its nearest neighbor, as cold and lonely as itself." Pasternak compares the new naked souls to Adam and Eve. Thus, in dissolving human relationships, yet allowing the naked soul to reach out to another soul, liberty restores human beings to their primal state of freedom and responsibility.

As already noted, society has in some ways spontaneously knitted itself together. Man's social and political inclinations have not been destroyed, or wholly suppressed, by the coming of liberty. Thus Tocqueville was forcibly impressed by the abounding life of private groups in the United States. Further, as Tocqueville foresaw, many have found significant human relations through the kind of political activity that democracy makes widely available. Such remedies no doubt help greatly to keep personal isolation from being as stark as it might otherwise be. Nonetheless, group life and political activity should not be idealized.

Group loyalty is a dangerous phenomenon. Not that groups are bad in themselves. On the contrary, they are good insofar as they further good human relations. But they are no better than the human beings within them. Indeed, they are probably worse in that individuals will often do things as members of a group that they would not do if acting solely for and by themselves. They will make demands in behalf of their families or businesses that they would not make for themselves alone. And they will act with greater ruthlessness to advance the interest of a group than if self-interest alone were involved. Conscience will sanction deeds in behalf of the group that it would not sanction otherwise. An allied issue here is idolatry. Group loyalty can tempt members into making the group into a kind of god. Not many individuals are presumptuous enough to deify themselves. But most of them, in some circumstances, will at least tacitly deify a nation, a race, a class, or a party. Much of the tragedy and turmoil of the twentieth century originated in group idolatry. All of this suggests that group activity not only repairs social atomism, although it may do this sometimes. In many instances it gives it a different form. The naked human soul, not yet humbled or driven to distraction, but proud and ruthless, is armed with collective powers.

As for political activity, one must be equally guarded. No doubt participation in public affairs can teach people to be more considerate of one another and can make them more skilled in defining and solving common problems. Politics and love are not mutually exclusive. But they do not usually go together, since politics involves power. The same is true of politics and truth. People seeking power do not necessarily lie. Still, when they speak they must calculate consequences, and speaking the truth will often not produce the consequences they desire. Someone whose highest aim is to find and uncompromisingly voice the truth is not fitted for political life. For such reasons as these, one should be wary of the Aristotelian dictum that "man is a political animal." If it means that the political arena is where we achieve our fullest humanity, it is certainly false. It presupposes a truncated version of the human soul. Even Aristotle, for all his idealization of citizen life in the polis, saw the best life as that of philosophical contemplation, not political activity. It may be that politics does less to moderate the pride that atomizes society than, by opening up an arena in which intoxicating prizes are offered to personal ambition, to exacerbate it.

Social atomism is clearly a paradoxical phenomenon. It does not mean that society visibly falls into as many disconnected individuals as there are members of the population. Society coheres. Individuals join together. They do this partly because they are not entirely evil. They are moved by impulses toward righteousness and truth. They join together also, however, in furtherance of selfish interests. The pride that sometimes leaves individuals "cold and shivering" is empowered rather than curbed. And if pride is eventually defeated, there may arise a drive toward distraction. This drive, like pride, calls forth associations — in this case associations that allow or require their members to lose themselves in the group. Bureaucracies and mass movements are familiar examples.

The Ordeal of Liberty

The modern conceit that the feudal order of the Middle Ages spelled unrelieved misery, while the liberal society of modern times opens up vistas of happiness, is far from true. There was unquestionably a great deal of misery in the Middle Ages, but it came more from conditions like poverty, disease, and war than from lack of liberty. Lack of liberty can be comfortable. Liberty can be distressing. We get an inkling of this in the prevalence among free people of drug use, mental illness, and other manifestations of unhappiness. If liberty is glorious, that is because it allows human beings to use their intellectual and moral powers for glorious ends. It is not because it provides lasting tranquillity and solid satisfaction. Where people are fixed in social stations involving definite duties, where the social order tells each one how life from beginning to end must be carried on, and where certain reigning dogmas are apt to be publicly uncontested, human evil is more or less curbed and obscured. Where there is liberty, however, appetite and ambition are released, doubt is encouraged, and evil becomes manifest in diverse and unforeseeable ways. In free societies, children and parents, siblings and friends, professional colleagues and business associates all become potential sources of highly unpleasant surprises. And it is not only others who make the loss of creedal fixity and prescriptive place painful. Being responsible for the whole course of your life, and all the beliefs and allegiances that define your soul, can be a burden and a trial, and the final outcome may be not satisfaction but poignant regret.

The strains of liberty can be summarily described by noting two conditions inherent in the lives of free people. One of these is estrangement, lack of close and stable personal relations. Liberated men and women are unlikely to devote themselves wholly to the cooperative and communicative relationships that liberty makes possible. They are apt to aim at personal advantage instead of cooperation, and domination rather than communication. Power and pleasure prove more attractive than truth and searching conversation. Also contributing to estrangement is the fact that people with liberty can behave in incalculable ways. Uncurbed freedom means unpredictability. It goes without saying that custom and law, personal promises and legal contracts, the demands of superiors and the necessities of situations all do much to regularize conduct. But liberty would be meaningless unless people often broke free of conventional constraints, in that way confounding the expectations of others and becoming strangers to them. If original sin is real, this will happen rather often.

The other major strain in the life of liberty comes from personal responsibility. Being free means simply that one must decide what kind of person to be — what to believe and how to live. One must choose a vocation, a mate, a place of residence. One must choose avocations, friends, and diversions. And one must choose a god, or supreme principle of life. Such choices are meaningful only by being continually and in

46

various ways reaffirmed. They must be made again and again. They can of course occasionally be changed. But they are serious only if they are exempt from casual change. At the same time, since we are finite and partially blinded by sin, our major choices must always be made with insufficient knowledge, for example, of our potentialities, of the basic character of our associates, and of all the contingencies associated with our existence. The mere fact that we set the general direction of our lives in the naïveté of youth is filled with implications. Few lives are carried on for long without serious mistakes, and the consequences of mistakes, such as choosing an unsuitable vocation or unworthy friends or a false creed, can be grievous, not only for oneself but also for others. Hence the burden of responsibility is often felt not only in making one's life choices but also in regretting them and trying to rectify them. One of the main consequences of our fallenness is simply that liberty and guilt are inseparable.

The weight of responsibility is increased by some of the conditions that commonly develop in free societies. Estrangement, for example, sharpens awareness of the unsharable nature of responsibility. When I make those critical decisions that determine who I will be, I must do so alone. I can seek advice, but I must decide by myself what advice to follow. Choice is in essence a solitary act. Estrangement makes it impossible to soften this disquieting fact. Another condition intensifying the discomforts of responsibility is moral and cultural relativism, which sows confusion concerning the standards governing choice. Anyone with liberty and a sense of responsibility must ask, what is a good person? But the one asking this question in late modern times is apt to wonder whether there is such a thing as goodness, and may even wonder (if familiar with philosophical fashions) whether there is such a thing as a person. Many alleviate such strains by looking around them and making the same choices everyone else is making. This, however, is unlikely to reduce the danger of making mistaken choices. And it means, in effect, surrendering one's liberty.

The ordeal of liberty, however, is by no means merely a product of social conditions. It arises from the very nature of things. A human life is essentially voluntary. We are condemned, as Sartre said, to be free. Moreover, the stress inherent in liberty is heightened by an ignorance that cannot be overcome by even the greatest intelligence or by the most assiduous and prolonged research. Ignorance is implicit not only in original sin but also in the very fact of our cosmic and historical imminence. We cannot gain any demonstrable and unquestionable knowledge either of the whole network of circumstances in which we live or of the moral considerations — for example, how much to concede to expediency — that should govern our choices.

Here someone might object that I am speaking — as modern liberals typically do! — as though individuals had to live wholly without authorities. Life is not lived (the objection might run) on a level plain, where every person and every reality are on a footing with every other person and reality. On the contrary, humans live well only where they can look upward and thereby discover what they should think and do.

I do not deny the fact of authority or its importance. There is, for example, the Bible and the pope. And there are lesser authorities — parents, writers, teachers, even occasionally a political leader. I do deny, however, that any such authority can relieve a person of the responsibility inherent in the ontological status of being a person. To follow an authority is a free act, and to follow an evil authority, as countless millions have in the course of history, is an evil act. The presence of authoritative figures may help in the fulfillment of one's responsibilities. But also it may lure one into betraying those responsibilities, and doing something evil under the sway of an evil authority does not lessen one's guilt. Moreover, given the radical evil affecting human beings, there are numerous evil authorities at hand in any period of history. These are not only the monstrous simplifiers prophetically foreseen by Burckhardt, but also the kings and bishops, the prime ministers and presidents who are rendered self-centered and insensitive by their power.

Liberty makes things worse in two ways. To begin with, stable and responsible authority is more or less eroded by liberty. The fact is that where there is liberty we do live mainly on a level plain. Liberty is incompatible, many assume, with deference to authority. And such deference is repellent to the sin that liberty unleashes. Pride renders one reluctant to admit that anyone else is wiser than he. And while a distracted man may become merely an object to be manipulated by some self-deified dictator, distraction robs him of the capacity to submit intelligently to one authority rather than another. In principle, liberty and authority go together perfectly. On the one hand, few if any are capable of choosing wisely without some guidance from others; in that way liberty depends on authority. On the other hand, authority is not real unless it is freely accepted; in that sense authority depends on liberty. Where there is very much liberty, however, authority is apt to be weak and beleaguered. For the confused individual, there is often no one to look up to. This is one of the results of original sin and one of the conditions underlying the ordeal of liberty. Beyond the general erosion of worthy authority, there is the multiplication of ephemeral and unworthy authorities. The level plain on which a free life is conducted is infested with swarms of petty self-styled experts in psychology, spirituality, politics, and every other area of general concern.

Deference to authority, then, is no more adequate an answer to the fraying of social bonds than is participation in private groups or in political activity. All alike provide ways in which the corrosive power of human sin can make itself felt. The subject of authority will be discussed more fully at a later point in the essay.

It is not, of course, liberty alone that renders personal responsibility onerous. It is liberty in the face of the moral law. No wonder relativism is popular, however disturbing it may be to an awakened conscience. When we say that moral law is relative — to time, to place, perhaps even to a person ("what is right for me") — we say, in effect, that there is no moral law. At least there is none that need cause spiritual anguish. Liberty becomes much lighter. Liberty becomes an opportunity to live as we like, not as a fountain of perplexities about right and wrong, and good and evil. Yet that wearisome inner voice, heedless of the best arguments for relativism, can rarely be utterly silenced. Almost everyone knows that it makes a difference — in some mysterious way a difference of infinite significance — how we conduct our lives. Regarding some matters we can no doubt do as we like, but other matters tell us, without equivocation, that we had better take care. It is conscience that thus troubles the lives of free people.

That liberty is arduous is the great unrecognized fact in free societies. It is not a fact that is difficult to comprehend. Both our religious traditions and our history tell us that not all human impulses are morally good. Yet faith, philosophy, and conscience all tell us that we ought to be good. There is a conflict between our natural impulses and our moral consciousness. Liberty means that this conflict is waged, or at least ought to be waged, within the soul of every person. Hence the ordeal of liberty. The ordeal is largely unrecognized, although it is plain to be seen, because it is not pleasant. Ambitious people do not ordinarily gain power and wealth by urging people to fight against the evil in themselves but by painting prospects of a carefree life. More surprising is that political philosophers, presumably free of base ambition, have done little more than leaders in commerce and politics to illuminate the character of liberty. Their lack of realism is probably due, as I have suggested, to the influence of Enlightenment optimism.

Before trying to determine what a more realistic liberalism would look like, however, we must examine somewhat further the present state of liberty.

Flight from Freedom

If everyone is in some degree lacking the inner restraints dictated by moral law, and at the same time largely free of outer restraints, one might assume that the general result will be anarchy, limited only by the most exigent requirements of order. In most matters people will do as they like, with little regard for others, and also with little regard today for what they did yesterday. There will be tumultuous diversity and ceaseless innovation. Life will be pleasurable and impulsive, displaying little constancy and little nobility. People will be unaffected and independent, but also unreflective and irresolute. This is the gist of Plato's critique of democracy (or equal liberty, which for Plato, as for Tocqueville, was at the core of democracy). Aristocratic in his political philosophy, as in his family lineage, Plato recoils from a society in which no moral distinctions are drawn, either among the numerous appetites clamoring for satisfaction or among the numerous personalities seeking attention in public places.

That there is a degree of truth in this portrait can hardly be denied by anyone who has experienced life in modern America. Americans are accustomed, in their social existence, to behavior that is more or less undisciplined and is constantly shifting in response to shifting fashions. The world around them has an anarchic flavor. Yet, to mention shifting fashions is to allude to a quality of democratic life that Plato did not notice and that perhaps was not so marked a feature of fourth-century Athens as of twentieth-century America. This is the quality associated often in modern times with terms like "conformity" and "masses." It tends to suppress the anarchic propensities natural to democracy.

Paradoxically, where everyone has liberty, most people are inclined to think and behave, not as their own unique impulses command, but as everyone else thinks and behaves. They incline toward conformity. Tocqueville was forcibly impressed by this quality in America — so forcibly, indeed, that he could say he knew of no other country where there was so little independence of mind. He saw that liberated people may, contrary to what one might expect, become much alike. It seems that a democratic populace may exhibit, rather than the amoral diversity that Plato saw as intrinsic to general liberty, a deadening uniformity. It becomes a "mass."

There is still liberty. Those inclined toward uniqueness are still, subject only to minimal restraints by the law and to the discomforts of nonconformity, at liberty to follow their own inclinations. For many, however, the liberty manifest in the uninhibited unfoldment of a particular personal life largely disappears. It is not so much deliberately nullified as tacitly and unconsciously abandoned. This is done from a longing in the hearts of almost everyone to take refuge from the uncertainties and difficulties of liberty by conforming with a life pattern exemplified and sanctioned by the lives of all those around them. Little thought is given to the question liberty puts before every individual: How should I live? Everyone falls back on a common answer.

Let us carefully note, however, that a common answer does not imply a community. In the relations among individuals, there is uniformity without authentic unity — without the shared concern for truth and the inquiring communication that create community. Hence arises a well-known byword for life in a mass society, "alienation." People are basically separate, even though outwardly alike and united, a phenomenon that has been intensively explored in modern literature by writers such as Kierkegaard and Ortega y Gasset. And we remember again Riesman's "lonely crowd." We can see in the prevalence of alienation that mass society does not do away with the atomization produced by liberty. Rather, it consolidates it. The uniformity of mass society is social atomism in a frozen state. Naked human souls cluster together but are not thereby clothed.

The motives behind the "revolt of the masses," as Ortega called it, seem clear. I can summarize much in the preceding pages by saying that liberty sets off tremors of nihilism. There are no authorities, truths, rules, traditions, guides that do not come into question. In these cir-

51

cumstances the task of designing and carrying on a life is formidable. At first, liberty may be welcomed. But suddenly one awakens on the high seas of primeval incertitude. How can one navigate? Inevitably, one will glance to one side and then the other to see how others are navigating. If everyone else is following a particular course, it will take uncommon courage and self-confidence to set a different course. The vast fleet one has joined will probably change course frequently and unpredictably, and its ultimate destination may be in doubt. But one will no longer suffer the desolation of sailing alone with no land in sight. In less metaphorical terms, by joining the mass, one alleviates the strains of liberty. That liberty itself has quietly vanished may scarcely be noticed.

The flight from freedom is not manifest solely in mass society. Dostoyevsky saw a certain kind of ecclesiastical order (perhaps he had the Catholic Church in mind) as catering to the nearly unbearable strains imposed on believers by the kind of faith Jesus demanded, faith in an improbable crucified and risen God. Dostoyevsky was struck by the Gospel account of the "temptations in the wilderness." In this account (Matt. 4:1-11 and Luke 4:1-13) Satan urged Jesus to provide his followers with assured bread, removing all economic worries; with indisputable authority, relieving them of responsibility for ordering their lives; and with miracles that would dissipate all spiritual doubts. Jesus of course rejected these temptations. When he did so, according to Dostoyevsky, he imposed on humans an excruciating freedom. In the famous "Grand Inquisitor" passages in *The Brothers Karamazov,* Dostoyevsky envisioned the great threat to liberty as not mass society, but a totalitarian church, a theocracy. Superficially, Dostoyevsky was looking back to the Middle Ages. Actually, however, he was looking ahead, prophetically. He seemingly foresaw the coming of the totalitarian church-state typified by Nazi Germany and Stalinist Russia. The underlying motive he discerned was the same as the one described by analysts of mass society: that of escaping the sweeping insecurity — economic, moral, social, and spiritual — intrinsic to liberty.

Yet another phenomenon reflecting the human recoil from freedom is what might be called "the culture of distraction." By this I mean the institutions, habits, attitudes, and practices that cultivate and express devotion to such ends as physical pleasure, entertainment, and accumulation of possessions. These ends constitute a single end to the extent that all of them minister to the universal desire to lay aside the burden of personal responsibility. They divert people from their humanity into a kind of bestiality — confined to the moment and to the immediate physical environment. In modern times the instruments of such diversion comprise magazines, television, films, and popular newspapers and books. Through such instruments people are transported into worlds of sports, melodrama, pacifying news, and other forms of light entertainment.

As the "bread and circuses" of ancient Rome illustrate, a culture of distraction can grow up in various historical situations and in response to various causes. But the modern culture of distraction is a product primarily of industrial capitalism. Not that capitalism creates such a culture from any intrinsic necessity. One of the most basic characteristics of capitalism is flexibility. It can be adapted to various purposes and circumstances. The pressures of competition and the necessity of profits do not generate the all-consuming and irresistible fate that Marx thought they did. And capitalists, with their fabled ingenuity and energy, are not driven by the mechanics of the system to any one end. Moreover, governments, workers, and consumer groups can infuse cooperative and communal relations into the economic order. Nonetheless, in the conditions created by industrialism, capitalism creates a material abundance that favors distraction, and it provides capitalists with powerful incentives to try to lure consumers into lives of distraction. Although capitalism does not preclude, and may even provide the necessary basis for, a truly communal culture, it also provides some of the main forces with which any effort to create a communal culture must contend.

Does industrial capitalism likewise tend to produce mass society? Here one must be wary of oversimplification. We are speaking of separable phenomena. Thus it is questionable that ancient Rome, with its diversionary practices like the games, can be considered a mass society. And Tocqueville saw multiple signs of mass society in America before the modern culture of distraction, and the capitalism underlying it, had developed very far. But still, it is clear that industrial capitalism and mass society fit comfortably together. If mass society represents a flight from freedom, it might be said that industrial capitalism, through the culture of distraction, gives wings to this flight. Witness, for example, the way in which both work to replace the profound dilemmas that make liberty onerous with the trivial choices facing the modern consumer. And this is not to speak of the root fact that industrial capitalism, by producing, advertising, and distributing uniform and similar consumer goods throughout a population, tends to call the masses into existence and to maintain them.

The flight from freedom may be outwardly benign. Liberty may be sacrificed behind a facade of liberal institutions. As twentieth-century history shows so starkly, however, liberal institutions may be affected disastrously. Mass society and the culture of distraction provide ready foundation stones for tyranny. As everyone recognizes, modern totalitarianism is essentially different, not only from the monarchical authoritarianism of past centuries, but even from the tyrannies that have infested history since the time of the ancient Greeks. It destroys virtually all private life. It is able to do this partly through the kind of mass support that, so to speak, turns every citizen into a policeman. And the masses are mobilized through the technology of distraction. The flight from freedom becomes not only very visible but also highly aggressive. It is not surprising that Tocqueville, one of the earliest writers to discern the onset of mass society, was also among the first to sense the imminence of tyrannies of a new, more all-consuming kind.

It would be hyperbolic to picture the flight from freedom in colors so garish as to suggest that it might lead the whole human race into some sort of totalitarian captivity. Totalitarian regimes have shown themselves far less efficient than liberal regimes, in spite of their formidable appearance. And liberal institutions, where they remain in place, are not apt to be meaningless. They protect numerous centers of individuality and communication. They allow many individuals to refuse to surrender personal responsibility, even though surrounded by people who in one way or another are inwardly enslaved. They safeguard possibilities of solitary reflection and personal decision, and these do not always go unused. Tocqueville found Americans, although subservient to public opinion, at the same time restless and discontented. This suggests that, among those unwilling to shed the garment of conscience, mass society and a culture of distraction may intensify, rather than eliminate, the labor and strain involved in carrying on a distinct personal life.

These phenomena may, however, exact a high moral price. A social mass by its very nature suppresses and obscures the distinct personality. It may render the very idea that personality is a primal reality and value puzzling if not incomprehensible. At the same time, the mystery of being, the mystery brought forth in great art, sought by philosophers, and worshiped in the major religions, may subside beneath the surface of an opaque and undiversified society. Authentic values may lose their luster or disappear. And with authentic values forgotten, common inquiry into the nature of such values can no longer occur. Dialogue is replaced by the "idle talk" that Heidegger saw as a significant element in modern society. If dialogue withers, then community — which is created through serious communication — also withers. Liberty becomes the institutional form of alienation, a condition suffered perhaps in the company of millions of others, yet suffered alone.

Tocqueville saw much of this in early America. He admired Americans in many ways and regarded numerous American institutions, such as strong local governments and highly respected courts, as powerful buttresses of liberty. Yet he also saw the lives of Americans disturbed and trivialized by the strains inherent in democratic liberty. Thus Americans were avid for money, as the sole means for gaining status and security in a free and egalitarian society. And long before capitalism had brought the material abundance enjoyed in the later twentieth century, Americans were preoccupied, Tocqueville noted, with physical gratification.

In sum, the common notion that liberty is an avenue to the good life is not true. The question of why, if this is the case, liberty should be sought and prized, is central to this essay. Before turning to this question, however, we must consider yet one more dilemma that liberty inescapably involves.

Masses and Minorities

It seems, in the light of the foregoing pages, that at any one time most people in a liberal society will be more or less adrift and distracted. They will not be in serious pursuit of deep truth; they will care little for beauty; they may for the most part be decent in their outward behavior, but they will not display, or even strive toward, purity and goodness. Idle talk will absorb them, while searching conversation will make them uncomfortable. All of this is to say that they will be wasting their liberty. They will not be reflectively or wisely choosing the ends for which they live. Their choices will be made with little thought for the highest standards of value. And choices made on one day or in one year will not be made with the choices of preceding days and years in mind. Life thus will be accidental and disjointed. These are the likely consequences — for the majority — of modern liberty.

To be sure, a few — mainly among the wealthy, powerful, and prominent — will seem to be living more purposefully. But their purposes will usually be nothing beyond the wealth, power, and prominence that give them standing in the eyes of others. In modern times these are gained by serving the masses, and people who do this must ordinarily share the attitudes of the masses. Although proud and self-assertive, they are not truly distinguished. They are merely conspicuous members of the majority that is wasting its liberty.

Here we see how imperfect is the correlation between the dichotomy of pride and distraction, on the one hand, and that of free minorities and unfree masses on the other. While pride may prompt one to the distinctive aspirations and actions in which freedom is discovered, and while distraction goes readily with membership in the masses, pride may precipitate one into the masses. This is the irony of pride. Pride connotes absence of humility, hence — to whatever degree it holds sway — insensitivity to other persons, to the commanding worth of truth, and to the beauty of creation. It may incapacitate one for the critical reflection and elevation of spirit in which true freedom resides. Pride no doubt often plays a part in the attainment of authentic distinction. But such distinction is authentic only by virtue of qualities, such as scientific understanding or perception of beauty, that are given and cannot be seized, and that therefore depend on receptivity and humility. True distinction can be maintained only if pride is conquered or at least, in critical areas, held at bay.

Where there is liberty, however, there will be minorities who are raised up, not mainly by the pride that often casts one down, but merely by their consciousness of their freedom and of their consequent responsibilities. These will face the ordeal of liberty and will refuse to flee. They will probably not be altogether wise or righteous. Nor will they be without deep personal complications and conflicts. But they will be inclined toward reflection and self-expression. They will be on the lookout for serious conversations and communicative relationships. Some among them may be people of visible distinction, such as writers and artists. But many of them, outwardly at least, will be quite ordinary, their distinction being only that they know they are free and are using their liberty as well as they can.

Liberty, then, goes with highly significant inequalities — significant according to the standard of liberty itself. Not that the line between the free minority and the self-enthralled masses will be sharp and clear, with everyone on one side thoughtful and free in every action and everyone on the other side invariably in flight from responsibility. There will be gradations of liberty, and these gradations will be constantly shifting. Nonetheless, this is to say something about liberty that is fundamental but is often either forgotten or accepted with undue equanimity. Liberty is a door open to all but used, at any one time, by only a few. Hence, in ironic contrast to the ideal linkage of liberty and equality, voiced in both the American and the French Revolutions, liberty in fact is always destructive of equality. Only a few accept the freedom it offers.

As everyone knows, however, the inequalities liberty brings are not spiritual alone. There are also inequalities of fame, of social status, of wealth, of power, and so forth. Liberty separates the few from the many in outward as well as inward ways. And in outward inequalities, the few always and necessarily enjoy a greater amplitude of liberty than do the many. This is troubling, but any effort to make it less troubling by denying the egalitarian implications of liberty would undermine the ethos of liberty. I will try in the following pages to show why. On the other hand, a determined effort to do away with inequality would inevitably do away with liberty as well. In this situation, it is essential for liberals to be loyal to the ideal of equality without attempting to realize it literally. How is this possible?

I suggest as a starting point the careful refusal of every form of elitism. By "elitism" I mean any affirmation of an ostensibly superior group of human beings as permanent, as perfect or nearly perfect, and as deserving power or some form of elevated status in the society and polity. Plato's ideal of the philosopher-king is an obvious example of elitism. Why is elitism always false?

1. First of all, while some will always choose more carefully and wisely than others, the power of choice is universal. Hence everyone has a claim to liberty. That is one of the most elemental principles of justice. It is subverted, however, by any form of elitism. In plain terms, the moral superiority of a few is less significant ontologically than the moral responsibility of all. The latter is integral to the very concept of humanity.

2. Every elite is imperfect and impermanent. It is manifest that no one achieves moral perfection, and few even approach it. And if righteousness is rare, it is also unstable. A good person who gains power or fame may be thereby morally worsened. Wisdom is no less elusive and unstable than righteousness. When we speak of a "wise person," we mean someone who, compared with others and in present circumstances, is wise. We speak of a human being, not God. Paul recognized such things when he expressed concern that he himself might in some way fail and, having preached to others, end finally as a "castaway" (1 Cor. 9:27). The very concept of sainthood is questionable.

3. Even if there were a perfect and permanent elite of the free, it would be undiscernible. There are two reasons for this. One is that the kind of personal distinction that underlies true freedom has no reliable, outward marks. The free "elite," the few who consciously live their liberty, is not coincident with any intellectual, creative, or highly cultivated set of people whatever. Many writers and artists manifestly belong to the masses. Many academicians are lacking in intellectual distinction, and many churchmen are spiritually mediocre. We must think that people of true spiritual eminence have lived and died entirely unknown to the world. Can one doubt, for example, that there were strong and courageous women on the frontier in nineteenth-century America who, perhaps through reading the Bible and enduring hard experiences, gained a spiritual depth that was never expressed and never recognized? Not every possessor of wisdom has written a book, nor has everyone keenly sensitive to beauty brought forth a painting or a musical composition. The other reason any elite of the free would be undiscernible is simply that human beings are undiscerning. This is one of the meanings of original sin. Not only do we fail to attain goodness, we also fail to see it where it exists. This is surely a major reason why Jesus enjoined us to refrain from judging (Matt. 7:1). To claim the ability to judge others with assurance is to claim a divine, not a human, power. Again we see how questionable is the concept of sainthood.

To summarize, it is doubtful that any group with the qualities suggested to us by the term "elite" has ever existed. If it has, it has been more or less invisible. Why, then, a reader might ask, bring up the whole matter? Why emphasize the inequalities that go with liberty only to conclude, seemingly, that we may as well ignore them? The answer lies in the close association of inequality and evil.

Our subject in this chapter is liberty and human evil or, more precisely, sin. The inequality implicit in such phenomena as mass society and the culture of distraction is our first encounter with an evil that constantly bedevils every effort to establish liberty. Admittedly, inequality is not evil always and in every way. It can be reflective of qualities such as talent, discipline, and understanding on the part of a few. The personal distinction due to uncommon courage, rectitude, or insight does honor to the whole human race. At the same time, however, inequality also is reflective of personal traits such as the will not so much to achieve excellence as to surpass others in some palpable way and look down upon them. Even the most admirable forms of human superiority are never purely innocent. Moreover, inequality incites the evil qualities that give rise to it — qualities such as arrogance and callousness. Just as "power tends to corrupt," so do renown and ascendancy of every kind.

Finally, this must be noted, that inequality means estrangement. It almost always divides: rich from poor, powerful from weak, learned from unlearned, and so forth. In this way, it precludes the community in which freedom is fully realized. This is manifest in the case of material inequalities. It is probably often true for moral and spiritual inequalities. Only in exceptional instances, as with Socrates or Jesus, and perhaps Abraham Lincoln, does moral and spiritual distinction seem free of divisive consequences. Washington was aloof, and difficult to approach. There is a vision, often called "conservative," of organic social unity, resting on the recognition and acceptance by all of the superiority of a few. Aristotle and Burke are names often associated with this vision. It is probably not wholly false, but given original sin it is largely so. Envy and pride are too prevalent, and social aristocracy inevitably too ambiguous, for the vision to have much validity. Elites even at their best are bound to be divisive. In the fact of inequality we see as clearly as anywhere the fallenness and imperfection of all human society.

The conclusion that inequality is inevitable under a regime of liberty, and that any resolute attempt to destroy it would destroy liberty at the same time, seems irresistible. To wage war on inequality would be to stifle the gifts and virtues that define our humanity. It would effect universal enslavement. And it would do this without effecting complete equality, for it would also effect the ascendancy of the equalizing enslavers. Clearly, we must acquiesce in numerous degrees and kinds of inequality.

What does need emphasis is that we must not acquiesce in inequality without in various ways questioning, protesting, and limiting it. No one who cares for liberty can settle down comfortably with fixed and extensive inequalities. Even spiritual inequalities reflect, and may enhance, estrangement. Economic, social, and political inequalities are far more threatening. Inequalities of every kind sit uneasily with liberty, however inseparable they may be from liberty. The tension inherent in this condition never wholly subsides. There is no ideal balance between liberty and equality, and there are no times of tranquillity in which peace between the two ideals reigns for long. There are always minorities struggling consciously or unconsciously on the side of inequality, and there are always other minorities, supported sometimes by multitudes, struggling for equality. How to deal with inequality is one of the major questions confronting anyone reflecting seriously on liberty, and we will face the question at several points in the following pages.

One question, however, is more fundamental still and claims our immediate attention. If liberty means the enfranchisement of creatures strongly inclined to live in evil and irresponsible ways, how can liberty be justified?

CHAPTER 3

Why Liberty?

—=◉=—

Choice and Value

If liberty has consequences that are virtually certain to be in some degree undesirable, given the pride and distraction to which humans are
predisposed, it might seem that its only possible justification lies in its
inherent value or rightness. As we shall see, however, consequences are
not entirely irrelevant. Indeed, I shall argue that liberty has no intrinsic
value. In itself, apart from the uses to which it is put, it is worthless. Yet,
with a force approaching unconditionality, it is required of us. We must
claim it both for ourselves and for other people. In our private lives we
must carry on our own, and allow other persons (assuming sanity and
mature age) to carry on their own, singular lives, and in the political
realm liberty is the primary claim every person has on the state. What
gives liberty this kind of standing?

The answer is not far from common sense, yet it has not often been
clearly articulated and focused upon by political philosophers. Good
comes into the world, that is, into the social and political order created
and sustained by human beings, only by being freely chosen. For example, there is truth in the world only if there are those who freely search
for the truth, and find it, and freely give voice to it. Likewise, there is
beauty in the world only so far as natural beauty is freely enjoyed and ar-
tificial beauty freely created. There is justice in the world only if there
are just people, and people are not made just simply by being forced to

61

behave justly. Liberty, it may be said, is the gateway into the realm of values. Things of worth can be found only by passing through that gateway. A gateway leading nowhere, however, would be worthless. This is why liberty in itself is worthless. Liberty does not provide a way that surely leads to the good, yet it provides the only possible way. This is what makes it a standard that is formally conditional yet has a necessity that is virtually absolute, giving it some of the authority of an unconditional imperative.

So unavoidable is the gateway of liberty that Christians might say that even God must pass through it to enter the human world. This does not imply that God must choose to be or to possess the good; perhaps he is good by necessity. But by giving men and women the power of choice, he determined that he could not enter their inner lives unless, so to speak, he was freely invited. The grant of freedom to the human species was an act of divine self-limitation. This is only to say that he created men and women with the power to sin and thus to lead lives from which their very creator is excluded. There will be more on this matter in the following pages.

The act of choice has a depth, and a consequent significance, which is easily overlooked. In modern society, people are continually making casual choices — among products in stores, among automobiles, among places to vacation, among programs to watch on television. The act of choice begins to seem as trivial as the things that are chosen. We readily think of it as caused — by advertisements we have seen, by the comments of friends, by passing moods and fancies. But choice as such is not trivial at all, and this is because of its depth, which lies in freedom. In choosing, we manifest our freedom, and in our freedom lies our personal being, as well as the drama and mystery of human life on the earth.

Freedom does not belong to the causal order. It is not among the things we observe and fit by inductive reasoning into causal sequences. It is not something we can learn to control from the outside. This may sound implausible, for we all know that our choices can be affected by outward conditions. And we know that we can affect the choices of others by pleading with them, or by threatening them, or perhaps simply by pointing out likely consequences of one choice or another. Otherwise, social life would be difficult or impossible. Yet there is a single ineffaceable fact that proves that we are free, and this is our sense of responsibility. Faced with moral, hence not trivial, alternatives, we know we must choose and that how and what we choose makes an enormous, if undefinable, difference. If we choose wrongly we feel riveted by guilt. These are experiences we cannot voluntarily shed, and we would not have them if our choices were causally determined. When we feel responsible, in contemplating either an upcoming choice or a wrongful choice already made, we know, unless we delude ourselves with determinist fancies that defy manifest facts, that we are free. We realize that we belong to a dimension of being that is not disclosed to objective observation. We are conscious of the depth that gives choice its significance. This was a major theme in the moral philosophy of Kant.

The centrality of freedom in personal life is not recognized, however, merely by assuming that at two or three critical junctures things truly of value must be chosen. A good life must be structured throughout by good choices. This means that the values chosen must determine the general course of one's life. They must therefore be renewed again and again; they must be reflected upon and, of course, sometimes revised. Occasionally, they must be repented of and entirely repudiated. But serious choices are those in which, at least by intent, one chooses one's whole life. Not that we can envision alternative lives, and then pick the one we prefer. But in every moral choice the choice of a life is implicit. And for every serious person, that life must be reflected upon and chosen repeatedly. To live freely is to weave a fabric of choices. Here it becomes apparent that freedom is not just one of life's many features but rather the fountainhead of every life. Seen from this point of view, and in company with the concept of radical evil, or original sin, it becomes apparent why humanist writers have sometimes considered freedom an almost impossible burden and why some Christian writers have insisted that freedom is of value only when infused with grace. There will be more on all of this later on.

When we understand freedom as belonging to a dimension of being other than that of mechanical cause and effect, we begin to understand the nature and mystery of sin. The evil human beings do is not caused, however extensively it may be shaped, by the objective order we observe around us. Sin is therefore, in the final analysis, inexplicable. It arises from a level of being we cannot comprehend in terms of natural causation — terms that enable us to comprehend the world around us. This is signalized in the biblical myth of the fall and in the Christian doctrine of original sin. Sin presupposes, not an outward cause, but sin. Evil arises from freedom, and this is why it is not a natural condition but a mystery.

To mark the depths of being that underlie serious choice goes a long way toward justifying liberty. As I have already explained, liberty pertains to the outward order, the complex of institutional and legal arrangements, designed for the protection of freedom. Hence someone unaware of the depth of freedom might assume that liberty has no greater manifest warrant than a variety of other social and political institutions that we accept, not for any metaphysical reasons, but merely because they seem to work. But in liberty, the outward order has a uniquely close relationship with the ontological abyss from which persons draw their being and their dignity, that of freedom. The purpose of liberty is to make room in the world for freedom and to guard freedom from the myriad kinds of human carelessness and animosity to which it is vulnerable. Liberty, then, has its raison d'être in freedom, although freedom, like liberty, would be pointless were it not used for the realization of values. It would be a gateway with nothing on the other side.

Still, it may seem that arguing for liberty as the only opening through which the good can come into the world is unconvincing, given the concept of original sin, or radical evil. That concept apparently implies that human beings are bound to make wrongful choices. They are unfit for liberty. How can liberty be so essential if it is so dangerous? Two comments may serve to answer this question.

First, liberty can be fruitful in spite of its dangers. The concept of original sin denotes strong inclinations toward self-magnification (pride) and self-abandonment (distraction) but not complete depravity. Also, in spite of original sin there are forces of life, sometimes called "inspiration" by secular reason, and "grace" by religious faith, that can counteract or supplant evil human impulses. More will be said about these later on in this chapter. Here they are noted only to indicate that liberty, even though sure to bring undesirable consequences, is not bound to be ruinous. It is a gateway through which it is possible for people sometimes to pass.

And second, no other gateway exists. Values cannot be realized by being forcibly imposed. An authentic human life cannot be carried on unless it is consciously chosen by the one whose life it is. Hence we can speak of natural rights — natural because they arise from the capacity for choice that inheres in human nature. Liberty is no doubt dangerous, but the danger must be faced. I do not mean to suggest that practical considerations should be banished. Some societies are probably unready for liberty. And any society may experience times of crisis in which liberty must be curtailed. Also, there are many ways of lessening the dangers of liberty, such as care for favorable traditions. My argument here is simply that the very conditions of our humanity give the imperative of liberty a commanding quality. Creatures who if free are likely to do some very bad things but may do some good things too, and if unfree could do nothing good, must be given their freedom.

The absolute necessity of liberty, not as a value in itself but as a precondition for the realization of value, may have been first recognized by theological rather than political writers. From as early as Paul there was an awareness among Christians that the greatest of all values, and the source of all values, God, had to be freely chosen. The act of faith was that choice, and faith and freedom could not be separated. Admittedly, Christians were slow in coming to see that freedom implied liberty, that the inward condition implied outward, or institutional, arrangements. For centuries they were at best lukewarm supporters of liberty. But Paul spoke eloquently of the freedom intrinsic to faith, and Augustine — no liberal! — was exceedingly reluctant to forcibly suppress the Donatists, a tumultuous multitude of heretics that for years tried his patience as bishop of Hippo. He did not want his churches filled with inwardly rebellious believers.

The strength of the link between faith and freedom in Christian thought, and its endurance in spite of the authoritarianism and intolerance toward which Christians have always been inclined, is illustrated in the thought of two writers of modern times, Kierkegaard and Dostoyevsky. Neither, it must be said, cared greatly about liberty. Kierkegaard was too centered in the realm of subjectivity and too preoccupied with the trials of "the existing individual" to give much thought to the outward order, and Dostoyevsky, in a manner common among Russians, leaned simultaneously toward anarchism and authoritarianism but was quite definitely not a liberal. Both writers nevertheless conceived of life as a drama of freedom. Faith placed a person in a position unsupported by reason, and in that way suspended over an abyss of doubt. Such a position could be sustained only by a strenuous and continually renewed act of choice, an act consisting in the affirmation of faith. To speak in terms of values, for both writers human life was formed and colored above all by an absolute good from which there issued the most urgent conceivable claim on personal responsibility.

To assert that good exists in the world only by being freely chosen is a "personalist" proposition. The personalist outlook will be discussed further along in this essay. Suffice it here to say simply that nothing good can be in the world if the intelligence and will of persons are disregarded or crushed. Of course, that is not literally true. For example, there might, in some sense, be truth in the world if there were an organization, such as a church or a state, formally committed to true doctrines, these perhaps inscribed in official documents and regularly read aloud, yet not understood by anyone. Most of us, however, would say that in such circumstances truth is not really present. Why not? Because it has no lodging in the mind and will of living persons. It is our respect for persons that predisposes us to believe that a value becomes real in our lives only by being chosen.

Plato, as we all know, outlined a political system designed to realize perfect justice. Plato was personalist to the degree that at least one person — the philosopher-king — had to be just. But Plato lived prior to the time when the idea of dignity as a quality intrinsic to a person as such had been fully developed. Moreover, his philosophical system, which allowed, or even required, heavy emphasis on universals, militated against a personalist outlook. It readily followed that justice could come into the world through a single just person, who, like a great architect and builder, would establish a just order of society. Justice would be transmitted into the souls of people other than the philosopher-king through habit, discipline, and the salutary untruths he called "noble lies." None but the philosopher-king would be fully just, however, because none would understand justice and therefore none, with fully illuminated minds, would choose it. Nowadays, most of Plato's readers feel that his ideal state, even though in some ways resplendent, does not come very close to depicting perfect justice. This is mainly, I think, because of its impersonality. It has become axiomatic that regard must be paid to the power of individual persons to deliberate and choose.

If free affirmation of justice by a single philosopher-king does not suffice to establish justice in the world, what number of people would suffice? How many must assent to a value for it to be given proper entry into the world? I am not asking, be it noted, how many must assent for a value to be a true value. Choice can only recognize, not establish, value. The question is how widely individuals must be allowed to exercise the power of recognizing values by choosing them. The answer is implicit in the principle of personal dignity as pertaining to every person. Personalism is radically democratic. Every person counts. Is this to prescribe unanimity? If that were so, it would be a principle without practical application. Here we enter on familiar ground. Liberty requires, first, that individuals be given as much room as possible to choose and to live in accordance with their choices. It requires further that so far as values need to be uniform, thus based on collective assent, and enforced by legitimate authorities, participation in the process by which collective assent — which can be variously defined but must necessarily come to less than the assent of all — be open to all. This is to speak in terms of rough common sense. The point is simply that a personalist political order pays heed to the freedom of every person.

Few societies, of course, have been altogether lacking in liberty. Modern totalitarian states, and ancient states like Sparta, may have come close. But many societies which we think of as unfree, like the aristocracies and monarchies of medieval Europe, left many people with a measure of liberty. In the Middle Ages it was not only the landed aristocrats who were in some ways free, but also traders and manufacturers in the towns, scholars in the universities, and monks, priests, and bishops in the church. Liberty was lacking in two ways: only a few enjoyed very much of it; and those few were ordinarily confined by an orthodox creed and by the detailed prescriptive duties associated with their various stations. The right of every person to a deliberately elected life, subject to prevailing circumstances, had little part in the reigning ethos. A modern liberal state opens the doors more widely. Its major premise is that the good is accessible only through a process of search and affirmation that is carried on, to the utmost practical extent, by every sane and mature human being in its purview.

It will be manifest that only moral choices, not choices of any kind, are significant. Modern commercial society sometimes boasts of the number of choices available to consumers. Those, unhappily, do little to widen liberty in any way that matters. The choices that matter are those concerning beliefs, friends, mates, vocations, and avocations — choices that determine how one lives and for what ends. Summarily, it might be said that significant choices are those determining what kind of person one is to be. Only cumulatively and indirectly do choices among products in the marketplace bear on that issue. Industrial abundance, which has its true importance in removing the need for a slave or servile class of any kind, and thus making possible liberty for everyone, has confused our minds concerning liberty. What counts is not being able to choose many things but being able to choose the good.

What, then, is the good? What value or values justify and necessitate liberty?

The Value of Truth

Strong claims can be made for truth — truth that is freely and fully shared — as the answer to these questions. A good society is one in which there exists a true and common wisdom. A good person is one searching for the truth and at every step in the search sharing his efforts and discoveries as fully as possible with as many others as possible — a person filled with light, shedding light. Such an ideal is to a limited extent Platonic. Plato's republic was centered on ultimate truth, and the highest human virtue was wisdom. But of course, there was little sharing of the truth, mainly because Plato thought very few were capable of sharing it. I believe, in contrast, that truth can be shared, perhaps not universally, but very widely, and beyond all definite limits. In this respect my view of the good is more Christian than Platonic. Christianity from the beginning has held that the highest truths can be apprehended by anyone — by fishermen and common laborers, according to the traditional story. And in line with this difference, my view is more democratic than aristocratic. There will be much throughout this essay on the relationship of democracy to liberty.

It may seem that according truth such eminence slights righteousness, understood in terms of virtues like fairness to all and help for those in need. I do not deny the importance of virtues of this sort, but I assume in Christian fashion that all virtues can be summed up in the virtue of love, and that the highest expression of love lies in carrying on with others the search for and knowledge of ultimate truth. As I will try to show at greater length further along in the essay, the common quest for truth implicates most of the other virtues, like fairness and helping those in need. Again, there is a Platonic aspect to this. While the *Republic* is about the centering of common life on the truth, it is also about other virtues — courage, justice, and temperance. Pursuit of the highest value entails observance of lesser values. I believe this is the case. In a good life, knowing the truth and sharing it go hand in hand, and through the sharing many of the major virtues are practiced. In Christianity, however, this is a far more egalitarian enterprise than in Plato. This is implied in Jesus' twofold command to love God and one's neighbor. The neighbor can be anyone and is thus implicitly everyone.

We need remember too that the search for truth cannot be carried on exclusively in private studies and university classrooms. It is carried on by trying to live it. Jesus speaks of "doing" the truth. And doing the truth, trying to live it, involves the practice — and in the practice the testing — of the major virtues, as we understand them. We inquire into and deepen our understanding of true values by trying to live in their light. Further, testing our understanding of virtues and values is also testing our understanding of the realities of the world around us. The "ought" is set within the "is." As pragmatists such as Dewey stressed, inquiry is a matter of practice as well as theory. More precisely, true theory emerges from observant and thoughtful practice. But practice, contrary to the relativism typical of the pragmatists, is moral practice. And moral practice is not simply conformity with the moral law. It is inquiry into the nature and source of the moral law and into the world in which it must be practiced. The search for truth is a search, so to speak, for a luminous and practical righteousness.

The egalitarian implications here must be noted. In some ways people who in their major occupations are practically engaged in the world are perhaps in a better position to seek and find the truth than are academicians, who are able to devote most of their time to the truth. And such people may obviously be just as concerned with righteousness as any select group of intellectuals or writers. Indeed, they may be less subject to the influence of morally subversive intellectual fashions. In sum, to set truth as the highest value for a society is not, in spite of its Platonic ancestry, to establish an ideal of philosophic detachment or intellectual ascendancy. Plato was a spirit of almost unmatched nobility, but Christianity comes closer to a sound understanding of the relationship of truth to the world with the concept of the neighbor — one who may not have studied extensively but who works and suffers and pays some heed to the promptings of conscience and thus is well positioned for seeking and apprehending the truth.

Organized humanity has always tended, however, to be more Platonic than Christian. Care for the truth has fallen to a few. The many, ordinarily impoverished and pressed by urgent physical needs, have been in no position to devote themselves to the truth as a grand value. Societies have therefore been divided into the leisured and learned, on the one hand, and the laboring and unlearned on the other. The industrial revolution sharpened the split. This was ironic, because the principal moral benefit of industrialism lay in the material abundance it produced, thereby making it possible for everyone to be in some degree leisured and thus in one way or another learned. The early decades of the industrial revolution witnessed the ruthless reduction of the laboring classes to a state of extreme material degradation. It was a state, as Marx so powerfully insisted, of virtual slavery. The irony of poverty amidst growing plenty was doubled, however, by the fact that the humanitarian response only renewed the diversion of the many from the truth. This response consisted in freeing workers from their enslavement and raising them from their material degradation. But this was accomplished while largely forgetting about truth. The urgent task seemed to be that of providing those in need with material help, not truth. The result is the twentieth-century welfare state — a relatively just material order attended by a signal defect, that of spiritual emptiness. Truth is smothered now not by poverty but by popular culture.

As we shall see, overcoming the spiritual impoverishment that has taken the place of material impoverishment for the populations of the Western nations is not easily done. Indeed, it may not be feasible as a collective project. In the meantime, however, the principle remains: liberty is meaningless apart from righteousness, and righteousness consists in seeking the truth — the truth concerning the good and its place in the world — and in drawing as many people as possible into the search. The welfare state has validity in that it lays a basis for such liberty. So far, however, the basis has not been built upon. Not only is truth largely forgotten in the public realm, but people are encouraged to devote themselves to the material values and the light entertainment that undermine authentic liberty. The demands this situation puts on those who care about liberty will be investigated in the following pages.

The idea of truth as the highest value is common to many who are traveling on the two major avenues toward the truth, humanist reason and religious revelation. This becomes particularly clear if we consider the metaphor of light. Truth is a kind of shining. Through truth, reality becomes radiant. Those who follow the avenue of reason celebrate one period of history in particular as a time in which their cause was triumphant. The celebrated period, of course, is the Enlightenment. Those on the avenue of faith celebrate an enlightenment that is recounted mythically in Genesis 1. The first day saw the creation of light. The establishment of values began, it might be said, when God saw that the light was good. This theme was carried forward at various points in the Bible, among them a cluster of ideas expressed in the Gospel of John. Christ was "the light of men," the light shining in the darkness, which the darkness has not overcome. John the Baptist came to "bear witness to the light." John proclaimed that "the true light that enlightens every man was coming into the world" (John 1:4-9).

Still, however ancient and honorable a lineage the ideal of truth may have, one can and should ask some philosophical questions. To begin with, why value truth so highly? The preceding argument suggests a preliminary answer. Choice can be a moral act only for those who know what they are choosing. To choose an authentic value without understanding what is being chosen, for example, hearing a Beethoven string quartet as a result merely of happening into the wrong room, would be morally insignificant. Significant liberty presupposes truth. This is a valid answer to the question but fails to go far enough.

The very idea that there are authentic values, waiting as it were to be chosen, assumes that reality or some part of reality is good in itself. Without that assumption the primary use of freedom would be to create values, not simply to discover and choose them. Thus the high value Christians place on light is grounded on the notion that all that is real is created by God and is hence to be revered. This notion underlay the stress on truth in later Christian philosophies such as those of Augustine and Thomas Aquinas. On the side of humanist reason there are no doubt many who prize truth, not because they believe in its intrinsic value, but because they see it as requisite for successful action. They assume not so much that reality is good as that human beings can make it good. Nonetheless, the historical roots of reason's high evaluation of truth lie in the ancient world, in the philosophies of Plato and Aristotle. And for these thinkers, as for ancient Jews and for Christians, the universe is good, and this is because it arises from or in some way expresses a ground that is virtually divine. This evaluation carries forward into the modern world in the reverence in which many defenders of humanist reason hold the physical sciences and the physical universe in its intricate harmonies and mysteries.

Here we face a dividing of the ways. A major premise of this essay is the principle, not only common to Plato and Aristotle, and Augustine and Aquinas, but restated in modern philosophies like those of Martin Heidegger and Gabriel Marcel, that reality in its depths, depths often dignified with the term "being," is good. Therefore truth is good, for truth is the clarity of being. Sin is fundamentally a refusal of that clarity. It begins in falsifying the self, in the self-magnification of pride or the self-erasure of distraction, and through that initial falsification falsifies all of reality. All things are turned into objects, over which pride exerts power or into which distraction plunges to lose the self. Sin is always deeply implicated in lying. These, at any rate, are major assumptions underlying this essay. Yet it is not logically contradictory, nor in flagrant conflict with manifest facts, to adopt very different assumptions, namely, that ultimate reality is chaos and night, that truth consequently is dismaying and scarcely to be borne by any but a few who are exceptionally strong, and that the human vocation is not discovery but creation. Nietzsche made such assumptions and built thereon one of the most impressive philosophies in the history of thought.

Making all of this clear is a matter of intellectual honesty. To hold that reality is good and that knowledge is therefore the highest value is not a provable position. It can be rendered plausible, and will be, I hope, in the following pages. It is more like a beginning of thought, however, than a demonstrable conclusion of thought. It is to take one fork in the road of intellect, that of inquiry and contemplation. The other fork is that of action and power. The former depends on receptivity, the latter on self-assertion. Plato can be taken as the great philosophic representative of one way, Nietzsche of the other. The present essay follows the Platonic way.

The Platonic way involves at least one serious problem, however, which must here be faced. Underlying Plato's exaltation of wisdom lay the Socratic equation of knowledge and virtue. In other words, righteousness had its sole and sufficient grounds in apprehension of the truth. To focus the life of an individual or society on the truth, putting all else aside, was safe because the truth, once understood, would issue naturally and inevitably in justice and all other virtues. To know the good was to choose it. But Christianity and common sense alike place this idea in question. It is one thing to argue, as I have, that making good choices, or righteousness, depends on knowing what is good. It is another thing to argue that good choices follow spontaneously and necessarily from knowing what is good, and that we can therefore ignore all other conditions of righteousness. Our understanding of the truth is always too imperfect, surely, for that to be feasible. And even if we could understand the truth perfectly, perhaps man in his freedom could act in defiance of it. The myth of Adam's fall suggests a wanton and rebellious streak in the human makeup.

There is no way of disposing finally of this challenge. Neither an individual nor a society can concentrate on truth and forget all else. Individuals must sometimes make choices that seem to them right even though they do not fully understand why. Many heroic acts have no doubt had their origin in such a state of mind. And everyone at one time or another has done something he has, at least vaguely, known was wrong. Like comments can be made on societies. Good societies cannot be founded solely on good schools, as Plato in a fashion recommended. They must give some thought to what virtue depends on aside from knowledge. Chapter 11, "Limits on Liberty," pursues this matter somewhat further. And nearer at hand, I refer the reader to a later section of the present chapter, "Righteousness and Receptivity." While there is no way of immediately resolving the issue presented by the Socratic equation of virtue and knowledge, a few additional comments may clear the road ahead for our present inquiry.

Although truth cannot be the exclusive concern of free persons and societies, it can and ought to be their central concern. We are never entirely bereft of light. Like the Israelites in the wilderness, who at night were accompanied by a pillar of fire, there is always a glimmering of truth to guide those who are willing to be guided. There may be trusted authorities — pastors, counselors, writers, traditions. And there is always conscience, which in indicating what is right, also indicates what is true. None of these deserve unconditional trust. Together, however, they enable us to carry on the journey exemplified by the ancient Israelites and made possible by liberty — toward a truth in which there is no misunderstanding or doubt. Furthermore, if there is always at least a glim-

73

mering of light to guide us, then we should surely do all we can to draw nearer to that light. As travelers, we must at the same time be inquirers.

The idea that choosing without full knowledge is a "leap" is unfortunate, I believe. It has to be granted that if we never know with absolute certainty what the good is, then in every choice there is a risk. If we are always in partial darkness, there is always danger that we will stumble when we begin to walk. There are degrees of risk, however, and there are wise choices and reckless choices. If we are never in total darkness, if even in the darkest night there is still a pillar of fire, then the challenge of liberty is to follow the light that we have. Doing this necessitates not a leap but a wager. Pascal's concept (applied here not only to Christianity but to truth in general) is ever so much better than Kierkegaard's. "Leap" connotes finality, "wager" a tentative move. The result of a leap may be a final fall into an abyss of darkness, or with better fortune a precarious foothold that one cannot safely abandon. Such was the case for Kierkegaard in his life of faith. A wager, in contrast, can be an experimental step. One can step back or take another step in another direction. A wager can initiate a process of reflecting upon and trying out uncertain truths.

The standard of liberty, I am suggesting, calls for a life of moral inquiry. One tries to draw nearer to the light or to discover a better light. Thus liberty involves reflection. To be free is to have a habit of thinking. Life for all alike, under a liberal regime, should have a philosophic dimension. Philosophy is simply the effort, better carried on sometimes by amateurs than by professionals, to perceive what is ultimately of worth. It is a striving toward truth, a striving to which we are called, not by any intellectual quirk, but by the dependence of life in human beings (as in plants and all other living things) on light, and by the small beckoning light that even in the greatest darkness is always somewhere on the horizon.

Moral inquiry also involves, for Christians, prayer and meditation. These are not entirely different from philosophical reflection. They are ways of seeking the truth when the truth is understood as God. Prayer is trying to speak directly to God, an effort any reflective Christian knows is somewhat quixotic. The God imagined by one who is praying is almost certainly a misrepresentation. God is not like a human mate whom you know intimately and can see when you speak. And one of the meanings of our fallenness is that we cannot, at any moment we desire, picture God clearly and enter his presence. But Christians pray in the faith that God can hear and see quite well in spite of our misconceptions. As for meditation, that is reflection carried on in the interpersonal space between the divine and the human that prayer endeavors to establish. Like reflection, meditation seeks truth. But it does this in the hope that one's queries, sooner or later, and in one fashion or another, will meet a divine response.

My final response to the Socratic equation is simply to say that it may, in spite of all doubts, be true. Is it imaginable that one might know, without a shadow of uncertainty, what the good is and then not choose it? Is it clear in the myth of original sin that Adam knew God fully before disobeying him? It seems manifest that one who does not know the good might deliberately will not to know it. To acknowledge this is to grant a good deal to the role of freedom in the attainment of righteousness. Does the Christian emphasis on human freedom require anything more? I am not sure that it does. In the Gospel of John, Jesus says, "You will know the truth, and the truth will make you free" (John 8:32). A rather Socratic utterance!

The conclusion to which we are led, I believe, is the one I have already hesitatingly voiced: that truth is our central concern, even though it is not our only concern. Righteousness no doubt depends also on things such as moral law, statute, tradition, and habit. These, however, cannot produce the kind of moral purity that flows from knowing — with no shadow of doubt — what is good. And surely the greater our knowledge of the good, the nearer will be our approach to righteousness. These are the propositions that justify making truth our central concern in carrying on the life of liberty.

These are the bare bones of my concept of value. They will take on flesh and come alive, I believe, as the inquiry unfolds. But first of all, more must be said about the very idea of choice, which has been forcibly criticized. This has been not so much on the much-trampled grounds that choice is illusory and all human behavior causally determined. The old argument over free will has at least for the time being been set aside — quite properly, in my opinion — by Kant and by succeeding philosophical movements like existentialism. The critique that demands our attention is that social doctrines emphasizing choice are implicitly individualistic, hence false to the social nature of human beings.

Individual, Society, Community

For the sake of convenience, I shall refer to the critics simply as anti-individualists. The anti-individualist argument starts from the proposition that humans are essentially social. They gain all the skills and powers, the attitudes and loyalties, that make them who they are from society. Their lives throughout are socially situated. They are heirs of a complex pattern of customs and practices. These provide the order and spirit of their lives. Selfhood thus is not found in an abstract point of transcendence, as individualists often seem to imagine, but in a personality structured in detail by the surrounding society. Liberty, accordingly, is not an abstract right prescribed by nature, and is not in any way antithetical to society. It is a set of opportunities provided by society. And it is always enjoyed within a network of social limits and under the sway of beliefs and attitudes that constitute one's very self and therefore cannot be transcended. To suppose that an individual possesses a liberty and selfhood not derived from society is a fantasy — a fantasy that afflicts individualistic liberalism. Such a fantasy is implicit in the famous idea that we should decide on the ultimate standards governing our relations with others behind an imaginary "veil of ignorance." This is a veil concealing from us not only our social position, as defined by such criteria as class and profession, but even our principal beliefs, standards, and goals. Needless to say, being socially situated is not regarded by anti-individualists as a handicap or even as a limit on our freedom. It is the very source of our humanity, hence the source also of any freedom worth possessing. The individual envisioned in the minds of individualistic liberals is an abstraction, a ghost.

There are truths in the anti-individualist argument that come close to being indisputable. These can easily be seen from a Christian vantage point. To begin with, their argument establishes close and dutiful relations among humans a priority that seems to be required by our highest moral standards. These, when voiced not only by Christians but by many others as well, might be summed up in Jesus' command to love others as you do yourself. We should be kindly and considerate and even, when circumstances so require, self-sacrificial. If individualism implies that an individual all alone can be good, or even human, it is ignoring the extent to which humans are in essence related beings. In short, anti-individualists insist on our primal and inviolable moral solidarity.

Further, seen from a Christian perspective, the idea of an unsituated self, capable of making life decisions from a position entirely beyond society, looks like self-deification. Only God is unsituated. To be immanent in a particular society, and shaped fundamentally by a particular social position, is surely inherent in our finitude. It seems that anti-individualists recognize not only our obligations to others but also a virtue inherent in our immersion in society, that is, humility. Individualism, at least in some forms, is replete with pride.

Anti-individualism, then, at least on its critical side, has a strong moral content. It tells us to think of others and not to make too much of ourselves. Individualism is apt to sanction selfishness and presumption. Anti-individualism also has the advantage, it appears, of realism. Society is an omnipresent fact in everyone's life, and this has important implications for our attitude both toward others — which should be an attitude of care and thoughtfulness — and toward ourselves — which should be an attitude of humility. If society is a manifest and all-embracing fact, it may be questioned whether "the individual" has ever existed except in imaginary versions of the state of nature.

In spite of all this, I want to argue that individualism is nearer the truth than the position of its critics. The truth of individualism over against anti-individualism is upheld by the same inescapable fact that upholds personal freedom over against all-inclusive causal determinism — the fact of personal responsibility. Indeed, anti-individualists build on an unacknowledged determinist premise. Implicitly, they regard society as a causal network enclosing the individual. How otherwise can they assert that personal identity is structured through and through by society? How otherwise can they deny that rights are rooted in nature, that is, in the freedom — inherent in human *nature* — that enables one to criticize society and demand things society withholds? And how otherwise can they deny the power of an individual to transcend, in some degree, his social situation?

My argument here can be usefully restated in terms of conscience. Conscience informs us of our moral responsibility, and in this way of our freedom, with an authority that ends all quibbling and doubt. I do not mean that conscience tells us infallibly what we should do. It is obviously affected by social environment and prejudice. It can spur people to do bad things. Conscience does, however, tell us with unquestionable authority that there is right and wrong, and that these ought to govern our lives — regardless of what society says. Right and wrong stand watch, as it were, over every choice. It is particularly noteworthy that the claims of conscience single out individuals. Each one is conscious of bearing moral responsibilities, and these responsibilities cannot be transferred to society. If I fail them, social influences may be an extenuating factor, but they cannot entirely remove the guilt I alone must bear. In sum, conscience is a power of social transcendence.

This, very briefly, is the argument against anti-individualism. Although I have used the words "conscience" and "responsibility," it will be clear that I am speaking of choice. And I am speaking of the choices that are made by individuals, that is, by each one alone, for responsibility bears on each one alone. Conscience tells us that our choices are of ultimate, irreducible significance. In some sense, they matter eternally. And it tells us that responsibility for choosing rightly bears on each particular person — not as a social being but simply as a being with an ineradicable concern for right and wrong. In a word, conscience is an individualist.

This argument does not involve a wholesale denial of the anti-individualist stress on the social embeddedness of individuals. Those who choose are always situated in a particular set of circumstances — physical, cultural, economic, and so forth — and are always in some degree products of these circumstances. Hence their options are limited. Some options they cannot even think of, and others are rendered impossible by their situations even if they think of them. And the choices they make will be shaped, in more ways than they can comprehend, by prejudices, impulses, fears, and other personal characteristics they have inherited and not chosen. Still, as everyone knows, options remain, and choices must be made. And making such choices carefully, that is, "conscientiously," or "responsibly" — *and if need be in defiance of society* — is essential to an authentically human life.

Anti-individualists speak of the "encumbered self," referring thereby to the individual who is never a mere individual but is a social being, a product of past social developments, living under the obligations of a present social role. Conscience tells us that we should strive to disencumber ourselves, whether by putting ourselves imaginatively behind a "veil of ignorance," or in some other way. This is not necessarily the self-deification some might fear — and should fear. It is, or at least can be, an effort to become a moral individual, that is, to rise above the laws and customs of a time and place, and put oneself under the authority of moral requirements that are absolute and universal. Such an effort is in essence not self-exaltation but moral responsibility. If the intent of those who attack individualistic liberals for their supposedly naive belief in the disencumbered self were merely to call attention to the difficulty of transcending society, even the impossibility of doing so fully, their argument would be irrefutable. Seemingly, however, their intent is to insist on the complete immanence of the individual in society. If they were right, then moral relativism would be unavoidable. It would in that case be illogical even to claim that social involvement is morally better than individual isolation. Disencumberment is no doubt a formidable undertaking, and one that can never be more than partially accomplished, but conscience requires us to carry it out as fully as we can. It does this by speaking of responsibilities that are not necessarily the same as those imposed by society — responsibilities that might call on me to jeopardize, or even abandon, my social situation.

Here we gain our first glimpse of a concept that is central in the theory of liberty to be developed in the following pages. This is the concept of "the liberal stance," as I shall call it. Broadly stated, liberalism represents primarily, not a political program or an ideal society, but — for every individual — a way of standing among others. It means first of all claiming the liberty to respond to my own personal responsibilities as I understand them. At the same time, it means realizing that others should have the same liberties I have. The basis for such liberalism is every person's capacity for choice, along with every person's responsibility for choosing the things that ought to be chosen. It matters little whether the "ought" be understood teleologically, as deriving from a good or goods to be sought, or deontologically, as prescribed in an unconditional moral law. The critical point is that liberty, for self and others, is a moral claim that singles out — that "disencumbers" — every individual.

The main author of moral liberalism, by which I mean the theory that liberty is essentially a moral opportunity owed to man as a moral being, is Immanuel Kant. Given Kant's philosophical authority, it is surprising how rarely the theory is clearly recognized. Prevailing views tend to polarize liberty and morality. On the one hand, proponents of liberty have often encouraged, or, more commonly among philosophers of liberty, have merely allowed, people to construe liberty as an opportunity to do as they please. Little attention is paid to moral responsibility. On the other hand, people acutely concerned with moral responsibility have not usually been much interested in liberty. The moral law, in their minds, implies hierarchy of some kind. Surely, however, both views are quite wrong. If liberty is no more than an opportunity for indulging personal preferences, it is trivial. If we are subject to absolute moral imperatives, however, liberty is indispensable, for there is no moral merit in doing what you have not chosen to do. Allowing liberty and morality to be set against one another is fatal to both.

From this point of view we can understand the strange fusion, often found at the height of moral life, of freedom and necessity. The idea that free choice is central in moral life has been attacked by anti-individualists on the grounds that moral acts are apt to arise from an awareness that they absolutely have to be done. Hence they are not really choices in the usual sense of the word. The point certainly has merit. When I make a difficult but morally obligatory decision, I may even exclaim, "I have no choice!" This phenomenon is exemplified historically in Luther's perhaps apocryphal words at Worms, "Here I stand. I can do no other." What must be noted, however, is that we admire people like Luther because in fact they could have done other. Instead, they chose to do what they "had" to do. What the anti-individualist objection brings out is that choosing is not like flipping a coin. It is choosing in a way that meets a moral demand.

It is also choosing in a very personal way. It is important to understand what this means. I have been using terms like "responsibility" and "morality." These suggest to many people something cold and impersonal. As I have said, however, the general outlook underlying this essay is "personalist." For the concept of choice being developed in this discussion to take on overtones of impersonality would indicate that the argument has somehow been derailed. Moral choice, as I understand it, is highly personal. This is so in two respects.

In the first place, choosing morally is choosing the self. One's own personal being is not suppressed by the good but rather is called forth, since the good is what each one desires, however unknowingly. Repeated choices of the good, consequently, do not gradually constrict and suffocate the self, as casual critics of morality often suppose, but allow the self to unfold. The purpose of liberty is that you be yourself, or, more precisely, that you *become* yourself. Freedom is therefore not realized in a single act of decision. It requires a series of decisions; indeed, it requires a lifetime of decisions. To choose reflectively and seriously is to choose with earlier and impending choices in mind. It is to choose an unfolding self. Personal freedom is thus far more complex, rich, and arduous than the bare concept of choice may suggest. It comprises developments that come about through experience and reflection, disappointment and repentance, anxiety and gratitude. Some choices may be built upon, others regretted and revoked. Yet others, our wisest choices, require repeated renewal. We can see more clearly why a significant choice is not like flipping a coin. It is more like committing oneself anew to a long and arduous journey. It is a journey toward the good and toward the selfhood that is found only in a person's relationship with the good.

In the second place — and here we come to a point particularly relevant to the anti-individualist critique — choosing morally is choosing not only the self but the other as well. The good may be defined provisionally as community, that is, the self and the other in a state of unity. If "the other" be construed as whoever happens to be on hand, that is, as "neighbor," then to define the good as community is not far from Jesus' command to love your neighbor as yourself. To link liberty with community is not arbitrary. As already noted, a rightful claim to liberty can be based only on the fact of one's freedom, one's capacity to choose. But this means that a rightful claim to liberty must be made in behalf of all who possess that capacity, and that is everyone. In this way the claim to liberty places one in a hypothetical community of free, hence responsible, persons. In the term coined by the philosopher who stands preeminently for the fusion of liberty and morality, one is placed in a "kingdom of ends" — of beings who choose ends, and deploy means in relation to them, but are not themselves to be used as means.

It may seem that making community the aim of liberty puts us back into the anti-individualist camp. This is not the case, however, for the anti-individualist concern is not with community, properly speaking, but with society, which is a different matter. The distinction between community and society will be made more fully at a later point in this essay. Here I shall say only that community is far more personal and subjective, hence more mysterious, than is society. It is a state of what has sometimes been called "intersubjectivity," and cannot be known through objective observation such as that employed for the study of society. Community is found not in any stable, outward reality but in the activity of communication. Communication, in turn, as one might anticipate from what I have said about the value of truth, has to do with inquiring into the depths of reality. It follows that the liberal stance, although assumed by one person independently of, and sometimes in opposition to, every other person, is communicative.

All of this is to speak summarily of matters yet to be explored. Let me say, however, that the whole history of social theory, from the time of Plato to at least the time of Hegel, is bedeviled by the failure to distinguish community and society. This has been disastrous for the understanding of liberty. I am by no means the first to make the distinction. It was clearly present in the ancient Christian distinction between kingdoms of the world and the kingdom of God. And it is very near the surface of the twentieth-century writings of various existentialists, such as Nicolas Berdyaev and Karl Jaspers. It comes near to being explicit in Martin Buber's distinction between "I-Thou" and "I-It" relations, even though Buber, a socialist, muddied the distinction in outlining the ideal society. At any rate, one of the main purposes of the present essay is to draw the distinction clearly and to show how it enables one to affirm liberty, which is necessarily *from* society, without falling into an anticommunal individualism.

Justifying liberty in terms of conscience, and of the personal freedom to which conscience testifies, thus does not burden a great ideal with a false individualism. It is true that any theory emphasizing personal responsibility will be individualistic. This is because personal responsibility singles out individuals. Each one in particular bears responsibilities that, strictly speaking, are unsharable. This is the individualism inherent in the fact of freedom. It is not, however, the false individualism that consists in denying the absolute value of human relationships. Indeed, the very same conscience that singles out individuals practically always places them in relationship with others. It informs them of what they owe to their fellow human beings. It separates them from society in order to bring them into community.

It is striking how acceptable the principle of personal responsibility is both to humanist reason and to religious faith. Protagonists of humanist reason often deny that there are absolute values or unconditional moral imperatives. It is doubtful, however, that many of them altogether mean it. Almost never are they willing to disavow normal responsibilities, like caring for one's children or telling the truth, or to grant that involvement in some monstrous practice, like slavery, is merely a matter of personal taste. By all evidence, the sense of responsibility, although occasionally weakened by adverse conditions and at times frivolously denied, retains a tenacious presence in human souls, whether or not it has good logical grounds for being there.

As for religious believers, they acknowledge with near unanimity the fact of moral responsibility and the authority of conscience. For them, the experience of personal responsibility carries a cluster of religious intimations. Whether in recognition of a duty that must by all means be fulfilled or of a duty grievously unfulfilled, it is an encounter with the absolute. And that encounter carries other religious intuitions — for example, of being subject to a judgment that is inescapable by dying, and is thereby an intimation of eternity.

Obviously the sense of responsibility may mean different things to humanist reason and to religious faith. Yet both can perceive the freedom of man, and both can realize that some uses of freedom are right and some are wrong. In this way they can, and often do, inhabit a common moral universe. My argument in this section might be summarily restated by saying that a human being is primarily an inhabitant of this universe, and only secondarily an inhabitant of society. The claims on one of the moral universe are absolute; here there is no room for individualism. But the claims of society are conditional, to be appraised, by each one singly, in every particular instance. Here individualism is inescapable.

Righteousness and Receptivity

The purpose and justification of liberty, then, is choice — not in a moment, but over a lifetime — of things worthy of choice. A life engaged in that enterprise we usually call "righteous." Liberty cannot be discussed, therefore, apart from righteousness. However, this puts before us a question that is easy to ask but hard to answer: How is righteousness possible? I have laid down the premise that human beings are strongly and persistently inclined toward unrighteousness and therefore almost certain to misuse their liberty. We have discussed ways in which people with the liberty to follow their unrighteous inclinations harm one another and society. It might seem that liberty is fitting only for creatures

83

with greater moral sensitivity and powers of self-discipline than human beings in their fallen state possess. I have argued, of course, that while liberty threatens society with widespread unrighteousness, it is nonetheless necessary, for otherwise there could be no righteousness. To put this in terms of truth: where there is liberty there will be much dishonesty and deception, but without liberty truth will be neither discovered nor genuinely known. Still, liberty is indefensible unless righteousness is possible. Is it? There are good reasons for thinking it is.

To begin with, radical evil does not imply total depravity. Radical evil means, as Kant defined it, living with an inner reservation to the effect that the moral law is not absolute. It will be followed only so long as the cost — measured in terms of self-interest — is not too high. Accordingly, someone might conform with the moral law most, or even all, of the time, but always with the inner understanding that under no circumstances would he sacrifice his life. Such a person would be radically evil but would strike most of us as quite a decent person. Of course, someone whose allegiance to the ought is qualified by concerns of self-interest might in some circumstances act in ways we would consider wrong. The point, however, is that the principle of radical evil, or "original sin," does not imply human behavior that is invariably vicious. This is part of the answer to the question of the possibility of righteousness. It is not the whole answer, however, because righteousness that carries a secret qualification giving primacy to self-interest is seriously flawed. If liberty opens the way only to righteousness so compromised, the case for liberty is weak.

We must therefore consider another answer — one offered by faith, and at first glance at odds with reason, yet, I believe, potentially meaningful to reason. Christians maintain, as everyone knows, that righteousness comes mainly or wholly through grace. Worthy choices are made possible by God. The principle of grace issues in a rather dramatic vision of humanity, one in which humans are thought of as extremely evil yet capable of living good lives and perhaps actually doing so. Usually Christian writers have seen the evil dimension of humanity as manifest in many or most people, and the good possibilities, due to grace, manifest in only a few. But there is no reason in principle why grace might not be given to everyone without exception. There can be great glory in human beings, according to the theology of grace. Yet, however glorious, a person can never be proud. Righteousness is a gift to those in need of it, which means it is bestowed on the unrighteous. It is unearned, or gratuitous. This is why it is grace. There is glory in God as well, yet not the glory that comes from implacable justice. God is above all merciful, for he is generous to the undeserving. The Jewish prophets, although often depicting a wrathful God, insisted always that God's final word was not wrathful but merciful. For Christians, this final word was Christ, whose life was the story of God's merciful engagement in the fate of lost and fallen humanity.

Humanist reason is apt to look on such views with puzzlement, indifference, or hostility, yet it is common for people with no religious commitments, perhaps even disdainful of those making such commitments, to sense their dependence on something beyond their comprehension and control, something apart from which they cannot accomplish anything of moment. Thus it seems almost universal among artists to acknowledge that only under the impulse of unbidden perceptions and energies, given perhaps as banal a name as "inspiration," can they create anything of worth. All writers, regardless of religious attitudes and convictions, know that fitting words come to them sometimes easily, sometimes haltingly, and sometimes not at all. And it is so common as to be unremarkable for scientists to declare that the most fruitful hypotheses cannot be summoned at will but must simply occur to them. Such attitudes have the look of a tacit acknowledgment of grace.

Is there any reason to think that righteousness is any more under the command of will than is original work in art, literature, or science? It is sometimes said that someone "found it in his heart" to carry out a generous act — an apparent acknowledgment of something given rather than summoned. And it seems that truly good people (as distinguished from people who are merely puritanical) never feel that they are very good. The goodness of their acts is a gift they have not deserved. Indeed, righteousness and self-righteousness appear to be mutually exclusive. The Christian idea that we can be all that we ought to be only through grace is not, it seems, utterly strange to humanist reason.

Associated with the idea of grace, or (in humanist terms) the givenness of our best works, is a principle of prime importance for understanding liberty. If human righteousness and wisdom are dependent on something beyond us, then a certain posture is appropriate to men and women, a posture exhibited, it might be said, not only by every authentic (as distinguished from merely professed) Christian but also by every authentic human being. That posture is one of receptivity. Good choices are made, and worthwhile works accomplished, by responsiveness rather than sheer will. Our lives are given to us not only at birth but at every moment, or at least every moment in which we are living well and are free. This is not to slight the creativity that is often seen as the quintessence of freedom. It is not to deny that we are in some sense creators not only of various works but also of our lives. It is only to observe that we do not create at will. To be fully responsible, it might be said, is to be fully responsive.

A staunch receptivity toward the source from which our humanity and freedom come to us is often called faith. To speak first in Christian terms, faith in the proper sense of the word is not "faith that" but "faith in." It is faith in God, not in propositions about God. And faith in God amounts to something that might better be termed "love" for God. Although Jesus sometimes called for faith, it was love for God that he named as our highest obligation — the substance of the "first commandment." It seems that faith consists less in a willful and stubborn affirmation of creeds than in wholehearted attentiveness toward and trust in the fountainhead of all things. God, in the Christian mind, is the source of values and of the grace that enables us to perceive these values. Love for God is an unwavering personal orientation toward this source. It is unconditional receptivity.

As thoroughly religious and theological as this may sound, there is an attitude not entirely unlike it available to humanist reason. I shall call it "openness toward transcendence." Such openness is not faith, for it is fundamentally agnostic. It is openness toward something unknown. It is informed, however, with an awareness of our need for insights and energies we do not command. Hence it must wait for these to be given. It is steadily receptive. While it does not claim knowledge of transcendence, it does know that our lives, along with the values that give our lives meaning, are not products of our will or subject to our governance. They come from beyond the self and beyond society. Openness toward transcendence might be seen as less a moral imperative than a practical necessity.

Some Christians would charge that such openness, ungrounded in revelation, is blind and willful. There may be an element of truth in that charge. Yet that humanist reason can be open toward transcendence without being flagrantly arbitrary or unreasonable is shown by two philosophical figures of the twentieth century, Martin Heidegger and Karl Jaspers. The former distinguished between being and beings — roughly a distinction between transcendence and world — and envisioned man as a sensorium of being. Man is not in command of being but can create only a kind of inner space for being and wait for its appearance. The latter, Jaspers, focused his philosophy on that mysterious dimension of reality that was left over after we have defined and understood all the objects around us. This reality, like Heidegger's "being," is roughly the same as transcendence. Jaspers saw the individual person as achieving authenticity only in relation to transcendence. Neither Heidegger nor Jaspers was a Christian.

While we have been considering grace mainly as a source of righteousness, it should be noted that it is seen equally well as a source of wisdom. Grace overcomes not only unrighteousness but also foolishness and ignorance. It brings truth to human beings who, from their own resources, have little capacity for acquiring truth. And if righteousness that is pure arises only from truth, such must be the way grace works. It must, to effect righteousness, bring truth into souls destined for righteousness. But use of the word "grace" here may obscure how relevant these matters are to humanist reason. When writers, artists, and scientists — most of them in late modern times humanists — speak of their dependence on words, ideas, and insights that come to them unbidden, they are speaking implicitly of their dependence, in their efforts to disclose the truth in novels, paintings, philosophies, and other human works, on transcendence. They are tacitly acknowledging the standard of receptivity.

Freedom is not compromised by construing it in terms of receptivity. The selfhood in which freedom becomes real is not diminished by its dependence on transcendence. This can be dramatized, I think, by casting it in Christian terms, that is, in terms of grace. Does the dependence of man on God inevitably entail, as Marx and Nietzsche charged, a diminution of man? To answer this question it may help to glance at the relationship, as Christians see it, of divine grace and human will.

The relationship is often depicted as rather simple. It is characterized in words like, "We need God's help to be good or to do anything worthwhile." Such a statement is easily understood. It allows us to think of the divine-human relationship as cooperative. God and man are like two business executives working out together the design and marketing of a new product, or like two horses pulling in unison the chariot of righteousness. Everyone knows from daily experience what it is to cooperate with someone else on a common project, and if receiving grace is the same sort of thing, we know what that is too. This view of grace is not only attractive. It may in some sense be true. As it stands, however, it involves difficulties.

The difficulties pertain both to the human and to the divine. On one side, not much weight is given to the evil in human nature. If men and women are capable of being in harness with God, it doesn't look as though they can be so very bad. On the other side, the notion that grace is mere assistance doesn't accord much importance to the power of God. God's role is about the same as man's. God and man are partners. God is virtually finite. In brief, too much is made of the human, too little of the divine.

In response to such difficulties some of the most respected Christian thinkers maintain that divine grace and human righteousness are not complementary but coincident. Divine power is not like human power, which always involves either curbing or assisting a free act on the part of others. In divine-human relations the power of God and the freedom of man flourish simultaneously. The power of God is unique among all powers. It is more mysterious than the power of a policeman or even of a prime minister. And in no way does it lessen freedom. On the contrary, it is liberating. Divine sovereignty and human freedom in some sense coalesce.

The resultant vision of grace and freedom is dramatized in the symbol of Christ as the God-man. Christ is not partly divine and partly human, according to orthodox Christianity, but rather is wholly and entirely divine — God incarnate — and at the same time wholly and entirely human. Jesus was God, in Christian eyes. But he was also a particular man, born in a province of the Roman Empire, during the reign of the emperor Tiberius, supporting himself with a trade, having a mother and father, as well as sisters and brothers, and finally so falling out of favor with the ruling powers that he was executed while still a young man. All of this, as Paul noted, is "foolishness to the Greeks." Yet it accords, strangely enough, with the vision of human grandeur and freedom suggested in Marx and enunciated with unsurpassable eloquence by Nietzsche. Christianity differs from these two humanists —

and profoundly — in its understanding of God and the relationship between God and humanity. But it does not differ from them in its estimate of human stature or in its stress on the possible amplitude and glory of human freedom.

From this summit of vision, where Christian faith and humanist reason, often to their mutual surprise, encounter one another, we must descend and examine more carefully the route by which the summit is reached. We must ask how grace works. Doing this will widen our understanding of freedom and its relationship with transcendence. It will show that grace works in a way that humanist reason is apt to see as peculiar — not simply by bringing us into conformity with the moral law but by enabling us, while striving toward righteousness, more or less to forget the moral law. The theory of how this happens may at first look like a fantasy of antiquated religiosity, unfit for modern minds. But the theory is not only at the center of Christian faith and the Christian idea of freedom. It coincides to a surprising degree with the image of freedom that haunts many modern minds, whether Christian or not.

Justification and the Life of Liberty

To feel justified is to feel that your life and being are warranted, or valid. Hence you have a right to live and be yourself, a right to be free. But the right does not come from other people or from the legal order, even though approval of others or legal acquittal may give you a temporary feeling of being justified. It comes from the very ground of things. All the authorities of the world are finite and affected by sin. How could any of them bestow justification? I have already pointed out that a sense of responsibility unmet, that is, of guilt, is a consciousness of being accountable to something beyond the world. Feelings of guilt, of unrighteousness, are agonizing because they carry fears of having, in the final reckoning, no valid claim to your own selfhood. On the other hand, assurance of justification may carry with it a mysterious sense of immortality. Your right to existence, arising from the ultimate ground of all reality, does not lapse. The connection with liberty is plain: to feel unjustified is to be unready for liberty. The sense of justification, on the other hand, carries the sense of being rightfully free.

It may seem that our need for justification, as a spur to righteousness, would be beneficent. In actuality, however, it is often harmful. It may, for example, arouse a will to power or wealth of such magnitude as to silence any doubts about the substantiality and significance of one's life. Thus the worst tyrants can sometimes be seen as men maddened by the need for dramatic, unceasing, and unquestioned validation of their being. They live exclusively in the company of sycophants and flatterers. They are hailed by multitudes. Critics are humiliated and destroyed. It is not implausible to see the totalitarian tyrannies of the twentieth century as massive enterprises of self-justification. Mass adulation and limitless power gave the tyrants and their cohorts unshakable assurance of rightful existence. Indulgence in wanton killing seemed the prerogative of people beyond all judgment and question. The masses, too, could derive a sense of justification from their identification with a leader whose life and existence were of unquestionable validity. And they might find in an ideology, sustained by propaganda and public spectacles, a seeming source of justification, such as the mysterious purity of a race, or the unique historical mission of a class or nation.

Another possible upshot of the hunger for justification is moral relativism. Since fear of offending against the moral law is one source of concern about justification, denial of the moral law, at least as anything more than the customs and rules of a time and place, may bring apparent liberation. By removing a threat to valid selfhood, one gains a right to live. The gain is illusory, as I have already shown. If there are no absolute moral rules, or absolute values, then choices are in the final analysis trivial, since none can be wrong. And if choices are trivial, then liberty is trivial too — merely something one happens to enjoy. Nonetheless, an amoral universe may, at least for a time, look like a setting for perfect freedom.

Perhaps the most natural and powerful result of the quest for justification is the one symbolized by ancient Israel: the aspiration toward exact conformity with the moral law. It is an answer of persuasive simplicity. If justification lies in righteousness, then it is presumably attained by adhering perfectly to all the rules by which righteousness is defined. Probably everyone who has not been lost in clouds of dissipation and distraction has felt drawn to the ideal of righteousness under the law. Christians have been no exception. According to orthodox Christianity, however, striving for justification through perfect conformity with the law is a very great error. There are at least two serious flaws in the ideal of justification through the law.

The one most commonly noted, and not by Christians alone, is the generality of the law. Legal prescriptions are indifferent to the particularity of every person and situation. Particularity is of course compatible with the reign of law. Law grants room for particularity by the very fact of its generality. Also, every legal order contains multiple devices, such as courts of equity and provisions for pardon, designed to recognize and accommodate cases that do not perfectly fit the law. But particularity is merely allowed, not affirmed. Hence a fundamental impersonality is implicit in the ideal of justification through the law. What matters is not being the one you distinctively are but perfect obedience to general rules that pay no heed to your distinctive being.

The other weakness of the ideal of justification through the law is particularly stressed by Paul and goes back to the condition discussed at the outset of this essay, namely, that humans are stubbornly and deeply inclined toward evil. In a word, they are lawless. In consequence, not even the most virtuous person, by the most arduous efforts, can perfectly fulfill every legal prescription. This is particularly the case if, as Jesus asserted, the law concerns not only outward behavior but also inward attitudes, such as lust. And most people will fall short in more than details. They will sometimes stumble and violate major commands of the law. It follows that the law condemns but does not justify. This is the gravamen at once of Paul's charge against ancient Judaism — to pursue justification through the law is a doomed undertaking — and of his defense of the law — it instills a spiritually salutary consciousness of our personal culpability.

At the very center of Christianity is a quite different principle of justification. It is often referred to as justification by faith, although the name is misleading. One is not justified basically by an inner attitude, such as faith. One is justified by a merciful God. Hence a better designation would be "justification by divine forgiveness." Yet this too, although accurate, is misleading. While pointing accurately toward the final source of justification, it allows for the impression that God forgives us because he is easygoing and indulgent. That is far from the Christian view. One great truth behind Jewish reverence for the law, as Christians see it, is that God is righteous and requires unconditionally that his human creatures likewise be righteous. It was that truth that enabled the

Jewish law to dramatize the depth of human unrighteousness. It follows that forgiveness cannot be in any way casual, even for the supreme power and creator of the universe, for whom, as the biblical saying has it, everything is possible. Even for God, forgiveness is difficult. Nevertheless, there is divine forgiveness. How does it come about? To answer this question we must note yet another deficiency of the law.

The major requirement of the law in relation to unrighteous men and women can be simply stated. It is condemnation and punishment. For justification to be achieved, justice must be done. This is logical. And in the most flagrant offenses against the law, it is more or less practical. Every day, year after year, the judicial systems of civilized nations mete out rough justice — thus bestowing a degree of justification — on the most flagrant offenders. Even at their best, however, human legal systems do not meet the problem of justification. They touch only a few people; they bear only on a few offenses; their judgments are often crude and superficial. The evil in people is too pervasive, too deep, too hidden from human sight for human beings to provide justification. Protagonists of the law are led inevitably to the ideal of a divine system of justice, imposing on every person, either within or beyond earthly life, the precise penalties that are deserved.

For many, such an ideal is irresistible. It is a vision of all time and existence as perfectly ordered, perfectly just. The vision has captivated even Christians. The doctrine of double predestination — that God decided before ever creating the universe not only on those he would save, but also on those he would damn — is in part an expression of the ideal. Yet it causes many to recoil in disgust and horror. This is because the universe it presents — following from the defects of the law cited above — is depersonalizing and remorseless. Even if God spares a few, such mercy is capricious and leaves all of us threatened by the murderous justice that rules the universe. On the premises of this essay, all of us are morally deranged, and deeply so. Even though we avoid flagrant misdeeds, such as murder and theft, we all are capable of them. In that sense those who commit sensational crimes are representative figures. All of us are deeply guilty and deserving of punishment. And the punishment due for our primal offense, that of effecting the total disorientation of the soul that is Kant's "radical evil," would presumably be severe and might be death, or eternal damnation. As a result, life under a law that reaches into every corner of space and time, and governs all eternity, inevitably takes on a grim, penal flavor. Every person is ceaselessly pursued by judgment and punishment. My point, in short, is that the ideal of justification by the law, given original sin, is a penal universe.

Christianity — which in its original, Pauline form does not affirm double predestination — dramatically changes this picture. The core Christian claim is that justice in behalf of every human being was done in the crucifixion of Christ. Since Christ was "the son of man," in a mysterious way the representative of every person, Christ's suffering and death brought justification to the entire human race. Every man and woman has been brought out from under the cloud of judgment and punishment created by the law. In this way Jesus' suffering and death was a work of liberation. Thus envisioned, the divine forgiveness that justifies humanity comes about, not through an easy act of indulgence from a lenient judge, but through the agony and death of a person who was both divine and human. The perennial spell of the cross lies, above all, I believe, in its telling us that we can now be ourselves and live freely regardless of our failures and transgressions. Contrary to the repressive spirit typically displayed by protagonists of the law — great Christians among them — Christianity is a religion of liberty.

Christian theology of course speaks of justification by faith. Where does faith come in? It signifies nothing more than acceptance of the new state of moral affairs. It is a refusal, authorized by the cross, to be imprisoned by an unrighteous past. It is surmounting moral failures, neither by obsessively grieving over them, nor by denying that they have occurred, but by accepting the revolution in the moral universe that occurred when Jesus was crucified. Admittedly, the Christian churches have in significant measure failed to recognize and support this revolution. They have often palliated the harsh and unpleasant doctrine of original sin and thereby have obscured the meaning of the cross. They have allowed believers and unbelievers alike to think that faith consists in professing certain doctrines rather than in seizing and cherishing the innocence — and the consequent freedom — regained by the human race on Calvary.

The Gospel of John speaks of Jesus being "lifted up" on the cross. Through the crucifixion — for Christians the axis of human destiny — every person is lifted up, every person exalted. This comes about through the act of justice that releases humans from the guilt pronounced upon them by the law. Released from guilt, they are righteous, and being righteous they are justified. In this lies the renewal of the dignity given to humans when they were created "in the image and likeness of God," and lost mythically when Adam cut his connection with God. To appreciate the miracle of this liberation, however, it is essential to keep in mind that even for God the process was arduous. It entailed the inferno of suffering and dying endured by a man who was also, in Christian faith, God. In this inferno, mercy and righteousness were fused. Justice was done, but it was done in a way that liberated, rather than crushed, the human race. Men and women came down from Calvary clothed again in the primordial splendor of their created being.

Up to this point we have considered primarily one dimension of the crucifixion: its bearing on the past. But to effect liberation, it must bear also on the future. How futile it would be to tell someone freed from subjection to the law, so far as past offenses are concerned, to become again subject to the law and try to do better! If past works have lost their power to condemn, then it would seem that future works have lost their power to justify. This is implied by the principle of justification by faith and not by works. Observance of the law, whether in the past or in the future, no longer determines one's eternal destiny. To maintain otherwise would be to jeopardize the new state of affairs effected by the crucifixion. It would give the cross an oddly limited, backward-looking meaning. If we have been set free from the *penalties* of the law, then we must in some sense have been set free from the *demands* of the law. Here the scope of the moral revolution brought about by the crucifixion becomes apparent.

Still, one must ask what it can mean to be freed from the demands of the law. Can we commit crimes and carry out atrocities without fearing punishment? Paul was aware that critics of Christianity had charged it with stripping away all moral restraints, and he indignantly repudiated the charge. He was shocked by the idea that the unrighteous, absolved of their guilt by the cross, might continue in their unrighteousness. Justification implied, in his mind, not merely forgiveness but also moral transformation. Forgiveness of past sins — that is, justification of those whose lives have not earned justification — without an ensuing change on the part of the forgiven, would be morally senseless. Forgiveness would be a moral absurdity if unrelated to moral reform. In traditional terminology, justification must lead to, or be accompanied by, sanctification.

While Paul's view seems quite reasonable, it contains a serious difficulty: it apparently brings law back to the center of things. What can it mean to strive for sanctity except to try very hard to obey the law? The law, after all, is a summary of what we should do and refrain from doing. Paul, echoing Jesus' warning that his ministry in no way diminished the authority of the law, explicitly accepted this implication. The law remains. It loses none of its majesty. What then has been changed by the cross?

Here we approach the most puzzling aspect of Christian morality. If I am not mistaken, however, we also approach the heart of the idea of liberty. To be truly righteous and free, one must claim freedom from the law without derogating from the authority of the law. This is the paradox of Christian goodness and of human freedom. The best way of explaining it, somewhat surprisingly, may come from the Far East.

The Bhagavad Gita calls on us to engage vigorously in worldly action but to do this in a spirit of inaction — to act, but to do so as though we were not acting. The theme is developed through mythical warriors, in battle, so the action is violent and absorbing. Even action of that sort, according to the Bhagavad Gita, should be carried on in a spirit of inner detachment. It seems that Christianity issues a somewhat similar call. Those justified by the cross, and set free from the law, must still struggle toward the righteousness prescribed by the law. They must do this, however, as though they were not struggling. They must strive for sanctity as though not striving. This may sound impossibly paradoxical. But in truth it is no more paradoxical than the ideal of a serious moral life that is free of moral anguish — of a dedication to goodness that is not ridden by remorse and legalistic compunction.

A state of this sort seems to be promised to us by the New Testament. Sanctity, although as yet unattained, is no longer an impotent ought. It will be given to us through the grace that forgives us. This is symbolized in the Christian declaration that Christ not only has been crucified but also has risen from the dead. Hence Paul can promise us here and now, in spite of our temporary unrighteousness, the peace "which passes all understanding" (Phil. 4:7). Justified by grace rather than the law, we can now heed and respect the law without being enslaved and frightened by it. Very simply, we can enjoy a state of moral liberty. We can live as creatures at once morally serious yet free of care.

Such a view of righteousness may at first sound strange to humanist ears. Yet it is not very far from some deep, common concerns. Many people, including not a few who have abandoned religion, strive to be morally decent, and even good. But they do not want to be "puritanical" — joyless, negative, censorious. They want to be moral but not moralistic. They want to live as responsible men and women, but they view with distaste preoccupation with every nuance of the moral law. They do not want to be burdened either with feelings of guilt or with anxiety about doing something that would bring down feelings of guilt. Summarily, they aspire to a life that is morally decent but not grim. That is approximately the life Christians believe is available to us through Christ's crucifixion.

I do not mean, by anything I have said, to intimate that one can rightfully forget the past or be lighthearted about the wrongs one has done or the wrongs one's society has done. One lives as human only by living in continuity with one's personal and historical past. And so far as past misdeeds are concerned, one lives as forgiven, and thus justified, only by remembering those things for which one is forgiven. It seems, accordingly, that the proper posture of a human being is one of penitence — for Christians, before God, for all others before the moral law. I suggest, however, that such penitence should be, so to speak, cheerful. The universe is not fundamentally a penal order. Nor is it altogether inhospitable to liberty.

Nor do I mean to suggest that one should be lighthearted about wrongs one may do in the future. This would be particularly inappropriate for beings affected by radical evil. To live unaware of, or unconcerned with, the human proclivity toward evil would be a mark of moral frivolity. It would also be inappropriate, however, at least for Christians, to live in a state of continual anxiety over the possibility, even the likelihood, that one will commit further wrongs in the future. That would be to forget the merciful firmament, so to speak, that was spread over humankind by what happened on Calvary.

To be righteous is simply to be yourself and thus to be free. A righteous man or woman is not a deformed or stunted human being but an exemplification of humanity in its fullness and perfection. In saying this, we must take care not to brush aside and forget the law. Being yourself is not the same as being different from everyone else. The full and undiminished humanity of your true self partakes of universality. Killing, stealing, lying, and other such acts diminish the humanity of anyone who commits them. Still, to be fully yourself, or fully righteous, it is not enough to measure up to universal norms. You must be human in your own distinctive way. You must be creatively human, and this means, as we have seen, being respectful of the law but at the same time unburdened by it. You must somehow do all that the law requires, and even more, without trying to. What does this mean? How is it possible?

Jesus and Paul both summed up the meaning of righteousness — which they saw as at once within and beyond the law — in a single word, "love." If you are moved by love, you simultaneously fulfill the law and are fully free. You are not even tempted to kill, or steal, or lie. Universality is spontaneous. Yet nothing is more personal, more deeply rooted in your own being, than love. Hence love comes out in free and unforeseeable ways. It brings out, rather than inhibiting, the uniqueness of the one who loves. Personal distinctiveness flourishes, not in isolation, but in good and deep human relationships. All other relationships, such as those involved in an economic enterprise or a bureaucratic organization, are in some measure restrictive. But not those based on love. Love gives more to the other than justice requires, but it does this in perfect freedom. It is at once generous and creative.

This whole essay is indirectly about love, for significant liberty is used for building relationships, and the highest standard governing relationships is love. Love prompts us to come together, and we come together in the most fully human way when we inquire together into the truth. The quest for truth is itself an expression of love — for Christians love of God, for humanists love of being. And the highest relationship among humans is found in sharing that quest. These matters, and their implications for liberty, will be explored in later pages. It is necessary first, however, to look into the philosophy that underlies love and all serious communication and that therefore underlies significant liberty.

This philosophy often is called "personalism," since it is centered on the primacy of personal being. Love and communication are important because persons are important. The depth of the reality into which we inquire when we search for truth is, at least as Christians see it, personal. Liberty is significant, then, insofar as persons are significant. The argument made for liberty in this chapter pointed in this direction. In arguing that good can come into the world only by being chosen, I argued in effect that values can be realized only when centered in personal being. Value is real only in correlation with persons. That is why, if a state perfectly just in form but containing no just persons were founded, nothing of moral significance would have been accomplished. In sum, if persons were not somehow fundamental in the whole order of things, liberty would be meaningless.

CHAPTER 4

Personalism

The Personalist Idea

Personalism concerns both reality and value. Fundamental reality, or being in itself, to use a phrase common among twentieth-century philosophers, is not to be understood in terms of something impersonal, such as ideas or matter. Idealism and materialism, among other philosophies, are thus ruled out. Reality is basically personal, made up of persons or in some sense centered in and subordinate to persons. Thus ideas, while real, are created and used by persons, and a person can never be exhaustively known through any idea or set of ideas (a principle flagrantly violated by most ideologies). In like fashion, matter is real but secondary. In the form of organic and inorganic realities, it provides the setting for personal lives and is the primary constituent of a human body. But the laws of matter do not determine human thinking and action. On the contrary, human persons use those laws to subordinate matter to their own ends. The impersonal in all its forms, then, is of secondary reality.

If persons are the primary reality, they are also the primary value. Humans are strongly inclined to put impersonal realities, such as the state, or administrative rules, or scientific knowledge, ahead of persons. This is partly because the impersonal can be more surely comprehended and controlled than can the personal. To inhabit an impersonal world is to enjoy security of a kind that is elusive in a personal world. While the urge to depersonalize arises from the desire for security, it also arises from sin. The pride that strives for power necessarily strives to suppress or eradicate the freedom that renders persons so incalculable and uncontrollable. And distraction, as a flight from freedom, tries to depersonalize the self. The personalist idea accords with the principle already set forth, that being is good. Being in its depths is personal, and our humanity is found as we enter into these depths, both in the self and in others.

The concept of person has been endlessly explored, not only in the social sciences, especially psychology, but also in novels, plays, and poetry. Yet the concept cannot be very precisely defined. We are all persons and therefore have an intuitive sense of what personhood is. But we cannot get outside ourselves and view ourselves objectively. Many of course have thought they could, particularly psychologists and other social scientists. But personalists take issue with them. Some objective knowledge of personal being is attainable, but no *comprehensive and final* objective knowledge of persons is possible. You can never possess exhaustive knowledge either of yourself or of another person. Even those you love and intimately know remain mysterious, and what you do know of them intuitively is far greater in extent than what you know of them objectively.

It is possible, nevertheless, to identify qualities that are reliable signs of personal being. Three are worth noting. One is particularity. This is among the qualities that make all-encompassing objective knowledge of a person impossible. Such knowledge concerns the general rather than the particular. Of course, even rocks and trees possess particularity (and thus, arguably, are persons of a sort). But we all feel that the particularity of a rock or tree is negligible and does not bar its being comprehensively known. But the particularity of a person is not negligible. In recognition of this every person is given a proper name. Of course, our dogs and cats also are given proper names. This suggests something of real importance, that personhood cannot be strictly confined to human beings. Anyone who has cared greatly for a particular dog or cat knows that this is true. Still, most of us would hesitate to regard every organic being as a person, and would confine personhood in its fullness to humans. The fact that we assign personal names to conspicuous natural entities like lakes and mountains is due (aside from the quasi-personal feelings we sometimes develop for such entities) to practical considerations making it desirable to mark their particularity even though we do not seriously regard them as persons.

A second quality marking personal being is the capacity for speaking and listening. A person is a conversational being. While I can learn relatively little about a person through detached analysis, I can learn a great deal by engagement in conversation. Here the person's proper name is indispensable. I do not normally enter into discourse with anyone whose name I do not know. And one of the most decisive expressions of respect for a person — the respect we owe every person — consists in according attention to, and addressing, that person in the course of sustained, inquiring talk. One way Martin Buber demonstrated the depth of his understanding of personal being was by elucidating the relations of persons in terms of dialogue. A person is a "Thou," not an "It," and can be approached, not by being objectively observed, but only by being addressed and listened to.

The third quality reliably defining personhood is especially pertinent to the idea of liberty. This is a sense of responsibility, or conscience. As a person, I am aware of being accountable for the things I do and the way I live. Two components make up this awareness. One is the consciousness that I am free, which comes, as I have pointed out, not from arguments in favor of free will but from facing situations in which I must choose. The other component of conscience is the knowledge that my choices make a difference, not only in terms of practical consequences but in far more mysterious terms, those of right and wrong. Moral responsibility is often a burden, but it is also a kind of exaltation. To face choices that are morally significant is to stand in some measure above the natural order, exempt from its necessities. It is to know that one is different in kind from mere natural entities like rocks, trees, and horses, which are denied both the misery of guilt and the glory of righteousness.

Personalist colors can be seen in various philosophies that are not personalist in substance. I have already alluded to personalist colors in Plato's philosophy, such as the dialogic form in which he wrote, in spite of the impersonalism implicit in his doctrine of forms. One of the most haunting works of personalist literature, the *Meditations* of Marcus Aurelius, was written by an adherent of Stoicism, a decidedly impersonalist philosophy. And personalist colors are vivid in some of the writings of Saint Augustine, who philosophically was a Neoplatonist. It could be argued, indeed, that Augustine founded personalism with his *Confessions*. Prominent heirs of Augustinian personalism in modern times were (all Christians) Luther, Descartes, Pascal, and Kierkegaard. It was probably Kant, however, who opened the door for personalism to enter the mainstream of philosophy. For Kant, both scientific truth and moral law, although rigorously impersonal in themselves, were, so to speak, presentations of the knowing and willing self, the person. To be sure, they were not freely constructed presentations. Kant did not, like later personalists, deal with a self that was deep, or impassioned, or mysterious. But he opened the way to such personalists. Setting bounds to the general, he made room for the particular; limiting the range of the objective, he opened up possibilities of intersubjectivity, or dialogue; and arguing that causal necessity does not govern being itself, he established a realm of moral responsibility. Much of this was implicit rather than explicit. Nonetheless, Kantian principles and distinctions reverberate through the personalist writings of later centuries.

If Kant opened the doorway to personalism, Kierkegaard was the first to pass through the doorway. It was the issue of eternal life, facing every individual, an issue to be decided by harrowing personal choices (harrowing because of the objective uncertainty of faith), that gave Kierkegaard's thought its personalist orientation. I have already pointed out that Christianity strongly affirmed personal freedom (even if not social and political liberty) by affirming a supreme value, God, who demanded voluntary allegiance. This tells us something about the Christian roots of personalism. Kierkegaard tells us more. He does this by his intense concentration on the drama of personal salvation and his mordant critique of a great but depersonalizing philosophy of his time, that of Hegel. We shall return later in this chapter to the Christian sources of personalism.

It is doubtful whether liberty can flourish anywhere but in cultural soil imbued with personalist ideas and attitudes. Such soil allows legal liberty to be grounded in the freedom of personal being. People must be free legally because they are free ontologically. It is true that the personalist soil that favors the growth of liberty was little emphasized by liberal forefathers such as Locke. This may be in part, however, because it was taken for granted. Owing to the long reign of Christianity, personalist attitudes pervaded the Western mind. Also, there was the rising optimism of modern man. Rendering liberty unproblematic, it may have disposed philosophers of liberty to be casual about their ontological grounds. But with the passing of Enlightenment optimism, due above all to twentieth-century savagery, protagonists of liberty find themselves in troubled waters. Now, without an anchor in deep personalist waters, they are in danger of being cast on the rocks.

The waters of liberty are troubled not only by the harsh experiences of the twentieth century but also by the growing impersonality of society. An interlocking set of causes has brought depersonalization. These include technology, total war, bureaucracy, depersonalizing habits of thought, and perhaps other causes not yet recognized. Modern impersonality may be seen as clearly as anywhere simply in the scale of modern society. Large populations and vast territories dictate impersonal laws and impersonal administrative practices. In contrast, the small populations and territories of the ancient city-state in Greece allowed for a relatively personal kind of polity. Most relationships were face-to-face rather than statutory and administrative; they could be determined by spontaneity rather than rule. Such conditions of course had drawbacks, such as the impassioned and volatile character of city-state politics. But there was much room for the personal. It is not surprising that the ideal of dialogue, and even, one might say, of a dialogic polity, was born in ancient Greece. Every society, however, is in some degree impersonal. Even the city-state classified people; there were citizens, resident aliens, women, and slaves. The personal was in that measure subordinate to the impersonal, the particular to the general. The modern state is compelled to a far greater degree to define and maintain itself through generalities. Extensive and sophisticated depersonalization is unavoidable.

Of course, depersonalization is not entirely unfavorable to liberty. To be under general rules is to be free at least from arbitrary and unforeseeable interference in your own life. Thus modern liberty depends on impersonal laws and on impersonal constitutional limits on the government. But these originated in personalist motives. In contrast, the depersonalization inherent in phenomena like bureaucracy and total war originates in obliviousness of persons. This is what renders modern depersonalization ominous. It suggests a sickening of the spirit. The cry for liberty comes from various spiritual sources, some of them confused or perverse. Its true source, however, is a personalist conscience. It is raised in behalf of the integrity and dignity of persons.

Reason, Faith, and Persons

Where does one find the deepest grounds of personalism, in reason or in faith? It is perfectly clear that personalist attitudes can be quite fundamental in irreligious minds, in the minds of people whose final reliance is on reason. A case in point is John Stuart Mill, in whose writings one can find eloquent expressions of personalist insight. I am thinking particularly of the praises of individuality in the essay *On Liberty*. Another such case is Friedrich Nietzsche, an extreme humanist and also, one might argue, an extreme personalist. The *Übermensch* can be seen as a personality exalted nearly to divine heights, and Nietzsche's disdain for the masses may have been done mainly to their stifling, as Nietzsche saw it, of distinctive personal life. The "will to power" might be construed as a will to uncompromising and undefeated personal being. Moreover, in Western history as a whole, it would be hard to show that humanist reason has shown less concern for persons than has religious faith. The Enlightenment in particular had a significant role in establishing political regimes that honored the person.

This too must be said, that personalism of some sort is present wherever there is love, and love opens a wide doorway for personalist attitudes no less among the irreligious than among the religious. Love for a person is an intuition of the infinite — that is, measureless or limitless — value of the person loved. One who is loved has no price. This of course is to speak of value rather than reality, but love may tend to fuse the two. One who radiates infinite value may seem also to possess being of a kind deeper or more enduring than the being of the ordinary things around us. Humanists sometimes assert that the concept of personal immortality is incredible. As a theory, that may be so. When it comes to the death of one who is loved, however, it can be argued that it is personal *mortality* that is incredible. Some part of grief may lie in the near impossibility of believing that the loved one is really nonexistent. Insofar as emotions like love and grief inhabit indiscriminately the hearts of believers and unbelievers alike, it can be said that personalism of a kind is virtually universal.

Such observations fall far short, however, of settling the question of where the grounds of personalism lie. One may wonder, for example, whether reason, as the faculty of dealing in universals, is not essentially a depersonalizing power, and whether, accordingly, people who rely exclusively on reason in approaching reality are not involved in ceaselessly undermining any personalist attitudes that may have lodged in their minds. Moreover, merely to show that personalist attitudes can find a place in minds reliant wholly on reason, is not the same as showing that reason can provide adequate philosophical grounds for maintaining the reality and value of persons. Thus while a rationalist (meaning one who relies on reason rather than faith) like Mill displayed deep personalist concerns, it would be harder to say this of a rationalist like Marx. Marx was acutely sensitive to the destructive impact on persons of early industrialism, but he was quite ready in the final analysis for persons to be obliterated by a vast historical destiny and by political and economic agencies working to advance that destiny. And much of the impersonalism of Marx's thought was derived from that most relentless of rationalists, Hegel. Personalist attitudes, after all, might have entered the minds of people like Mill and Marx from traditional sources — Christianity, for example — which they did not explicitly acknowledge.

At the most, then, we can conclude only that humanist reason is able to accommodate personalist attitudes, and often has. As for religious faith, something stronger must be said. Christianity is *radically* personalist in that the *roots* of all reality — of the heavens and the earth, and everything within them — lie in a person, in a particular being who has a name and who speaks and listens. The universe is created by God. And not only that, it is redeemed by God as well, and redemption comes about through the incarnation of the divine creator in a particular human person, Jesus. The figure of Jesus, both God and man in Christian faith, and as man mysteriously incorporating or representing every man and woman, manifests with great dramatic force the personalism intrinsic to Christian faith.

The Christian ethic follows quite logically. It is, as we all know, centered on the most personal of all relationships, love. Love is first of all for God. But it is also for every human person who is encountered, one's "neighbor." The qualities of the person encountered are entirely irrelevant, which shows that love is not for anything general — not for beauty, or courage, or wisdom, as in Plato — but for a particular person. The circumstances of the encounter also are irrelevant, which means that the most accidental or even dreaded encounters impose a duty of personal recognition, of love. Jesus apparently loved even those who crucified him. He prayed that God would forgive them. The basis for this ethic lies in the supreme model of good, that is, God. The Christian universe, created and redeemed by God, is held together by love.

The personalism of the Christian outlook is strikingly expressed in a daily discipline, prayer. Such a discipline is striking because from the standpoint of humanist reason it is so thoroughly irrational. It means looking, or trying to look, into and beyond that inconceivably vast array of things we call the "universe," and speaking with utmost seriousness to someone who is invisible, incomprehensible, and, so far as we can know objectively, nonexistent. It is not surprising that Pascal was frightened by the infinite spaces about him, for they seem to show that reality is vast and impersonal, and a person almost nothing. In Christian faith, however, if we look out on the universe with sufficient discernment we will see, not the ominous emptiness of endless space, but the countenance of one who speaks and can be spoken with. The practice of prayer is a way of expressing and cultivating a personalist faith.

These considerations, however, do not completely settle the question of where the grounds for the personalist idea are to be found — in reason or in faith — and what those grounds really are. To pursue this question we must address the principle that constitutes the most extreme expression possible of the personalist idea, namely, that every person, without regard to many of the traits often counted as standards of human excellence — traits such as beauty and intelligence — is of infinite value, a value often signalized with the term "dignity."

The Question of Personal Dignity

It is unfortunate that "the dignity of the individual" has become a cliché, for it refers to one of the principal moral insights in the history of thought, namely, that every human person possesses value of a kind that is measureless. A person cannot properly be used solely as a means, for that implies a measurement of value. Granted, in a world where there are social purposes, and humans organize to achieve them, practically everyone must at some time and in some way be used as a means. It is part of the ethos of liberty, however, that they not be used carelessly or unjustly, that is, without recognition that they are fitted to be ends, not mere means. Thus even ordinary soldiers whose lives have been lost are said to have served and not to have been used, if they fought in a good cause and were justly called on to fight. It is also part of the ethos of liberty that every person has the right of carrying on a life outside the network of means-ends relationships. Those who can at any time be used by someone else are slaves. According to the principle of personal dignity, each one should be seen as having a value that cannot be measured in terms of any utility. However hackneyed the term "dignity" may be, it is hard to think of a suitable replacement for it. Hence I shall continue to use it in this essay.

As commonplace as the words may be, however, it is not obvious what we mean by "the dignity of the individual," nor is it obvious what grounds we have for attributing dignity to every individual. This is dangerous, for it means that the mystery and the measureless value to which the phrase refers are being forgotten. It is like classical concertos and symphonies being used as background music in grocery stores; they are cheapened. I speak of the person's dignity as a question to draw attention to this situation. In the present section I shall discuss the question itself, in the following section the answers it calls forth.

The question is particularly pertinent in relation to the subject of liberty. Respecting the liberty of a person and respecting the person are inseparable. Liberty is granted from a sense of the dignity of the one to whom it is granted. Correspondingly, the sense of a person's dignity is left stranded, and is apt to die, unless it unfolds in a grant of liberty. We may of course leave people free out of mere indifference, and liberal states — perhaps exemplified by America at the end of the twentieth century — may rest mainly on mutual unconcern. But in that case liberty is merely accidental, without moral significance. Also, unsupported by moral determination, such liberty is vulnerable to every kind of historical mischance and is unlikely to endure. We may of course leave people free merely because we expect them to behave in ways advantageous to ourselves and the whole society. But that, as the doctrine of original sin implies, is to base liberty on an illusion. Liberty is morally estimable and historically durable only so far as it expresses a realization that persons have a moral right to determine the shape of their own lives. And they have this right (with such exceptions as those specified in the criminal code) in spite of the damage many of them will do in using it. We grant liberty to persons because we regard them with respect, not indifference, and because our respect for them is not effaced by the radical evil they embody. If persons had no dignity, slavery would be morally unobjectionable.

The idea of personal dignity is, then, that every person possesses immeasurable worth. It may help us see why such an idea is questionable if we mark the word "every." What reason is there to attribute dignity to *every* person? Some people, in the eyes of most of us, possess a degree of dignity. The dignity of those we call "great," for example, and of those we love, is as visible as their faces. Such dignity is apt to be more or less ambiguous, however. The "great" can always be caricatured and shown thus, from another perspective, to be small, or even ridiculous. And their achievements can always be questioned, and their failures, such as those to be found in every person's life record, can be pointed out and set against their achievements. The dignity of those we love is sometimes more vivid and enduring than the dignity of the great. But love is rarely so blind that the faults of the one who is loved are never glimpsed. In sum, our clearest perceptions of dignity are considerably clouded. They do not provide the idea of personal dignity with stable and adequate empirical grounds.

Moreover, they pertain to only a handful of people. If I am asked to name the great men and women, I may think of quite a few, but the list is not endless. And while I may very much like numerous people, there are probably no more than three or four whom, in the strictest sense of the term, I love. Beyond the great and the loved, then, are multitudes of people whose dignity is not very apparent. Many of them may be appealing or interesting to me, but I would not, without the spur of a moral norm, speak of their "dignity." And beyond the appealing and interesting, there are more than a few who are either uninteresting or quite definitely offensive. Where is the dignity of those who are dirty, drunken, and socially irresponsible? Where is the dignity of those who are criminally insane, or severely retarded in mind and ruined in body? Can we seriously ascribe dignity to tyrants and to the sycophants and bullies who always cluster around them?

To a dispassionate observer dignity will seem very unequally distributed. The human race will appear as a great hierarchy. A few, by virtue of achievements or personal charisma, will stand at the summit. All others will be ranked, however roughly, in descending order below them. Most people will arouse neither profound respect nor biting scorn. Long centuries of Christian culture, teaching the sacredness of every soul, have made most of us hesitant to acknowledge these hierarchical perceptions. They were, however, explicitly and unapologetically embodied in the political philosophies of two pre-Christian figures of unquestionable intellectual and spiritual stature, Plato and Aristotle. For either of them, the idea that every person possesses a dignity equal to that of every other person would probably have been puzzling and would certainly have seemed dangerously at odds both with manifest realities and with the consequent imperatives of social and political order.

The question of personal dignity, then, concerns a worth that belongs to every person, irrespective of personal characteristics or personal circumstances, a worth that is measureless and absolute. On what grounds can we believe in such worth? What gives us the right, even the duty, to affirm something so in conflict with manifest facts? It is the indiscriminate character of the idea that makes it particularly challenging. Dignity is ascribed to the person as such, that is, to every person without exception. And the modern idea of liberty requires nothing less than this. We do not hold that some people have rights and others do not. All alike have rights. Hence the intimate linkage in our time of liberty and democracy. If we lost our belief in equal dignity, we would sooner or later lose our liberty too.

What basis has this belief?

Reason, Faith, and Personal Dignity

I shall argue in the following pages that Christianity can mount a more coherent defense of personal dignity than can humanist reason. This defense depends on tenets of biblical revelation that humanist reason by its very nature cannot accept. I believe, however, that grounds for affirming the dignity of persons can be found in humanist reason. The solidity of those grounds is open to question, but I shall not argue that humanist reason necessarily slides into nihilism. If that were so, there would be a great chasm between religious faith and humanist reason, and one of my main purposes in this essay is to deny any such chasm. It would preclude serious, searching communication between two major portions of the human race; it would contradict the universalism inherent in both reason and faith; and it would remove all grounds for the major theme of this essay, which is not sheer liberty but liberty of a kind realized only in boundless dialogue.

The Christian case for personal dignity is an unfoldment of what was said above about the radical personalism of Christianity. It contains three main points. The first is centered on a well-known proposition in the biblical account of creation. Men and women — presumably all of them, no exceptions are noted — are created "in the image and likeness of God." The sublime personhood of God is thus reflected in every human person. The general idea (as well as its connection with liberty) is embodied in America's Declaration of Independence: "All men are created equal." This clearly means that they are equal, not in intelligence, practical ability, physical strength, or any other visible quality, but in their claim to respect. And the main consequence of this claim is immediately stated by the author of the Declaration. Human beings in their created equality are "endowed by their Creator with certain unalienable Rights," and among these are "Life, Liberty, and the pursuit of Happiness." Persons are equal, not because their dignity can be measured, but because it cannot. It reflects the goodness and glory of an infinite and eternal being.

A second major way in which Christianity undergirds the idea of equal dignity is found in the divine act of redemption, the central tenet of Christian doctrine. Redemption may be regarded as supplementary to the divine act of creation. It is restoration of the dignity that is diminished or lost when human beings sever relations with God. It may be that something more than restoration occurs through divine forgiveness, in view of the suggestion, in both the Old and New Testaments, that a forgiven sinner is paradoxically more precious than someone who has never sinned at all. (See, for example, Psalm 32:1-2 and Matthew 18:12-13.) In any case, the dignity-destroying power of sin is nullified. Human beings are cleansed of the stains of radical evil. Every man and woman is glorified now not only by the creative generosity but also by the merciful generosity of God. In this sense, the main symbol of personal dignity in Christianity is the figure of Christ, crucified and risen.

As a result of the two divine acts of human glorification — creation and redemption — the Christian God, in the words of the King James Bible, is "no respecter of persons" (Acts 10:34). These acts are at the basis of the ethic of love for neighbor, for anyone encountered. Jesus is completely unconcerned with the wealth, power, social standing, or educational background of those he addresses. He is unconcerned, in a sense, even with their morality, as shown in his complete openness toward prostitutes and Roman collaborators. Paul observes to the Christians in Corinth that "not many of you were wise according to worldly standards, not many were powerful, not many were of noble birth" (1 Cor. 1:26). The distinctions humans proudly establish on such grounds as learning and wisdom, and prestige and wealth, are jeopardized if not entirely overthrown in the twofold mystery of creation and redemption. All that counts is that human beings come from the hand of God, and having renounced that origin, that they have been lifted up by the same hand.

A third major way in which Christian faith conduces to equal dignity lies in the belief that every person will live eternally. The idea of eternal life accords persons a kind of primary ontological standing; they are not like the trees and the beasts that (we assume) quickly pass away. The idea also accords persons a primary moral standing. It implies that they possess a value of an entirely different order from the value of rocks, and rivers, and stars. This is often forgotten because the thought of life after death has become so familiar as to have lost all interest for many. It is brushed aside with some such phrase as "belief in the afterlife." Eternal life is no doubt beyond imagining, and, as is often pointed out, to think of it merely as unending earthly life degrades it. One may even recoil before the prospect of a life that goes on and on without ever ending. The force of the idea, however, lies partly in its very incomprehensibility. It tells us that a human being cannot be evaluated in the way we evaluate the transitory things around us. It lifts every person above time and decay, and above history and nature. After the firmament has been rolled up as a scroll, and the last trumpet has sounded, even the most despised among us will be alive before God.

We can begin to see, at this point, that dignity is closely connected with goodness, or, more precisely, with the human capacity for knowing the truth and doing it. Men and women as created by God, in his own image and likeness, were wise and righteous. Dignity was a manifest human characteristic. After they had lost their goodness, and with it their dignity, the act of redemption that Christians believe occurred through Christ was an act of re-creation. And Christian anticipation of eternal life may be understood as faith that the dignity bestowed through creation and redemption will never be lost. Here, however, most humanists will balk. What sense is there in attributing wisdom and righteousness to people who manifestly are not very wise or righteous, who are, as Christians put it, still "fallen"? A full answer to this question will be given in the section "The Idea of Destiny," which concludes this chapter. A short answer, however, is that human beings are destined to recover the wisdom and righteousness on which their dignity rests. Their lives have been given an orientation toward their unabridged humanity, an orientation that can be nullified only by a persevering refusal of divine mercy. Thus in Christian theology the justification that is bestowed with the acceptance of God's forgiveness initiates a process of sanctification, a process by which those justified recover their original goodness and dignity. On these grounds, human beings deserve respect of a kind that looks beyond their still-fallen state. If God can impute righteousness to men and women (the standard definition of justification), in view of their destined righteousness, then these men and women should do likewise with one another.

Divine grace, in the Christian view, is a wellspring of personal exaltation. It calls forth and makes manifest, in the twin dramas of justification and sanctification, the glory of a human personality. The ultimate source of this glory is God, of whom every person is an image and likeness. "Original sin" symbolizes the severance by humans of their relations with this source, and thereby the diminution or loss of their divinely created personal being. Divine forgiveness is an offer of reconciliation. Were humans to accept this offer — thus being justified by faith, and setting out on the road to sanctification — they would recover their similarity to God (without, of course, losing the dissimilarity inherent in characteristics like finitude, temporality, and multiplicity). They would begin to mirror the wisdom and righteousness that constitute the divine personality. This they never fully accomplish on earth. Only Christ, the Word of God and the righteousness of God, shows forth in its plenitude the primeval glory of the human person. Through Christ, however, every person, in spite of the horrors and deformities etched in the human visage by sin, is liberated from the impersonality effected by sin and placed within reach of the full glory of personal being.

To summarize the Christian view, every man and woman reflects the divine (as created by God); is the potential or actual recipient of a grace that is indifferent to human rank and honor (as redeemed); and transcends the limits of mortal life (lives eternally).

Can humanist reason provide a comparably cogent answer to the question of human dignity? Many of its representatives, of course, do not try to. The question is of no interest to those with no allegiance to liberty. People spellbound by the ostensible glory of some collective like a nation, class, or party are quite willing that individuals be suppressed and liberty forgotten. Very different in ideology, but often no less oblivious of the question of personal dignity, are those assuming that humans are for the most part good. Universal goodness renders liberty natural and unproblematic, and no concept of personal dignity seems to be needed. A slightly complicated version of this faith is implicit in Marxism, which does not affirm universal goodness as a fact but does affirm it as a possibility. Marxists adhere in principle to the ideal of liberty, even to a tacit anarchism. They would, however, defer the establishment of liberty until human nature has been so transformed by economic evolution that liberty would arrive spontaneously (except for forceful assistance from agents of economic evolution) and be attended almost altogether with agreeable consequences. The issue of human dignity does not arise.

Another way of bypassing the question deserves somewhat more careful attention. This is the idea of the social contract. The idea has been worked out and defended by numerous religious thinkers. It is particularly congenial, however, to the irreligious liberals of the modern age, for it renders the social order independent of religious presuppositions. It allows morally responsible people to ignore with good conscience the question of personal dignity. The idea is simpler than centuries of discussion would suggest. It is not necessarily connected with any legendary state of nature or contractual act. It comes down to a simple agreement, supposedly more or less implicit in any functioning liberal order: I will respect your liberty if you will respect mine. Plain practical considerations replace philosophical and theological speculation. We all want liberty. Let us, then, by mutual consent have it. I will grant human beings their liberty simply so that they will grant me mine. The question of personal dignity does not arise.

One weakness in this famous doctrine lies in what its advocates sometimes see as its chief strength, that is, the absence of explicit moral presuppositions. This means the absence, in our terms, of any postulate of personal dignity. The strength, if such it be, is that moral doubts and disputes are avoided. Liberty rests on self-interest. The weakness is the obverse side of the strength: liberty is robbed of moral significance. It becomes nothing more than a common preference. Why I want liberty for myself I need not explain, not even to myself. I simply want it, and that suffices. As for the liberty of others, I am concerned with that not because I respect or even feel affection for others but only because their liberty is a condition of mine. Such an attitude not only devalues liberty. It destabilizes it as well. It makes it merely a conditional imperative, hence vulnerable — as a moral faith is not — to every shift not only in historical conditions but in personal feelings as well.

The chief weakness in the social contract idea, however, may be in its underlying view of human nature. Mutual consent can provide a firm basis for liberty only if human beings uniformly and steadily care very greatly about liberty. For those who in many if not most circumstances would just as soon let someone else shape and guide their lives, luxuriating in the absence of responsibility, the idea of the social contract is meaningless. It is also meaningless to those who care less for liberty than for power — who aspire to do the shaping and guiding of lives that some want done for them. As we have seen, there are many of both kinds. Given the impulses and ambitions set free under a regime of liberty, there can arise very compelling (which is not to say morally valid) reasons for rejecting liberty. In a social and political setting like the Weimar Republic, great numbers of people may flee from their freedom. And there are always people who thirst for power. To political adventurers the idea of mutual agreement to a common liberty smacks of timidity and mass mediocrity.

We now can see that social contract theory is a variation on the theme of universal goodness. Liberty is unproblematic, and the principle of personal dignity is unneeded, because people are, if not very good, not very evil either. They are selfish, but only to the extent of wanting their own liberty. And they are good enough, or at least sensible enough, to grant liberty to others as the price of their own.

It seems, then, that humanist reason cannot provide a defense of liberty unless it can provide a defense of the proposition that dignity belongs to every person. Can it? The obstacles in the way are apparent. The very premise of humanism seems to place in question any appeal to a source of dignity beyond human beings themselves. And while human beings can *recognize* dignity in one another, they cannot *grant* it.

114

They can grant only the liberty that presupposes dignity. It does not follow, obviously, that every exponent of humanist reason must be lacking in respect for persons or concern with liberty. We have already noted that humanist reason has been more impassioned in defense of liberty than has religious faith. We have noted also, however, that humanist defenders of liberty often seem insensitive to the evil in human beings. Hence we must ask whether these defenders have the philosophical resources to remain steadfast once they fully face the fact of human evil.

The question has no conclusive answer. Humanist reason may not be trapped in the cul-de-sac suggested by its inability to appeal to or beyond the human level. But it may be. The theoretical situation is unsettled. At the very least, this may be said: those who reject the God of Christian revelation, and even more so those who reject any other version of the divine, are under challenge — if they care for liberty — to show how the dignity of the individual can still be affirmed. How might this challenge be met?

To begin with, account must be taken of the fact that humanist reason does not necessarily reject every version of the divine. This is made amply evident by the examples of Plato and Neoplatonism, to say nothing of the various kinds of natural theology. Might reason develop a version of the divine adequate to the present exigency, that is, that serves as a source of dignity capable of somehow nullifying or overruling the deficiencies of dignity inherent in human finitude and moral perversity? The question obviously precludes any sure and decisive answer. But to my knowledge, no major humanist thinker has done this. Plato and Neoplatonism did not affirm the dignity of every person. No doubt there are natural theologies in modern times that have done this. Whether they have done it successfully would of course have to be judged in every particular instance. But given the modern status of human dignity as a conventional and almost irresistible piety, a rationally affirmed transcendental being that bestows dignity on every person has the look of reading into a concept of the divine the results you want to get out of it. Is there any other way humanist reason might find grounds for affirming the dignity of every person? Perhaps there is.

For one thing, it might be argued — circumventing the question of source — that personal dignity is a natural intuition. Personal love, as we have seen, is arguably such an intuition. To love is to perceive absolute worth in the one who is loved. To be loved is to be, in a fashion, exalted, or dignified. The love of a man for a woman may be aroused by the woman's beauty but, as numberless examples prove, remain undiminished with the loss of her beauty. All love has a neighborly, or indiscriminate, component in that anyone can love and anyone can be loved. It is also arguable, as we have seen, that admiration for a great figure on the world scene is an intuition of human dignity. Heroic figures like Pericles and Alexander of Macedon seem to reveal momentarily a realm beyond utilitarian calculation, a realm where it is not true, as Hobbes put it, that "the value of a man is his price." Finally, literature contains powerful, if inexplicable, intuitions of human dignity. The idiot in William Faulkner's *The Sound and the Fury* has a dignity that is not only anomalous, given the visible qualities of the idiot, but also strangely microcosmic, since the idiot is symbolic of the disordered state of a family and perhaps of a whole society.

Such intuitions can incite a sense that there is something mysterious and sacred about a human personality. It may be argued, however, that adjectives such as "mysterious" and "sacred" smuggle into the discussion principles that are essentially religious. Also, intuitions of personal dignity are so various in character, often so ephemeral, and in many instances so subjective, as to throw doubt on their significance. As already noted, love for one person does not normally predispose the lover to respect persons other than the beloved; and high regard for "great men" may be (indeed, ordinarily is) accompanied by disdain for ordinary men. Rarely if ever has anyone shown signs of perceiving dignity in every person without exception. Is there any plausible example of such a phenomenon other than Jesus? And in any case, are such "natural" intuitions of human dignity really natural? Do they originate with humanist reason or are they incursions into humanist minds of an idea they have unconsciously drawn from religious faith?

Where, then, might humanist reason find ground on which to rest the principle of personal dignity? The most likely answer lies in the fact that man is a moral being. As already argued in connection with conscience, humans cannot easily confine their minds to the expedient and inexpedient but feel compelled to think also of right and wrong. And it is doubtful that anyone who is sane — capable of calculating the expedient and inexpedient — is altogether lacking in this moral compulsion. In other words, conscience appears to be a universal human characteristic. Its significance is twofold. It marks its possessor as more than a thing, with only finite value. And, in its universality, it marks in this way every human being. It equalizes.

As far back as the Hellenic age, in the philosophy of the Stoics, human equality was affirmed on the basis of man's moral nature, and on this basis Rousseau founded the ideal of democracy. This moral egalitarianism, so to term it, was given its classical formulation, and used to undergird the cause of liberty, by Immanuel Kant. (For my point to be clear it needs to be noted that any attribution of equality that is free of illusions of factual equality — as of intelligence, strength, etc. — is implicitly an attribution of dignity.) In none of these cases was the idea Christian or explicitly religious. For Kant, as we know, man is a moral legislator. This is evident in a capacity, present presumably in every person, for casting the rules governing human conduct not merely in hypothetical terms ("I must do this if I want that") but also in categorical terms ("I must do this regardless of consequences"). The power of framing such laws, and placing one's life under their authority, distinguishes humans from animals and bestows a dignity Kant expressed by drawing an explicit distinction between person and thing and insisting that a person never be treated as merely a thing, that is, as merely a means to another end.

Kant's moral theory has of course been endlessly debated. We are concerned here, not with its general validity, but with its suitability as a basis for the principle of personal dignity. For this it has a grave weakness. This is the incontrovertible fact of moral inequality. A few people are apparently very good, but only a few. Most people are morally mediocre, and a few are very bad. Even if there be a distinctively human capacity for making moral judgments, it is exercised unremittingly and wisely by only a small minority, and it seems to be exercised hardly at all by another small minority. Perhaps everyone possesses a conscience, but not very many follow it assiduously, and a few regularly defy it. Most of us consult it now and then and follow it spasmodically — conforming in this way with Kant's definition of radical evil. So does the fact of man's moral nature imply equality, or does it ground a moral hierarchy? Again, the examples of Plato and Aristotle are instructive. For both thinkers, moral excellence was of utmost importance, but this did not lead them to egalitarian political views. It led them in the opposite direction. As already noted, they showed little if any awareness of the idea that every human being possesses dignity. People were as unequal in dignity as in moral excellence.

Of course, Christians too confront the fact of moral inequality. To the extent that they rest the dignity of the individual on the wisdom and righteousness restored in the divine act of redemption, they are in the same predicament as the humanists. If moral goodness is an index of dignity, then the idea that dignity belongs to every person is groundless. In the Christian universe, however, the morally imperfect individual is in quite a different situation than he would be in the humanist universe. Behind him is the dignity of divine creation, ahead the wisdom and righteousness to which he is divinely destined. At the risk of over-simplification, it might be said that the individual in a Christian context, although sinful, is dignified by his origins in a divine creative act and by a destiny in a divine redemptive act. The same individual in a humanist context seems to be deprived of every dignifying relationship.

It is sometimes held that the sheer capacity for choice, the freedom, possessed by every person is good ground on which a humanist might defend the principle of personal dignity. There is no question that freedom is a distinguishing mark of the human species. It elevates every human over every animal and over every other natural creature. The trouble with this idea is the same one that invalidates the notion that the capacity for morality is a source of dignity. This is the fact of moral inequality. Freedom is grossly misused by a great many people, and misused in considerable measure by virtually everyone. It provides a better basis, therefore, for a hierarchical rather than an egalitarian view of the human race.

It is not clear, then, that the principle of personal dignity can be upheld on other than Christian premises. Practically all the assaults on human dignity, the scale and ferocity of which distinguish the twentieth century from all other civilized eras, were carried out by anti-Christians, and most of them by Marxist protagonists of humanist reason. The preceding analysis indicates that this may not be accidental. That every person without exception must be respected is probably the central principle of Western morality and the basis of the most humane political institutions yet devised by the human race. It is uncertain, however, whether that principle can survive if it comes to depend on reason alone, unsupported by faith.

The lifework of Dostoyevsky amounts to a profound and impassioned argument that it cannot. The weakening of Christian faith in his time left Dostoyevsky facing, as he saw it, an era of tyrants, assassins, and insurrectionists. He expressed the principle of personal dignity in his early *Notes from Underground* when he asserted that a human being is not merely a numerical unit. Two plus two does not equal four when we are dealing with persons. But this, as Dostoyevsky saw it, is a principle that derives from God. In the final analysis personal dignity is given by God. Hence if God dies, so will persons, except as things to be used as the most powerful and ruthless among them desire. In a universe without God, the human race will inevitably fall under the dominion of the terrible maxim "All is permitted."

Dostoyevsky may have been right. His novels prophesied the twentieth-century's monstrous assaults on liberty and personal dignity. Admittedly, the relationship between religion and morality is complex and undecided. At the very least, however, this may be said, that the common humanist assumption that with the "death of God" everything in the moral universe can go on as always is shallow and thoughtless. The assumption was derided by one of the greatest of humanists, Nietzsche. One who gives up the Christian God, he asserted, has no right to retain Christian morality. Very plainly: an atheist cannot affirm the dignity of every individual. It is surprising how few humanists have matched Nietzsche's discernment and courage in saying this. Almost without exception they deny God and affirm personal dignity. Does this make sense? No question before us at the outset of the third millennium is more urgent than this one.

It is clear, however, that humanist reason and religious faith share a concern for personal dignity even if not an understanding of it. Hence they may "reason together," as Isaiah enjoined. They may engage in searching conversation about the basis, nature, and consequences of such dignity. Christians would bring the ground principles of their faith into such a conversation. Non-Christians would bring their belief in the moral resources and power of reason. Paul, as little inclined as he was to make casual concessions to those outside the faith, nevertheless asserted that those who "have not the law" may "do by nature what the law requires," and he saw them as showing in this way that the law was "written on their hearts" (Rom. 2:14-15). Reason and faith have common ground — ground for conversation even if not for agreement.

The Christian vision of salvation — the restoration of human dignity — is incomplete as I have outlined it up to this point, however. The righteousness and wisdom that constitute a person's dignity, and are restored in the life of Christ, are not, as noted above, observable facts. They are matters of destiny. What does this mean?

A useful starting point for answering this question is provided by the apparently irresolvable antagonism between persons and time. Every person's life is immersed in time, and time is wantonly inconsiderate of persons. Without consultation or consent, it recurrently throws personal lives into disarray. It continually threatens even the most prudent and fortunate with unforeseeable and undesired changes. And it dooms every personal life to being sooner or later extinguished and finally forgotten. In sum, it spells the reign of accident and oblivion. Doesn't the universe itself in this way tell us how absurd it is to think of every person as being an end and not a mere means?

The Idea of Destiny

Time, of course, appears in some ways benign. Processes like physical growth and intellectual development take place in time. Creative activity, as in the arts, is carried on in time. Various animal species, including man, have evolved in time. Indeed, so impressive are benign appearances of this sort that time as a whole has often been envisioned optimistically, as in the doctrine of progress, or in Henri Bergson's idea of creative evolution. Marx's writings constitute an ingenious and seductive affirmation of time.

Such visions attain plausibility, however, only by neglecting particular persons, and all the agony and hopelessness that have filled countless lives. And they largely ignore the death that pursues and finally overtakes every person without exception. Attention is given mainly to the human race as a whole. Individual persons are quietly sacrificed to the cause of a vast imagined historical triumph, yet to occur. If we attend to particular persons, however, and set aside dreams of collective glory, the antipersonal nature of time becomes manifest. It promises even the most fortunate individuals years of physical and spiritual insecurity and, in the final outcome, total extinction.

I am speaking of worldly time, time as perceived by humanist reason. To mark its character, let me introduce a useful term: "fate." Worldly time bears the aspect of fate, of a force indifferent to persons and ultimately irresistible. There are periods of history when the fated character of worldly time becomes conspicuous. During these periods the future is massive, ominous, and uncontrollable. War, revolution, economic anarchy — such events and conditions tell individuals that their possessions, their loves, and their lives may be taken from them at any hour. The personal, embodied in exposed, mortal men and women, is overshadowed by the impersonal, in the form of warring, oppressing, and uncomprehending powers and necessities.

If the term "fate" is useful for characterizing worldly time, how is time in its essence, time in its ultimate range, to be characterized? A convenient counterterm is "destiny." To claim that time fully understood is destiny rather than fate is to claim that, in spite of appearances, it is fundamentally personal and meaningful. While glimmerings of destiny can be seen in the works of a few non-Christian writers, such as Hegel and Marx, it is mainly through Christianity that the idea has become explicit. In Christian faith every person has been created for membership in a lasting community, symbolized as "the kingdom of God." All that happens, every mischance and tragedy, serves this ultimate end. When Paul says all things work together for good for those who love God (Rom. 8:28), he is speaking of time as destiny. In the life, death, and resurrection of Jesus worldly time was relativized. The coming and going of earthly friendships and kingdoms can no longer be seen as the final truth about time and history. That truth is the coming of a community open to all persons and beyond the reach of fate. Such, at any rate, is the Christian idea.

Above all, destiny is personal. Even though it is universally human, it is mine. Whereas fate comes upon a person as an enemy breaking into one's life, destiny comes as the very emergence and realization of the person. So far as I fulfill my destiny, I become the person that in some sense I already am. Destiny is the temporal form of my own personal being. Illness and accident, loneliness and confusion, guilt and death, while not unreal, in the context of a destiny are not all-powerful. They do not make the lives of particular persons meaningless. Rather, they contribute, in ways beyond the comprehension of reason and objective observation, to the realization of personal being.

If time is truly personal, then every person must have a destiny. That this is the case is implied by the Christian concept of God as all-powerful love. "Even the hairs of your head are all numbered" (Matt. 10:30). This is to say that every human life, however short and miserable, is meaningful if seen in relation to its ultimate end. Every person is dignified by the destiny that governs the unfoldment of his days and years. In the lives of some — Socrates, Alexander the Great, Washington, Beethoven — there are dramatic signs of destiny. But in most lives the signs are dim; fate is far more conspicuous. This in part is because most or all of us fail our destinies in some degree. Sin consists in the neglect or betrayal of our destiny. We welcome fate. We do this in objectifying reality — always in the proud conviction that thus we can master it, but always at last falling victim to it.

Although destiny is personal, it is not created by persons, either individually or collectively. Contrary to the popular liberalism that prompts us to speak of letting people decide their own destinies just as they decide what products to buy and consume, and contrary also to the revolutionary romanticism that envisions a nation, a class, or a party forging the world's destiny, a destiny is given. Your identity is discovered as you carry on your life. Where, then, does freedom come in? In the receptivity already discussed. Just as value is found and not created, so it is with one's destiny. Freedom is manifest in watchfulness — for the self and for the selves of others. "To be free," as the adage has it, "is to be yourself." But selfhood is paradoxical. It seems somehow present, yet still to be realized. It would therefore be better to say, "To be free is to *become* yourself." This is an enterprise of watchfulness and acceptance. It is also an enterprise calling for liberty.

Humility, then, as a willingness to watch for and receive one's life and being, is a prerequisite of destiny. Ironically, when human beings set out to create their destiny, what they always create instead is fate. This is particularly evident in history. Proudly confident in their ability to direct the course of events, men initiate revolutions and start wars of conquest. The results are always greatly at variance with those anticipated. The degree of variance depends on the scale of the creative ambitions behind them. When those ambitions are great, their results may contradict them disastrously. Time, supposedly under human command, assumes vast, opaque, and destructive forms. This is perfectly illustrated by the Bolshevik Revolution, aiming at total liberation and ending in something close to total enslavement.

This is the irony of fate. Forces destructive of the self come upon those who assert the self absolutely. It is the irony of destiny that only those who relinquish illusions of mastery, and hold the self in a posture of openness and waiting, can transcend fate and find themselves in the hidden contours of time. It is clear when we speak in this way that somewhere in the background is transcendence, or God. If our destinies are given to us, it cannot be by nature or by society, both lacking in the requisite power and wisdom. They must be given by something transcendent and personal. In Christian language and understanding, they must be given by the one who creates and governs all things, by God.

It may seem, then, that destiny is an idea that can have little meaning for humanist reason. This is far from true, however. Destiny has long been of major concern to humanist, as well as to religious, minds. It has indeed been of major concern to all civilized peoples. This concern is expressed in the simple and age-old act of storytelling. This becomes apparent when we realize that destiny is the meaning of a temporal unfoldment — of a person's life, of a nation's history, of humanity's evolution — and meaning is inherent in every story. All storytelling is a search for meaning in our personal and collective lives, that is, for destiny. Good stories are satisfying mainly because they forcefully convey the impression that time, beneath all appearances to the contrary, is not at enmity with personal being.

Stories always, of course, in some measure fail. Never can we see deeply enough into others, or even into ourselves, to tell stories that are completely true. Histories and biographies are never definitive; autobiographies and memoirs are often unconsciously skewed. And many stories are deliberate misrepresentations of destiny. They may be official versions of the past of a leader, a movement, or a nation, or sentimental deceptions devised for commercial purposes. And even the best stories afford mere glimpses of destiny, no more than that. They are provisional interpretations, always subject to criticism and in need of revision. In any case, humans are in practically all times and places engaged in weaving and reweaving stories and in this way prosecuting an unceasing war against fate.

In recent centuries this war has depended for its victories more on novelists than on any other group. Historians, biographers, journalists, and others have of course played important parts in the contest with meaningless time. But our inability to tell completely satisfactory stories is an inability to make sense of all the facts, of all those stubborn bits of reality that we find to be undeniable, however inconvenient or even intolerable they may be. For the infinite mind of God, Christians believe, even the most refractory facts dissolve into one all-encompassing vision of glory. For finite minds, however, they doom every story to partial failure. While responsible historians and journalists cannot ignore them, novelists can. The genre of fiction allows imagination to disregard facts that cannot be integrated into a coherent and meaningful narrative. It permits, in this way, an unobstructed vision of personal being in time.

But surely, someone may object, stories frequently show people defeated and crushed, and the stories that do this are not always among the worst stories. Some of them are carefully and conscientiously written. This is clearly true. It is true particularly of stories in newspapers. Many of them deal with grief and dire misfortune. Even among the classics of fiction, however, there are stories that seem to exhibit an irresistible and all-consuming fate. Some of these, I think, are unproblematic. The authors exhibit the human capacity and inclination to neglect and destroy whatever meaning their lives might have. People cast aside their destinies. In novels and stories dealing with such events, however, destiny still is displayed. The source of fate is shown to lie not in time but in human nature. Still, there are stories — these among the greatest works of world literature — that seem to show persons destroyed by forces out of all proportion to their personal faults. The hero may be flawed, but the point of the story seems to be very far from any theme so common-sensical as the adverse consequences of folly and pride. They seem to show forth a tragic incongruity between human beings and the deep currents of reality. They seem to say that time can strip a person of every dignity.

Do such stories demonstrate that storytelling, as an assault on fate, must finally fail? Do they tell us that time in its depths is an enemy of personal dignity and always, in the end, will win? It will be evident that they do not, I believe, as soon as we note that these accounts of humanity engulfed in darkness ordinarily belong to the genre of tragedy. While there are no doubt different kinds of tragedies, practically never do they leave us cast down, as they would were they mere tales of disaster. In a fashion hard to understand, they seem to exalt and console us. Under their instruction, something within us says, "In spite of everything, all is well." The reason for this, I suggest, is that by exhibiting the tragic end of persons whose dignity indicates a different end, they evoke a

124

consciousness of transcendence. They hint of an eternal fulfillment of temporal occurrences.

It goes without saying that there are false and shallow and misleading stories. Stories are spoiled by sentimentality, and prurience, and various other sinful motives and emotions. Hence not everything that calls itself a "story" reflects the meaning of life and the dignity of a person. There are tales full of sound and fury, signifying nothing. My argument is that honest storytelling is a search for meaning, and that stories in which there is truth show us meaning in time. Stories are engrossing, and always have been, because we very much need the sense that the things we go through and the events that unfold around us are not senseless. We need to be assured that our dignity is not laid waste by a wanton and impersonal universe.

If honest storytelling is a search for meaning, one can think that there may be a single definitive story, a story containing the heart of all true stories, of which storytellers are in quest. Christians believe that the life, death, and resurrection of Jesus is that story. Every human life is in some way a journey in search of God, beginning at a great distance from God, in that far country, the world. The journey progresses through the suffering and death that strips men and women of worldliness, of the proud illusion that the universe is made up of things they can comprehend and control. This stripping is a preparation for life in an eternal community. It is a crucifixion. The Christian claim that Jesus is the Christ is the claim that his story is not merely an objective chronicle, to be registered in our minds. It is every person's story. From Jesus' crucifixion we can draw the strength to go through our own crucifixions, and the wisdom to find new life in them.

Pilate's exclamation *"Ecce homo!"* points to the tormented Christ as an image of stricken humanity. In contrast, the risen Christ is an image of exalted humanity. The crucifixion of the God-man reveals the presence of God in all human suffering and dying. The torment Christ endured on the cross is thus only a preface to the glory he attained in the resurrection. This means for humankind that the agony of losing all that one owns and is in the world becomes the road to human transfiguration. The life of Christ is the definitive story because it is the definitive glorification of the human person. The risen Christ is, or can be, for every individual dignity regained.

A Christian might argue, then, that the life, death, and resurrection of Jesus is the story all storytellers are striving to discern in some particular set of temporal circumstances. Every meaningful story must show death in some form, perhaps the defeat of high aims, the disappointment of fervent hopes, or physical death itself, surmounted in some way by new life. Stated generally, the story may sound trite. Realized in concrete lives, however, it may constitute the only pattern that gives meaning to the lives of mortal, erring men and women. The proud determination of each person to reduce every reality to a comprehensible and controllable thing, which deprives creation of its glory and the self of its dignity, must be defeated. Only thus can glory, in creation and the self, be rediscovered. Christians believe that the Gospels recount the story, not just of one man, at one time, but — at least so far as we take on the dignity proper to a person — of all of us, at all times. In this sense the life of Christ is the definitive story for the entire human race, and destiny is universally human even though it is also sharply particular for every person.

A serious theoretical difficulty in the concept of destiny — a difficulty lavishly illustrated by Marxist controversies — is the impossibility of treating the concept as simply either prescriptive or descriptive. In a fashion the concept is prescriptive. A destiny *ought* to be fulfilled. Yet the "ought" in this context is peculiar. It has weight of a kind that an ordinary moral norm, like telling the truth, does not have. To live your destiny is to discover and be who you are. Hence, to fail your destiny is not simply to be guilty of a wrong. It is to fail to be. This may be why powerful personalities in history are apt to speak of their deeds in terms not so much of what they felt they ought to do, but of what they *had* to do. A destiny is in some sense a necessity. Yet it is not a causal necessity. It can be unfulfilled. Hence the concept of destiny, although not merely prescriptive, is not descriptive either.

I am not aware of any theory that resolves this difficulty. A teleology such as Aristotle's is suggestive, fusing as it does norm and reality, prescription and description. But traditional teleology has a biological coloring. It is debatable whether a theory meant to apply universally to living nature can be usefully applied to the mysteries of personal existence. Hence reflection on the idea of destiny may leave us feeling suspended in the air. The impossibility of either prescription or description seems to deprive us of ground to stand on. Yet experience indicates that such ground exists. Our lives are not always carried on either under a moral norm or in conformity with causal necessity. In some of our best and most difficult times we labor to discover that which we might fail to do yet are bound to do. We are, of course, back on familiar ground — the fusion of freedom and necessity. The main task of freedom is to discover that which, in some sense, we have no choice but to do. The idea of being forced to fulfill your destiny is logically contradictory, for your destiny is your innermost self. Yet your destiny commands your unconditional allegiance. A destined life, with all its necessity, is the same as a free life.

Finally, we must consider briefly a theological difficulty involved in the concept of destiny. It appears most dramatically in the death of infants and children. Some destinies are apparently aborted. Some individuals never have a chance to work out their life stories. Are such individuals robbed by natural accident of the destiny and thereby the dignity that, Christians believe, God bestows on every person? If so, the idea of divine omnipotence is refuted. Also refuted is the concept of destiny as I have presented it. Here time seems wantonly brutal.

The first thing to be said is simply this, that the death of infants and children, however distressing, is not uniquely problematic. Every destiny is aborted. No individual on earth lives a life perfectly crafted and rounded out in a whole that constitutes all that a person seeks and is intended to realize. To say this is not to voice a willful pessimism. It is common knowledge that few lives unfold coherently and end triumphally. Most people, even those who enjoy good fortune over many decades, do not exhibit in their lives a clearly meaningful story. And many of them spend their final years in a state of confusion and wretchedness that calls into question the direction and significance of all their past. And at last the very fact of death seemingly pronounces over every life a verdict of nullity. Every life ends in nothingness. The death of infants and children, then, is only a poignant appearance of the evil that sooner or later overtakes every person.

To speak of aborted destinies is to speak, simply, of our fallenness. As the Bible says in a hundred ways, the human story on earth is that we sin and we die. Hence we face at this point more than a theoretical difficulty. We face human existence in the world. There is therefore no "answer" to be made except the one I have pointed to already, that inherent in Christian faith and in the lives of noble protagonists of humanist reason such as Socrates. Human existence is encompassed by a mystery —

sometimes referred to as "transcendence," sometimes as "eternal life." Entry into this mystery is the destiny of every person. This is a destiny ordained and proclaimed, Christians believe, in the resurrection of Christ. It is also, one may believe, depicted and foreshadowed in the *Phaedo,* Plato's account of the death of Socrates. It defines the hope that lies at the heart of liberty and enables many — not all of them Christians — to carry on lives that rise above fate and point toward things unseen in the world.

CHAPTER 5

The Flawed Society

―――=•(())=―――

Liberty and the Good Society

Liberals typically are attached to liberty not only because they want it for themselves, so that they can live as they please, but also because they believe it will lead to harmony and happiness for everyone — to the good society. They see humans as basically good and liberty therefore as mainly beneficial. Only rare liberal voices have spoken in a different vein, out of awareness of the evil in human beings and of the consequent evils that characterize liberal societies. The greatest of these voices was probably Tocqueville, who believed steadfastly in liberty but showed, in his study of America, that a liberal society was unlikely to be unambiguously good and happy.

I described, in chapter 2, some of the major evils, such as personal estrangement and mass dominance, that are apt to be manifest in liberal societies. These evils suggest how far from a good society a liberal society may be. Liberty enhances the opportunities for creatures in which there is much evil to spread evil into the world around them. There are of course criminal statutes and social restraints. But the very idea of liberty is that of allowing people as far as possible to do as they please, and people in whom there is much evil are bound often to do things that are wrong and harmful to others. They would not be free unless they could. Liberty must therefore be affirmed in spite of the evil it is bound to bring. It must be affirmed because it is just, recognizing the freedom that distinguishes humans from animals, and because only by allowing humans to bring evil into the world can it allow them to bring good as well.

It follows that liberal political theory is (or at least ought to be) essentially different from other political theories. Most political theories are stated in terms of an ideal society. In contrast, liberals thinking in a Tocquevillean mode are mentally prepared for the nonideal society that liberty is likely to call forth. Their minds are not governed wholly by calculations of worldly consequences. They are cognizant of the moral imperatives arising from the fundamental fact of freedom. And insofar as they calculate consequences, their first concern is that the liberty of individuals be shielded from threats posed by the liberty of other individuals and by society as an organized entity. The ideal society is merely one that provides protection.

Setting liberty against society in this way implies that liberty is primarily negative. Much has been written concerning the contrast between "negative" and "positive" liberty. Broadly stated, negative liberty is "liberty from" — state, society, corporation, and so forth — while positive liberty is "liberty for" — following a vocation, helping others, and engaging in other constructive activities. The former is realized by anyone who is not hindered from the outside from doing as he likes, the latter by one who is carrying on the kind of participatory and productive life that befits a human being. Positive liberty is apt to come out of these discussions looking far more noble and wholesome than negative liberty. Positive liberty is usually presented as principled and responsible, negative liberty as self-indulgent and amoral. Nonetheless, as shown in the writings of Isaiah Berlin, positive liberty does not look as good under close examination as it does at first glance. Positive liberty is almost always envisioned as dependent on conditions created by society, conditions such as a good educational system. And quite often positive liberty is seen as the fulfillment of a function in society, with the activities that render liberty positive those prescribed by society. Society in these ways is more or less idealized. And in the measure that society is idealized, liberty in its commonsense meaning, that of unconstraint, disappears. It was in the spirit of positive liberty that Rousseau spoke of people being "forced to be free."

The reason why positive liberty usually ends in betraying liberty in the ordinary sense of the term is, I think, readily explained. The ideal of positive liberty has practically always been, not simply that people should have liberty in order that they *can* be moral, but that, if they are given liberty, they almost certainly *will* be moral. But for this to be argued, human nature must be falsified. The evil in people must be denied. The only way to do this plausibly is by maintaining that in a social and political order yet to be constructed — a democratic one, perhaps, or a socialist one — human nature will change. The selfishness and malice we see everywhere in people will disappear. And their newly acquired goodness will become manifest in the positive roles they play in the new society. If, somehow, these results do not emerge, then society must take a stronger hand. It must reshape and discipline those who have failed to be free.

The concept of negative liberty, it is vital to note, does not imply moral indifference. Central to the present essay is the proposition that liberty has a moral purpose. Liberty is wrongly used unless it is used for choosing things worthy of choice. In this limited sense, I argue on the side of positive liberty. Also central to this essay, however, is the proposition that society cannot be counted on to inform us of our moral purpose or to tell us what is worthy of choice. And it certainly cannot be counted on to change us so that we will make the choices we ought to make. Hence moral responsibility falls primarily on individuals, not on society. This viewpoint has two implications. The first is that individuals must be given room to fashion their own lives apart from society and even in resistance to society. The second implication is that individuals must be allowed to make erroneous judgments of value. People are not free to do the right thing unless they are free to do the wrong thing. Liberty that cannot be misused is not real liberty. This is not to preclude moral leadership on the part of private powers such as churches and universities, or even on the part of government. It is, however, to preclude social and political arrangements designed to obviate all the evils that arise when liberty is possessed by fallible and malicious human creatures. In these ways I argue on the side of negative liberty.

The first requirement of negative liberty is constitutionalism — government under publicly known and enforceable limits. The limits may be defined in a fundamental law, less readily changeable than ordinary laws, as in the United States, or in customs, traditions, and historic documents, as in Great Britain. The essence of constitutionalism lies in

131

the existence of areas reliably free of governmental interference. Such is the primary requirement of negative liberty because the primary threat to such liberty is government. Society can interfere with liberty in numerous ways, with familiar examples being the power of employers over employees and social pressure to conform with general patterns of dress and behavior. But only the state can render society irresistible and totalitarian. When all liberty is lost, it is necessarily lost, above all, to the state. Under a constitutional government there is bound to be at least a modicum of liberty.

Still, while government is the most serious threat to liberty, there are other threats, such as families and employers. Thus liberty is not assured by constitutionalism alone. If it were, then one could say, "The smaller the government, the greater the liberty." The best guarantee of liberty would be a government incapable of action. That is not the case, however. If government checks a nongovernmental group that is interfering with someone's liberty, then, while it narrows the liberty of the interfering group, it widens the liberty of the one being interfered with. If both sides are left with equal liberty, then it may fairly be said that the government, by acting, has increased the liberty of the governed. This is why liberalism is not the same as "libertarianism," which is usually understood as the philosophy of minimal government. Much less is liberalism the same as anarchism, the philosophy of no government at all. To use a phrase of Kant's, the state can "hinder hindrances" on liberty. When it does this, it widens liberty. The classic instance of this, which established the principle in Western thought, is legislation in the nineteenth and early twentieth century that limited working hours and regulated working conditions in factories. Government in this case, without depriving factory owners of any liberties to which they had rightful claim, widened the liberty of the workers.

We may therefore conclude that enlarging the sphere of government, in order to "hinder hindrances" on individuals, can enlarge the sphere of liberty too. In drawing this conclusion, however, we enter an area where it is difficult to draw sharp boundary lines. Negative liberty shades gradually into positive liberty. For example, an illiterate person can hardly be free, even negatively. Governments quite properly, therefore, provide public education. Only by an artful twisting of words, however, can this be called "hindering hindrances." In plain terms, it is helping, and there are countless ways governments can help. To argue that it never should do so is virtually impossible. To acknowledge that it should, however, blurs the boundary lines between negative and positive liberty. A government that helps individuals find jobs, for example, must decide what kinds of jobs to help them find. When it does that, it is not only helping them; it is guiding them, however gently. Guiding of some sort is probably inherent in all helping. In providing education, for example, government cannot confine itself to cultivating literacy. There is no such thing as value-free education, and surely should not be. This, however, implies that public education involves public guidance concerning the ends for which life should be lived.

These blurred boundary lines surround the sphere of negative liberty. It would be perversely rigid to say that a government devoted mainly to the protection of negative liberty should do nothing to provide areas in which such liberty can be fruitfully exercised — areas created by public parks, clean and safe streets, libraries, beautiful public buildings, and pristine nature. And if a liberal government may help individuals in realizing a fruitful freedom, surely it is reasonable for it to help them in uniquely worthwhile efforts like creating works of art and founding symphony orchestras. And finally, to argue that governmental leaders should never stand for some values in preference to others, or set moral examples of any sort, would be self-defeating, for there is no leading that is purely political and not implicitly moral as well. A leader like Washington was primarily political but inevitably set a moral example and thus provided moral guidance. It is obvious that in these and other ways liberal governments are bound to be drawn into supporting positive liberty. Whether intentionally or not, they will encourage certain ways of life — liberty *for*, not merely *from*.

What we see here is not that the theory of negative liberty is false but that theory as such never conforms exactly with reality. In politics there is no substitute for prudent officials, leaders guided not by theory alone but by the circumstances in which they work and by their own discerning minds. In liberal politics there is no substitute for officials fully alive to the principle of negative liberty yet aware that the principle must be applied with discretion. Protagonists of positive liberty may render them more sensitive to ways in which individuals carrying on their own chosen lives can be helped by the government. Protagonists of negative liberty, however, may play a more vital role. Keen to publicize the dangers in public education, public art, and other such undertakings, they can help keep political leaders mindful of the basic aim of liberty: that individuals, with the aid of whatever private groups they choose to call on, such as churches and schools, and perhaps guided too by public education and political leadership, work out and live their own distinctive destinies.

There are two basic principles of liberty. The first is that people ought to use their liberty to make wise and righteous choices. The second is that they have a right to make unwise and unrighteous choices. It is the second principle that is problematic. It prescribes a right to be foolish and immoral. There is no use in saying, "Very well, so long as they don't hurt anyone else." Foolish and immoral actions always hurt someone else, if only by way of hurting oneself. This is discussed at length in chapter 11. At the same time, there must be limits, for otherwise society would be engulfed in anarchy. The nature of such limits is also discussed in chapter 11. What needs emphasis here is that the second principle, with all its problems, is absolutely indispensable. The first principle is merely a pious and impotent sentiment without the second. One who is not at liberty to be foolish and immoral is not at liberty to be wise and moral. There are very great dangers in the practice of the second principle. This is demonstrated by such catastrophes of freedom as the Peloponnesian War in ancient times and the advent of Nazism in modern times. There is no way of recognizing the freedom — which is to say the dignity — of individual persons without facing these dangers. Hence it is vital, as government verges into the area of positive liberty, that there be prudent officials to remember, and jealous private guardians of liberty to remind such officials, that if people do not have liberty to do things they ought not to do, they do not have liberty at all.

Some may feel that if liberty promises only an ordeal, and has no vision of a good society to offer, it is not very attractive. Perhaps not. One should bear in mind, however, that in spite of all the pessimism and negativity proper to it, the theory of liberty is centered in something glorious, or at least potentially glorious. This is the single and singular human being — "a wonder, a grandeur, and a woe," in Herman Melville's words. Liberty may lead to ordeals of one kind or another. But it opens the doors into the human condition, where one may experience to the full not only the misery but also the splendor of human existence.

Liberty against Itself

It does not suffice, however, to say that liberty produces (and provides protection against) a flawed society. The flaws produced by liberty are not just those of a kind that would mar any social order. Many of them tend to destroy liberty itself. Moreover, a liberal society must accept, and in a certain sense rest content with, such flaws. I do not mean to suggest that it cannot take expedient measures to protect itself — that it cannot, for example, suppress revolutionary agitation for fear of destroying freedom, or curb inflammatory speech out of respect for free expression. Dilemmas of that sort are serious, but in a stable and sensibly governed society are manageable. I am speaking of conflicts between actions allowed by liberty and conditions undergirding liberty that cannot be readily managed even though they can finally be fatal.

To understand these conflicts it is necessary to see that strong and enduring liberty rests, in some measure at least, on customs, beliefs, and practices supportive of a free life. While these are too numerous and variable to be exhaustively listed, examples are obvious. It is questionable whether liberty can arise or endure among a people unwilling to take on personal responsibility, lacking in respect for individual persons, unskilled and unpracticed in the use of reason, inept in the formation and leadership of groups, or devoted mainly to merriment and pleasure. Moreover, the needed qualities are unlikely to be widespread or lasting without some support from society. In short, it is highly desirable that a liberal polity be grounded on a liberal culture. Such a culture may not be indispensable. Liberty in all circumstances entails risks. But the risks will be less numerous and severe where liberty has appropriate cultural foundations.

Not only is a liberal culture conducive to liberty. So is a liberal philosophy, not as a systematic, precise, and polished expression of a particular school of thought, but as a more or less coherent set of general beliefs about the nature and purpose of human life. People cannot think just anything about human reality, however untrue and however disrespectful of major values, and still prize and practice liberty. One of the aims of this essay is to sketch out principles of a sort that might structure a liberal public philosophy.

The assertion that a stable structure of liberty is greatly helped by a substructure of liberal culture and philosophy is little more than com-

mon sense. It may seem scarcely controversial. Among political thinkers, however, the assertion is intensely debated. It is faced by a potent
counteridea — often called "proceduralism." The gist of proceduralism
is that a liberal polity is grounded not in any particular set of values or
any one concept of the common good but rather on certain generally accepted procedures that are followed in the conduct of public business
and even in the formation of the polity itself. There are few if any established public values, and there is thus a great deal of room for private
values and for debate concerning the value-choices necessitated in the
formation of policy and the conduct of public business. Even liberty is
not so much a moral premise of the system as it is a natural outcome of
procedures empowering people of diverse values. The procedures are
just in the sense of assuring a fair hearing to all parties and persons.
They are morally neutral in the sense of allowing diverse values to be
embodied in private lives and advanced in public debate. Certain values
might be incorporated in public policy, but not in a way that would foreclose the affirmation of different values and the formation of different
public policies in the future. In short, a liberal polity is fair but morally
uncommitted.

The best-known representative of proceduralism may be John
Rawls, with his famous concept of "the veil of ignorance." Designers of
the polity, indeed all who reflect on the best order of society, are called
upon to forget not only their economic condition, social status, and political situation, but even their moral creeds, their philosophies, and
their religious (or antireligious) convictions. They are, in short, to be ignorant of their very identity. In consequence, they are to be morally neutral. Yet they are led, in Rawls's account, simply by common sense and
self-interest to form a polity that is liberal and egalitarian. Imagine you
are a political founder, working behind the veil of ignorance. Not knowing, once the veil is drawn aside, in what sort of economic, social, and
political situation you will find yourself, and not even knowing what
your fundamental beliefs and values will be, you will naturally want to
organize a society in which no particular beliefs and values are officially
sanctioned, and people are left free to live according to whatever beliefs
and values they may have. In short, you will favor liberty but not a liberal
culture. Issues before the society will be settled, not on the basis of certain values, but only through fair procedures, such as open elections.

At least superficially, proceduralism is a plausible point of view. It seems to show that a liberal polity does not depend on a liberal culture and philosophy. Since these are difficult to attain, and once attained can be sources of repression and strife, that is a considerable advantage. It indicates that the public pursuit of liberty can skirt the intractable and divisive dilemmas encountered when it comes to affirming some values rather than others. These dilemmas can be confined to the private sphere, to be dealt with, or ignored, as individuals choose.

There is a serious weakness in the proceduralist argument, however, and that is simply that no set of procedures is self-justifying. Common sense and self-interest will not do. The very idea that procedures, rather than, say, a great leader's inspired but inexplicable insight, ought to be followed in the conduct of public business presupposes a substantial cultural and philosophical commitment. It rules out authoritarianism in every form. Moreover, every set of procedures presupposes standards differentiating good from bad procedures. For example, procedures designed to assure that all representative voices are heard in public debate rest on the assumption that all segments of a society should be taken into account; procedures designed to assure thorough analysis of proposed public measures presuppose principles concerning the power of reason and its role in public life; and procedures intended to safeguard the right of every person to participate in elections derive from beliefs about the nature and worth of a person as such. In sum, procedures rest on the philosophical and moral principles — the values — implicit in any set of procedures.

It is doubtful that Rawls resolves this difficulty in the proceduralist argument. The veil of ignorance is a device to assure that even though you are only prudently concerned with your own interest, you will treat all others fairly by according yourself no special privileges. This is to say, however, that the veil of ignorance *presupposes* an ethic of fairness. Why would anyone not adhering to that ethic be willing to choose a government in the state of moral oblivion Rawls recommends? Rawls answers that you would be willing to do this simply to give yourself the best chance of having a free and decent life, unoppressed by others. And if you ask why, once behind the veil of ignorance, you would vote for equal liberties rather than for privileged classes, he gives the same answer. You would do it just to be on the safe side, since you don't know what your own position in society will turn out to be. But that is to assume another ethic, that of prudent care for one's own interests. There are people who don't accept such an ethic, people who would, for example, will a society in which a privileged class enjoys vast pleasures and powers, and do this gambling that they themselves would be members of that class. There is no telling what kind of government would be designed by people working behind a total and effective veil of ignorance, that is, in a state of complete moral neutrality. Indeed, it is questionable whether they could design any sort of government at all.

It must be admitted, on the side of proceduralism, that moral concerns embroil us in endless perplexities and dangers. Humans are threatening to one another not because they are mere animals but because they are humans and therefore apt to be inflamed by righteous indignation, self-righteousness, and other morally derived yet murderous emotions. It is unquestionable that liberty is often endangered by people burning with a certainty of their own moral purity. It is therefore tempting to infer that confining morals to private life, and founding public life on morally colorless procedures, would be a boon to peace and public amity, and to liberty especially. Proceduralism is quite understandable. But it fails because it tries to separate things nearly identical, that is, the human and the moral.

This brings us back to my claim that stable liberty is far more likely in a culture that renders liberal morality widespread and habitual. It is more likely too where there prevails a liberal public philosophy. Liberalism is no different in this respect from other ideologies. Socialists, fascists, conservatives: adherents of creeds such as these have never doubted that they needed to cultivate convictions and practices supportive of the politics they promote. Liberals have been tempted to think they are different. But they are not. Liberty — *even negative liberty* — presupposes moral commitments as definite and irrevocable as does any other collective ideal. Thus people who possess liberty must readily accept personal responsibility; normally treat their fellow citizens with consideration and respect; be disposed and able to reason about personal and civic problems; be inclined toward and adept at rational discourse; and find life bearable in the absence of entertainment and physical pleasure. And for such an ethic to be widely accepted, there must be a culture through which it is sanctioned and inculcated. This is not, be it noted, for the sake of positive liberty, but rather to enable people to bear the strains of negative liberty, to meet the responsibility inherent in being distinct, free, and moral beings.

Liberal political culture obviously differs from other political cultures in its content. And it differs in another way that deserves careful attention. Here we reach the point of this section. Liberalism must expose its supporting culture and philosophy to contradiction and defeat. Otherwise there would be no liberty. Liberalism is unique, not in being able to do without moral and metaphysical premises, but rather in having to place those premises in peril. It must expose them both to direct attack and to subtle erosion. In a liberal society people must be free to live where they please and to follow any vocation to which they feel called; to be educated in the manner and to the extent they wish; to choose as friends, mates, and associates those who appeal to them; to indulge in such recreation as they find attractive and appropriate; and finally, and worthy of particular note, to profess, promote, and conform with whatever moral creed, political philosophy, and religious vision strikes them as true. There are of course limits, but these must be few where liberty is real. Of course, all political ideologies and all political cultures are subject to erosion. This is because they all depend on voluntary support. They must leave people with a measure of liberty. But only for a liberal society is the liberty that is filled with so much danger the very purpose of its existence.

We have already noted some examples of the liberal assault on liberty. Mass society arises because many people refuse responsibility for their own minds and lives. They allow public opinion to dictate their own opinions, and common ways to prescribe their own ways. Likewise, a culture of distraction can come into existence only because many are unwilling to pursue distant and serious purposes. Hence they embrace frivolity. In a liberal society people are at liberty to be conformists. They are at liberty to be frivolous. Yet both practices undermine liberty and such liberal culture as may exist. In other ways as well, liberty comes into contradiction with itself.

Various minorities, for example, use their liberty to the detriment of liberty. Groups that are openly dissident and superficially alarming are probably not among the most dangerous of these. This is precisely because they are dramatic and undisguised. Communism and fascism have never seriously threatened American liberty. However, there are less dramatic, but in consequence more dangerous, ways in which small groups may turn liberty against itself. Examples come readily to mind: professors teaching a moral relativism that is implicitly antithetical to personal responsibility; philosophers and literary critics preaching an epistemological relativism that undermines reasoned discourse by rendering truth inaccessible or insignificant; advertisers cultivating selfishness, greed, and vanity; communications executives purveying entertainment while neglecting public affairs and serious drama; lawyers who encourage frivolous and unjustified lawsuits, thereby striking at the friendship and trust that bind together a free society.

Another example pertains to social coherence, which in some forms may support a liberal culture. America in the latter part of the twentieth century experienced the collapse of the family, with half of all marriages ending in divorce. This could do serious damage to liberal culture by destroying the matrix of liberal values such as personal responsibility. Most of those alarmed by the problem evaded it by blaming it mainly on homosexuals (many of them striving to create their own particular kind of family) and largely ignoring the prevailing acceptance among heterosexuals of divorce and extramarital sex. This happened with the connivance of intellectuals beguiled by prevailing fashions and businesspeople profiting from sexual license.

A final example of how liberals must allow liberty to come into conflict with itself is pornography. Where there is freedom of speech and other forms of communication, there will almost certainly be pornography. There will even be reasoned defenses of pornography. And among those indulging in it will be people who in most of their relationships are morally responsible. But pornography surely weakens liberty. By reducing people to objects of lust, it subverts personal dignity and thus subverts liberty. The fact that in pornographic films and books there are often vivid depictions of violence is not accidental. Not that limits on pornography are precluded. Certain neighborhoods and urban areas, as well as public schools, may banish purveyors of pornography without seriously compromising liberty. It is doubtful, however, that a modern liberal society can suppress pornography completely and remain liberal. Not only must it allow people to do things they ought not to do in order that they may freely do the things they ought to do. For the sake of decent culture itself, the indecencies of pornography must be permitted. Long experience has shown the futility of censorship. People of literary and artistic sensitivity are normally unwilling to serve as censors, and when people lacking such sensitivity serve as censors, damage is inevitably done both to literature and to culture generally.

There is another conflict, sure to arise in every liberal society but essentially different from the conflicts we have been considering. In rough terms, it is a conflict not between good and evil but between good and good.

Liberty and Equality

Liberty and equality are companion concepts, as we have already seen. They are the two indispensable ways of expressing, in the political order, respect for individual persons. They are therefore inseparable. We have also seen that the relations of liberty and equality are difficult in practice, even if relatively neat in theory. Liberty inevitably brings inequality, and inequality in various ways threatens liberty. We need to look again at this matter, for the unavoidable evils of inequality are among the major flaws of a liberal society.

It is manifest that social inequalities — these comprising inequalities of wealth and power, as well as of social status — are not wholly evil, since people really are unequal. They are unequal in practical ability, in theoretical intelligence, in artistic creativity, in personal force and charm, in physical agility, and in every other desirable characteristic. We may call these *"real* inequalities." Given the existence of real inequalities, social inequalities are fitting. Any effort to create a social order without such inequalities would be contrary both to justice and to efficiency, and it would also be destructive of liberty. It does not follow, however, that a liberal society can settle down comfortably with whatever inequalities arise. There are numerous and grave evils associated with every set of social inequalities.

Some of these evils are quite apparent and need little comment. One of the most glaring and painful is that social inequality rarely corresponds more than roughly with real inequality, save in narrow and technical fields of endeavor such as science and medicine. In the larger society, preeminence often seems to reflect, not real personal excellence, but rather qualities such as intensity of ambition, personal charm, and even unscrupulousness. Thus the wealthiest entrepreneurs and the most powerful politicians do not usually strike us as the best human beings. Indeed, wealth and power and other forms of high social standing often are offensive because they command so little spontaneous respect.

Another evil attached to social inequalities is that they are always, even though a product of liberty, in some degree hostile to liberty. The very meaning of having greater wealth, power, and prestige than others is having a greater range of enjoyment and action, more diverse opportunities and prospects — in a word, greater liberty. Correspondingly, the meaning of inferiority in wealth, power, and prestige is constricted liberty. As Marx showed so powerfully in relation to workers in early nineteenth-century England, very great social inequalities can amount to virtual enslavement. Numerous instances of inequality based on race also illustrate the enslaving effects of inequality. As we all know, when slavery was abolished in the United States, blacks were immediately subjected to a kind of social enslavement.

A third evil inherent in social inequalities is that they usually work against community. They may divide society into classes that live differently and think differently and therefore can scarcely communicate with one another. Rich and poor, rulers and ruled, elite and commoners live in separate universes. Promotion of social equality is often taken to be a "leftist" cause. But conservatives have traditionally been devoted to social coherence and to order and, at least to that extent, to community. They have supported traditional rank, but that is not the same as supporting radical social divisions. The former can be conceived of in ways compatible with community, the latter cannot. Conservatives, then, cannot affirm social inequalities of every kind. The willingness of some purported conservatives to acquiesce in the social chasms created by unrestrained capitalism suggests a disregard for the traditional meaning of conservatism.

Yet another evil connected with social inequalities is their encouragement of inordinate self-esteem, or pride. They incite sin. For most people the urge toward self-glorification is nearly irresistible. People competing for wealth, power, and prestige are not simply trying to realize their own potentialities. They are striving for heights from which they can look down on their fellow humans; and when they gain those heights, that is what they ordinarily do. Social preeminence rarely instills humility. Although it is just and expedient that some be first and some last, being first encourages the centeredness on self that is the essence of sin. Such qualities, in civilized societies, are usually carefully concealed. But in certain circumstances they break out in horrors that fascinate and shame the human race. And in all circumstances they cultivate personal qualities that subvert liberty and its proper uses.

Finally, it must be asked whether, apart from specific evils caused by social inequalities, there isn't something morally dubious in any social hierarchy whatever. Surely it is questionable, in view of the dignity we attribute to every person, to place persons in definitive ranks. Personal dignity is a mystery, hence persons are incomparable. Even someone who is mentally retarded, or emotionally disordered, or morally vicious, or physically ruined and repellent — or all of these together — cannot be said, at least not by us humans, to be absolutely and essentially inferior to others. The mystery of personal dignity, so far as it renders persons incomparable, renders them equal. Thomas Aquinas claimed that even in heaven the saved would be ranged in ranks. Such a view is understandable. Uncommon righteousness and wisdom must have lasting significance of some kind. Still, one may wonder whether Thomas's heavenly hierarchy does justice to the transfiguring power — the dignifying mercy — of a God who is not indifferent even to the fall of a sparrow.

Hence, while Thomas's inegalitarian vision is understandable, so is the egalitarian vision of modern socialists and communists. Considering the number of evils arising from social inequality, the idea of abolishing such inequality altogether is in some sense right. But of course, even if the *idea* is right, the *politics* is impossible. If anything in the field of political science is certain, it is that a determined drive toward complete equality will fail. It will not only destroy liberty, given the scale of coercion needed for eradicating an established set of social inequalities. It will destroy equality as well, for the equalizers will become a new ruling class. This is all so dramatically written in the history of the twentieth century that illustrations would be gratuitous. And it has to be added that even if, by a miracle, complete social equality were achieved, then the real inequalities distinguishing people would be unjustly neglected, and a workable society and polity would be impossible.

The most beguiling answer to the dilemma of equality and liberty is usually encapsulated in the phrase "equality of opportunity." Inequalities of wealth, power, and social standing need cause no alarm, we are told, so long as there is equality of opportunity. We can rest assured, in that case, that social and real inequalities correspond and that liberty remains intact. It is surprising that this formula is so often repeated, for it is quite empty. The very essence of social inequality is inequality of opportunity. If that were not so, no one would aspire to superior power, wealth, and social status, which offer openings and possibilities not available to the powerless, poor, and despised. The idea of allowing extensive inequalities while preserving equality of opportunity is a contradiction in terms. The best one can say for the gospel of equal opportunity is that it can remind us that inequalities must not become rigid and enslaving. It can help us define the point at which inequalities must be curbed. Taken literally, however, it makes little sense and serves mainly to obscure the problematic relations of liberty and equality.

It used to be thought that the growth of *equality* was the great menace to liberty. Tocqueville, for all his perceptiveness and wisdom, did a great deal to cultivate this illusion. The dream of equality, he thought, was particularly enchanting in free societies, and the growth of equality was thus a relentless historical destiny. He joined other thinkers of his era in supposing that a populace empowered by equal suffrage would assault all wealthy and powerful minorities, bringing everyone down to a common level. The groundlessness of these apprehensions is shown by the ease with which private wealth and political advantage have been preserved, and even enhanced, through a century or more of social reforms in behalf of the poor and powerless. If there is any general truth in this matter, it is surely that, so long as liberty is preserved, inequality will survive and will tend to grow. The communist conviction that inequality could be eradicated only through sweeping violence was not absurd, however terrible its consequences.

It must be admitted that inequality can be tempered and curbed, and that this can be done without destroying liberty. This is conclusively demonstrated by the American New Deal and by the welfare states created in western Europe during the latter half of the twentieth century. It is clear that even though power and wealth can always defend themselves in a free society, they do not necessarily bring in their train powerlessness and poverty for the general populace. Liberals must of course see that they do not. For the sake of liberty, there must be a measure of equality.

Yet here again we are far from anything ideal. It seems to be a general law in politics that no society can enjoy all good things at once. The welfare state can provide a pleasant life for a great many people, but it entails serious imperfections. It will no doubt cause many people to work less hard than they would under the spur of economic necessity. Hence society will be less wealthy than it otherwise would be. And there will be a degree of injustice since some people receiving social benefits will not, by standards either of need or of performance, deserve them. Correspondingly, some will suffer losses of wealth and power that cannot be objectively justified, for there are, after all, rich and powerful people whose riches and power are deserved and are used for the benefit of the society at large. And there may be accidental imperfections, appearing only occasionally. For example, it seems that a high level of social benefits sometimes brings a high level of unemployment. To be economically secure, yet without a vocation, is about as severe a deprivation as is poverty.

Worse, many people will feel, is the spiritual mediocrity that seems to accompany a high level of material prosperity. Nicolas Berdyaev, a Christian and a socialist, argued that once people were free of poverty and were economically secure, they would perceive more clearly than ever the tragic essence of human life and would move toward higher spiritual levels. The welfare states created in the twentieth century present little evidence that this is so. On the contrary, it seems that widespread enjoyment of material comfort and security is spiritually stultifying. Worldliness can be almost irresistible where the world is a highly agreeable place; hence Jesus' assertion that it is hard for the rich to enter the kingdom of heaven. A populace whose lives are materially secure and pleasant may not turn against God in dramatic defiance but simply lose all interest in religion and come scarcely to know what religion is or why people ever were religious. They fall into a state very different from that either of the great believers or of the great atheists of the past, a state of religious imbecility.

That liberty and equality are at once consonant and contradictory is a rich source of the flaws that must always affect free societies. Even very wise citizens and officials could not find the right balance between liberty and equality, for there is no such balance. And when this nonexistent balance is sought by sinful and foolish people, by heedless champions either of liberty or of equality, the consequences can be grievous. Thus liberal societies will always, in varying degrees and ways, incorporate the defects that go with inequality: wealth and power in unworthy hands, deprivation of liberty ensuing on economic deprivation, obstructed communication, and the reign of pride and selfishness on the higher social levels — the latter hidden ordinarily behind professions of humility and dedication to public service. And if steps are taken to moderate these evils, then the drawbacks of the welfare state, such as economic inefficiency and spiritual lassitude, are likely to appear. We see in all these conditions how far liberty is from bringing the good society that so many liberals have assumed to be a natural product of liberty.

Some light may be shed on the flawed society that arises from liberty by considering two different reactions to that society. Both stem from the difficulty of acquiescing in a radically and conspicuously imperfect society. They employ, however, opposite strategies.

The Dangerous Passion for Purity

It may sound strange to hear of a passion for purity on the part of a species as infected with evil as humans are, and even stranger to hear such a passion characterized as dangerous. It would be overly cynical, however, to infer from the evil in human beings that they are altogether indifferent to good. Sometimes, of course, they are, but sometimes they exhibit a fierce drive toward righteousness. The fallenness of the human race does not, as I have already said, connote utter depravity. People often are affronted by evils they see around them and are aroused by a desire to cleanse the world and establish a reign of righteousness. America's beginning, in the Puritan regime in seventeenth-century Massachusetts, testifies to this desire, as do various sectarian movements in Christianity. Figures like Savonarola are raised to power by the indignation incited by evil. To witness, and feel helpless in the face of, evil in others can cause nearly intolerable pain. Hence the vehemence often evident in the drive toward moral purity.

The flawed society arising from liberty invites such a response. In a liberal setting the passion for purity must take the form of a revolt against liberty or at least against the liberal movement that has brought liberty to the modern world. Marxism is a clear example. Marx was moved above all, perhaps, by the moral indignation aroused by the state of workers — free men, women, and children — in industrial England. And while he was not opposed to liberty as such, he was profoundly opposed to liberty of the kind that prevailed in England and other capitalist nations. He was perhaps the most ardent and effective enemy liberalism has ever had to contend with. What we see in cases like this, it may be said, is the passion for a flawless society.

The dangers inherent in this passion become apparent on examination. People outraged by the evil they see in others are apt to be more or less unaware of the evil in themselves. They are inflamed with anger yet uncurbed by humility. Hence the spectacle of evil men dedicated to the eradication of evil. Fiercely determined to cleanse the whole world, they are captivated by the illusion of their own innocence. Their own malicious impulses, veiled within that illusion and exacerbated by moral indignation, flourish. Such a psychology is plainly hostile to liberty. It obscures the strange and trying truth that, even though we are armed with the powers of science and technology, and can deliberately work all manner of changes in the physical world around us, we cannot change evil men into good men.

The passion for purity has clearly figured in the great revolutions of the twentieth century. Revolutionaries of course have varied motives, and not all of them are moral. But one motive is rage for a flawless society, the kind of society liberty precludes. Dostoyevsky exhibits the dynamics of this rage in Ivan Karamazov. After speaking bitterly of the terrible and meaningless sufferings endured by the innocent all through history, Ivan exclaims, "I must have justice, or I will destroy myself. And not justice in some remote infinite time and space, but here on earth, and that I could see myself" (*The Brothers Karamazov,* trans. Constance Garnett, Modern Library, p. 253). In late nineteenth-century Russia Ivan was a prophetic figure. He shows us the wellspring of communist totalitarianism. Blinding us to our own moral flaws, and to the dependence of goodness on freedom, the passion for purity blinds us also to historical possibilities. For people such as Ivan Karamazov, the limitations imposed by human nature and historical situations have to be defied and broken.

We can begin to see the precariousness of the spiritual balance on which liberty depends. On the one hand, there must be moral seriousness. Unless liberty is prized for the moral opportunities it provides, it is insignificant and is likely to be ephemeral. Lacking moral purpose, it is merely something some people happen to enjoy. If a valid and stable regime of liberty depends on firm moral purpose, then it depends also on principled opposition to evil. However, it depends also on a willingness to endure indefinitely a good deal of evil. Otherwise one becomes an enemy of all those in whom evil is present; one becomes an enemy of liberty.

There is one word, a not-very-stirring word, that denotes exactly the quality required, and that is "patience." This word, with its connotations of resignation and self-control, is not often associated with the idea of liberty. But perhaps nothing is more requisite to liberty than patience on the part of liberal governments and peoples. It is a spirit that is sensitive to evil, and disturbed by it, yet disinclined to attack it with violence. Patience was signally lacking in Ivan Karamazov. It was also lacking in Lenin, whose historical impatience was so catastrophic for Russia and other nations.

But how is patience possible? How can one abhor evil deeds without abhorring, and attacking, the people who commit them? Or, to reverse the question, how can one be tolerant of evil without becoming indifferent to it and thus losing the moral temper that underlies liberty? These questions have no single and simple answer, but there are several interlocking answers, and noting these can help us understand the possibility of patience.

To begin with, there is a partial answer in Christian eschatology. History has meaning, according to orthodox Christianity, in that all human events reflect and further the gradual coming of justice and community. But this is a prolonged development, requiring perhaps many millennia; it results primarily from divine and not human powers; and it will not all be accomplished on the plane of visible history. History will end with the cataclysmic irruption of a just and eternal kingdom, a climax prepared for but not fully realized during the course of earthly events. Although historical developments are cryptic, the final eradication of all evil is certain. In these circumstances the first requirement is patience, an attitude of watchfulness and responsiveness.

Very different is the attitude of modern revolutionaries. History has no meaning except for the meaning imposed on it by human action. And history has no end; history is all there is. The human situation envisioned by revolutionaries is very different from that envisioned in Christian eschatology. It renders patience all but impossible. If there is no divine force at work in events, then human action is urgent. And if such action fails, then history is meaningless, and if that is so, the entire universe is meaningless. The spectacle of unrebuked and uncurbed evil in those circumstances can be nearly insupportable. For Ivan

Karamazov, the horror of evil was that of an absurd universe, mocking humanity. He had to have justice immediately, visibly before him, or he would go mad.

Christian eschatology indicates that the human situation is one in which patience is possible, even essential. Humans can and must practice a politics of waiting, which can be a politics of tolerance for varied human words and actions. In itself, however, it is an insufficient answer to the questions asked above. This is partly because it lacks clear meaning for humanist reason. It does not seem to show how all of us together can be patient, and thus sustain liberty, in the face of evil. Moreover, although eschatology can be patient and liberal, it is not necessarily so. It can be vengeful. Eschatological expectancy can be a way of exulting in the thought of the misery and terror to be finally visited on one's enemies. The thirst for vengeance is candid and unrestrained in many Old Testament passages, and it is scarcely hidden in the writings of Christians such as Augustine and Calvin. The apparent satisfaction with which some people of faith have contemplated the prospect of hell as the final destination of all those they feared and despised reveals a frame of mind not very favorable to liberty.

So we must ask again, How is patience possible? As we have seen, being liberal on the basis of an unrealistic optimism is easy. What is necessary, however, is being liberal while being realistic, and therefore in some degree pessimistic, and that is not easy at all. How it can nevertheless be done — how patience is possible — seems to be shown by the concept, and the occasional fact, of forgiveness. To forgive is simultaneously to acknowledge evil but not to let it define those who harbor it. It is to see evildoers for what they are yet to retain that strange respect for them that we have already discussed in connection with personal dignity — a respect grounded, not in their visible nature, but in the mystery of their being. It is also, when circumstances permit, to leave them their freedom. A forgiving person can be, so to speak, a liberal without delusions.

A serious question, however, remains. How is forgiveness possible? Forgiving someone for a wrong done to someone else may sometimes be relatively easy, but it seems presumptuous. Who am I to forgive an evil from which I have not suffered? Further, if the evil is large in scale, and sustained in time, like the things done by white Americans to African Americans and Native Americans, forgiveness can seem not only presumptuous (if bestowed by anyone not a member of the affected groups) but also disproportionate to the enormity of the deed. Some things, one might suppose, cannot be forgiven. And finally, forgiveness may seem in conflict with the necessities both of social order and of justice. Vengeance is not only at times a compelling inner drive; arguably, it is a condition of social order and an imperative of justice.

It is worth observing, I think, that in spite of all such difficulties, forgiveness seems to be among the powers belonging to human nature. It is not the greatest of those powers, but occasionally it is manifest. It is dependent partly, perhaps, on the "troubled spirit" and the "broken and contrite heart" spoken of in Psalm 51. Those conscious of their own moral failings may be able to enter sympathetically into the hearts of others who have failed morally and thus be able to forgive them. Vengefulness is likely to march in company with self-righteousness. Mercy is encouraged by humility, particularly by the kind of humility that resides in those who are aware of being themselves in need of forgiveness.

Still, humility and mercy are mere moods, as weak and variable as any other moods, unless they have objective grounds of some kind. To have any weight they must be sustained by an authority no less indisputable than the authority that sustains the moral law. Indeed, it must be the same authority. Who can authorize forgiveness for offenses against the moral law except the author of the moral law? For Christians, of course, this is God. Most Christians would argue that there cannot be any other author of a law that is authentically moral and not merely a custom, with nothing behind it but social habit or considerations of prudence. The right and the ability to forgive, it would seem, are drawn from religious faith.

Another line of thought leads to the same conclusion. Forgiveness not only needs the authority of the author of the moral law. It must somehow be warranted by qualities in the one to be forgiven, the wrongdoer. A wrongdoer *as such* is evil, and to pronounce forgiveness on someone who is evil is arbitrary. This brings us back to the author of the moral law. In the Christian view, divine forgiveness does not decree that a deed, once done, has not been done. Even God cannot do that. What it does may be summarily described by saying that God looks on the wrongdoer as though he is righteous. This is not just make-believe. For the creator of all things to look on someone as righteous is an act of re-creation. The creator of the universe creates a righteous person out of an unrighteous one. In human eyes, this event becomes visible as destiny. Divine forgiveness inaugurates a moral change. The wrongdoer is no longer merely a wrongdoer, but rather is destined for righteousness. This way of thinking is fundamental in Paul.

In a word made familiar to us by earlier discussions, the wrongdoer is justified. "Blessed are those whose iniquities are forgiven, . . . blessed is the man against whom the Lord will not reckon his sin" (Rom. 4:7-8, in which Paul quotes Ps. 32:1-2). Forgiveness, seen from this perspective, is human recognition of the strange dignity bestowed by divine forgiveness. It is not so much a prerogative as a duty. Who am I, merely human, to be merciless toward someone to whom the source of the moral law and of all earthly and heavenly reality has been merciful? The question has particular force if I myself am a wrongdoer and in need of mercy. But all of us, in the view of Christians, are in that position. All of us are in need of forgiveness. All of us are unjustified unless we are justified by grace.

Where does all this leave humanist reason? This is a difficult question. The biblical doctrine of forgiveness comes to a climax in the figure of Christ and his atoning sacrifice on Calvary. There is no like figure, and no comparable emphasis on forgiveness, in any other religion, or in any secular creed. Even Christians have had trouble absorbing the implications of the crucifixion. Representatives of humanist reason have often found those implications offensive, in conflict both with justice and with the necessities of earthly order. The principle of retribution is exceedingly powerful. Instinct and conscience alike impel us to demand an eye for an eye. And a realistic apprehension of the importance and the conditions of orderly society reinforces the demand. It may be that the idea of mercy — and accordingly the patience on which liberty depends — is more dependent on revelation and faith than humankind has recognized or wants to admit.

Here and elsewhere, however, I think we should hesitate to admit any absolute breach between Christian and universal human understanding. Doing that encourages the former to be rationally incomprehensible and the latter spiritually shallow. And it disallows in advance all efforts at communication and common inquiry. Hence we should note that the idea of gratuitous mercy is not always absurd or repellent to ordinary human reason. This is true especially, as we have seen, of those who are cognizant of their own need for mercy. Remorseless justice can be disquieting even to those to whom the name of Christ is meaningless or unfamiliar. And those who have suffered some great wrong, like American Indians, sometimes realize that to escape a self-destructive hatred of those who have wronged them, they must find a way of forgiving them. If Christ is the Logos, the deep order of reality, then the meaning of his life and death will not be completely senseless or insignificant to anyone who is sensitively human. All of this is to suggest as I have in many other places that Christ, although certainly puzzling to human reason, can help awaken everyone to the hidden nature and claims of the good.

We should remember that our present concern is patience, or the possibility of facing evil without being overwhelmed by the proud and repressive passion for purity. Of course, there is a cynicism that contemplates evil with a shrug of the shoulders. But moral insensibility gives no support to liberty, for it renders it trivial. Liberty needs the support of a principle that allows us to abhor evil but hold back from merciless retaliation. Liberty needs widespread awareness that the moral structure of things is more complex and paradoxical than the ideal of strict, unvarying retribution allows for. Christ may offer some degree of that awareness for all who are interested in liberty.

Also we should realize that we are speaking of a spirit — the spirit of mercy — and not a set of practices. To explore the ways in which forgiveness can be practiced in a polity and a society, and to consider such matters as the relationship of mercy and penal order, would require far too much space to be undertaken in this essay. The key point is that a disposition to forgive, in whatever ways circumstances permit, seems to have an important place in a liberal society. It deflects the passion for purity into less destructive channels, possibly even into channels of truth-seeking communication. Moreover — and it is noteworthy that this comes to the same thing — it undergirds the idea of the dignity of the individual. A merciful spirit enables us to look into the undignified person before us and see one who is mysteriously dignified. In sum, to grant liberty is to treat with forbearance and respect people who excite our anger and arouse a fervent desire for implacable justice. A merciful spirit can enable us to do this.

The craving for pure righteousness on earth, however, is not the only impulse that endangers liberty. Another such impulse is, not to obliterate the wickedness manifest in every liberal society, but to live wholly apart from it.

The Lure of Withdrawal

The idea of withdrawal into private life, abandonment of society at large, can exercise a powerful attraction. This is partly because the social world in some historical situations can be an almost impossible place for a serious person to inhabit. In a tyranny, for example, where most social life is colored by adulation of the tyrant, a conscientious person may be impelled toward a life cut off entirely from the world around. And even in a society dominated by the uniformities of mass society or by a culture of distraction, private life may look far more attractive than any form of public life. In almost any historical circumstances, however, withdrawal can be an appealing, and even apparently worthy, act. As we have seen, even at its best, society is shaped by practical exigencies and human impulses that lead to the objectification of persons, their reduction to function, class, race, and other impersonal categories. Society is not community, although it may contain partial and passing communities. This means that withdrawal is not necessarily from community. On the contrary, it may be for the sake of community, that is, for communication of a kind that can be carried on only among a very few or perhaps only, through inward conversations, with oneself.

Communication — in more philosophical language, "dialogue" — is best represented probably in the ordinary activity of serious conversation, and is at the center of liberty. This is because liberty is meaningless without moral purpose, and the great moral purpose of all human life is the attainment and sharing of ultimate truth, or the good. This sharing is sought through communication, or dialogue, and as an aim and achievement constitutes community. But earthly society, constrained by imperatives of economic and military security to objectify its members, and disfigured by pride and diversionary inclinations, is a setting always more or less unfavorable to communication. Gossip is more common than serious conversation even in highly literate societies. It follows that withdrawal can be a communal, and seemingly moral, act. Not only that. As I shall try to show in the following chapter, it can actually be a moral act.

It can also, however, be a wrongful act. Its motive can be evasion of trials of collective existence that one ought, as a communal being, to share with others. Or the motive may be indulgence, without interference or shame, in private pleasures. In such cases it is a refusal of community. Even though society is in many ways antithetical to community, there can be no community entirely apart from society. All possible interlocutors, after all, are in society, and all subjects of serious conversation, or dialogue, are embedded in the common experience undergone in society. Many of the forms and courtesies required for communication are learned from society. Only a society stifling all communal relationships would justify complete withdrawal, and it is doubtful that even the totalitarian states of the twentieth century were such societies. Hence refusal of all social relationships would amount to a refusal of communication, and thereby to a refusal of meaningful liberty. It would be using withdrawal as a personal privilege rather than a common right needed for the health of common liberty.

For the sake of convenience, let us name these two kinds of withdrawal. The kind that accords with the demands of a communal conscience I shall call "provisional." Its purpose may be recuperative, providing momentary relief from social pressures; or it may be reflective, solitary meditation in preparation for a return to society. It may be carried out in response to social conditions rendering communication for a time difficult or impossible. It is not in any of these instances taken as a permanent and intrinsically appropriate state. The other kind of withdrawal might be called "final." It is a tacit declaration that now and always one is better off alone. Its premise is that man is not a communal or social being but is solitary in essence. Provisional withdrawal is essential to the health of liberty, as I will try to demonstrate in the following chapter, whereas final withdrawal undermines liberty.

The case against final withdrawal is ancient and familiar. For the Greeks of antiquity, and for many representatives of humanist reason, human beings are political in essence, that is, beings whose powers can be developed and exercised only when devoted, in common with fellow citizens, to the furtherance of the common good. Anyone who can live fully in solitude must, in Aristotle's famous words, be either a beast or a god. This is an argument from self-realization. The self is essentially social, and the social self is exercised and developed most fully in politics, the realm of common affairs. Man is therefore a political being.

This theme, classically formulated by Aristotle, is still persuasive to many people over two millennia later. There is no doubt a measure of truth in it. Its signal defect (setting aside for the moment the question of the value of political as opposed to other social activities) is that it idealizes society. In spite of the realism for which he is noted, Aristotle was not fully sensitive to the manifold ways in which even good societies obscure the truth and reduce human beings to the status of things. Somewhat surprisingly, Plato, who is accurately reputed to have been more idealistic than Aristotle, was more realistic about society. His idealism allowed him to see the glaring defects of society, or at least of every existing society. Plato's appraisal of society is expressed in the myth of the cave. Society is an underground cavern, lit by a fire — not by the sun. The cavern is inhabited by chained prisoners who, all of their lives, have seen nothing but the shadows cast on the cavern walls by the fire. The shadows are naturally mistaken for ultimate reality. Some prisoners, however, are set free and allowed to ascend from the cave into the sunlight, where they can look on true reality. These, of course, are philosophers. In the cave there can be neither truth nor community. For those who have reached the sunlight there can be both.

If Plato saw society more realistically than did Aristotle, however, he did not present an equally compelling case for living within society. Rather, he dramatizes the lure of withdrawal. Why should those who have ascended into the sunlight return to the cave? Plato has no doubt that they should. They alone, with their philosophical wisdom, are fit rulers. For them to rule, therefore, is clearly in the interest of society. It is not in their own interest, however. They should go back into the cave of society, Plato asserts, simply because the good of the whole takes priority over the good of the part. The welfare of the whole society requires the sacrifice of the welfare of the individual philosopher. Philosophers must live in darkness for the sake of society. Eventually, in Plato's prescription, they will be released from their kingly imprisonment and allowed to return to the sunlight — and the solitude — of philosophical contemplation. Only there, not in society, can they realize their full humanity.

The Christian case against final withdrawal is very different from the Greek case but no less definite. It is, indeed, more sweeping. This is because it rests on that rank-destroying and boundary-breaching concept — the "neighbor." The Greek outlook is hierarchical and parochial. Only a few can attain to the full human stature of citizen (and even fewer to the stature of philosopher), and those few are confined to the life of a city-state. The Christian outlook, in contrast, is egalitarian and universalist. Every human being on earth is a neighbor, or poten-

155

tially a neighbor, and therefore to be treated with care. Class distinctions are irrelevant and no one is a foreigner or barbarian. It is an ancient complaint that Christianity is subversive of civic life, in this and other ways as well. Perhaps it is, although the matter is open to debate. Christianity is not, however, on the side of final withdrawal. Neglect of one's neighbor would be disobedience to — and in that sense neglect of — God, creator of the neighbor and author of the command that the neighbor be loved. This implies that turning away from society, where all neighbors dwell, would be tantamount to turning away from God. Moreover, it would be turning away from God in a more radical and mysterious sense.

For Christians, the story that defines their faith gives dramatic emphasis to the imperative of social participation. The story is summed up in John's statement that "the Word became flesh and dwelt among us, full of grace and truth" (John 1:14). God, in the form of the Son, entered into human society. Not that society is good. The self-sacrificial character of the divine descent into the world is brought out in Paul's well-known statement that Christ, although having been in the form of God, "emptied himself, taking the form of a servant . . . and being found in human form . . . humbled himself and became obedient unto death" (Phil. 2:6-8). Life in society, compared with life in either primal or redeemed creation, has as little intrinsic worth for Paul as for Plato. But for Paul, God himself (as the Word, the Son) has come into society. The sun has come down into the cave. For Plato, the light of truth could be found only by leaving the cave. For Christians, the shadows have by no means been completely dissipated. Yet all of the light humans on earth are destined to behold is to be found in society, among the shadows. This at least is the basic thrust of Christian doctrine, in spite of exceptions such as monasticism and hermitism. Jesus occasionally withdrew into the wilderness for prayer, but he always returned to society. Men and women should follow this example. They should enter into society because that is what God did, and only in society is God to be found. The Christian condemnation of final solitude is more paradoxical than the Greek condemnation, but it is also more radical.

The challenge to humanist reason, barred from the paradoxical realism that Christians derive from the basic articles of their faith, is that of resisting the lure of withdrawal without idealizing society. Twentieth-century intellectuals have shown a strong propensity toward an Aristotelian evaluation of political life. This is a readily available and highly attractive way of summoning people to take part in the collective life around them. Yet, obscuring the flaws inherent in society as such, it does tend toward idealization. A stirring alternative was offered by Albert Camus in a great, but more or less unrecognized, work of political theory, *The Rebel*. Camus's leading idea is conveyed by the title itself. Society is always a scene of injustice and estrangement. A person of conscience, therefore, can live only as a rebel. Through rebellion one affirms the human solidarity that society denies. But rebellion against society can be carried on only within society. Rebellion is not withdrawal. Camus was an outspoken atheist, yet his ideal of social involvement was broadly similar to that of Christianity. Society is seriously disordered. It is nevertheless where one is obliged to live. Perhaps the most serious issue connected with Camus's political outlook is whether the "absurdist" philosophy he affirmed provides adequate ground for the rebel to stand on.

The Christian case against final withdrawal, however, also gives rise to a troublesome question. If authentic life can be carried on only in society, yet society is always more or less degraded, what kind of life can this be?

CHAPTER 6

The Liberal Stance

Standing Alone

In the *Republic,* after conceding that his ideal city is unlikely ever to be realized in the outer world, Plato suggests that individuals must serve as founders and rulers of their own inner cities. Statecraft becomes soulcraft, the art of forming and governing the self. The present essay has come to a position not unlike Plato's, however different the liberal ideal may be from Plato's ideal. The liberal ideal first of all is merely a liberal society. But the purpose of liberty being that of wisdom and righteousness, manifest in community, the ultimate liberal ideal is that of a society in which liberty is well used. The former ideal can often be realized, but by no means always. The more ultimate ideal is never realized. Morally fruitful liberty, carried on by all or most of a populace, is an ideal beyond the reach of practically all peoples and societies. At the same time, even in an illiberal society or in a gravely flawed liberal society, every individual remains personally responsible for standing on the side of liberty and for using his own liberty, so far as he possesses liberty, as wisely and as well as he can.

Liberals are impelled, as was Plato, to think of their political ideal as pertaining less to the polity than to the individual. If liberty is often lacking, and when not lacking leads to a flawed society, then the task of being free in a persevering and morally fruitful fashion falls forcibly on individual persons. The society I live in will probably betray the liberal ideal in various ways, not only by infringing on liberty unnecessarily, but also by giving rise to serious misuses of liberty. In my own personal life, however, I may do better. At least I am obliged to try. I am responsible for my own life in a way I am not responsible for the life of my society. The former I can control, the latter I cannot. Hence, uncoerced, I must support the cause of liberty in every way I can, and I must strive to see the truth and to live in its light. In this sense liberalism prescribes not so much a kind of society as a kind of human being. And the human being who embodies the liberal prescription may be more or less isolated in society. In this sense liberalism rightly understood is a lonely creed.

These statements can remind us of earlier discussions. In exploring the grounds of liberty in chapter 3, I argued that liberty is required, in spite of the evil in human nature, because men and women have the power of choice and are therefore responsible for (even though not the creators of) their own destinies. They either choose the good or else the good has no place in their lives or in the world they inhabit. This shows clearly how the nearly inevitable failures of a liberal society place a new kind of emphasis on personal responsibility. It is not just that a liberal society needs responsible members. Rather, the very standard of liberty is apt to be met and exemplified mainly by free individuals, perhaps only a few of them, and these will always be individuals living in some degree apart from and in tension with society.

Every ideology, of course, seeks to form individuals in accordance with its highest standards. Socialism, for example, envisions compassionate and cooperative citizens; conservatism counts on people to be respectful of tradition and faithful to the duties of their various stations in society. Liberalism is not absolutely unique. Yet it is different. Other ideologies are primarily collective. They aim at giving society a certain shape and at society transmitting that shape to individuals. Individuals are in this sense subordinate to society. Also nonliberal ideologies typically rely on a leading group, like a disciplined party or an aristocratic class, to be the shapers of society. Thus communists, conservatives, and fascists all think primarily of a certain kind of society, under a certain kind of authority, and only secondarily of the kind of people who will make up the society. Liberals, so far as they are realistic, think first of all of free individuals. Liberalism is born in the project, not of giving society a certain ideal form, but of setting individuals free of society. Once this happens, no one knows just what shape society will assume. Diverse policies can be pursued, so long as individuals are left with their liberty. Grievous failures may be sustained, and society badly damaged, without discredit to the liberal ideal, so long as there are individuals in the society who are responsibly and wisely carrying on the life of liberty. Finally, a realistic liberalism differs from every other ideology in not counting on any kind of ruling class or party to found and maintain it. In these ways liberalism fully justifies the main charge levied by its critics. It is highly individualistic.

Liberalism is individualistic because it is centered on freedom, the power of choice. And because it is so centered, and is cognizant of the evil in human beings and the moral vulnerability of society, it subordinates the question of the good society to that of the good individual. Through freedom, societies and persons can take on varied forms. And through the freedom of deeply flawed human beings, serious evils are almost certain to emerge. This is not to hint at any sort of moral relativism. As I have said repeatedly, the point of freedom is to choose the good, not simply to do as you please. But liberals do not believe that humans are capable of collectively defining the good or of collectively assuring that individuals will choose the good. Hence, when all is said and done, there is no alternative to leaving people free to envision and affirm the good for themselves. Not that this will make them happy. It will only make them human. The conviction defining true liberalism is that freedom is at the core of personal reality. Hence anyone who abandons freedom abandons his own selfhood and alienates himself from the good, which can come into the world and life only by being freely affirmed.

A critical reader might feel that what I am saying here is in conflict with what I said above about liberal culture. Fruitful freedom can be rendered more likely through the examples, influences, and instruction provided by a free society. This suggests that liberalism, like every ideology, accords society a certain primacy over the individual. It suggests too a certain human plasticity. All of this I grant, provided the qualifications in these concessions be noted. A liberal culture is desirable but not indispensable. And where it exists it may fail to inculcate in the individual an ethos of freedom; indeed, it almost certainly will so fail in some degree. Nonetheless, the individual still is free and must responsibly live his freedom. Moreover, a liberal culture differs from every other political culture in striving to produce individuals who are capable of criticizing and living independently of the culture. The standard of loyal opposition has far wider application than to party politics. A good liberal citizen is a participant in society through potential, and sometimes actual, dissidence. A liberal culture strives to cultivate a capacity for such dissidence. Many who possess this capacity will devise and pursue evil ends. But some will display the human nobility that defines the liberal purpose. It is that possibility that renders liberty imperative.

The concept of the liberal stance presupposes that the responsibilities accruing to my freedom are my own and no one else's. Not that my responsibilities are unique; there are general moral ends and rules that govern all lives. But the responsibilities are mine alone, and guilt for failing to meet them also is mine. This is the individualism inherent in liberalism. Still, to grant that the general ends and rules that govern my life are the same as those that govern all lives is to see that the liberal stance is not purely individualistic. Standing alone is paradoxically a way of standing together. This is true in three ways.

In the first place, as we have already seen, my very claim to liberty has a universalist dimension. That claim is based on the fact that I possess the power of choice. If liberty is withheld from me, then my very humanity is denied. I am treated as something other than a being who can choose. But if my claim to liberty is based on my power of choice, then it is implicitly a claim in behalf of everyone who possesses that power. It implies that every human being should be free. Otherwise, my claim lacks any color of justice and is morally baseless. It is an expression of mere desire or of a will to power, not an assertion of right. In this sense, in possessing liberty I stand not alone but in the company of everyone. My claim to liberty is arbitrary, mere self-assertion, unless it is just, and it is just only if I grant that everyone has a like claim. It follows that the liberal stance is implicitly political even though maintained by a solitary individual. Standing responsibly apart from all others, while recognizing the right of everyone to do this, is a way of standing with them.

The liberal stance is universalist also in being an orientation toward values that are universal. As I have said, the responsibility of a free person is to discover things that are truly good. It is a moral responsibility. It is fulfilled, therefore, not merely by choosing things I like, but by choosing things worthy of being chosen by everyone. This does not imply social uniformity. The life of a philosopher who tries to see the truth may be quite different from the life of a scientist or an artist with the same goal. It will be radically different from the life of a businessperson, a computer technician, or a worker who is trying to see and deal with reality as it is. It may be quite different even from the life of another philosopher bent on discovering the truth. Nonetheless, responsible liberty presupposes a concern with values that are objective, not mere matters of personal taste. It is to stand, even in deepest solitude, in the company of all human beings.

There is a third way in which the solitary stance inherent in liberalism is a form of unity with all others. The liberal stance is communal, and community consists in more than abstract universality. We must think further along this line.

Standing Together

The word "communal" here is equivalent to "communicative," and a communal stance is understood as a readiness to engage in communication (it will be convenient sometimes to speak of "dialogue" or "conversation" as roughly synonymous with "communication"). To restate my main theme, to be free, or in full possession of liberty, is to maintain an attitude of communal readiness — of attentiveness toward others, and of readiness to speak, or otherwise make known one's inner mind. The meaning of communality obviously varies greatly according to personal situations, skills and training, and media employed. Some follow communicative professions, such as teaching and the arts; others, deprived of literacy and condemned to laborious, time-consuming jobs, have only constricted opportunities for communication; most people, it seems, have some skills and opportunities for communication, but largely waste them. The most common medium of communication by far is words. But words are used in very different ways by philosophers, poets, natural scientists, businesspeople, and workers. And some, such as painters, dancers, composers, and sculptors, communicate with unsurpassable effectiveness while using no words at all.

The most numerous callings, as in business, armed services, trades, and so forth, do not necessarily involve very much communication in the proper sense of the term (a sense I shall shortly explain). It does not follow that these callings are on a lower human level than the communicative professions. For one thing, they are essential to the maintenance of the private and public realms in which communication occurs. Further, however, they may paradoxically provide the basis for acts of communication that surpass in authenticity the communicative acts of people professionally engaged in communication. The latter may be vulnerable to the kind of stultification symbolized in the case of professors by the term "ivory tower." Professional communicators may lack the inestimable advantage of being in close and continuous contact with concrete reality. Great poets have been doctors or insurance executives. It is far from unthinkable that a soldier or a day laborer might have more significant things to say than a professional philosopher.

Not every verbal or other exchange is communication in the present sense of the term. In fact, relatively few human exchanges are. Communication properly speaking is that which constitutes community. But community is not merely social cohesiveness. There is community only where people are united in their concern — a concern that might be expressed in disagreement — with things that matter to them in their essential humanity. People often, of course, are united in their *accidental* humanity, say, in their fervent attachment to a sports team, or in their hatred of a foreign group. Authentic community, however, exists only where the bond of unity is a fundamental and universal human concern such as justice, education, or environmental beauty. Authentic communication occurs where people are engaged together in searching for and showing forth the truth that bears on such concerns. Information, useful instructions, gossip, prurient sexual details, and the stuff of sentimental fiction are not suitable matters of authentic communication, and this is because they do not engage us in our fundamental humanity. They are distractions, leaving to one side and forgotten the essential, as distinguished from the accidental, self. To be worthy of respect, communication must be serious, and to be serious it must have to do with matters of ultimate concern to all humankind — matters that may, even should, also be of personal concern.

An ideal life is often thought to be one that is creative. It is the artist, writer, composer, inventor, original thinker, pioneering scientist that usually commands greatest respect. Why assign priority to communication over creativity? I would ask in response, whether there is a difference between them. A creative act normally, perhaps even always, has a communicative intent. A creative work, such as a painting or a poem, is put in front of others. It is not discarded or set aside for mere

163

private contemplation. Further, if creativity by its nature moves toward communication, it seems also that every act of serious communication is creative. To speak seriously to someone (whether in words or in paint, stone, or some other medium) is to express insight that is achieved after effort and is not merely casual. Not only the great works of literature and art, but also the most prized remarks in personal conversation are other than mere disclosures of the person at their source. They are disclosures of the world and of humanity. In a word, they are true.

Let me note one assumption that does not underlie these statements and one that does. As for the former, to define communication in terms of basic and universal human concerns is not to condemn all those forms of self-expression that aim at amusement and recreation; it is not to enthrone a wearisome solemnity. Times of relaxed sociability, unburdened by serious purpose, have a place in a good human life. Idle talk is not indefensible. We must recognize, however, that human beings come together on very different levels, sometimes on the level of the ephemeral and trivial, sometimes on the level of common utility, and sometimes on the level of the deepest human interests. Only meetings of the third sort are truly communicative. All other "communication" is wrongly named because not very much in fact is communicated.

The assumption I do make is that the deepest concern of one person is the same as the deepest concern of every other person. The particular and the universal in this sense coincide. When I am fully at grips with the issues at the center of my own selfhood, I am universally human. All human beings are in some sense one human being. A version of this truth is present in the Christian idea — an idea meaning different things to different Christians — that all humans fell with Adam and that all are crucified and raised from the dead in Christ. This, it may seem, is to slight uniqueness as a mark of personal being. It is doubtful, however, that uniqueness, as the polar opposite of universality, is essential to personal reality or significance. I may be indistinguishable from many others in opinions, emotions, and manner of life. The only question relevant to my distinct personal being is whether I have made these my own by reflecting on them and choosing them. It is freedom — the act of thoughtfully choosing, not of choosing things different from those chosen by anyone else — that makes me a person.

The reasons for regarding communication as the primary work of liberty are, I believe, embedded in much that I have said in the preceding pages. My argument begins with the claim in chapter 3 that truth is the highest value. Conscience commands righteousness, and righteousness depends on knowledge of the good. The primary vocation of every person is therefore that of trying to gain knowledge of the good. The second main principle underlying my argument is stated in chapter 4: the dignity of every person. This principle implies that each one is bound morally to consider the welfare of every other person, to the extent that this can be done within the severe limitations inherent in our finitude. This means that one must consider, in every interpersonal situation, what the welfare of other persons requires. The basic answer, meaning very different things in different situations, must always be: assistance in coming to an understanding of the truth. Physical assistance, such as gaining food and shelter, may be more urgent, yet it is pointless unless it finally serves someone in fulfilling his human vocation, pursuit of the truth. Assistance in this supreme task is provided by opening the doors to the realms of serious communication. This means in the larger society cultivating a public realm, open to all persons and all matters of common interest. This will be discussed in chapter 9. But helping people move toward the truth has a more personal meaning: attentiveness in relation to the persons one encounters, and a readiness to speak to them. To be shut out of the realms of communication is to suffer the most serious deprivation that people can impose on one another. We are human together in seeking to know and live in accordance with the most comprehensive truth we can gain.

This can be put in terms of justice. The same moral logic that compels me in claiming liberty for myself to claim liberty for everyone, compels me also to recognize the interest that everyone has in the truth and thus to will universal possession of the truth. Willing a liberal society, I will a society given to serious communication. By this route the ideal of liberty leads directly into the imperative that liberty be used principally for seeking and sharing the truth. The standard of justice, as equal liberty, is not merely legalistic. It can be translated into the ideal of a communicative society.

It is particularly important to bear in mind that my emphasis on communication is not meant to slight action. Communication and action go together. The truth we know must be lived. Only in that way do we prove our sincerity and show, both to ourselves and others, that our professions of truth are not mere ornaments but reflect the substance of our being. Moreover, only if the truth we profess is lived can we know whether it is really true. As pragmatists hold, truth is tested in action. It follows that action, carried on reflectively and if possible in communication with others, is a form of inquiry.

It makes sense to speak of a communal *stance* for the same reason it makes sense to speak of a liberal stance. As already shown, the evil in human beings makes it certain that a liberal society will be severely flawed. This is the same as saying that communication will ordinarily be degraded and obstructed in a liberal society. The air will be filled with entertainment, obscenity, and trivia. Most people may behave in decent, and often kindly, ways, yet be distracted or subtly selfish and proud. A communicative person is apt to find few who speak to his concerns or are willing to listen understandingly to expressions of them. Acts of true communication will be rare and difficult. A communal (or free) person may have to be satisfied with maintaining a communal posture in relation to the world, while forgoing very much actual communication.

One of the main allegations of critics is that liberalism is neglectful of man's communal nature and needs. This criticism is largely without merit. It arises partly from a failure to note that even though liberalism has an individualistic dimension, and numerous liberals have been indifferent to community, there is nothing in the concept of liberty or in that of personal responsibility that is antithetical to community. Liberty allows each one to decide what is truly of value, and that gives liberalism an individualistic cast. But the individual may decide that the highest value is community, thus transcending individualism. At least two distinguished liberals of the nineteenth century saw selfhood, and therefore liberty, as realized only in the company of others. These were Alexis de Tocqueville and the English idealist Thomas Hill Green. Such liberals perhaps are outnumbered by liberals of a different stamp. But they show that liberalism is not essentially indifferent to community. If it often has been, that is a historical accident, largely without philosophical significance.

It was argued earlier in the essay that liberty leads to atomization of society. This may seem to concede that liberalism is hostile to community. Atomization is a result, however, not of liberal aspirations but of practical pressures and of sin. Moreover, what is atomized is society, not community. The distinction between these two, already explained in principle, will be elaborated upon as the essay proceeds. Suffice it here to underscore the plain fact that not every way of uniting people brings them together in their full humanity. An army platoon and a factory assembly line are familiar examples of cohesive social units that are not communities. "Society" is a convenient term for designating these merely apparent, or outward, unities. It is not that they are unnecessary, but only that they are not communities. They are properly means, not ends. Social atomization, then, is a product of our fallen condition and not of our essential humanity or of the liberal ideal.

Critics might press their case by pointing out that society cannot be atomized without having an adverse effect on community. People must be in social contact with one another to engage in communication. That is no doubt so. It remains true, nonetheless, that nothing in the liberal *ideal* is in conflict with the communal ideal. There might, in an atomized society, be a good deal of communication, in spite of difficulties. And in any case, since liberty is the main condition of authentic choice, there can be no community where liberty is denied. And finally this must be noted, that liberty at the very least allows one to maintain a communal stance, that is, a reflective and attentive posture, and thus, like a Platonic philosopher, to create a community in his own inner city.

It may seem at first glance that the theme I am advancing is not very Christian. It sounds more like Socrates than like Jesus. For Socrates the ideal human relationship lies in searching conversation, whereas for Jesus the bond is charity. But what does charity require of us? First of all, we are apt to say, physical assistance, like food to the hungry and shelter to the homeless. And no one can doubt the frequent urgency and the elemental humanity of providing such assistance where it is needed. Yet we often provide the same sort of assistance to animals, so charity must call for something more. Simone Weil (a Christian) saw what this is, I think, when she spoke of *attentiveness* as "the rarest and purest form of human generosity." Attentiveness, of course, is communality. After urgent physical needs have been met, we recognize the full humanity of men and women by listening to them, and of course speaking to them as well. Real listening, however, presupposes liberality — letting people act and speak in full sincerity, that is, letting them discover and show who they really are by unconstrained life and speech. Charity, liberty, and community are concepts belonging together and summarizing the tenets of true liberalism.

Just as the idea of liberty as communication may look at first more

Greek than Christian, so it may look more elitist than democratic. It may seem that communication seriously concerned with truth must be carried on largely by an elite of the intellect and the arts. If that were so, then liberty — as essentially communal — would be mainly for a few. This impression, however, may derive from underestimating the communal opportunities and abilities of ordinary people. Granted, conscious dedication to the discovery and sharing of truth is rather rare. Most people, if catered to by a vulgar culture, financed and systematically used for purposes of power and profit, readily forget about truth and devote their hours and days to sports and other forms of light entertainment. But at least as long ago as Hegel and Marx there arose the insight that nonintellectual people, such as manual laborers and slaves, may experience unyielding, everyday reality with far greater force than elites of intellect and art. If so, then there may be in the minds of the common people a basis for communication of a depth that elites fail to reach. And common people may not be as lacking as is often supposed in the power of articulating their experience. Ordinary conversation is not necessarily lacking in wit and penetration. Moreover, ordinary people are capable of enjoying good art and literature. This is indicated by various historical experiences, such as the popularity of great drama in ancient Greece, the leadership of fishermen and other workers in the rise of Christianity, and the fact that modern mass democracies, while just as foolish and irresponsible as earlier aristocracies and monarchies, are also apparently just as wise.

Until around the beginning of the twentieth century, the range of authentic liberty — communal liberty — was limited by economic stringencies. Multitudes were necessarily confined to long hours of hard labor and thereby to ignorance. These stringencies have been relaxed due to the industrial revolution and the material abundance thus produced. Now the main obstacle to liberty — egalitarian and communal liberty — is popular culture, which is a way of saying sin. Sin in this case is avarice and disrespect for truth and persons by the minority that contrives popular culture. It is also irresponsibility by the multitudes that willingly indulge in such culture.

Plato's "inner city" seemed relevant, earlier in the essay, even to the bare idea of liberty, before liberty had been defined as communal. It helped focus on the possibility of maintaining a liberal stance in defiance of illiberal surroundings. Now, having considered the essential communality of liberty, Plato's idea is more apropos than ever. The liberal stance can be thought of as the forming and governing of an inner community, a community centered in one person, yet potentially global in scope. The foundations of this community are laid when I recognize that the liberty I claim for myself must, in justice, be acknowledged as the right of everyone possessing the power of choice, that is, all human beings. The foundations are reinforced when I recognize that the values for which a free person is responsible are not merely subjective but are universally human. Since the first of these values is truth, my inner city begins to take shape only as I stand ready to listen and speak (or otherwise express myself). Even in solitude, attentiveness, along with a readiness to respond, becomes the practice of an inner statecraft.

The liberal, or communal, stance may be characterized by two terms, one accentuating its Greek lineage. The term "civil" invokes the ancient polis. Attentiveness and responsiveness are in a broad sense political. Whether the polis be imagined or real, global (a "cosmopolis") or parochial, a readiness for communication inescapably involves a concern with common affairs and, as a responsible stance, a willingness to act on one's perceptions. This is the sense in which the liberal stance is a civil stance, the posture of a citizen. Liberty so conceived can in some measure be realized through participatory politics. It is important, however, that the "can" in this proposition not be transmuted into a "must." Deep and daily involvement in political activity is not a prerequisite to full humanity. The idealization of participatory democracy symbolized by ancient Athens and expressed in modern times by Rousseau jeopardizes a balanced understanding and appreciation of liberty. *Communication,* not *participation,* is the key to liberty. It might therefore be misleading to call the liberal stance "political." It is civil, however, in incorporating a communicative and responsible concern with common problems.

The other term for characterizing the liberal stance, suggesting perhaps a biblical lineage, is "universalist." The term indicates a stance maintained not merely in the midst of one's own people but also with an eye to universal humanity. And it indicates an orientation that reaches out limitlessly not only in space, to all present humanity, but also in time, both to humanity's earliest experiences and to its final destiny. It may seem that extending the breadth of communicative concern so far as this is implausible. Who can think about the whole human race and all of human history except for a few historians and philosophers? It is arguable, however, that the unqualified universality of the liberal stance is implicit in the ancient maxim that nothing human is alien to any human creature. Humanity is defined primarily not by observable uniformities among members of the species, as in animals, but by the attentiveness and communicative availability of every member of the species toward every other member. Such mutual involvement may not be a fact. But, like humanity itself, it is a norm. And it is not without practical relevance. Travel, study, and technological means of communication enable many to live in some measure as global citizens.

It should be carefully noted that this norm does not imply that one must strive to live at the center of a gigantic abstraction — the concept of humanity in all times and all places. The human race is incarnate in every particular human being. This is the gist of Jesus' concept of the neighbor. Your proper concern is with the concrete person who is here and now before you. But this can be anyone and is therefore, in a certain sense, everyone. In caring for this one person you are caring for every person. Moreover, this one person is a product of the whole human past and is thereby microcosmic, or, more precisely, microhistorical — a kind of focal representation (even though only fragmentarily decipherable) of all that has happened to the human race. Your neighbor thus fuses particularity and universality. The liberal stance is shaped by a recognition of this universality. It consists in a conversational openness to the person in your immediate presence, with this person thought of as an embodiment of humanity in all nations and ages. If I am speaking with a black American, I do so perceptively only if I am conscious of the long periods of slavery and discrimination that have had much to do with defining my interlocutor; if I am speaking with a Jewish person, I may remember the uprootedness and suffering of the Jewish people back to the time of the Egyptian captivity. In such ways, it might be said, one exhibits a universalist imagination. Through the idea of the neighbor, justice is done both to the limitless scope and to the personal immediacy of communality.

The concept of the liberal stance is paradoxical. The idea of a stance that every particular person is responsible for maintaining, all alone if necessary, is individualistic. But the stance is defined in terms of attentiveness and responsiveness, and in that way is communal. To probe further into the matter, it may be useful to examine two closely connected concepts, both suggestive of individualism, yet both communal when fully understood.

Solitude and Private Property

To deal with these two concepts we must go back to the issue of individualism. A major premise of this essay is that *ontological* individualism — the idea that a human being is in essence alone, and that life apart from others is a primal or proper human state — is false. We belong, in the depths of our being, together. This is a highly plausible principle for protagonists of humanist reason. Countless studies and theories have exhibited humans as radically dependent on one another, not only for physical survival, but also, in some way and degree, for their human qualities and for their fulfillment and happiness. As for protagonists of religious faith, we need only recall such core Christian concepts as the kingdom of God as the destiny of every person, and the standard of uncalculating and unqualified love signalized by the word "agape." There have been great individualistic thinkers, such as Nietzsche, but they have been dissenters from a consensus embracing both faith and reason.

A second major premise of this essay, however, is that *historical* individualism is valid. False ontologically, it is provisionally true. The perfect communal unity proper to man's uncorrupted nature has been lost. In the circumstances of historical existence we are factually, even though not essentially, more or less alone. The best life one person can live is bound to be in some degree separate from the lives of others. This is the human condition on earth. The grounds of this appraisal — the radical evil in human beings — have already been discussed. Our fallenness is plainly evident, within societies and in the relations of societies with one another, in the indifference, callousness, and cruelty with which we treat one another. Sin is simply a failure to love, and it leaves individuals more or less stranded and alone.

The historical estrangement of the individual cannot be fully understood, however, in terms of a general erosion of good relationships due to sin. Human fallenness is, in a limited way, structured. While sin affects both individuals and societies, it is generally less restrained in societies than in individuals. Since this is a major premise underlying both my contention that the individual person is normally more or less estranged from society and the distinction I draw throughout the essay between society and community, it may not be amiss to quickly review the reasons for thinking it is so.

In at least four ways societies tend more strongly toward evil behavior than do individuals. Roughly, the larger the group the more readily these considerations apply; nations, for example, are apt to be morally worse than families. They apply in some measure, however, to all groups. (1) Society by its very nature is organized for the sake of urgent practical ends, such as military security, economic sufficiency, and the raising of children. These ends constrain every society to mobilize and objectify its members, and thus to be impersonal and illiberal. (2) All societies and groups are in some measure hierarchical. Some rule and some are ruled, some are managers and others are managed. The higher stations are always invitations to self-magnification, and the lower stations are invitations to self-abandonment. (3) Whereas individuals are able sometimes to feel something of what other individuals are feeling and to view them with sympathy and compassion, such relations are far more difficult between groups. An American has little sense of how it feels to be an Egyptian or a Ugandan, and therefore has little empathy for the members of such societies. (4) Groups — particularly nations, but even families — are usually unapologetically selfish. An American president can unashamedly confess, even boast, that he cares solely for America and little for other nations. People will do things in behalf of the tribe, nation, or family that they would not do just for their own sake. The violence and terror of the twentieth century were primarily a phenomenon of group life.

Owing to such conditions, there are no saintly societies. It is doubtful even that there are morally admirable societies. The societies we look back on with greatest admiration — ancient Athens, medieval Florence, perhaps the Roman Empire — are known not only for their achievements but also for their terrible deeds. Moral preeminence, even moral experience, belongs largely to individuals alone. To only a small degree, and seldom, do societies sin and repent. The most abominable acts are likely to pass without expressions of official regret. In America at the turn of the millennium, it is mainly dissident groups that deplore slavery or the massacres of Indians. Saintly individuals, even good individuals, necessarily are strangers in society.

The other circumstance that renders historical individualism true has been spoken of repeatedly in earlier pages and underlies the idea of the liberal stance. That is personal responsibility. In the midst of the fallen human race there is no getting out from under the weight of this responsibility. This is not to attribute infallibility to conscience but only to highlight the untransferable responsibility conscience imposes. No person or agency beyond the individual can relieve you of the burden of personal responsibility. You cannot escape responsibility by pledging unconditional allegiance to any party, race, or nation, nor by submitting unquestioningly to any earthly power or leader, nor by conforming uncritically with any institutional order. Sooner or later you must ask yourself, "Am I thinking and living as I should? Are my opinions true? Are my actions right?" In facing such questions, as every person sometimes must — at the cost of altogether forsaking personal being — you acknowledge and take on individual responsibility. You realize the necessity of making decisions that may not coincide with the demands of society and may not be approved of or shared by any other person — indeed, may not even be right — but that an inner moral voice compels you to make. In short, you realize the provisional truth of individualism.

Here again we come upon that primal distinction, the one between society and community. In society the provisional truth of individualism becomes starkly clear. To speak summarily, man is communal whereas society is anticommunal — a variation on Niebuhr's "moral man and immoral society." All the conditions mentioned above as militating toward immorality militate also against community. Being organized for practical purposes, as well as for community, and being compelled thereby to objectify its members, society is compelled to limit community. And, luring people into pride and distraction, it is much more anticommunal than its practical ends compel it to be. The relatively moral individual, more or less estranged from the relatively immoral society, is the communal person, compelled for the sake of communication to disengage himself in some measure from society. The estranged individual, even though in solitude, must, for the sake of community, establish and maintain his own inner community.

Society and community never exist, it must be granted, in their abstract purity. They are always mixed together although more or less in tension. Some social groupings, like monasteries and parliaments, are relatively favorable to community, while others, like totalitarian states, render communal relationships, aside from those that are secret and perilous, impossible. Groupings of the former sort provide many openings for community, for serious listening and speaking. Those of the latter sort attempt, through propaganda and terror, to stamp every particular relationship with the will of the leader and the leading party. Even such extremes as these, however, are far from pure types. The nearest approximations to community, such as a conversation led by Socrates in the agora or a meeting of Jesus and his disciples, are small and ephemeral. And even within their narrow bounds they are highly imperfect; Socrates was badgered by men like Gorgias, and among Jesus' disciples was Judas Iscariot. On the other side, totalitarianism is a malign aspiration, not an achieved reality. Not even the most efficient and ferocious despot can stifle every breath of community.

The issue of individualism needs to be seen against this background. For an individual to negotiate the currents of historical life is exceedingly difficult. Vigilance, good sense, and an independent mind are needed. Both society and community make legitimate demands. The demands of society have to do with maintaining the order on which community depends, and a responsible individual cannot ignore them. The demands of community come from the individual's deepest self, but for these demands to be met society must offer suitable openings and possibilities. Ontological individualism, denying the value of community and the communality of human nature, can only sow confusion. Historical individualism, on the other hand, illuminates the individual's real situation, made up of circumstances in which the pressures of society and the possibilities of community are inextricably mixed together. It can in this way undergird personal responsibility. It can provide a perspective enabling the individual to view every group, institution, and authority critically, complying with demands that directly or indirectly further liberty and community, and resisting those that do not. It can help one know when entry into a social complex is obligatory, either because it meets the basic necessities of life and order or because it offers immediate possibilities of communication. And it can help one know when withdrawal from society, in one way or another, is absolutely requisite.

These considerations, I think, offer a basis for accurately construing the perplexing subject of solitude. The subject is perplexing because of the ambiguity of solitude. Often it is evil. In the form of solitary confinement, for example, it is tormenting and potentially destructive.

It is evil also when embraced voluntarily as a desirable state of life. This may happen from motives of hedonism and self-indulgence; solitude is seen as allowing unhindered and unembarrassed sensual enjoyment. Solitude may be embraced also out of resentment or fear, causing the company of others to seem in one way or another threatening. In instances such as these the self is conceived to be essentially unrelated. Solitude, consequently, seems a fitting and final human state. In a word, solitude is evil when it manifests ontological individualism. As Dostoyevsky showed in *Notes from Underground,* solitude of this sort is a matrix of nihilism.

Nonetheless, solitude is essential to human life on earth. Just as individualism is a provisional truth, solitude is a provisional norm, and this is due, of course, to the nature of life in history. Where humans are separated from one another by time and space, and by pride and distraction, solitude can protect and nourish our communality. One enters into solitude not to enjoy a life outside of community but rather to protect oneself against society — to cultivate the sensitivity to truth and to persons that is the main condition of community but in danger of being stifled by society. Solitude of the right kind is precommunal. In solitude one founds and governs the inner community that may, at some time and in some measure, take shape in the outer world.

All this has important bearing on the principle of private property and, by way of this principle, on liberty. Let us begin with the general concept of privacy, which forms a kind of logical bridge between the concepts of solitude and private property. Very broadly, privacy is the right of exclusion. I have such a right if, with legal sanction and support, I can sever any or all human connections (excepting those involving a legal responsibility, like a parent for a child) for as long as I like. Legally protected privacy is in part a right to solitude. Hence everything said in behalf of solitude applies to privacy as well. These things need not be repeated here to make it clear that the right to privacy is essential to our lives in history, and that this is the case, not because there is any truth in ontological individualism, but because we are communal beings fated to dwell in the more or less anticommunal circumstances prevailing in all historical societies.

To characterize privacy merely as the right of exclusion, however, is misleading even though accurate. Rightly used, it has more to do with inclusion than with exclusion. For one thing, as implied in the preceding discussion of solitude, it is an opportunity to free oneself from outer discord in order to realize the inner harmony of prolonged and careful thought. Earlier I referred to solitude, so used, as precommunal — a preparation for entering into community. Without greatly misusing language, however, one might call such solitude, and the privacy that provides access to it, simply communal. It allows one to build through inner conversations, or reflection, an imaginative inner community — a community that may be in some measure actualized in the outer world.

Further, while privacy presupposes a right to exclude everyone, it also presupposes a right to exclude only some, while admitting others. Private life is not necessarily solitary. Privacy consists in choosing one's own company. As a realm of selective communities, it is midway between solitude and the public realm, where an all-embracing community can be sought. In this way it is vital to all of us in our communal being. One can go forth from solitude without entering immediately into the alien world of society. The kind of soulcraft learned in the founding and governing of one's inner city can be employed in the fashioning of small cities of friends. If the proper use of solitude is the readying of the self for community, then privacy, as an opportunity to form selective communities, draws its legitimacy from the ideal of community. In privacy, the communal work of solitude can be practiced and tested.

It is only realistic, however, to say that the ideal of community may come nearer to realization in these miniature private cities than in any of the cities of the world. The nearest approach to community in the world at large may be in nations, with their common languages, cultures, and governments. Patriotism is an emotion that sometimes allows for and spurs communication. Yet nations are both too large and too small to be real communities. They are too large in that they far surpass most possibilities of face-to-face communication, and they usually comprise groups too diverse and mutually antagonistic to achieve much in the area of dialogue. They are too small in that they leave out most of the cultures and peoples that make up the human race. Even the greatest of them are parochial, not global. Modern nations thus are more societal than communal.

The ideal community comprises everyone without exception — people of all nations and faiths, of all classes and interests, and of all levels of intelligence. The modest little concept of "neighbor" allows for no limits. Much more will be said about this further on. It is manifest, however, that an all-embracing community is impossible. If even two people cannot be united in a perfect friendship or a perfect marriage, obviously the multitudes making up humankind cannot be perfectly united. The human race is not and cannot be a "human family," if we take "family" for an emblem of the perfect community that no family ever is. The meaning of the concept of original sin, it might be said, is simply that humankind exists in a state of deeply rooted estrangement. Community is achieved with difficulty and is always fragmentary and fragile. Hence the best communities may be those ephemeral understandings sometimes reached when a few people, like the interlocutors in Plato's dialogues, speak seriously to one another and listen.

Without privacy, liberty would wither away. This is true not only of private liberty but also of public liberty, the right to engage in various kinds of action and speech out in the world, in the sight of everyone. What would freedom of speech amount to if there were no solitude, where thinking could be carried on, and if there were no thoughtful private conversations? It is scarcely an overstatement to say that privacy is the soil in which liberty of all kinds has its roots. Only in privacy can liberty, with its intrinsic communality, be conceived and born. These are not merely theoretical statements. Twentieth-century totalitarianism invariably involved the subversion of privacy through such practices as inciting children to spy on their parents and encouraging adults to report not only suspicious activities on the part of others but also suspicious attitudes and remarks. In his novel *1984*, George Orwell imagined a regime that mandated a television set in every room of every private home that could not be turned off and through which one could be observed from a central police center. Even facial expressions at times of unguardedness and repose might be carefully observed. Thus it was shown that a state at war with liberty is necessarily at war as well with private life.

If liberty depends radically on privacy, it must also depend radically on private property. While solitude and serious conversation often flourish in public places, like the ancient agora and the modern sidewalk cafe, they would be exposed and vulnerable were their only possible settings public. They need places of private refuge. Withdrawal from society for the cultivation of community would not be a reliable possibility without physical places where one could be alone or with selected companions. If privacy is a right of exclusion, then to exercise the right one must have legal command of a particular piece of the earth from which others can be excluded. Notably, thinking along these lines brings a particular kind of property to the fore, that is, real property. All kinds of property, such as books and furniture, contribute to one's capacity to live apart from society, but these would not amount to much without a place where they can be used and safely kept. In this sense a piece of land and a house are the basic forms of property. Homelessness is tantamount to the loss of everything. If private homes did not exist, then neither would community, except in its most fugitive forms, and neither would liberty.

In the nineteenth and twentieth centuries the idea of public property, "public ownership," took on a glow of idealism. Liberty was seen mainly as public liberty, the common life of the whole society, and this carried with it the idealization of public property. It must be granted that some kinds of public property, such as public parks and libraries, and the meeting places of legislatures and courts, deserve a degree of idealization. Normally, they are attractive areas to which everyone has rightful access. All who are there can see others and be seen, and spontaneous, if ephemeral, communities can coalesce. And in political and judicial areas, all may meet and carry on common business, or witness it being carried on. The ideal of public property probably draws life, however tacitly, from the impulse toward community, which impels us toward the vision so eloquently voiced in the book of Isaiah and the letters of Paul, clearly formulated by writers such as Cicero and Marcus Aurelius, and symbolized by the Roman Empire and the Roman Catholic Church: the vision of a community comprising all nations and peoples and — taken to its eschatological finale — all historical eras. This vision sheds light on the concept of property. It suggests the grandest of all public places, the whole earth, as the common possession of humanity. The concept of private property looks mean and pinched in comparison.

If a global, or even national, community in any full sense of the word is impossible, however, then public property in any full sense of the word also is impossible. There is no public to own it, only the government, and government and public are by no means the same, even in systems of representative government. Does any modern citizen think of himself as owning the postal service or the public highways?

The very fact that we live in space and time, to say nothing of our selfish and quarrelsome proclivities, is fatal to all ideals of public ownership that are not severely qualified in theory and carefully circumscribed in practice. Where such ideals are pushed to an extreme, all property is apt to fall into the hands of the government, with the deadly danger in which this places liberty obscured by the fiction of public ownership. In this way the concept of public ownership, though gilded by idealism, comes close to being an apologia for tyranny.

Many supporters of liberty are concerned far more with public liberty, like that exercised in political activity, than with private liberty. It is therefore worth noting that the argument for private property is not only that private liberty depends on it. If privacy is essential to the nourishing of all communal inclinations and capacities, then *public* liberty too depends on *private* property. The quest for communal relations in places open to everyone calls on abilities nourished in private. Thus the vibrant political life favored by many proponents of liberty (with good reason, if often with insufficient reserve) could not arise without a settled system of private ownership.

Enthusiasts for public ownership might protest that laws of private ownership protect not only individuals and their private lives but also giant organizations that are careless or oppressive in their treatment of individuals. The point is incontestable. It is classically illustrated by businesses and factories and the ways they exploit employees and consumers. The liberty of the great does not always readily harmonize with the liberty of the small. This fact has done more than anything else, probably, to discredit the idea of private property. In principle the issue presented is not serious. That liberty is not limitless is a commonplace as old as liberalism itself. All liberty is under regulation, and the liberty of the great needs to be limited for the sake of the liberty of the small. Subjecting factories to this rule in the early decades of the industrial revolution formed a critical stage in the evolution of modern liberty.

In practice, however, the issue is not altogether simple. On one side, the great, by virtue of their very greatness, have power and influence that enable them to threaten the regime of equal liberty. Often, for example, they obstruct just and needed regulations and gain tax advantages that are indefensible in terms of the public interest. On the other side, however, while large nongovernmental organizations threaten liberty, they also support it. They are centers of potential resistance to any government transgressing constitutional limits. Were they deprived of all independence, liberty would be imperiled.

Such problems are in most circumstances neither completely soluble nor completely insoluble. This is perfectly clear from the history of liberal institutions in the nineteenth and twentieth centuries. Maintaining liberty is not easy, but it is not impossible. Hence a liberal society always comprises a multitude of arrangements that are more or less unsatisfactory yet are not worthless. This is to restate the theme of the preceding chapter: a liberal society is always flawed. And this brings us back to the main theme of the present chapter, the liberal stance.

Founding and maintaining liberty is, to be sure, a political and institutional task. More basically, however, it is a personal task. A liberal society will always be rife with evils and imperfections. It will never be a good society. It cannot mold citizens to its own pattern, first of all because its primary aim is to protect their freedom, not to mold them; and also because its own pattern will be flawed. This is why a liberal society places a heavier load of responsibility on the single individual than does any other ideology or society. Of course, individuals always are flawed too. But the best individuals attain a moral level higher than do the best societies. It is a great achievement when a society can form and live within a set of liberal institutions. However, this achievement aims at and is justified by a greater one — an achievement usually requiring both solitude and private property: a free man or woman, often more or less in opposition to society, carrying on the arduous work of discerning and living in accordance with the highest values.

Liberty is an ordeal, and an ordeal cannot be undergone properly in pure spontaneity. It requires a firm and structured personality. This is particularly the case when it has to be undergone alone, as a solitary stance.

Liberty and Character

Character signifies constancy, a state of personal being in which freedom is given moral form. Thereby the incalculability inherent in the freedom of a fallen creature is overcome, or at least greatly reduced. A person of character is someone you can count on. A society without a goodly number of such people would be one in which liberty, dissolving all calculability, would be impossible. And a person without character would be unable to maintain the liberal stance. Character is both transcendental and worldly. Its structure is determined by an orientation toward the unconditional in some form, with Jewish people, for example, toward the Law, with Christians toward God. Yet a person of character, although looking toward transcendence, is rooted in the earth and adept at dealing with the concrete realities involved in earthly life. Further, character is both Christian and pagan. It can be a crystallization of virtues like faith and charity; it can also be a product of classical virtues such as wisdom and courage. As a settled structure, character rests on habit; as a vital order, it is animated by love of truth and by respect for those with whom truth can be shared. If anything like a good society were attainable through liberty, it would be populated mainly by men and women with character testifying, like the scarred hide of an old lion, to moral battles waged and won.

The transcendental aspect of character is manifest in its constancy. As a provisional victory over the worldly, changing self, it is a distant intimation of divine immutability. It is a prophetic foreshadowing of the eternal and changeless selfhood suggested by the concept of redemption. In this way it is a sign of destiny, both as personal salvation and as historical eschaton. The transcendental aspect of character is manifest also in the end toward which it is oriented, namely, a good that is unconditional, hence beyond time and place.

Thus defined, character involves a certain otherworldliness. That is not to say, however, that the world is abandoned, but only that it is not treated as the total environment of life. If character meant world-abandonment, it would be irrelevant to liberty, since liberty is a standard pertaining to worldly institutions and conditions. Character raises one above the world in a way that leaves one standing more firmly than before within the world. It is expressed in resistance to worldly temptations — to the immersion in sensual pleasures that obstructs our vision of the good; to confinement within empirical truth and thus within the visible, objective realities that natural reason readily comprehends; to subjection to conventional opinion, which tells us ceaselessly that the world is all there is. Character is the ability to look steadily beyond the world while remaining an interested and responsible dweller within the world.

It is this two-dimensionality that renders character pertinent to liberty. It guards simultaneously the moral vision and the mundane prudence on which liberty depends. It provides liberty with its discipline. There are, of course, other sources of liberal discipline. Some of these are social, such as custom and tradition; some are legal, whether in the form of statutes or of enforceable rules of other kinds; and some are economic, exemplified mainly by free markets. These are far from ineffective. Indeed, they have inspired ideologies investing one or another of them with an authority that is virtually religious; Burkean conservatism and laissez-faire economics are well-known examples. Nonetheless, they are unreliable. Custom and tradition can sanctify gross prejudice, as in the matter of race; long-standing laws, like those regulating the status of women, can be unjust; and free markets, while often producing material abundance, normally give rise to economic instability and intolerable inequalities. And all of them are fundamentally impersonal. To count on them unconditionally is to subordinate the personal to automatic relationships, and thus to undercut both community and liberty. That is why character, with its inner, personal discipline, is indispensable. It brings order without impersonality. The pervasive immorality that denotes absence of character renders order dependent on power. People who cannot discipline themselves must be disciplined by someone else.

For humanist reason, character consists in a stable and well-ordered soul. What this means is succinctly described in the classical ideal of the cardinal virtues: passions that are moderate and docile (temperance), faculties that play their proper roles (justice), a spirit capable of forcefully defending justice against all threats (courage), and a rational understanding of the final values from which the rules of character are derived (wisdom). These are natural virtues, attainable through the normal powers of will and reason, not depending on faith. The ideal of character implicit in the cardinal virtues runs through classical thought. Major portions of both Plato's *Republic* and Aristotle's *Nichomachean Ethics* can be read as disquisitions on character and on the ways, through reason and not faith, that it can be deliberately cultivated.

The Christian concept of character is not antithetical to the classical concept. It can be construed, indeed, as an amplification of it. The key to the Christian concept lies in the so-called theological virtues: faith, charity, and hope. *Faith* amplifies the wisdom sought by natural reason by setting before it a supreme reality and object of knowledge,

God, unattainable by unaided reason yet not unintelligible. Hence it is that faith can inspire and guide a rational search for understanding it rather than obstructing it. In like fashion, *charity* amplifies justice. Granted, aspects of charity, such as forgiveness, clash with justice as commonly understood. In general, however, justice enjoins the very least that charity requires, and charity departs from justice by going beyond it, for example, by giving more to the other and taking less for oneself, than justice prescribes. Finally, *hope* may be said to amplify all the classical virtues by giving them impetus. Virtues like wisdom and justice would have no place in life if they could never be practiced with favorable consequences. Christian hope, looking at all things from the perspective of eternity, holds that such virtues, in the long run, invariably have favorable consequences. Hope harmonizes moral and practical reason, saving morality from a fatal collision with practicality (a major theme in the moral philosophy of Kant).

The way Christianity amplifies the concept of courage is especially worthy of note. If courage be understood as a state of internal tension, with the ruling parts of the soul mastering fear, then it is questionable whether Christianity affirms courage as a virtue. Courage, so understood, is heroic rather than saintly; it affirms a degree of human self-sufficiency that Christianity does not grant. But Christianity affirms something very similar to courage, if it is not courage itself, and that is fearlessness. It is an amplification of courage in the sense of being based on what Christians would see as more solid grounds. Thomas Aquinas explains this in an interesting way. Aquinas distinguished between *servile* fear and *filial* fear in relation to God. We experience servile fear when we are afraid of God's judgment, when we are frightened by the thought of damnation. We experience filial fear when we apprehend God as "an unfathomable and supreme good" and realize, accordingly, that there is nothing to fear but separation from God (*Summa theologiae*, q. 7, art. 1). Fearing God in a filial way, however, is not the same as being frightened of him. It is more like feeling awe and reverence. And since neither God nor anything else is to be feared in the usual sense of the word, it is a kind of fearlessness.

How deeply situated in the theological virtues such "courage" is can be seen by noting that it rests, as Aquinas construes it, on a particular kind of faith, a faith shaped by charity. Charity comprises love both for God and for neighbor, and it arises spontaneously when God is apprehended through a fully developed faith. Hence Aquinas's characteriza-tion of it as "formed faith." This is the kind of faith that gives rise to the "filial fear" that in truth is fearlessness. The point is simply this, that Christian courage has foundations in the depths of being, as appre-hended in faith and charity. Some will prefer the more purely human courage of the ancients and of humanist reason. Christian courage, it can be argued, is both more realistic concerning human weaknesses and more deeply grounded.

This discussion brings us close to what is probably the fundamen-tal difference between reason and faith in their conceptions of charac-ter. Confidence in reason, and lack of anything like the Christian doc-trine of original sin, inclined ancient paganism naturally toward a conception of character as a human achievement. And so it usually is with protagonists of humanist reason and all who trust in human facul-ties above all else. In contrast, the Christian sense that reason and all other human faculties are more or less deformed by sin necessitates re-liance on divine grace. The natural powers of man are not adequate for the building of character. The issue, broadly, is whether character is a human artifact or a divine gift.

The classical view is appealing, and is rendered plausible, by the ex-istence in ancient times of numerous men of character. Plutarch's *Lives* testifies to the reality of pagan character. Christians should not be as grudging as Augustine was when he characterized the virtues of the an-cients as "splendid vices." This is partly a matter of fairness to the an-cient world and of acknowledging the manifest merits of many inhabit-ants and leaders in that world. But also it is partly a matter of recognizing the sweep of the grace that Christians believe is necessary to human character. Nothing in their faith requires them to deny that grace, and true moral character, might be given to non-Christians. It should be noted, moreover, that Christianity argues the need, not for the *replacement,* but only for the *empowerment,* of human faculties by grace. Reason, for example, is not negated by grace but is given efficacy and guidance. Something of the same sort might be said about the hu-man faculties that give rise to character. Even by Christian standards, then, pagan and humanist character can be reckoned as genuine.

While Christians can and should respect humanist character, they aspire to character in a different way. It is original sin and grace that make the difference. They cannot rely for character on their own qualities, such as their intelligence and determination, for these are weakened and disordered by original sin. Character must be given them. Not that the qualities making for character are despised or neglected, but at the center of character (or one might say making up the circumference of character and giving it form) is something undefinable but fundamental. And it is something given, not willed or deliberately cultivated. To the extent that will and deliberate cultivation enter into the matter, they come out of the given and undefinable element and do not control it. The mystery at the source of character is exemplified by Lincoln. The very survival of America as a unified nation is due to the strength of Lincoln's character. There were times during the Civil War when everything was disintegrating. Not only was the nation split in two. The Northern part was split by diverse factions and personalities. Only Lincoln, at the center, was not distintegrating. But it is hard to explain the strength of his character. He had almost no schooling at all, and his family was broken and more or less unsupportive. Yet there emerged a character that shaped the course of history.

Dependence on grace gives an ironic cast to the Christian concept of character that is not, so far as I know, paralleled in humanist thought. Although human faculties are called into action by grace, they may at first be conspicuously weak, and their initial weakness may stand in striking contrast with their final strength. This can be seen as clearly as anywhere in the figure of Peter. Certainly Peter was a person of character; otherwise he could not have led the early Christian movement, with Paul, nor could he have undergone martyrdom. Yet he is presented in the Gospels as a man without very much natural strength and balance. He is inclined to panic (for example, when walking toward Jesus on the sea), is sometimes spiritually obtuse (as in heatedly denying that Jesus might be crucified), and is easily intimidated (illustrated above all by his denial of Jesus on the day of the crucifixion). He is quite unlike Socrates, who is depicted by Plato as evincing throughout his adult life exceptional discernment, courage, and self-command. That as sorry a figure as Peter, who in his denial of Jesus at the end committed a sin not entirely dissimilar to that committed by Judas, was a recipient of grace nicely illustrates the relationship of the human and divine in the Christian understanding of character.

As the examples both of Lincoln and of Paul suggest, the crucible of the grace that bestows character may be suffering. No doubt factors such as family discipline, personal example, and a good education in many instances play a part. But they may be less essential than is often supposed, and they may not work at all unless tried and shaped by suffering. What may be the most interesting short statement ever made about the sources of character was formulated by Paul in his letter to the Romans. "We rejoice in our sufferings," Paul wrote, "knowing that suffering produces endurance, and endurance produces *character* ['experience' in the King James translation], and character produces hope, and hope does not disappoint us, because God's love has been poured into our hearts through the Holy Spirit which has been given to us" (Rom. 5:3-5). It appears that character, for Paul, is the axis of human destiny. Giving rise to hope and then to love, it is like a raft that carries us on the stream of time into community, into the kingdom of God. The answer to how character is gained lies in the first part of the statement. The source of character is the endurance required by suffering. It would be close to numerous Pauline utterances to say that character is realized through crucifixion with Christ and involves a foretaste of what it means to be risen with Christ.

Christ's crucifixion represents, of course, not only suffering but also dying. And it is arguable that every kind of suffering, as an experience of loss, is a partial death. This suggests that character is cultivated and shown forth in confronting our mortality, whether as the partial death experienced in suffering or as literal death. Rather than being a flight of Christian fancy, this is a staple of pagan wisdom and therefore congenial to humanist reason. It has been etched into Western consciousness by Homer's depiction of men in battle, in the *Iliad,* and by Plato's portrait of Socrates defying the Athenian people in their efforts to silence him and finally, judicially condemned, calmly dying. Owing partly to Socrates' example, dying with composure became a settled standard and test of personal character in the Roman world. As for Christianity, it happens that Jesus did not, in undergoing the crucifixion, evince the imperturbability idealized in ancient thought. But the idea that enduring selfhood is attained not by avoiding but by passing through the ordeal of death is dramatically symbolized by the resurrection.

What has to be said finally is simply this, that character is what makes possible the liberal stance. Character is the inner strength of a free person, perhaps in communication with others, but often more or less alone, watchful of surrounding realities, alert to glimmerings of truth, attentive toward others, and disposed to converse seriously whenever that is possible. The bedrock of such a person is resolute assent to the liberty of others, which is the justice forming the soul of a free person. These things are not always easy. The outer world often arouses fear and resentment in us, and our own fallenness disposes us toward viewing others with hatred or contempt or indifference. It is character that enables us to stand fast. Lincoln again can serve as an example. He is, in many ways, the model of the free person. His life mission was the saving of a liberal America and the liberation of American slaves. He reflected at length and learned continually about the realities of the American situation. He was thoroughly sociable, and conversation was one of the main pleasures of his life (almost anyone with the patience to stand in line could come off the streets and converse with Lincoln if he wished). Yet he was despised and ridiculed by many of the leading men of his time. Even though he passed his days in the midst of frenzied human activity, and dealt with dozens of people every day, he was essentially a solitary figure. Nonetheless, he stood fast, and he did that in a way that shaped the course of the history of liberty.

If the development of character forms the axis of human destiny, as Paul seems to suggest, and freedom lies in the realization of a destiny, then it is a concept we are bound to encounter again in this essay. First, however, it is necessary to probe more deeply into the communality at the heart of the liberal stance.

CHAPTER 7

Dialogue

The Dialogic Ideal

To be in close relationship with others is not to be marching with them in time to stirring music; nor to be united with them in a momentous political cause; nor to share in a common language, culture, and past. While many such experiences may contribute to community, they need to be reflected upon, in solitude and in conversation, to become fully communal. To be closely related to others is to speak reasonably with them, and to hear them, concerning serious matters. We are reasoning beings, and if our lives lose their moorings in reason, they become deranged. If we are reasoning beings, however, then we are speaking and listening beings, for reason lives only through speech. It does not follow that all people should spend all their time speaking and listening. That would abstract them from reality and thus deprive their speech of some of its truthfulness. We have already noted the ivory tower difficulty experienced by professors, most of whom do spend all their time speaking and listening. And not only is it better for the human spirit to be involved in the world and its material urgencies, it is also essential for the human race. There are practical needs to be met, such as food, clothing, and shelter. Even with machines, human beings collectively cannot devote all their time to speaking and listening. These define the ideal center, not the whole shape and structure, of human association.

I have referred to serious speaking and listening as "communication." That is a useful term because of its connection with the term "community." It helps bring out the fact that community is not an established reality, like an ethnic neighborhood, but an act — the act of communication. However, the mere transmission of information, and even advertising, has come to be spoken of as communication. This has become so common as to render the term misleading. I have also called serious speaking and listening "conversation." That is a pleasant and unpretentious term, and suggests the humane and leisured quality that belongs to community. But it has been as carelessly applied as the term "communication." Most of us think of gossip and random exchanges of various sorts as conversation. Hence there is no substitute, I believe, for the term "dialogue" — so overused as to be almost trite, yet retaining a certain philosophic weight and also, being rarely if ever applied to mere exchanges of information, gossip, or idle observations, carrying connotations of seriousness.

Dialogue is directed — owing to its nature and not to passing circumstances — toward the truth. It is a search for truth. Moreover, it is a reasoning search. In this way it has a humanist accent. It is what is often called "dialectic," the kind of argumentation carried on by Socrates in the agora and gymnasia of ancient Athens. Dialectic was the process of question and answer, hypothesis and critique, in which Socrates, as a mission, not a mere diversion, entangled his fellow citizens, finally at the cost of his own life. It is a process of progressive intellectual refinement through setting idea against idea. The term "dialectic," however, like "communication" and "conversation," has been damaged by being excessively broadened. A dialectical schema, often characterized in terms of thesis, antithesis, and synthesis, was used by Hegel for the interpretation of world history. This was done brilliantly and provocatively. History was seen as a kind of grand cosmic argument leading toward a conclusive and all-encompassing truth. It was not a dialogue, however, for it did not necessarily involve listening and speaking, nor did it necessarily involve thinking persons. This basic impersonality had fateful consequences. By virtue of Marx's use of it in developing a different concept of history, it led into modern totalitarianism. In this way it became different from, and antithetical to, dialogue, which presupposes, not merely a reasoning process, but reasoning persons. Dialogue is a personalist concept.

Or better, perhaps, dialogue is an *interpersonalist* concept. The

189

dialogic ideal is not that of a single, thinking person, but of persons thinking together. The questions and answers, hypotheses and critiques, should come from different minds. The dialogic ideal is that of community as enacted by persons engaged in communication, or truth-seeking conversation. Dialogue, then, is a standard prescribing not only a particular human orientation — toward truth — but also human relationships of a particular kind, relationships cast by the necessities inherent in reasoning together. If persons are essentially reasoning creatures, then the interpersonalism of dialogue is a matrix of persons as well as of truth.

Although the dialogic ideal was introduced into Western consciousness mainly by Socrates, it is not confined to the world of Hellenic rationalism. It is represented in Jewish scripture by a listening and speaking God. It is not surprising that the most eloquent defender of dialogue in modern times is a Jewish biblical scholar, Martin Buber. And in spite of the doctrinal proclivities of past Christians, it is powerfully undergirded by the Christian affirmation of truth and of neighborly love. That Christians through the centuries have made so little of dialogue is indicative of their captivity to the potentially antipersonal and antirational ideal of dogma. In any case, the dialogic ideal has deep roots in Western culture.

To identify dialogue and community may seem implausible because dialogue even at its best is unfixed and incomplete. Nonetheless, we are far more nearly at one with other persons in dialogue than we are in any visible outward association. Social entities like small towns, ethnic neighborhoods, sports clubs, and political associations may on casual observation seem like communities. Such groups can no doubt provide emotional satisfactions of a kind not often found in conversation. But such satisfactions attain the summit of intensity in nations at war, in fanatical sects, and in totalitarian states. This shows how treacherous they are. Momentarily satisfying our hunger for community, they can in fact betray community. A true community unites us as the persons we truly are. Dialogue can do this, whereas the impassioned groups often mistaken for communities cause the self to be more or less forgotten. The very ephemerality and fragmentariness of dialogue guard against the group idolatry that so afflicted the twentieth century. The imperfections of dialogue make it plain, contrary to the most virulent ideologies, that community is something we can taste and glimpse from time to time but cannot, in its fullness, ever enjoy on earth.

If we take dialogue as a standard of community, the importance of liberty comes clearly into view. It is not only that dialogue is plainly incompatible with coercion. One must be able to stand off from every idolized group — not because standing off from others is good in itself but because, given the conditions of earthly life, community depends on it. Here, as so often in this essay, the imperfections of all social arrangements direct our attention to the single individual. Dialogic readiness — a predisposition toward speaking and listening — is uncommon among societies, even among free societies. It can be steadily maintained only by individuals able to keep their critical distance from everyone around them. From time to time dialogue may spread from these personal centers into society at large. Hence the importance to society that individuals have the legal right and the moral strength to disentangle themselves from society and be sociably and reasonably separate. The liberty to do this is important to individuals, of course, even if society at large is unaffected. Dialogic readiness, given the rationality and communality of man, has some claim to being called the human posture.

It may seem that allying dialogue and liberty so closely is an excessively academic view, as though a university seminar were the highest realm of liberty. Dialogue needs to be understood, however, as a broad and spacious activity. It comes about not just through words but also through various expressive media, such as paint, stone, and dance. And words are not seriously employed just when philosophic abstractions, like those discussed by Socrates, are considered. Any subject, such as illness, sexual relations, or fighting, takes on dialogic gravity if seen in relation to ultimate human concerns. Hence dialogue can unfold in many places aside from university seminar rooms, for example, in courtrooms and churches, in kitchens and living rooms, in sidewalk cafés and coffeehouses, in legislative halls and business offices. Wherever people are observant, serious, and sociable, there can be dialogue. This is evident in the range of life covered in films and sculpture, in poetry and novels, in philosophy and theology. Dialogue is favored by certain physical settings, such as secure homes and accessible public places. Above all, however, it depends on the spirit of human beings. To prepare people for a dialogic life, and thus for liberty, is the aim, it might be said, of a liberal education.

The dialogic ideal is broad and spacious in its range not only of media and concerns but also of persons. It is, if not precisely egalitarian, universalist. Socrates brought significant truth to light by querying a young slave, and he carried on his conversational investigations in the marketplace and gymnasium, where anyone who wanted to could listen in and take part. Many recoil from dialogue, fearing that the tranquillity resting on their pride or on their state of distraction will be disturbed. It is not clear, however, that anyone is incapable of dialogue in some form. Every person has, if nothing more, a unique story and experience to communicate. The most ordinary lives, as shown in James Joyce's *Ulysses,* involve matters of profound interest to everyone. Martin Buber remarks that in dialogue the other "fills the heavens." By this he means that a dialogic partner is not looked at from the outside, is not appraised objectively, is not compared with anyone else. In this way dialogue equalizes. I don't mean to suggest that dialogue is easy. Its very infrequency indicates it is not. The main obstacle it encounters, however, may be the radical evil that affects everyone rather than deficiencies of intelligence affecting only some. It is therefore arguable that the doorway to dialogue is open to all, and that those who pass through it may dwell for a time in a realm where there is no established rank or social standing.

Admittedly, there are forms of dialogue, such as those between teacher and student, or psychoanalyst and patient, in which there are leaders and followers. Socrates was regarded with unusual respect and was allowed to take the initiative in most conversations. He could be challenged, however, and often was. And he always disclaimed any superior understanding, except for that inherent in his awareness of his fundamental ignorance. Such inequalities may tell us simply that dialogue in the world is never pure, never entirely free of the objectivities that prevail in worldly societies. They suggest, however, without telling us definitively, that some inequalities are compatible with full community. Authority, as a free relationship between persons who have reached varying depths of understanding, can perhaps be truly communal. When Aquinas maintained that there would be inequalities even in the kingdom of heaven, he presumably meant to affirm ontological grounds of inequality. But even if there are such grounds, there is no reason to think they bar anyone from the realms of dialogue.

Because dialogue is essentially personal, it is particularly at home in small groups, where relationships are face-to-face. Large numbers make for impersonality. There can of course be dialogue, or something very much like it, in larger groups, such as representative legislatures and even citizen assemblies, such as New England town meetings. There can even be national dialogues of a sort, as in some political campaigns. And global conferences, political and cultural, seem to exemplify international dialogue. Where a multitude of interlocutors are involved, however, most of them are unavoidably mere listeners, so dialogue is diluted. This is why privacy, or the right of exclusion, is essential to the dialogic ideal. Dialogue could not live were it not cultivated and practiced in numerous small associations, such as university classrooms, courts of law, and groups of friends.

Still, the larger dialogues are no less necessary than the smaller ones. The dialogic ideal dictates openness to all participants and all subjects. Dialogue in essence is a search for all truth and for a communal state in which all persons share in that truth. Exclusive dialogic groups, however indispensable to the life of dialogue, unavoidably compromise the ideal. They need to be balanced by spheres of comprehensive dialogue. The dialogic ideal can be approximated only in societies where there is a polarity of private and public dialogue — where face-to-face speaking and listening can be fully practiced but where the essential openness of dialogue also is recognized and in some fashion practiced.

Reason and Dialogue

We have already noticed the age-long effort, driven often by deep personal conviction, as well as less worthy motives, to set humanist reason and religious faith at enmity with one another. Both sides have contributed to these efforts. Some of the most devout and able Christian thinkers have dramatized their faith by stressing its incongruity with any results attainable by reason. Tertullian and Kierkegaard, both avowing the "absurdity" of true faith, are well-known examples. A comparable antagonism has been encouraged in the opposing camp. Protagonists of humanist reason have contended for the power and integrity of reason by deriding faith. Marx and Nietzsche exemplify the humanist side of the conflict.

In the preceding pages I have argued against this kind of polarization. Freedom is realized only in communication, or dialogue, which is a common effort to see and make known the truth. Dialogue is essentially boundless, not only in seeking all truth and therefore being open to all reality, but also in being open to all willing and competent interlocutors. Authentic dialogue strives toward a universal human community. The impossibility of attaining this goal does not nullify the goal itself or the course that participants are compelled by the very nature of their enterprise to steer. This at any rate is my argument. Following from it is a companion argument: that reason and faith are not completely and irrevocably divided. Not that they can ever reach agreement on all things. There are Christian principles that a humanist must, as a matter of philosophic integrity, reject. And humanist reason will often reach conclusions that a Christian must regard as profoundly wrong. Nonetheless, many of the truths held on each side are comprehensible, and some even acceptable, to the other side. Hence communication is possible. These are considerations, I contend, to which the polarizers on both sides have given insufficient weight.

I discussed the ideal of boundless communication in chapter 1 under the rubric of the universality implicit in both humanist reason and religious faith. I return to these themes here for two reasons. The first is that the purpose of liberty — that of truth-seeking communication — has now been defined. To suppose that the two elemental relationships with being that are represented by reason and faith create a chasm so profound that human voices on one side cannot carry across to the other side is to envision a radical split in humanity. If there actually were such a split, liberty as herein defined would be unthinkable. But not only has liberty been defined, so has communication. The concept of dialogue has enabled us to conceive of communication more accurately and fully. By defining serious communication as dialogue, we may have gained a vantage point that will make it worthwhile to look at the subject again.

Turning first to the side of reason, I can restate my argument in chapter 1 by saying that reason ought not to discourage engagement in any issue. It can clarify, and thus contribute to resolving, every disagreement that divergent human persuasions can create. God's words in the book of Isaiah, "Come now, let us reason together" (Isa. 1:18), should be near at hand, in every human mind and in every human conflict. Reason is the faculty that enables us to elucidate and interrelate everything we think we know. In this sense reason is the faculty of universality. Certainly reason has its limits. As Kant showed, however, to establish these limits is a task belonging to reason itself. It may be that ultimate truth comes from beyond reason. Faith must hold that this is so. However, no human intuitions or insights can do without reason, both to be clarified and to be brought into relationship with one another. And there is nothing that comes into human experience before which reason must halt and say, "We can go no further."

This is to argue for the power of reason. It is also, however, to argue for its responsibility — a responsibility often spurned by ostensible protagonists of reason. No claim to truth can justifiably be rejected unexamined. Reason must accept a fair encounter even with ostensible truths based on faith, as long as their proponents are willing to speak reasonably with them. Avowed rationalists who think they guard their integrity by precluding any dialogue with faith in fact do the opposite. To rule certain arguments out of court without a hearing is irrational. It is not only the cause of reason that is damaged by such attitudes but also the whole world, which can hardly remain a human habitation without the sobering and clarifying power of reason.

The concept of dialogue offers a fuller understanding of reason's universality. Dialogic reason is universal in its relentlessness; it does not allow the process of reasoning ever to stop. There is always room for one more question or criticism. The endlessness of dialogue implies openness, toward arguments from any quarter, toward arguments raising new doubts about conclusions already reached. This is the universality of reason: not that everything is encompassed by reason, but that nothing is shut out. Nothing has a right, or can safely be allowed, to remain unexamined. Dialogic reason in this way is both self-assured and humble — self-assured in refusing to accept any permanent boundaries to its own operations, humble in recognizing that it cannot itself draw such boundaries by reaching a totality that renders all further reasoning needless.

It is possible, of course, to exaggerate the power of reason. There is a modesty befitting to reason. This modesty lies in recognizing its dependence on intuition. A reasoning person needs some strong impressions concerning the overall nature and meaning of reality. The sense that all physical things cohere through causal necessity is an intuition.

So too is the belief that sense experience is somehow veridical, that we are not dreaming. Intuitions can be mistaken, partially or wholly. The materialist concept of history, the purity and proper supremacy of the Aryan race, and the infallibility of the free market are all false intuitions. But all the great truths also are intuitions, in that they are forcibly felt, entirely persuasive, but undemonstrable. The meaningful character of history, the dignity of the individual person, the very power of reason to clarify experience — all arguably are true, and all are intuitions. Without compelling impressions of this kind, false or true, reason would be paralyzed. As Thomas Kuhn has shown, even scientific reason depends on paradigms. Deprived of intuitions, dialogic reason, whether in philosophy, politics, or any other area, would drift into triviality or bombast.

Even in the most mundane matters — those dealt with by secular governments — reason depends on intuition. In the conduct of public affairs, protagonists of reason sometimes suppose that they employ objective, hence public, knowledge, whereas protagonists of faith appeal only to subjective, hence private, convictions. This is manifestly false. Although public debate may involve a good deal of information that is indisputable and in that sense public, it is not decided by objective considerations but rather by convictions that, although sometimes strengthened by factual data, are basically intuitive. Questions like the proper role of government in the economy, the propriety of heavily taxing the rich, and the level and kind of support owed the poor are all answered only on the basis of inner certainties that differ among persons and cannot be translated into outer, or demonstrable, certainties. If this were not so, there would be no competing parties in democratic countries and no split votes in legislative bodies. On every issue, all sides would be brought to agreement. Unanimity among politicians would be as normal as it is among natural scientists. The persistence in politics of deep disagreements among reasonable people testifies to the fact that public discourse is necessarily shot through with intuitive judgments.

Obviously intuitions can be dangerous. The great aberrations of human history occur when people are captivated by false intuitions such as those represented in Nazism. We are not at the mercy of intuitions, however, for reason is not only dependent on intuitions but also is capable of examining them critically and even, in some circumstances, of destroying them. Reason can deal with intuitions in a way that takes into account at once their absolute indispensability and their treacherous potentialities. In short, reason can plunge the fires of fanaticism into the waters of dialogue. Intuitions are at their most dangerous when shielded from dialogic consideration, as happens in political totalitarianism and religious fanaticism.

If reason depends on intuitions yet can master those that are dangerous, then it need not fear or resent the presence of faith in public dialogue. To begin with, Christianity is not necessarily an alien presence in the dialogic realm. What Christians call revelation is simply a powerful intuition concerning the ultimate source and end of all things. This being the case, Christians in the public realm stand on the same ground as does everyone else. Granted, their public positions come from beyond reason. But so do the public positions of all participants in public dialogue. Granted too, Christians have often behaved irrationally. But so have proponents of reason. Christians remain within the bounds of reason so long as they speak in ways that permit a reasoned response. They may readily do this. If they assert that the death penalty should be abolished, or abortion rights restricted, or the poor cared for, they need not simply claim the authority of the Bible. They can discuss practical consequences and can appeal to everyone's intuitions of right and wrong. And they can be attentive to the contrary views of others. Nothing in their faith forbids them to do these things.

Moreover, humanist reason may draw intuitions from Christian sources. Kant's intuition of the ultimate harmony of morality and happiness came from Christian revelation, and Kant was not embarrassed to accept the intuition even though he was not a Christian. And as we have seen, the intuition of human dignity may have originated in Christianity even if reason can defend it on other grounds. The idea of progress was almost certainly an adaptation of Jewish historicism to another context of thought. I do not mean to suggest that reason depends on Christianity, but only that it may, following the example of Kant, find it a source of useful intuitions.

In sum, reason should not unthinkingly recoil from or damn anything whatever. There are many unreasonable things in the world and in human minds. But some of them may be true intuitions, useful to reason. And while many are no doubt false, the world, and even religious faith, need for these to be uncovered and denounced. Dialogic reason possesses both the power and the responsibility for doing this, and for spreading out through the whole of human experience, thought, and discourse. By doing that it reaches its own full stature and it helps in a way no other power can to save the world from the illusions and deceptions that bedevil its affairs.

To argue the dialogic character and role of reason puts one on the side of a familiar and plausible connection. A like argument concerning faith appears much more problematic.

Faith and Dialogue

It is the stubbornly dichotomous propensity of Christians that, above all else, sets them — contrary, I believe, to the deepest implications of their own faith — in opposition to dialogue. This propensity is clearly evident in the New Testament, particularly in Paul's ironic contrast between the "wisdom" of the Greeks and the "folly" of Christians. It was cast in dramatic and enduring symbols in the Augustinian contrast between the city of God and the city of man. It issues naturally in a vision of humankind as divided between two primal categories, destined in eternity to be segregated into heaven and hell, and doomed here on earth, while intermingled physically, to remain so deeply divided spiritually that mutual understanding is impossible. The consequences for dialogue are apparent in the pages of that great primordial Christian, Saint Augustine. Rarely if ever does Augustine try to do that which is so essential to dialogue, and was so warmly recommended by a great humanist thinker of modern times, John Stuart Mill: to enter sympathetically into the minds of those he disagrees with. As already noted, he habitually speaks of them in tones of asperity and outrage, attaching to them such adjectives as "foolish," "vain," and even "insane." In the framework of Augustine's dichotomized universe, such an attitude is understandable. You can't converse thoughtfully and sympathetically with someone God has irrevocably condemned.

We have already seen why Christians should be very worried by this propensity. It is contrary to several major Christian intuitions: that God is love and cannot be understood simply as subsisting in a state of settled enmity with a large part of the human race (or, indeed, even with a small part of the human race); that God is omnipotent and that his merciful regard for fallen men cannot be unavailing; that every person has a dignity that comes from a God so concerned with each of his creatures that he marks even the fall of a sparrow; that God is light and that the greatest human task is therefore seeking the light and sharing it as widely as possible. All these intuitions (with others yet to emerge in the course of the discussion) suggest the possibility of a dialogic Christianity.

The dichotomies pervading Christian attitudes and thought, however, are not purely adventitious. The doctrine of original sin plainly suggests the untrustworthiness of human reason and of human perception generally. And the fact that much of the human race spurns or neglects Christian revelation invites dire inferences. Thus arise the dichotomies. The primary dichotomy in the Christian mind is probably that of believers and unbelievers. Every other dichotomy — between church and world, saved and damned, heaven and hell — seems to start here. Christian scripture relentlessly poses the issue of belief or unbelief. Voiding this dichotomy would, from a Christian standpoint, be reckless, even absurd. No serious Christian can regard it as a matter of indifference whether someone is a believer or not. What needs to be questioned, therefore, is not the existence of the dichotomy, but its meaning. To do that, taking advantage of the perspective offered by the concept of dialogue, is our main task in this section.

I have already argued that true belief is far from the same thing as formal assent. Belief is never altogether stable nor altogether unmixed with doubt. And it is always more or less hidden, even from the believer himself. Actual and professed beliefs may, in the same person, differ considerably. There are no doubt a great many professed believers who are very far from Christian truth. On the other hand, it appears that there are unbelievers who see deeply into the truth, even into truth as Christians understand it. I have already cited the example of unbelievers who fight heroically on the side of personal dignity. I have suggested that the signal weakness of traditional evangelism is its insensitivity to the mysteries and ambiguities of faith. The New Testament hints of a more nuanced view of faith. This is shown in the story I have already cited of the two sons told by their father to go to work in the vineyard, one of whom said he would but didn't, and the other of whom said he wouldn't but did. It is shown also in the story of the father seeking healing for his afflicted son, as recounted in the Gospel of Mark. Charged by

Jesus with the necessity of believing in order for his son to be healed, he cried out, "I believe; help my unbelief!" (9:24).

The distinction between believers and unbelievers, then, is neither clear nor unambiguous. In these circumstances, surely belief should be open to development. It should be the beginning, not the end, of a search for understanding. It should set Christian truth against the doubts that it naturally prompts. It should lead not only to solitary reflection but also to inquiries carried on in the company of others. It should, in a word, be dialogic. This is to restate an earlier point: that a Christian is properly an inquirer — one who knows what he is looking for, but knows it only by looking for it. Christians, however, have ordinarily been highly reluctant inquirers. Not that they have refused all manner of inquiry. The history of theology testifies to the contrary. But Christian inquiry has frequently been attended by tumult and bloodshed. This has happened because the doctrines that define beliefs, and can help believers reflect, have been turned into bulwarks against thought. By objectifying and freezing the mysteries of Christian truth in dogma, faith has refused the unsettled state proper to its own obscure and ambiguous nature. It has foreclosed the possibilities of dialogue.

Dogma is not the same as doctrine, as I have already suggested. A doctrine is a carefully worked-out theory, framed to clarify and help in the transmission of truth. Christianity could not exist without doctrines. They are needed for grasping the intuitions underlying faith, for assisting communication and mutual understanding among the faithful, and for help in identifying and alerting believers to the ill-founded and illogical opinions that are bound to arise within a vital faith. Also, they are needed for evangelical purposes. And finally they are needed for guiding inquiry, for aiding Christians in seeing what it is they are trying to understand more deeply. But this purpose cannot be served if doctrine is given a sacred exemption from all question, doubt, and change. Dogma is presumptuous, a way of closing one's mind against God and withholding the gift of attentiveness from one's neighbor. Dogmas are set in polar opposition to dialogue. Doctrines, in contrast, are potentially dialogic. They provide material so grave and mysterious that it cries out for attention and examination.

Christians have shown throughout history a strong tendency to harden doctrine into dogma. The motives for this are scarcely mysterious: the pride and will to power of priests and clergy, who strive to solidify believers into a mass subservient to ecclesiastical order and discipline; also the insecurity of believers who want to escape from the anxiety of not knowing whether their beliefs are adequate to their salvation. Dogma is a way for proud prelates to suppress doubters, and for anxious believers to suppress doubts. The results are not mysterious either. Dialogue disappears. The hardening of doctrine into dogma entails the hardening of the dichotomies into chasms that render truth-seeking communication out of the question.

To understand the idea of a dialogic rather than dichotomous Christianity, it may help to glance back at the nature of dialogue. A major premise of dialogue, as I have said, is that it never reaches an absolutely perfect and comprehensive truth — a truth foreclosing all further dialogue. Being transcends theories of being. In dialogue the realities being explored and the explorers themselves can never be entirely encompassed by any principle or system of principles formulated in the course of the inquiry. Further questions always can be asked. If dialogue has any proper ending, it is in a state of reverent silence in the face of mysteries that language and theory cannot comprehend. Thus Socrates' final state of ignorance. It was not that Socrates somehow failed, but rather that he carried through the spirit of dialogue to the end.

Particularly useful for understanding the impossibility of formulating doctrines that foreclose all further inquiry, that is, the impossibility of dogma, along with the necessity of continuing dialogue, is the fact that in certain crucial cases — cases concerning matters vital to theology — reason falls into conflict with itself. Its conclusions are not refuted; on the contrary, they are proven. But they are confronted with contradictory conclusions that are also proven. Kant thoroughly investigated and explained this remarkable fact in the *Critique of Pure Reason*. He called these contradictory but equally demonstrable propositions "antinomies of pure reason." He discussed four such antinomies. The third one is convenient for purposes of illustration since it enters into the daily experience of almost everyone. This is the contradiction between personal freedom and natural causality (pp. 384-421).

Leaving to one side the refinements of Kant's formulation of the antinomy, it will suffice for present purposes to note that no one can avoid assuming in the course of everyday life both (1) that freedom is a real factor in all that happens and (2) that all that happens is governed by strict causal necessity. Without the first assumption no one could live in the world as a responsible human being, deliberating on present problems and making decisions concerning them. Without the second assumption, however, one could not count on the people around him to act predictably and thus could not carry on a prudent and responsible life. He could not even navigate in the physical world, for he could not rely on the things in his environment to conform with physical laws. But the two assumptions are mutually contradictory. For Kant, they were not mere assumptions but were demonstrable principles. I maintain here only that they are unavoidable premises of daily life. Common sense juggles them, as in courts of law dealing with crimes and with possible extenuating circumstances. Such juggling is necessary for life in the world but has little philosophical weight. The truth is, strangely, that theory contradicts itself.

It is vital to realize that the contradictory truths, at least in the instance before us, are not nullified by the contradiction. Each remains standing, sustained by reason, even though contradicted. We cannot declare either personal freedom or natural causality to be illusory — a strange state of affairs! What is one to make of it? For Kant, it demonstrated the limits of reason. More broadly, it demonstrated the incapacity of the human mind to grasp the ground and totality of all things — an end toward which reason continually impelled us. It is this incapacity, I believe, that concerns us in trying to understand the relationship of Christianity to dialogue.

To apply Kant's theory of the antinomy of pure reason to religious doctrine, someone might charge, is to play fast and loose with Kant, who was concerned, not with any claims to revelation, but with the effort of reason all on its own to reach ultimate truth. I grant that such was Kant's intention. But reason, as he conceived it, was the human faculty that drove toward comprehension without limits. When religion frames doctrine, it casts ostensible revelation in rational form and makes itself subject to the Kantian critique. Someone might charge as well, in relation to my use of the Kantian antinomy, that Kant did not work out a concept of dialogue or ally himself with Socrates' method. I grant that too. Yet Kant believed that we must continue to reason, striving toward one unified conclusion, in spite of reason's limitations. Dialogue, even though unrecognized by Kant, is reasoning of a kind that meets these demands. It never reaches a general theory in which all reality is comprehended, yet it never gives up the effort to reach that unreachable theory.

It is not surprising to see, then, that some of the most important Christian doctrines are antinomies. The doctrine of the Trinity, for example, states that God is Father, Son, and Holy Spirit — fully each one of these three — yet one God, without qualification. As a rational claim, that is an antinomy. Also, the doctrine of the incarnation maintains that God became man; Jesus was not just godlike, or inspired by God, but was simply and completely God. According to the same doctrine, however, Jesus was simply and completely a particular human being, living in a particular time and place, finite and mortal like every other human being. That is another antinomy. Finally, orthodox doctrine holds that human beings are free, hence responsible for their deeds, and properly punished (if not forgiven) for their misdeeds; at the same time, they are totally dependent on divine grace for any righteousness they achieve. It is arguable that Christian truth is not weakened by such antinomies. Rather, it draws vitality from the tensions thus generated — a rather Socratic view.

Properly apprehended, the antinomies compel us — Christians and non-Christians alike — to maintain a dialogic stance. We cannot give up either of the principles that enter into a genuine antinomy, yet we are forced to regard each principle as being, so to speak, on the defensive. Each principle claims to be the whole truth, yet must concede the presence of a countertruth. Inquirers face a mystery that can be explored indefinitely but cannot be exhaustively enclosed in any verbal formulation. Dogma obscures this mystery by freezing believers in verbal formulations. This happens even when the dogma formally embraces an antinomy. The dialogic life that arises from the limits of reason is stifled. Thus the doctrine of the Trinity, or of the dual nature of Christ, is traditionally treated as something to be *confessed,* not discussed. But a Trinity that is confessed but never probed dialogically becomes a dead deposit in the believer's memory, weighing down rather than vitalizing faith.

The antinomies tell us that the doctrinal enterprise (in which Christians necessarily are involved) must remain unfinished. As reason passes beyond the sphere of ascertainable facts and approaches being itself (or God), it falls into irresolvable contradictions. The ultimate questions cannot be definitively answered. This is not skepticism, since each of the contradictory propositions is held as true. But such propositions are not settled and final. They invite further thought. The evil of dogma is that it not only refuses the invitation but also tries to revoke it. In doing this it falsifies the nature of reason and forecloses dialogue. Also it falsifies reality, both worldly and transcendent. It would put human theories in place of being and of the intuitions in which being is humanly apprehended. From the Christian quarter the objection might be raised that the intuitions embodied in the great Christian doctrines are not human but divine. Indeed, such an objection seems to derive from the very idea of revelation — truth that is given to us. But while revelation is (for a Christian) divine, the doctrine is human. And as human, it is subject to question, doubt, and revision.

I do not contend that the need for dialogue lies solely in the antinomies. The human mind is notoriously fallible, diverted from truth both by finitude and by sin. Only by being questioned does it become reasonable, and only by being continually cognizant of questions does it remain reasonable. This is to say that reason in all its realms is essentially dialogic. This is largely a matter of common sense. We are little tempted by dogmas in matters of everyday life. It is mainly as we touch the great issues concerning the meaning of life that the dogmatic temptation begins to invade our minds. And it is here that the theory of the antinomies stands guard. It dramatizes the fact that nowhere can reason legitimately come to rest, and above all not in those ideas in behalf of which men are inclined to die and kill.

The dialogic and antidogmatic position may be expected to appeal to most adherents of humanist reason. There are, of course, exceptions, mainly humanists who anticipate the eventual attainment of one final, all-encompassing truth through science. They anticipate, in effect, that reason itself will give rise to dogma. Among these was John Stuart Mill, who believed that reason would eventually comprehend all things. But he was alarmed by this prospect. Mill believed not only in science but also in dialogue, and consequently discussed the possible need for "devil's advocates" whose job it would be to question truths that had in fact been scientifically settled. Since Mill's time, however, such apprehensions have subsided. Schools of thought like existentialism and deconstruction have rendered the idea of a final, all-encompassing, scientifically certain truth incredible. The more serious defense of dogma, and consequent hostility to dialogue, comes from the side of religion. How are Christian dogmatists to be resisted?

Partly, of course, on the grounds laid out above. The inherent limits of reason, as manifest in the antinomies — both those laid out by Kant and those inherent in major Christian doctrines — as well as in the whole course of daily life, imply the inconclusiveness of all doctrine. There is, however, in Christianity itself a principle that undermines dogma. It figures prominently in Christian thought from the beginning, and has already been discussed. God, the creator of freedom, seeks from human beings a free response. More precisely, God seeks a genuine response. A forced response can only be one feigned in order to evade a physical threat. And a response elicited through psychological manipulation, as in "brainwashing," or in "hell and brimstone" sermons designed to frighten people into conversion, cannot engage the whole being of the believer, and thus can be no more genuine than a forced response. Faith has to be undertaken and sustained in freedom or it is worthless. But if that is so, faith entails thought. A genuine response is a thinking response, and a thinking response is one in which every proffered doubt, whether from within or from without, is faced and reasonably dealt with. In other words, the matrix of faith is dialogue, inward or outward.

This brings us back to one of the core ideas of this essay — that Christianity is properly Socratic. If Christ is the Logos, the order and meaning of all things, and if reason is given to men and women by God, then an unreasoning Christianity is untrue to itself. A Socratic Christianity entails no watering down of the gospel. To embody a truth that is unique, unsurpassable, and a source of salvation for the entire human race is of the essence of Christianity. Someone who regards Christ as just one of numerous ways of approaching God; or as a tentative truth, destined sometime to be surpassed by a better one; or as effective for some people but not for others, is not a Christian. Hence the irrepressible issue of belief and unbelief. But belief does not imply a dogmatic refusal to deal reasonably and carefully with doubts from within or from without. Dogmatism can seem like spiritual strength, but actually it is weakness. A strong faith would not recoil from dialogue.

What is at stake here is one of the primary attitudes called for by the human situation, that of openness toward transcendence. I argued earlier that this attitude is incumbent on humanist reason. But it is also incumbent on religious faith. Openness is an acknowledgment of our fundamental dependence. Knowledge and insight are given us, not created on our own initiative. That revelation, too, is given us is implied by the very name. It consists in what is revealed. As we have seen, our fundamental dependence — on the unbidden insight or sudden inspiration — is a commonplace among thoughtful scientists and artists. It should be equally commonplace among those who claim that they apprehend things revealed by God. That it is not suggests, paradoxically, mistrust of the very source of revelation.

Christians, then, are not in a completely different epistemological position than anyone else. Not only must revelation, like a scientific hypothesis or an artistic inspiration, be given to them. It must, so to speak, be given to them afresh every morning. Faith needs continual renewal. Christians are not masters of transcendence any more than scientists or artists are. In relation to encompassing being, they are dependents. Dogma, however, would reverse this relationship. It would seize the gift of revelation and make it a human possession, no longer a gift. It would replace a divine truth with a human artifact. Christians maintain due respect for God only so far as they remain open toward transcendence. And this they do only by maintaining dialogic relations with the human world around them.

I argued earlier that secular rationalists ought to accept Christians as fellow interlocutors in public dialogue. Here we are led to the converse proposition, that Christians should, *in accordance with the deepest requirements of their faith,* enter into public dialogue with humanist reason. The church is not enough. Christians are open toward transcendence only so far as they are open toward all human beings, and they remain thus open only by resisting the temptation to withdraw from the world and sequester themselves in enclaves where they can cultivate the stark dichotomies toward which spiritual pride draws them. I do not mean to argue that a dialogic faith incurs no risks. It is obvious that faith can be shaken in encounters with reasonable doubt. There is, however, no alternative. By withdrawing into dogma, faith betrays revelation by reducing it to a human possession. And it betrays doctrine, with the help of which faith can increase its own depth and breadth, by transforming it from a guiding light into an intellectual fortress. Christians who find the sociable and inquiring spirit of the great Athenian questioner strange or threatening have not fully taken the measure of their own faith.

But where does dialogue lead? Certainly not to a single, rationally demonstrable, universally held conclusion. And not to a settlement of the controversy between humanist reason and religious faith. Then where? Dialogue leads, as we have already seen, to the boundaries of all that can be comprehended through concepts. It leads to realities we cannot clearly speak of because they lie beyond the conceptual realm.

The Mystery of Being

All of us, given the pressures of practical life, the objectifying powers of our faculties, and the urges of pride, tend to think of being, or the real, as made up altogether of objects — of things of the sort we can perceive through the senses, analyze through reason, and locate in space and time. In that way, we can master them. This is apt to be so whether we look at reality through the eyes of humanist reason or of religious faith. For the former, the world of objects is often taken to be all there is. For the latter, there is another world. It is different, presumably, from the world of objects. It is still, however, usually thought of as a world of things that can in principle be seen and touched and rationally understood, that is, objects. This is one of the hazards of doctrine. So perfectly fitted to the work of objectification are our sensuous and intellectual faculties, so essential to the practical exigencies of life are the operations of these faculties, and, finally, so strong is our drive toward preeminence and power, even when touched by truths we believe to be revealed, that for most of us imagining anything as real is very nearly the same thing as imagining it as an object.

It is not surprising, then, that we objectify not only each particular thing, experienced or imagined, but also all things collectively. We picture the universe as a whole as a vast conglomeration of objects. And it follows, since we imagine this conglomeration as bound together in a system of causal relationships, that we imagine the universe itself as a single great object that we might sometime, somehow, examine and rationally understand.

This spontaneous objectivism, however, even though deeply rooted in our nature and situation, produces profound misconceptions both for humanist reason and for religious faith. To begin with, the universe as a whole (assuming that such a phrase has any meaning) is not an object. It is not accessible either to sensible intuition or to rational analysis. Where

— outside the universe — could one stand in order to examine the universe? Space and time presumably are comprised in the universe. It follows, however, that the universe cannot occupy a location within space and time — an essential characteristic of an object. We think of the universe as limited in space and beginning in time, yet in doing that we fall into the first of Kant's antinomies of pure reason and are compelled immediately to think of it as limitless in space and without any beginning in time. What is the universe, then, if not an object? That is very hard to say — simply because it is not an object. The universe is a mystery.

It is a striking fact, however, that not only is the universe a mystery. So is every particular reality within it. Some realities, like rocks and machines, do not seem very mysterious. Accessible to sensual observation in every detail, and knowable in every element and part, they impress us as thoroughly objective. Yet even these, the least mysterious of realities, cannot be exhaustively objectified. *This* rock and *this* machine are mysterious, at the very least, in being characterized by a "thisness" that is rationally incomprehensible yet is unquestionably "there." In short, every particular thing is mysterious by virtue of its very particularity.

When we realize the mystery of *all* reality and of *every* reality, we become aware of being immersed in mysteries. It is borne upon us that the reach of our concepts is far shorter than we had imagined. And we are compelled to think that the world of objects, hitherto assumed to be the sum of reality, is only an aspect of reality, as implied by the philosophy of Thomas Aquinas, or merely a human way of looking at and understanding reality, as argued by Kant. How is sense to be made of a reality that transcends all concepts?

One noteworthy feature of this transcendent reality is that it is hierarchical, or at least appears to be. A tree strikes us as more mysterious than a rock, a horse as more mysterious than a tree, a man or woman as more mysterious than a horse. And humans have long conceived of beings — angels and God — that are, so to speak, pure mysteries, entirely beyond sensual intuition and rational comprehension. Noteworthy too is the fact, presupposed by the hierarchy just sketched, that dignity is proportional to mystery, at least in our eyes. The more mysterious the reality, we seem to feel, the greater the respect we owe it. We do not hesitate to discard a rock we have no use for, but to think of a human being as something that might be used and then discarded — we regard that as the work of an evil mind.

The mystery of human persons is particularly worthy of comment. We cannot doubt the reality of persons, as we can the reality of angels or of God. And in casual encounters they do not usually seem very mysterious. They are all around us, every day. Yet their mystery in many instances is as evident as that of the whole universe. I can no more understand completely the particular person with whom I work or live, and therefore intimately know, than I can the totality (whatever that may mean) of the things that exist. One way we acknowledge this fact is by attributing to humans the quality of freedom, the capacity for choice. There is a sense, of course, in which freedom is known very well by all of us, for all of us are free. We apprehend freedom in some fashion whenever we choose or face a responsibility. Yet it is noteworthy that Kant denied that freedom was something we know on the evidence of inner experience. It is merely an inference from the moral law. We know our own freedom only in knowing our subjection to the categorical imperative. And in ascribing freedom to someone else, we are not so much claiming knowledge as we are confessing the presence of something incomprehensible, that is, the power of initiating unpredictable actions and of carrying on a life that is unforeseeable. In both cases, we are facing a mystery.

It is surprising that the mystery of being is much of the time forgotten, for it is quite plain and undeniable once pointed out. And even when it is not forgotten, it is apt to be subordinated somehow to the objectivity of being. The objects around us seem like hard, indubitable realities, the mystery that attends them like shadows cast in the sunlight — derivative and less than fully real. Such mental habits are seemingly reflective of human nature and the human situation. As we have already seen, however, they are also reflective of human fallenness. Not only out of practical necessity, but also out of pride, of a will to dominion, I strive continually to objectify. If something is real, I assume that I can specify its qualities and say what it is. But if something evades my efforts to look at it squarely and to speak about it definitively, its indubitable reality begins to fade. And, consciously or not, I want it to fade. As a mystery, it humbles me. In some such fashion as this we come to think of the objective character of a thing as primary, its mystery as secondary. And often we forget the mystery altogether.

Actually, however, the mystery is primary, for the object is an abstraction from the fullness of reality — the reality not only of the particular thing but also of the encompassing universe. We experience this fullness when we love someone, and even when we love a particular place or thing. To forget the objective character of a reality leaves you with the reality in its wholeness and mystery. To forget the mystery leaves you with a mere abstraction — with nothing, even though you may think you possess the reality. This matters relatively little when we are dealing with things like rocks, which are nearly pure objects (although insensitivity to the mystery of the physical world is no doubt at the source of much environmental damage). But it matters very greatly when we are dealing with persons. Even the classifications of social scientists and organizational managers can be dangerously depersonalizing. Abstractions arising from racial prejudice or ideological commitment, as was learned during the twentieth century, have potentially murderous implications.

The mystery of being cannot be dissipated, it is vital to note, by extensions of human knowledge. Some mysteries undoubtedly can be rationally elucidated; that is, knowledge can be extended. Presumably the range of psychological knowledge will be widened in coming centuries and in that sense some of the mystery surrounding and pervading personal existence will be drawn into the realm of objectivity. But will the mystery of someone you love ever disappear? The mere idea is repellent. To think merely of the degree to which knowing someone depends on forms of insight like empathy, which is the very opposite of objectification, makes it possible to sense the perdurable mystery of a person. And even in the humblest of realities, the mystery of particularity, of *thisness,* will always be impervious to objectification. The tiny margin of mystery surrounding the pebble in my hand will survive every triumph of science. And so will the mystery of all things together. No scientist, we can safely assume, will ever discover how to get outside the universe in order to examine it objectively. Knowledge, then, can be indefinitely extended, but the incongruity between reality as intellectually known and reality in itself cannot be eliminated. Indeed, this is an element of the mystery: that objective knowledge can be enlarged further and further while the mystery of being remains irreducible.

Given our drive toward intellectual and practical command of things, some will look on the mystery of things impatiently. They will bridle at the limits thus placed on human comprehension and control. Yet "the mystery of being" does not refer to mere refractory matter; it refers to the sacred depths of the universe. Even though we try ceaselessly to objectify all we encounter, if we could accomplish such an aim, and render the world around us purely and translucently objective, we would, so to speak, spiritually freeze to death. The concept of bureaucracy is worth contemplating in this connection, as in others. Ideally, a bureaucracy is a group of human beings reliably rational in their relationships and actions. The risks of impulse and treachery have been removed, or at least greatly lessened. We cannot help being attracted in some ways by the prospect of the human race so thoroughly and perfectly organized. It suggests a time without tension, war, or historical uncertainty. Yet it is chilling, for the indwelling and encompassing mystery of things has vanished. We see a world without danger, but also without love or reverence. This shows how ambiguous our relations with the mystery of being are. On the one hand, we are continually in contention against most of the mysteries we encounter, and try to comprehend and control them. On the other hand, we do not wholeheartedly want to succeed. The way reality so ceaselessly eludes and defies our objectifying enterprises is exasperating, yet it is also strangely reassuring.

Seen from the Christian standpoint, the mystery of being is a congenial concept. God, after all, is not an object. And the feeling of awe we sometimes experience in the face of things we cannot comprehend or master, such as a great storm or a mountain, is appropriate. It is a recognition of the mystical glory of God's creation. This does not mean Christianity opposes all efforts to understand and control the world around us. On the contrary, it sees such efforts as sanctioned in principle by God's injunction that men and women "fill the earth and subdue it; and have dominion over the fish of the sea and over the birds of the air and over every living thing that moves upon the earth" (Gen. 1:28). However, this is not a grant of absolute sovereignty. People who acknowledge no limits on human dominion are engaged, even if they call themselves "Christians," in a project of self-deification. On the other hand, those who pause before the mystery of being show their respect for creation, and this is so even if they call themselves "atheists." Standing before the mystery of being, believers and unbelievers alike are on numinous ground.

Why discuss these things in a chapter on dialogue? Simply because dialogue keeps us more or less continually in contact with the mystery of being. This is inherent in the fact I have already emphasized, namely,

211

that dialogue is inherently inconclusive. The proposition that dialogue never reaches an all-comprehensive theory is another way of saying that we cannot meaningfully speak of the universe as a totality. The concept of dialogue is paradoxical. It is thoroughly rationalist, for it says that we should never cease from reasoning. At the same time, it recognizes the limits of reason, for it is those very limits that command us to continue to reason. To live dialogically, as Socrates did, is to reason tirelessly about realities that yield themselves endlessly to rational exploration but are rationally unconquerable. It is to live on the edge of the mystery of being. And there is another way in which dialogue places one in proximity to the mystery of being.

There are always, in dialogue, the persons who are carrying on the dialogue but are not wholly comprised within it — the "I" and the "Thou." These provide another means of access to the mystery of being.

The Mystery of Personality

The mystery of persons we care for is less likely to be overlooked and denied than is the mystery of any other reality, and it is noteworthy that the better we know someone the more mysterious we may feel that person to be. The mere particularity of someone we have loved and known intimately for many years sweeps us helplessly outside the bounds of the objective world. The mystery of a rock, although perhaps profound for a poet such as Blake, who saw the world in a grain of sand, is negligible for most people. The mystery of a mountain, a tree, or a horse, while momentarily striking, may be soon forgotten. Even God, the most compelling and absorbing of all mysteries for some, for many is easily overlooked and neglected, or else is reduced to a hardened doctrinal formula of one kind or another. Almost all of us, however, greatly care for one or a few human beings, and the utter inscrutability of that one or few is apt to engross our minds, especially when death steps into the picture. Here the notion that a person is on no account to be used merely as a means to some desired end is not a moral theory but an immediate and compelling imperative.

In spite of this fact, most of us, most of the time, deny or fail to notice the mystery of persons. The reasons for this are various and familiar. In crowds, particular persons are lost from sight; in business and governmental organizations, members have to be judged in terms of their functions. When we are alarmed, as in time of war, we see many as mere embodiments of enmity and danger; when we are tired or self-absorbed, we are inattentive. Many seek a standpoint of superiority by reducing others to the level of a supposedly inferior race, class, or nationality, while some, for the sake of science, systematically reduce personality to observable and quantifiable characteristics. In such ways as these, we are engaged more or less continuously in the enterprise of depersonalization. At times and in limits, this is clearly legitimate and perhaps unavoidable. At other times, as starkly shown in the annals of war and tyranny, it is gratuitous and gravely evil.

How can the tide of depersonalization be resisted? The Christian imperative of love for neighbor — for anyone you happen to encounter — is a possible answer. It seems to say that the mystery in a person you love should, and therefore can, be discerned in every person you meet. It calls us to a venture in universal personalization. Hardly anyone, of course, can *love* every person who is encountered. Jesus may be the only plausible example in history of someone who actually did this. It seems worth noting, then, that there is another standard, similar to love, but nearer the capacities of ordinary people.

This standard is respect — an attitude toward others that is weaker than love but still cognizant of their mystery. Respect can emerge more or less spontaneously. In the ordinary course of life we repeatedly come upon certain "things" — persons given little attention at the moment — that refuse to be mere things. They may do this by behaving unpredictably or, with a mere look, making those looking at them realize they are being looked at. We may at first try to kill or enslave these exasperating "things." But the time comes, as argued by Hegel in celebrated passages in his *Phenomenology of Mind,* when we realize that these supposed things are beings like ourselves. Something like respect begins to emerge. We realize that they cannot be fully known through rational analysis and cannot be effectively examined except by being given proper names and being questioned and listened to. What has happened is that I as a subject, intent on attaining security and mastery in a world of objects, have encountered another subject. Thus arises the possibility of intersubjectivity, or community. If respect is not a fully satisfactory substitute for love, it may at least serve as a way station on the journey to that goal.

It may seem that attention to the mystery of personal being might best be sustained by attention to a mystery immediate to every person — the self. Without question the self is a constant presence and a mystery. The mystery sooner or later becomes apparent to anyone who tries to follow the ancient maxim of the Greeks, "Know thyself," for the task it sets is arduous and beyond completion. You may, of course, undergo psychological analysis and engage in earnest and prolonged introspection. You may write memoirs or an autobiography. You may in such ways paint a detailed and vivid picture of yourself. But every such picture has one large lacuna. That is the self that painted it. You can no more get outside yourself for purposes of objective examination than you can get outside the universe. Moreover, the self that paints a picture of the self is not a passionless source of light but rather is a center of remorse, pride, aspiration, and countless other feelings related to the self. These feelings inevitably shape every project of self-analysis. Even the best autobiography is by no means definitive. The mystery of personality is nowhere more evident than in the irony of a self that is intimate and ever-present yet forever beyond objective knowledge. The mystery of being, then, is immediately present to every person simply in the self.

It would be a grave misunderstanding, however, to suppose that the self is, as it were, a private universe. The self is real only in relation to others, and one is fully related to others only through love. For self-exploration to be fruitful, others too must be examined and their relations with the self must be examined. To become absorbed in the self and forget about those who are loved and respected, and also those whom one failed to love or respect, would cause the self to disappear. Illustrative is the fact that good biographies and autobiographies are concerned mainly with friends and associates, as well as enemies, of the subject.

In the Christian vision, the mystery of human personality is not just one mystery among many others. It is a key to the mystery of all being. This is partly because, as we have already seen, all being is personal in Christian eyes. Created by a personal being, God, reality in its deepest and most distant reaches is personal. Not that a stone, or tree, or lake in itself is a person (although the fact that we give names to lakes and mountains and occasionally have a strong emotional attachment to some natural entity like a tree or river may raise a question in this regard). Every such reality, however, is created by and thus reflects a personal being. God is in the whirlwind and the sea and the light. Further, all these things were not only created by God, they were created *through* the Word that became flesh, that is, through a human person, Jesus (John 1:3). The Christian universe originates in divine and human personality. And beyond that, humans are in some sense the preeminent creature. They were created in God's "image and likeness," and were given custody of all the earth. Somehow they are more important even than angels. Christ became a human person, not an angel. In sum, the Christian universe is drenched in personal being. Our access to such being in ourselves and others is access to all reality.

If the key to the mystery of being lies in the mystery of human personality, the key to the latter (still looking at things from a Christian standpoint) lies in the drama of sin and redemption. The drama begins, of course, with original sin. Man is morally ill and near to death. The illness lies in being turned in the wrong direction, away from God, the primal person. Following from that initial repudiation of personality, those affected by original sin repudiate every finite person. All sin is depersonalization, and a life of sin consists in the creation of a world of objects. In pride, one objectifies for the sake of mastery; in distraction one welcomes objectification as an escape from finite, responsible selfhood. Either way personality, in the self and in others alike, is denied.

Human resources (still looking at the matter from a Christian standpoint) provide no way out. Captivated by pride, or lost in distraction, humans can only throw themselves again and again into hopeless enterprises of self-salvation. Such enterprises are hopeless because man has cast away his created capacities for love and understanding. Stricken with radical evil, he cannot save himself. He depersonalizes all that he touches. He is imprisoned in a world of objects. The power of recognizing and esteeming personality, that is, the power of love, can be restored only by God, the primal person. This is a work of grace, and it is a saving work because, in the community created by love, lost humanity is rediscovered. Only as this happens — only as a drama of sin and redemption — does human life have meaning. The gist of Christianity is the belief that this drama was set on foot by the life, death, and resurrection of Christ. Through Christ the doors of human destiny were opened to all humankind. And the heart of being itself was thereby revealed.

Within this drama there are numerous mysteries, or more precisely, enigmas that take on an aura of mystery in the context of the drama of redemption. One of these — inherent in the antinomy of freedom and mechanical causation — is the impossibility of assessing objectively the degree of guilt in any particular act of wrongdoing. The guilty person knows infallibly of his guilt. Yet from a strictly objective standpoint, there is no guilt at all since every human act is causally conditioned in its entirety. On the other hand, from a moral standpoint, like that assumed by Kant in the *Critique of Practical Reason,* every misdeed, regardless of the circumstances surrounding it, involves an irreducible element of personal responsibility. Indeed, it is not immediately apparent how, from a Kantian perspective, there can even be extenuating circumstances. The issue thus presented is theoretically irresolvable. To say that the truth is "somewhere in between" the extreme positions is an evasion of the issue, not a solution. And the issue is far from academic, even though it involves the kind of philosophical complications that only academicians are apt to feel at home with. It plants at the center of every life a disconcerting enigma: rarely if ever can I judge conclusively of guilt and innocence — for someone who has injured me, for example, or even when I have inflicted the injury. Courts of law have to rely on rough approximations of common sense, fusing mechanical causation and moral freedom, and these have little or no philosophical standing.

Another mystery involved in the drama of redemption has to do, not with the nature of human guilt, but with its seemingly incurable character. How can there be such a thing as radical evil? It is a puzzle familiar to every morally serious person and is consequently as well known to reason as to faith. Everyone experienced in the struggles of moral life knows that selfishness (which we can take as roughly equivalent to sin in general) employs a rich variety of forms and disguises and is nearly unconquerable. Repressed in one form, it immediately emerges in another, perhaps at first unrecognized. It is often subtle and hidden, yet seemingly always present. It can easily be envisioned as an ingenious and tireless demon. It is almost universally condemned. It has been assaulted in innumerable moral struggles. Yet it is always at hand. How can its tenacity be explained? It cannot.

No less familiar than guilt, yet no less mysterious, is the forgiveness that in some sense overcomes it. It seems to be a kind of nullification of the past. But how can what has been done be undone? And who may forgive, and what may be forgiven? May so enormous a crime as the Holocaust be forgiven? If so, by whom? May an Arab or an Oriental, born long after the Holocaust, forgive its perpetrators, or must forgiveness come from the victims, most of whom are dead? Or must it come from the ultimate ground of the moral law, that is, God? If so, does that mean that humanists cannot be merciful? Does forgiveness replace punishment, or must the principle of retribution ("eye for eye, tooth for tooth") be in some manner observed? If a misdeed is punished in proportion to its gravity, is forgiveness still necessary? And what role is played by moral change? Can a criminal who is penitent but morally unchanged be forgiven? Such questions can be multiplied indefinitely, and they point toward the mysteries that well up when people are free to fashion their own lives, thus becoming involved in the drama of sin and redemption.

This drama, in Christian eyes, is in no way merely an epiphenomenon. It is the unfolding of being itself. As already noted, all things were created through the Word, that is, with a view to the divine plan of redemption. This means that the created universe was not neutral ground, where anything at all might happen. It was formed as a theater of salvation. And in its archetypal enactment — the crucifixion of Jesus — the central role in the drama of salvation was played by God himself, incarnate in a human being. The creator of the universe was the principal figure in the tragedy through which the human race is redeemed. These articles of Christian faith, although rationally incomprehensible, express as strongly as anything could the sense that the redemption of a person is not an event on the order of saving a species of fish from extinction. It involves the deepest ground of all reality.

While humanist reason cannot by its very nature fully accept the Christian understanding of the mystery of redemption, it is by no means lacking in personalist insight. To begin with, humanists have unquestionably been sensitive to the mystery of personal being. Just to recall the Greeks will suffice to show this. Homer, the tragedians, the histories of Herodotus, the dialogues of Plato: works such as these demonstrate that even though the *dignity* of every person, simply as a person, was not fully perceived by the Greeks, the *mystery* inherent in personal being was well known to them. As for the modern world, the names of non-Christian writers such as Proust, James, and Joyce place beyond question the ability of humanism of various kinds to look into and explore the mysteries of personal being. Indeed, it seems manifest that literary sensitivity to the enigmas of personal being is a kind of love. Beyond this, the idea that authentic human life is an enactment of the drama of fall and redemption has captured the imagination of humanists no less than Christians. Sometimes the drama has been construed in collectivist rather than personalist terms. In the case of Marxism, this had terrible consequences for the whole earth. But in a humanist such as Plato one sees the drama depicted in a way that is quite congenial to Christians.

A reader is unlikely to ask what all of this has to do with dialogue. I have already brought out the personalist character of dialogue. Dialogue is reasoning of a kind that bars the persons who are reasoning from ever disappearing into their conclusions. There is always someone with one more question to ask. And not only that, but for dialogue to concern itself with sin and redemption seems particularly fitting. Dialogue is the form of our common quest for truth, and the most important truth we seek in our universal humanity is that of human destiny, and this destiny is shaped largely by human selfishness and irresponsibility, on the one hand, and by acts of repentance and reform on the other hand. This is a statement to which, in broad terms, humanists might readily assent. The great question before us is what happens to and is done by the human race — a race deeply inclined toward both moral squalor and spiritual grandeur. Every person is deeply implicated in that question. But the answer to the question is beyond the sure and demonstrable comprehension of us all. In this way it calls on us to reason together, to engage in dialogue to explore in common our common destiny. And doing this is not only of spiritual but also of practical importance. As the nineteenth and twentieth centuries showed, interpretations of human destiny have a decisive impact on the things nations and leaders and parties do. If such interpretations had to sustain themselves in a dialogic public realm, not only might our understanding of ourselves and our neighbors be enlarged, but historical tragedies might also be avoided.

To speak of our common destiny may remind us of the activity through which humans bear collective responsibility for bringing that destiny to light and pursuing it.

Politics and the Dialogic Ideal

The dialogic ideal plainly implies a political ideal. Major decisions of the polity should — however rarely they actually do — arise from searching public discussion. In the same way that scientific, philosophical, and religious dialogue ideally eventuates in common agreement on the truth, political dialogue ideally arrives at a wise consensus on public policy. Governmental authorities should normally be confined to this consensus. The ideal is that of a dialogic polity. Political action should follow from, but normally not go beyond, the results of political dialogue. The means of reaching, or at least striving toward, this ideal are at once so well known and so various that it is neither necessary nor feasible to discuss them here. The Western nations have developed numerous forums for public discussion, such as parliaments and courts, universities and newspapers, radio and television. These are supplemented by informal forums, such as cafés, coffeehouses, and private gatherings. Forums of this kind can be arranged and used in diverse ways. The force of the ideal of a dialogic polity derives above all from the moral necessity of giving truth as wide a rein in human affairs as possible. If man is a creature made for seeking and dwelling in the light, then politics should to the utmost possible degree be carried on in the light.

Not only does the well-being of society dictate that dialogue govern political affairs, so also does the well-being of dialogue. Disconnected from practical urgencies, dialogue is apt to suffer a loss of sobriety and pertinence. Reason often resists this connection. As we see in the philosophy of Plato, it has a celestial inclination, drawing us upward, toward ultimate truth. But even Plato prescribed earthly roots for reason. From the philosophic heights reason enables them to attain, philosophers should descend into the world and reenter the cave of society. Surely Plato was right, even if not for quite the right reasons. Reasoning that abandons and forgets the cave of concrete circumstances becomes in some measure unrealistic and thus, in equal measure, false. Illustrative is the impractical, and sometimes intoxicated, atmosphere in which Russian intellectual life was carried on prior to the Bolshevik Revolution. Few Russian philosophers or writers, given the age-old autocracy reigning in Russia, had learned to think in terms of real political possibilities. And Tocqueville, notably, makes a like point about the French aristocracy in the period prior to the revolution of 1789.

The ideal of dialogic politics has significant implications for the political order. For one, a liberal society should be democratic. Very simply, the personal dignity that requires liberty for all requires not just equality, as I have already argued, but democracy too. I use the term "democracy" in its literal, political meaning: sovereign power in the hands of the people, at least to the extent that major governmental actions are based on informed common consent. The ideal of democracy does not derive from the wisdom of the people. A populace at large comes no nearer to infallibility than does any other group or power, and sometimes it displays great folly and unrighteousness. The democratic ideal cannot be justified even in terms of the goal of compelling government to heed the welfare of everyone. In practice, democracy contributes less to the achievement of this goal than one might expect; witness how frequently democratic governments cater to frivolous and unwise popular desires, and also how often they serve the interest mainly of wealthy and powerful minorities.

The principal justification for democracy is simply that it compels people in power to address and to listen to the people at large. The justification for democracy is dialogic. It accords every person the dignity of rightful participation in public discourse. This is not to suggest that the demos, although fallible and ineffective in other ways, does well at dialogue. The state of dialogue in a democracy is often, if not ordinarily, deplorable. Popular culture is more or less indifferent to beauty, to truth, and even to decency. Such phenomena as murderous violence in schools and the dissolution of marriage owe much to the conduct ceaselessly displayed, in search of popularity, in the media of popular culture. Political campaigns and legislative debates may occasionally display subtlety and discernment, but more often they manifest demagoguery, prejudice, and abject submission to popular sentiment. "McCarthyism" endangered liberty in America for a time simply because Senator McCarthy, in spite of his egregious disdain for truth and for the decencies of public discourse, was popular and widely applauded.

The fact remains that democracy is the condition of fully open political dialogue. In the absence of democracy, ordinary men and women, lacking power and public standing, can claim no right to speak, or to be spoken to, about public issues. Democracy accords them that right. Like all things human, it almost always fails to be what it ought to be. But one of the worst things about power is its aversion to dialogue. Having to listen to the populace is an encumbrance. Having to explain itself means exposure to embarrassment and to the risk of repudiation. This is to say that people in power prefer darkness to light. For all its customary flaws, democracy brings a measure of dialogue, and thus of light, into places that otherwise would be hidden from sight.

In discussions of democracy and popular involvement in politics, not only is democracy often unduly idealized, but the importance of politics is also overemphasized. So it is well to bear in mind that politics is not everything. The political realm is not the summit of life or the garden of all virtues. There are other spheres of life, such as art and religion, that are no less important, and may be more important, than politics. No one, given our finitude, can participate fully in all of these spheres, even though no one can rightfully ignore any of them. People have distinctive vocations. Some have political vocations, but others may rightfully place politics on the periphery of their lives. In short, we are not political animals. No sphere of earthly activity can accommodate the full amplitude of our humanity. Every such sphere is in some degree partial and confining. This is one reason why liberty is imperative. People must have room to piece out their necessarily imperfect lives in the ways commanded by their own particular destinies.

Nonetheless, a complete neglect of politics cannot be justified. Political responsibility is indispensable for maintaining the mind and bearing of a member of the human race. One of the things being human depends on is an attitude of attentiveness toward one's fellow human beings. And there is no limit to the scope of this attentiveness. Nothing that human beings are doing or suffering anywhere can be a matter of indifference to other human beings, even though, being finite, there are severe limits to the possible range and depth of their attention. This does not imply that one should try to be a citizen of the world. One belongs to the world by belonging to a particular society within the world and from that position paying attention to the world and taking responsibility for the relations of one's society to the world. But political attentiveness, although maintained from the standpoint of a personal situation within a particular society, is global in scope, and that is why it is obligatory. Political attentiveness is a manifestation of one's humanity.

These comments pertain to the liberal stance. Standing for liberty involves standing politically. This is largely implicit in a principle discussed earlier in the essay: that the liberal stance is essentially communal. Even the bare claim to liberty, as I have pointed out, is a claim in behalf, not of oneself alone, but of all who are inwardly free and thus morally responsible. Recognition of others is in this way implicit in the assertion of one's own rights as a free being. Fully understood, however, recognition of others implies listening and speaking. When such listening and speaking is done in full awareness of our universal humanity, it must be concerned with our common circumstances and our common troubles. It must amount to political dialogue. Care for one's neighbor, where everything implicit in the concept of neighbor is recognized, is necessarily expressed in dialogic politics.

Such politics requires not just liberty in general but also a particular kind of liberty — a kind that has its occasion when others do not appear as welcome interlocutors but rather as offensive or dangerous — as people whose presence is hard to bear. Without it, a dialogic politics is impossible. The practice of this liberty has been slowly and agonizingly worked out in the course of modern Western history, and its theory has been extensively discussed. Yet it remains both difficult to exercise and difficult to understand.

CHAPTER 8

Tolerance

The Issue of Tolerance

The word "tolerance," as usually understood, denotes an allowance of room, perhaps to troublesome acts of any kind, but particularly to troublesome acts of communication, for example, to speech that attacks widely accepted beliefs or that violates established norms of decency. Charges of sedition or pornography are among those apt to be heard where the issue of tolerance has come to the fore. There has been a good deal of tolerance at many times and places in Western history, as in Periclean Athens and, in spite of the occasional persecution of Christians, in the Roman Empire. But there was not much conscious reflection on it. Such reflection arose mainly from the murderous religious conflicts ensuing on the Reformation. The earliest ideals of tolerance represented a quest for peace through mutual forbearance. The issue was mainly religious tolerance. However, with the passing of religious conflict and the cooling of religious passions, at least within Western societies, and with the subsequent rise of ideological, cultural, and ethnic passions, the issue has broadened. At the beginning of the third millennium the idea of tolerance pertains to all areas of concern and media of expression in which human beliefs and attitudes clash — political ideology as well as religion, and art as well as literature. In short, it pertains to communication of every kind. Sometimes, of course, it pertains to action too, and rarely can action and communication be neatly distinguished. But here I shall consider it as primarily a matter of dialogic liberty.

We should note that the issue pertains not only to justifying liberty but also to justifying limitations on liberty. Tolerance cannot ever be unconditional. There are situations that necessitate intolerance. Many liberals are reluctant to recognize such situations. They seemingly imagine intolerant officials as always bad men and opinions not tolerated as harmless, if not true. Sometimes of course that is the case. But not always. There are creeds subversive of liberty and deeply offensive to the conscience of most people. The superiority of one race to all others, with another race fit only for slavery or extermination, is an example. And such creeds sometimes have powerful supporters with real prospects of gaining ascendancy. In the twentieth century there was of course such a creed — that of the Nazis. It is obviously arguable that Nazism should have been suppressed well before 1933. No more than any other abstract standard does tolerance authorize neglect of concrete conditions.

Even with limits at its outer perimeters, however, tolerance is more problematic than is often realized. In the West, it has come to be accepted by almost everyone as a matter of course. Granted, a few things are so outrageous or threatening that their suppression is justified, but only a few. For the most part we need merely to "live and let live." In most circumstances, that is a workable maxim. It does not, however, begin to provide an adequate rationale for tolerance. To see this let us briefly note a few of the most common and casual defenses of tolerance, along with their manifest insufficiency.

1. *If someone calls for the suppression of a dangerous error, someone else is likely to answer, "Who are you to say which ideas are true and which are false?"* But surely every person must say; every person must adopt at least a few firm principles on the basis of which to live. The only alternative is drifting aimlessly, doing and believing whatever others suggest. Someone without convictions and the courage to stand by them can be only a cipher. And the same may be said of peoples and nations. A society that cares nothing for the truth, that tries neither to find it nor, having found it, to cultivate and protect it, is surely doomed to a trivial life at best, and at worst to premature extinction. Once an individual or a society has embraced what it considers a basic truth, it cannot responsibly allow it to be crushed and forgotten. Otherwise, sooner or later we

would have to submit unprotestingly to the destruction of the very standard of tolerance. The issue is how to be committed both to the truth and to tolerance.

2. *At this point someone is apt to say: you can decide for yourself what ideas to live by, but the ideas other persons live by are none of your business. You need not worry yourself about the opinions of others any more than they need to worry about the opinions you hold.* In the first place, the ideas of others can have a decidedly harmful impact on your own life. Not only sticks and stones, but words and thoughts as well, can break your bones. This is abundantly illustrated in modern history, from the time of the Reformation to that of the various communist revolutions. But even with ideas that do not threaten the peace and order of your own life, to base tolerance on mutual indifference is to set it in opposition to community. Just as tolerance is condemned if it presupposes indifference to the truth, it is also condemned if it presupposes indifference to the common search for and communication of the truth.

3. *Nonetheless, runs a common rejoinder, you must recognize that your truth is not necessarily the same as another's truth. The convictions on which you base your life may be true for you, but probably will not be true for everyone else around you. Liberalism, in recognizing the independent reality of every person, recognizes that every person's truth is unique, and not to be forcibly fused with anyone else's truth.* There is obviously a measure of healthy common sense in such an attitude insofar as it acknowledges that we cannot expect people wholly to agree with one another. What it says, however, and what it usually means to those who say it, is something else, namely, that there is no truth common to us all. But this is simply a denial that truth exists. When you call something true, you do not mean merely to announce what you happen to believe. You mean to assert what everyone ought to believe. While the idea that no objective truth exists is surprisingly common, it is doubtful that anyone can or wants to live by that idea. Even to assert it is to assert an objective truth.

4. *Hoping to lay the matter finally to rest, some would say, let people thrash out competing ideas, let them argue with those they think are mistaken. Granted, there is such a thing as truth, but you can trust people to come up with it on their own. A "free market for ideas" can be as efficient as a free market for goods and services.* What is problematic in this view arises from that intractable condition we have been concerned with from the outset, that is, "original sin," the radical evil in every person. A

common form of evil is that of ignoring or flouting the truth. How can you trust people deeply inclined toward the evil of untruth to save and guard the truth merely by allowing them openly to discuss it? Again to the point is the example of Nazism, generally recognized as flagrantly false, yet winning general assent under conditions of free debate and in a nation steeped in a rich intellectual culture.

Plainly, the principle of tolerance is not self-evident. This is one reason why tolerance has not been the usual practice in past societies, even though there have been periods of tolerance. And it is the reason why the principle of tolerance did not come into the world and gain wide acceptance until late in the second millennium. Tolerance is unproblematic mainly to practical-minded people like the British and Americans, whose lives are relatively stable and prosperous, and are blessed with strong, stable, and lawful governments to keep the peace. It is not, however, unproblematic to anyone who finds it threatening or burdensome.

Two values indispensable to our humanity are involved in tolerance. One is truth — a good understanding of the natural and human universe we inhabit, not drifting endlessly on seas of doubt, and not being forever ignorant of whatever there may be of ultimate and saving worth in the universe. The other value is community — a life at least in peace, and so far as possible in searching communication, with our fellow human beings. To defend tolerance on the grounds that we cannot know what the truth is, and do not care what our fellow human beings think so long as they leave us alone, is to sink into a void in which nothing deeply matters, not even tolerance. If tolerance is viable only in such a void, it hardly deserves allegiance, nor is it likely to last. Nihilism does not make for tolerance.

On the other hand, the opposite of nihilism — the affirmation of values — does not make for tolerance either. Speech that questions or seems in any way to threaten whatever values are affirmed is apt to seem intolerable. And in some circumstances it may actually be so. I shall argue, nonetheless, that there is no necessary conflict between tolerance and the affirmation of values. They belong together. Tolerance, after all, is itself a value, and if values cannot be affirmed, neither can tolerance. To mark off tolerance so understood from the apathy we often carelessly dignify with the name of tolerance, the phrase "true tolerance" will often be used. True tolerance is a moral attitude. More spe-

226

cifically, it is animated by values already discussed — by love of truth and by respect for persons.

In modern times, tolerance among religious groups seems to have depended largely on doubt and indifference. In the eighteenth century it was nourished by the exhaustion following the religious wars and by the religious doubts cultivated by the Enlightenment. By the end of the twentieth century, peace among the creeds was sustained above all because they were not passionately embraced. As for tolerance among political groups, major exemplars have been Great Britain and the United States — nations marked by a pragmatic disinclination to press principles very far. In Great Britain, as the middle class rose in power, no one raised a banner proclaiming Liberty, Equality, and Fraternity; and in the United States, the upheaval that began in 1776 was the least ideological of modern revolutions. What all this seems to show is that modern tolerance represents a triumph of common sense but not of philosophy or moral principle. Tolerance may be relatively easy among people unimpassioned about the truth.

Not only is the value of such tolerance apt to be overestimated, however; so is its stability. Tolerance that depends on spiritual irresolution and indifference may in some circumstances be quickly weakened and dissipated. This is illustrated by the unanticipated outburst of communist and fascist fanaticism in Europe in the twentieth century. People who are spiritually adrift may try through violence to recover a sense of direction. The tolerance prevailing in the liberal democracies at the dawn of the third millennium expresses, more than anything else perhaps, a desire for undisturbed enjoyment of the pleasures and diversions of industrial abundance. What will become of such tolerance if industrial productivity falters or if people grow bored by its benefits?

Misgivings of this kind do not come merely from a sense of the errant and incalculable ways of human beings and human history. More fundamental are the claims of conscience. Truth and community are irrepressible human needs. They may be forgotten for a time but not forever. A permanent state of ignorance, long subjection to systematic deception, or confinement to relationships based on superficial interests and pleasures is incompatible with human nature. Sooner or later people will break out and will strive — or perhaps violently lunge — toward something that is, or seems to be, more significant. Tolerance can be

227

adequately defended, then, only by showing it to be among the prerequisites of community and truth.

The problem of justifying tolerance — of demonstrating its necessity for the attainment of ultimate values — may be suitably approached by leaving Christian ideas aside for the moment and trying to sketch out a defense of tolerance that might be acceptable to all reasonable people. Then we can try to determine whether it might be acceptable to people who rely not only on reason but also on faith.

Tolerance and Reason

As readers may realize, we already have on hand the basic principles of tolerance. They are the principles underlying liberty in general and were set forth earlier in this essay. The realization of values presupposes freedom. Good things do not become real in a world of persons, each of them possessing the power of choice, unless they are freely chosen. In other words, the only way in which persons can become meaningfully related to a value is by freely affirming it. Truth is the primary value we seek. As a value, it is apprehended only so far as it is willingly embraced. There is an intrinsic antithesis between truth and coercion. Another of the primary values is community. Community consists in sharing and searching for the truth — which is to say, in serious communication — and this occurs only when engaged in freely. Community and coercion, like truth and coercion, are antithetical. In sum, tolerance is an allowance of space in which persons may freely meet, either in a particular version of the truth or in a contest between alternative versions.

Is this, as a quick summary of my main argument for liberty, an adequate defense of tolerance? Not quite, since tolerance as a particular kind of liberty — liberty pertaining particularly to the intellect and communication — is subject to difficulties not involved, or at least not so pressing, in liberty generally. These must be resolved, not only for the argument to stand securely, but also for the very nature of the argument to be clear. There are two such difficulties. Both are serious enough to overturn simplistic defenses of tolerance. One, however, is relatively easy to resolve. The other is very hard to resolve and will absorb most of our attention in this chapter.

The former difficulty might be called "the problem of the third party." While I cannot force the truth into someone's mind by direct co-ercion, I can nevertheless silence anyone who is voicing what I see as untruths that pose the danger of misleading those I am trying to sway. In other words, it seems that I might advance the cause of truth by mo-nopolizing the channels of persuasion. This is probably the rationale of most policies of intolerance. They are not aimed immediately at chang-ing minds but at preventing the changing of minds by presumed pur-veyors of error. Thus Gnostic writings were suppressed by the early Christian church, not so much to force orthodox doctrines into peo-ple's minds as to free their minds from distracting errors. Can we then imagine a society in which a single belief or set of beliefs, taken by the reigning powers to be true, receive authentic, uncoerced credence on all hands simply because no other beliefs are expressed?

I think we cannot. Credence is not authentic, even though uncoerced, unless it arises from reflection and debate. Affirmation of the truth amounts to little unless alternative "truths" have been consid-ered, at least within the minds of individuals and if possible in conver-sations among individuals. Likewise, communication among people with no serious issues to ponder is not communication in any signifi-cant sense of the word. Hence it cannot achieve community worthy of the name. Tolerance is a dialogic practice. To accord tolerance is not simply to admit people into a wasteland where they can believe any-thing they like but have no stimulus to consider what is worthy of belief. Tolerance is of worth only in circumstances favorable to thought and serious speech — that is, only if it is tolerance of the third party.

A possible objection to such an argument runs as follows. Most people do not make up their minds on the major issues of life by dia-logue, either within themselves or with others. Thus they may listen to candidates for public office, but they will ordinarily choose, without much thought, the one whose views match their own. Or they will choose among candidates on the basis of nonintellectual traits such as personality and character. They will rarely engage in serious reflection or conversation. The ideal of dialogic tolerance is compelling (if for any-one) for people with a taste for abstractions and with experience in con-flicts among them. Most people, however, lack such taste and experi-ence. They spend their lives dealing with concrete realities. They do not find the free marketplace of ideas very profitable. Thus John Stuart Mill, a strong supporter of the kind of liberty realized in open discussion, was wary of the multitudes of ordinary people. Liberty of thought and speech was primarily for a natural aristocracy of the intellect. In short, the "third party" argument is elitist.

This objection obviously has factual grounds. People at large appear to be far more interested in things entertaining and sensational than in truth. And even at their most serious they have little taste for reflection. Thought and debate are the province ordinarily of minorities. In that sense the argument for dialogic tolerance is no doubt elitist. But not, I think, in a way that need greatly disturb proponents of liberal democracy. Liberal societies — even those with the most degraded cultures — have numerous dialogic arenas, such as universities, parliaments, courts, churches, town meetings, and the mass media. While relatively few take an active part in just one of these arenas, the few are different people in different arenas; their conversations may be widely heard; and almost anyone who wants to can, in one way or another, join in. Conversations in a vital liberal society are multifarious and shifting. The "elites" are diverse, relatively open to new participants, and their dialogues are sometimes widely heard. Two inferences may be drawn from these considerations.

The first is that the spirit of civil debate, as well as some of the truths glimpsed therein, may affect the intellectual tone of a whole people. Tolerance of the third party can foster an atmosphere of dialogic reflection. This is exemplified in the influence flowing from an effective parliament, like the British House of Commons, or from numerous great public and private universities, such as those scattered over the United States. Even those who never discuss serious issues may be drawn into a more thoughtful frame of mind. This is one way in which free dialogue can be relatively democratic. The second inference that may be drawn from the multifarious and shifting character of conversations in a liberal society is that even though relatively few, at any one moment, are engaged in serious deliberation, over the long run many, on one issue or another, may become thus engaged. Dialogue occurs not only in parliaments and university seminar rooms but also in restaurants, coffeehouses, and private dining rooms.

We come now to the second difficulty mentioned above — the one that is not at all easy to resolve. We might call it "the problem of uncertainty," although in reality it is the problem of how uncertainty and certainty can be combined. Tolerance does, as is so often said, presuppose a degree of uncertainty — at least if we are speaking of it as a form of attentiveness and not merely as a manifestation of indifference. I cannot be a dialogic partner to someone I see as unquestionably and entirely wrong. Hence I cannot be truly tolerant of such a one. If I am to be a tolerant person, I must be in some degree uncertain of my own views and cognizant of the possibility that I may learn from others. All of this is simply to acknowledge the widespread assumption that absolute certainty is dangerous to tolerance.

Far less widely recognized is the dependence of tolerance on certainty too. Dialogue would be unpromising if not hopeless unless people with deep and unshakable assurance of certain truths, or supposed truths, took part. Thus, one cannot be steadily tolerant, in the face of the temptations to intolerance that abound in any vital society, without being certain of the value of tolerance itself. And that certainty depends on other certainties: concerning, for example, the dignity of human beings, the respect shown them by listening and speaking with them, and the power and the limits of reason. And one who stands in readiness for serious dialogue must feel some confidence that truth can be known and is worth knowing. One exercises tolerance, not by plunging into an abyss of doubt, but in the strength of convictions of the sort that undergird one's life as a whole. Anyone who has taken part in truth-seeking conversations, and reflects on the experience of doing that, will realize that they generally are buttressed about with numerous unquestioned certainties.

Uncertainty has been too uncritically commended by defenders of tolerance. A human being cannot live in a world in which all outlines are indistinct and every reality a shadow. All-embracing skepticism is not a vital option. Nor does such skepticism promote tolerance. Anyone who is uncertain of everything will be uncertain of the value of tolerance too. Skepticism can issue as logically in mindless violence as in tolerance. And it might often do so. The horror of inhabiting a universe where everything is in doubt would not be conducive to peaceable human relations, not to speak of probing dialogue. And even if all-embracing uncertainty happened, in some set of uniquely favorable circumstances, to lead to tolerance, it would be a tolerance manifesting only the lassitude of despair. It would be morally worthless.

Acknowledging the need for certainty, however, we are thrown back on the question with which we began. If I possess the certainties that give me ground to stand on, why should I enter into relations of dialogic openness with people who try to weaken those grounds? Why should I guard the liberty of, and be prepared for serious conversation with, people saying things I feel sure are either wrong or trivial?

There are two conceivable — although, as I shall try to show, inadequate — arguments for tolerance as based on certainty alone, a tolerance conceding no uncertainty. The first can be summarized in the claim that an attentive and communicative tolerance might express a zest for intellectual combat. Taking pleasure in the carefully reasoned possession of certain sure convictions, one might feel like a splendidly caparisoned knight, eager to show one's strength. Tolerance is no doubt difficult in many circumstances, as I shall try to show. But the tolerance of a well-armed knight would be joyful. It would be a way of confronting the world, empowered by truth. University faculties offer apparent examples of such tolerance. Colleagues with differing opinions typically enjoy arguing with one another, and this is less because their opinions are held with any uncertainty than because they are held with a certainty that enables them to relax and find pleasure in intellectual combat.

This argument contains an element of truth but also a fatal weakness. The element of truth is the one suggested in the preceding pages, namely, that certainty is not unambiguously hostile to tolerance. Surely the refusal of tolerance, the suppression of challenging speech, has sometimes come from weakness and fear. The intolerant lash out at ideas counter to their own, not because they are confident that their own ideas are true, but because they fear they are not. If this is so, then we see again that tolerance must in some ways come, not from the uncertainty so recklessly commended by some liberals, but from certainty. When it does, it would be a way of standing ready to test and prove, in the eyes of everyone, the truths that are already the sinews of one's life and mind.

The fatal weakness in the argument is that tolerance motivated by certainty alone would not be inquiring. Tolerance is not genuine unless it is openness to the mystery of being and to the truths that enable us to enter into that mystery. There can be no such openness in the mind of someone who regards the full truth as already a secure possession. The intellectual banter of people afflicted with no doubts of a serious sort is necessarily oblivious of the value both of truth and of community. It is, in a word, frivolous. It must, then, also be unstable. People who are tolerant only for the sake of the passing pleasures of encountering and rebutting ideas unlike their own are not tolerant from principle but only from taste, and taste is highly changeable.

The second argument for tolerance without uncertainty, beyond the knightly argument (if I may so term it), involves an inner state that may look, at first glance, like uncertainty but is not the same. It was discussed with great force and insight by John Stuart Mill in his essay on liberty. As good a word for the inner state as any is "lukewarmness." Everyone knows that a conviction quite fundamental in one's life, and unshaken by any contradictory experiences or ideas, may somehow lose its grip on one's mind. One does not find it doubtful, but neither does one find it stirring. Mill was convinced that such apathy is apt to arise in the minds of those whose beliefs are never challenged. It might consequently be dispelled by confrontations with contradictory beliefs. These compel one to recall and think through the reasons buttressing one's convictions. This means that a person who is attentively and communicatively tolerant may be less likely to fall into intellectual and spiritual apathy than a person encased in unconsidered certitudes. Unthinking certitude is no doubt sometimes tyrannous, a motive to aggression and oppression. At other times, however, the harm it causes may be mainly to the one harboring it. It induces that seemingly innocuous but nevertheless debilitating inner state, lukewarmness. To be tolerant — attentively tolerant — of those you are sure are wrong is to turn the tables on them. They enliven the very beliefs they set out to destroy.

This argument, like the preceding one, contains both truth and a fatal weakness. The truth was brought out by Mill. Dogmatism is no friend of the kind of vital certainty needed for living well. Such certainty may be owing in part to irrational sources, such as a harsh experience or a trusted mentor. It must arise in part, however, from rational sources. It must have grounds that one can enunciate before others. If it does not, it is not humanly fitting, since humans are reasoning and communicating animals. Mill's argument follows. To listen to and answer those who question one's convictions is a way of nurturing those convictions by calling to mind the reasons undergirding them. In other words, tolerance conduces to intellectual vitality.

The weakness in the argument is the same as that in the preceding one. Tolerance that seeks only to strengthen one's own convictions, and does not envisage the possibility of changing them, is not inquiring. It is therefore not oriented toward either truth or community. This is not to say that Mill's argument is worthless. Far from it. As I will shortly try to show, it comes close to my own argument. As it stands, however, it fails to show that tolerance is a relationship with the truth and with other persons. Recalling the reasons underlying one's convictions is not quite the same thing as searching for the truth. And attentiveness that hopes, not to learn anything, but only to reinforce one's present views is not really attentiveness. The other is not a possible truth-bearer but only a means for restoring the vitality of one's own beliefs. Indeed, Mill envisaged the one to whom you should listen in order to cure lukewarmness as a devil's advocate.

My argument so far might be summarized in terms of an apparent contradiction. On the one hand, true tolerance depends on certainty. A steadfastly tolerant person must be certain at least of the value of tolerance, and that certainty presupposes other certainties. These I noted above. On the other hand, tolerance also depends on uncertainty. Without uncertainty it cannot be an orientation toward truth and community, and if it is not that, it is not morally significant. To be absolutely certain of my own views on every significant question is to place myself on a kind of pinnacle from which I look down on everyone except those who entirely agree with me. True tolerance is a form of listening, and listening is not morally significant unless it involves respect for persons and a concern for truth — truth that another might possess but I do not.

The problem before us at this point, then, is not the need for certainty or uncertainty but the possibility of combining them. The difficulty of the problem becomes clear only if we note that both the certainty and the uncertainty must concern matters that are foundational, that is, matters having to do with the grounds and orientation of one's personal being. To be humanly alive — to think and to act — presupposes certainties that cannot genuinely be doubted without projecting one into an abyss in which tolerance and every other ordered practice collapse. Hence the problem cannot be solved by saying that the uncertainties must concern only matters that are not of utmost concern to us. Were that the case, they would not be matters of serious dialogue nor of serious tolerance. Our uncertainties, as well as our certainties, must be foundational. The problem, therefore, is that tolerance rests on a seemingly self-contradictory, hence entirely unreasonable, state of mind.

Most people seem to have little difficulty with this problem. When taking part in discussions involving differences of opinion, they are apt to say something like, "This is what I believe, but I may be wrong." They profess simultaneous certainty and uncertainty. They may in this way enhance good feeling among interlocutors and thus promote dialogue. Can they, however, be altogether sincere? To believe something is to believe, quite simply, that you are not wrong. On the other hand, to begin thinking (not merely saying) that you may be wrong is in some degree to cease believing. Thus the popular answer to the problem — "This is what I believe, but I may be wrong" — begs the question. It takes for granted the very point at issue, the possibility of fusing the certainty and uncertainty on which communal tolerance depends.

The issue is put before us, we should bear in mind, not only by the desirability of tolerance but also by those two vital needs — truth and community. On the one hand, assurance of apprehending something of the truth is a primary condition of spiritual health. Someone skeptical of everything could live only in response to mere biological urges, and doing even that would probably require periodic suspensions of doubt. To say we need truth, however, is to say we need certainty. On the other hand, we need community too. But this means we need relationships with people most or all of whom harbor opinions and attitudes in varying degrees different from our own. Such differences can be reconciled with community only by being engaged dialogically. But doing this requires uncertainty. In this sense we need not only certainty but uncertainty too. The possibility of fusing these, and achieving dialogic tolerance, thus pertains to the possibility of fulfilling our primary needs. The problem of justifying tolerance seems to concern the very possibility of human wholeness.

The only solution to the problem that I can see rests on a fundamental distinction pertaining to the human intellect. The distinction is that between inward vision and outward form. Inward vision is your primal apprehension of your own identity and of the realities around you. Outward form is visible and audible and may be inscribed in language, paint, sound, stone, or other media. Vision is one's view of reality at large and comprises one's sense of the truth concerning such issues as the existence or nonexistence of God, the benevolence or malice of human beings, and the nature of the right and the good. Form most often is in words, although these may be badly articulated. Most people de-

LIBERTY

rive it from the society around them. In that way it enters consciousness and becomes a force in their lives. Vision without form would be hidden and almost nonexistent. But form without vision would be empty, mere bombast and pretense.

I speak of vision as "inward" and form as "outward." These terms, however, should not be taken literally. If someone has cast his inward sense of the nature of the world and his own place in it in a few propositions that he could readily write down or state before others, then vision has taken form and is effectively outward, even though it has not been made manifest to anyone else. It follows that vision is preconceptual. Religious faith, for example, does not begin when I say to myself, "There is a God." It begins often with a mystical or awed, or perhaps disturbed and frightened, intuition of a reality beyond all I can see and know, and of utmost significance to me. Likewise, atheism does not begin when I declare to myself, "There is no God." It begins with the vision of an empty and meaningless universe. As in Genesis 1, first God calls forth the reality (light, firmament, and so forth), then he names it. I may hasten, once a vision has appeared, to name it, to capture it in propositions, and to clarify it by reasoning about the propositions. But I may not. I may not welcome the vision I have of the world, or I may simply not be very introspective or thoughtful. Vision is always closely associated with concepts, but it is not the same.

It is doubtful that any adult person is entirely bereft of vision. It may be a very superficial vision, perhaps amounting, if formulated, to little more than a proposition like "Things will go along all right if you just use your head and treat others decently." But without vision of some sort, however superficial and unexamined it may be, one cannot live, whereas without a *formulated* vision one can still live, if only confusedly and unsatisfactorily. Hence the fact that most people are more or less inarticulate when it comes to the "deep" questions of life does not mean they are wholly lacking in vision.

That vision and form, although closely linked, are not the same is a point particularly to be emphasized. Even the multitudes of people who are more or less averse to philosophy, and uncritical of reigning customs and beliefs, are not likely always to feel perfectly at one with the society around them. As for the thinking and critical few, they are typically very much dissatisfied with prevailing opinions and ways. And even the most precisely formulated expressions of philosophical, aesthetic, or other insight do not usually still their restlessness. Although an insight is not firmly apprehended until it is well expressed, it can always be expressed in a different, and perhaps better, fashion. This is shown by the way key theological concepts, such as the Christian idea of the life and death of Christ as an act of divine forgiveness, are endlessly altered and elaborated upon. In a very different medium, it is shown by the way a great painter like Cézanne struggles to show forth in canvas after canvas a core vision of primeval nature.

Particularly noteworthy is the fact that the core insight is not necessarily lost, and may even be deepened, when its original formulation undergoes criticism and change. Illustrative is Plato's doctrine of forms. In its usual explanations the doctrine is easily criticized. Plato did this himself in the *Parmenides.* It does not appear, however, that he gave up the vision represented by the verbal formulas he criticized, and few scholars would hold that he finally disposed of the doctrine, which haunts the history of philosophy. By exposing usual formulations to doubt, Plato may have rendered the core insight more mysterious and in a paradoxical way more plausible.

How does this distinction pertain to tolerance? It makes possible, I believe, the fusion of certainty and uncertainty that tolerance demands. One can be certain of an inner vision but see its verbal or other formulation as in some way inadequate or inconclusive — in a word, as *uncertain.* And it is possible, on this basis, to say and mean, "This is what I believe, but I may be wrong." What one believes, without any doubt, are things that are ultimately inexpressible even though they are vital to one's being. What one can doubt at the same time is the adequacy of the forms in which the inner certainties are put before oneself and the world. Here we can see the nerve center of tolerance. A tolerant person can approach potential interlocutors with a profession of uncertainty that expresses genuine openness but does not abandon those certainties without which one would lack personal identity and be incapable of coherent conduct. The distinction between inner certainty and outer form is thus vital to the life of tolerance. Inner certainty is concerned with truths one cannot forsake. Outer form, however, is the clothing those certainties wear when they appear in the world. The clothing can always be changed even though one cannot appear in the world unclothed.

Making the distinction between vision and form is not a difficult intellectual maneuver. It is regularly and spontaneously done by philosophers, artists, and other such people. A serious thinker cannot live without being in steady contact with thinkers who are expressing very different visions; poets and novelists are always attentive to the contrasting works of other poets and novelists; architects and painters flourish only where they are conscious of the work being done by other architects and painters. One vision thrives only among other and different visions, and people who seek and cultivate vision normally know this naturally. And not only that. They know too that they are not imperiling their own visions through coming into contact with people cultivating contrasting visions. Rather they are hoping to deepen their own insight and express it more fully. In this sense they spontaneously practice an attentive and communicative tolerance. Who, then, is intolerant? Primarily, it seems, those for whom form is absolute. These are mainly protagonists of political ideologies and religious dogmas. Their aim may be certitude. Since there is no distinction in their minds between vision and form, they cannot tolerate any questioning of form, for that puts them on the brink of an abyss of bottomless doubt. Or their aim may be power, which is often based on a political ideology or a religious dogma.

I have emphasized that vision and form are not the same. It is also to be emphasized, however, that they cannot be cleanly separated. I do not fully apprehend my vision of things until I have created or found a fitting form for it. Hence when the form is attacked or altered or broken down, the vision underlying it is necessarily affected. Saying this admittedly requires a qualification in the argument. True tolerance cannot be entirely free of risk. If you don't really apprehend an inner vision until you have given it outer form, thus putting it before others and before yourself, then to expose the outer form to assault places the inner certainties in a degree of danger. There is no getting around this fact. I think introspection reveals, however, that the core certainty is always something deeper, more mysterious, and more tenacious than any verbal or other expression of it can be. A person who believes in God or in the dignity of a reflective life, for example, does not believe mainly in a particular theology or philosophy but rather is rooted in a sense of the depths of the human situation. This sense will not usually melt into thin air when the words expressing it come into doubt. One knows this and can open his mind to different and antagonistic views without tremors of anxiety.

On the other side, however, it is precisely because vision and form are interdependent that tolerance can play a part in the search for truth. While the inner vision may be threatened when its outer form is attacked, the vision may be deepened when its outer form is changed. A new form for an old vision may reveal new facets of the vision. Or it may open up a wider and more comprehensive vision than did the old form. The effort to perfect the outer form of a vision is an effort to extend the reach and deepen the roots of the vision itself. Of course, just as both vision and form may be destroyed in a dialogic encounter, both may remain unaffected. To say these things is simply to note again that liberty is an ordeal. The distinction between vision and form enables us to see it as an ordeal that should not be shunned.

The difference between this and Mill's "lukewarmness" argument lies in their respective implications for inquiry. Mill, as I read him, is talking about a truth already fully known. The motive of tolerance is that of recovering one's initial apprehension of it after time has allowed it to grow dim. The argument I am making is that a truly tolerant person hopes, not merely to recover an old truth, but to deepen the truth one knows. Moreover, one proposes to do this, not just by laying fresh hold of old reasons (old forms), but by working out new forms. One might say, of course, that to combat lukewarmness is always to strive toward deeper understanding. If it is, then I willingly ally my argument with Mill's, which is, as I noted, a strong one. But Mill was not, as I read him, talking mainly about a struggle for truth, whereas I am.

The importance of tolerance lies in its dialogic grounds. It is a readiness for deeper truth. A Christian, for example, can embark on a study of Marx, Nietzsche, or Darwin not only fearlessly but also in the hope of better formulating, and thus more deeply understanding, his own faith. Plato publicly criticized his own doctrine of forms, as I have suggested, not because he had begun to doubt it but because he wanted to give it a depth it could not have so long as it was identified with a particular set of words. In this, one sees the dialogic consciousness that governed Plato's entire lifework.

If tolerance is a readiness for deeper truth, it is also a readiness for more profound human relationships. If critics of one's foundational certainties can be listened to in the hope of penetrating more deeply into the certainties themselves, in like fashion the critics may be listened to in the hope of bringing about an act of communication. Tolerance is incipient communality. Just as one cannot search for truth without having, in some way, already found it, so one cannot address or accord attention to others without having a sense of primal solidarity with them, even though that solidarity has yet to emerge in communication. Tolerance is a preparatory posture, a readiness for the communication that will render the sensed solidarity a communal reality. True tolerance is not an individualistic posture. It cannot arise from indifference either toward the truth or toward other persons. It is a way of awaiting the other person as a possible source of understanding, and it comes to fruition in community.

When all else has been said, however, it is vital to bear in mind that tolerance may not, indeed probably will not, "work." It is an allowance of liberty. It is based on respect for the freedom of others, and by its very nature such freedom is incalculable. In a sense, it is standing off from others, giving them space in which to work out their own thoughts and lives, and to express themselves as they will. Tolerance that is morally significant, and not mere indifference, arises from the hope that the space thus given will become a meeting place in the search for truth. It arises from the realization that we cannot assure ourselves of some of the things we most care about. We can only be open to them. Tolerance is that openness. In that respect it is not merely a means. It is good in itself. It is a rudimentary relationship with truth and other persons, and even if it develops no further it is still that rudimentary relationship, and that is better than nothing.

This brings us back to the liberal stance. Truly tolerant societies are rare. Collective humanity tends toward one or the other of the polar states of repression or indifference. Indeed, it may be that almost never is an entire society, over an extended period of time, truly tolerant. A state of tolerance may prevail only for limited periods of time and only, perhaps, among limited numbers of people. Consequently one must often be tolerant alone: attentive to others, ready for conversation, but largely lacking in conversational opportunities. This, the above argument indicates, is to maintain a human posture in a fallen world.

The preceding argument has at least one signal limitation: it is, so to speak, written in Greek. It is addressed to those with a strong allegiance to reason. But this is a relatively easy audience. Greeks are traditionally tolerant. Can the argument be cast in a language acceptable to Jews and Christians, to those who are traditionally less tolerant than are Greeks?

Tolerance and Faith

One of the most frequently made and least carefully considered assumptions in modern discussions of tolerance is that religious believers are uniquely certain and therefore uniquely intolerant. Preceding arguments have placed that assumption in question. No doubt certainties of some kinds, such as those that possessed the minds of Lenin and his followers, imperil tolerance. And no doubt religious certainties have sometimes been of this sort. As I have shown, however, certainties as such are not in conflict with tolerance. On the contrary, there can be no tolerance without them. They free one from the fear of being thrown into a void of doubt and confusion by opinions counter to one's own. And there can be no stable and morally meaningful tolerance without at least one certainty — that concerning the value of tolerance itself.

Why, then, someone might ask, have Christians in the past so often been intolerant? Why has established Christianity been so given to suppressing opposing views? Why the Inquisition? Why the religious wars?

There is no simple or certain answer to these questions. Various factors have been involved. For one thing, tolerance was not an established standard of conduct anywhere in the West until sometime in the nineteenth century. A good deal of diversity was allowed in the Greek and Roman worlds, but that was a casual rather than principled practice. Also, after Christianity became an established religion in the fourth century, intolerance was often motivated by political, as well as religious, concerns. Roman emperors were apprehensive about the political repercussions of religious dissidence. And presumably the motives of intolerant prelates often were political too; in suppressing dissent they were suppressing threats to their position and power.

Religious intolerance has no doubt sometimes, however, had religious motives. In pursuance of my argument about the dependence of tolerance on certainty, I suggest that a major motive of Christian intolerance has often been *uncertainty,* rather than certainty. If religion is distinctively intolerant — which might be questioned in view of the intolerance of secular ideologies — it may be on account of the foundational character of religious beliefs. People ostensibly, and often in fact, base their lives on their religious convictions. Hence they naturally fear finding that those convictions are false. If doubts begin to assail them, it is as though the earth under their feet were being shaken. It is natural

241

for them to strike out at those encouraging their doubts. Detailed historical investigation would be needed to establish the motives for any particular episode or era of intolerance. To take a single instance, however, it is surely reasonable to think that the ferocity of the wars of religion was owing in part to doubts sown by the Reformation and the succeeding breakup of the Christian church. Religious parties sought to eradicate opposing parties not because they were sure of their faith but because they were not, and desperately wanted to be.

To attribute Christian intolerance to anxieties born of uncertainty is to suggest that basic Christian principles militate in the opposite direction — toward tolerance. Is this, however, true? I believe it is. Some of the most familiar and basic Christian principles make for tolerance. That Christians have so often been intolerant tells us less about their principles than it does about human nature — how inclined toward intolerance human beings are. What are these principles?

Three are fundamental. These, I believe, only supplement, and do not replace, the principles of tolerance discussed in the preceding section. Christians, like everyone else, are bound by necessity to respect the freedom that belongs to the human essence. And like everyone else, their minds are structured by the distinction between inner certainty and outer form. My present point is that Christian faith does not contradict these principles. Rather, it reinforces them.

1. One of these, discussed already in other connections, is love of neighbor. This love does not lead to tolerance quite as spontaneously as is often supposed. Someone who believes in using force to compel belief can argue that real love for others is properly manifested in using every possible means, including violence and intimidation, to open their minds to truth. A logic of this sort presumably operated in the mind of Augustine when he summoned imperial authorities to suppress the Donatists. There is, of course, one great fact that stems this logic, that is, freedom. True belief presupposes choice, and choice presupposes free thought. This means that love for neighbors has to be expressed first of all by stepping back and letting them possess their own minds. This is why it was only after prolonged hesitation that Augustine resorted to force against the Donatists. One of the most important gifts love can bestow on others is intellectual and spiritual (as well as physical) space in which they can be themselves. But since it is love that grants this space, stepping back from the other implies no indiffer-

ence, nor does it entail an attenuated relationship. Liberty motivated by love is a form of attentiveness. Hence it issues, quite spontaneously, in a dialogic tolerance.

2. Another Christian principle that makes for tolerance is humility. If pride is the quintessential sin, humility is the quintessential virtue. Humility is closely connected with the forgiveness Christians believe was granted humankind in the life, death, and resurrection of Jesus. But forgiveness implies something to be forgiven. If Christians live as forgiven people, they live as people who are guilty and have failed in significant ways. Thus human fallenness, and the humility to acknowledge it, is as central in Christian belief as divine mercy. As we have seen, this wickedness is not a condition easily remedied, nor is it a characteristic found in some but not in others. All of us alike persistently forget our finitude and indulge in extravagant, or sometimes subtle and therefore easily hidden, pretensions. All, then, are in need of forgiveness. Christianity is the religion that recognizes this and centers its teaching and life on what is held to be a decisive act of divine forgiveness. Only by accepting this forgiveness is a human being freed from guilt and thus free to live. But accepting the forgiveness depends on humility, which is acknowledgment of one's need for forgiveness. A Christian without humility can hardly be a genuine Christian. And a human being without humility, according to Christianity, can hardly live in a way that is authentically human. How does this bear on the issue of tolerance? In particular, how does humility affect the certainties supposedly essential to tolerance? How can one be both humble and certain?

The answer to these questions lies in the distinction between inner vision and outer form. The proposition that I can never be as sure of the form in which I cast my faith (I assume that faith is a kind of vision) as I can of the innermost certainty behind the form is readily applied to religious doctrine. The doctrine is the outward form of faith, not faith itself. My faith may be unfaltering. But to grasp it and to put it before others I must cast it in finite and fallible words, and this I must do with a humility that makes it possible to treat others' doubts and certainties with a measure of deference. The great Christian doctrines, such as the Trinity, belong among the greatest intellectual achievements of the West. But the idea that these doctrines are identical with the truth, rather than expressive of the truth, is a great and dangerous misunderstanding, expressive of pride. It leads directly to the identification of inner certainties with their outer, doctrinal, forms. Thence it leads to the suppression of anyone who questions those forms. Someone may suppose that if I am truly humble then I will entertain doubt about not only the outer form but also the inner vision, the faith itself. As I have said, however, if I doubt the vision, then the vision is dissolving. And with the dissolving of the vision, humility too dissolves. Humility does not consist in complete bewilderment and despair but in an awareness of one's own foolishness and unworthiness before something unqualifiedly wise and worthy. It is an element within a vision.

3. Love and humility are familiar norms and can readily be understood without reference to the Christian idea of God, even though they are derived from that idea. This is not the case with the third principle. The norm is trust in God. To understand the relevance of this norm to tolerance, it is necessary to attend briefly to the unique character of the Christian concept of God. Informed Christians do not simply believe, as do some religious people, that "there is a God." They do not rest even in so general a concept as divine mercy. They believe that God has characteristics that to many, throughout the ages, have looked quite peculiar and even wrong. As already noted in another context, the Christian God is present in three divine persons, Father, Son, and Holy Spirit. It is the latter, the Holy Spirit, that has particular importance in relation to tolerance. The Holy Spirit is God as the one who enters into our emotions and thoughts, inspiring and teaching us. Thus God is not only immeasurably far beyond us, the creator and lord of all things, but is also deeply within us, leading us toward righteousness and wisdom.

The implications such an understanding of God has for tolerance can be expressed in a simple proposition. Responsibility for the fate of truth in the world belongs primarily to God, not to human beings. In the book of Isaiah, God declares that the word that goes forth from his mouth shall not return to him void. "It shall accomplish that which I purpose, / and prosper in the thing for which I sent it" (Isa. 55:11). Hence when humans busy themselves with stamping out falsehood, and forcibly establishing truth in every mind, they display a lack, not only of love and humility, but also of trust in God. They can of course teach, and indeed they must. But as every teacher knows, the results of teaching are never sure in advance. Teaching is a far chancier enterprise than enforcing outward allegiance to an official creed. True teachers leave the minds of the students to the students themselves and to powers beyond both students and teachers. Those who practice forcible indoctrination, however, are determined to leave nothing to chance, or to any power beyond themselves. Judged according to the Christian principle of the Holy Spirit, they take on for themselves a divine responsibility. By Christian standards, intolerance is not only presumptuous, it is also faithless and untrusting.

The idea of the Holy Spirit is integral to the viewpoint being developed in this essay. At the outset I argued that human beings are a deviant species, that their proper nature is affected by a radical derangement, that of "original sin." The main political inference drawn in the past from such a view of man — an inference drawn even by Christians — is that liberty is intolerably dangerous. Human nature requires strong, unquestioned authority. My whole argument in this essay has been counter to this inference. In humanist terms, I have argued mainly that the risks must be run. Liberty is not so much desirable as it is unavoidable. Nothing of value can enter the world without it. If persons are the primary realities, then all efforts to establish the good by circumventing the hazards of personal reflection and choice must be self-defeating. If the good is community, and community is sharing in the truth and in the pursuit of truth, then the only gate leading into it is liberty — or, more specifically, the liberty of intellect and communication often called "tolerance." At this point I can put my argument in distinctively Christian terms. The risks of tolerance are supportable because there is a divine teacher, the Holy Spirit, who can enter into human minds and emotions to far greater effect than can any human teacher.

Here, however, I believe that we see the deadening effects of dogma on human minds. The concept of the Holy Spirit long ago became one of the main dogmas of the church. It has been professed through the centuries by people having little or no sense of its meaning. Hence the meaning has been largely lost. It needs therefore to be said that the "Holy Spirit" is a way of naming a God who is able and mercifully inclined to enter into and illuminate human minds. Christians understand God as light, and the light is not distant but is found within every person by those humble enough to watch and wait for it. Those who find it there, with any comprehension of its source and of their own relationship with ultimate truth, are unlikely to turn it into a dogma to be forced upon others. They are likely to be tolerant.

The Christian view of tolerance might be summed up by saying that tolerance is a norm arising from the Logos, the basic order of all things, the Word of God. It is therefore inherent in key Christian virtues — love, humility, and trust in God as the Holy Spirit. Christians believe that the Logos can be fully apprehended only through faith. They must grant, however, that, as the basic order and meaning of reality, it can be partially apprehended through reason. They can, accordingly, readily embrace the humanist argument for tolerance. Humanists, on the other hand, have no necessary quarrel with the Christian arguments for tolerance. The third argument, that of trust, they presumably cannot endorse. But they can readily affirm a tolerance arising from humility and love. There is, then, a possible accord between faith and reason on the imperative of tolerance. This accord would open up a realm of discourse, a public realm, in which faith and reason could meet. Such an idea is obviously not appealing either to traditional faith, which is viscerally inclined to a dogmatism that stamps out anything contrary to the reigning creed, or to traditional reason, convinced as it is that faith has nothing of interest to say and should not be admitted into the public realm. My argument, in contrast, is simply that faith and reason alike tell us that tolerance befits human beings in all regions and seasons. It is the human stance, a universal norm, befitting humanity as a communal and truth-seeking species.

In spite of all this, tolerance is not natural in view of human fallenness. Nor is it easy. When I said above that tolerance is a highly civilized attitude, I implicitly granted its difficulty. Civilization connotes discipline rather than sheer spontaneity. In concluding, we must look briefly at this aspect of the matter.

The Burden of Tolerance

Professions of tolerance are often intended to signify a sophisticated worldliness, superior to naive concerns about truth and righteousness. They are quiet expressions of epistemological and moral indifference. Such tolerance is at once morally worthless and intellectually shallow, indicative of an unwillingness to put forth moral and spiritual effort. True tolerance requires determination and strength. It imposes tasks of differentiation — between truth and error, and between good and evil. And it demands difficult balances — between certainty and uncertainty, and between the hostility aroused by particular voices and the forbearance, and even protection, that is owed them. Tolerance is no exception to the notion that liberty is an ordeal. It is fitting that the word "tolerance" derives from the Latin word *tolerare,* meaning to bear.

Nothing is harder, in the stance of tolerance, than making and steadily acting upon the distinction between the inner substance and the outer form of our vital certainties. We cannot be tolerant, as I have tried to show, unless this distinction shapes our minds and wills. Yet we spontaneously cling to outer forms and thrust them into our social relationships. This is no doubt partly from pride. Sometimes we are arrogantly sure of our own beliefs. But just as intolerance sometimes reflects uncertainty, rather than certainty, so thrusting forward the outer forms of our beliefs sometimes comes from the fear that there is no inner substance behind them. Exposing the outer form to criticism is like abandoning a life raft and simply swimming. All security is gone. If preceding arguments are valid, however, we must learn to swim. Unless we can loosen our hold on the words, or other forms, in which our most cherished certitudes are embodied, we cannot be tolerant.

The Christian grounds of tolerance are no less difficult to stand on than the humanist grounds. They comprise, in addition to the distinction between inner vision and outer form, love, humility, and trust in God as the Holy Spirit. Each of these is continually weakened and subverted by that quintessential human sin, pride. We love the self far more deeply and tenaciously than we love any but a very few others; far from being naturally humble, we will the ascendancy of the self over all others and fall into despondency when such ascendancy is threatened; and we recoil from entrusting the self to a God who cannot be seen and in times of crisis may seem no better than a flimsy hypothesis. One might say that Christian tolerance has the same quality Kierkegaard and Dostoyevsky attributed to Christian faith generally. It is excruciatingly difficult.

It is not surprising that tolerant persons and societies are somewhat rare. It is not surprising either that where tolerance of some sort is established, there are repeated and stubborn efforts at oversimplifying it and thus lightening the burden of it. One of these, already noted, is to treat it as limitless. Every restraint on speech or any other form of communication is seen as the beginning of a swift slide into tyranny. Tolerance would be easier to maintain if this were so — if it involved no difficult balances of liberty and restraint. That it is not so, however, is evident in the fact that tolerance, while an end in itself — as a communal stance — is also a means — to ends such as dialogue and truth. Failure to consider consequences is thus inconsistent with the very nature of tolerance. It would be irresponsible, for example, to tolerate speech that is likely to weaken or destroy the very institutions on which tolerance depends. In a word, tolerance requires prudence.

Pornography is an example. It is obvious that sexual candor can have a vital role in a work of art or a process of inquiry. It is thoroughly unfitting for writers like D. H. Lawrence and James Joyce to be censored, as they often were. But they were not pornographic. Properly speaking, pornography depicts the human body in ways designed to arouse lust. It objectifies. It is thus disrespectful at once of persons and of truth. Far from being a form of communication, it is hostile to communication. Yet it is not entirely easy to discriminate between candid works of art and works of pornography. So it is probably prudent ordinarily to leave the works of pornography unfettered. But this cannot be done invariably, and pornography has no intrinsic claim to liberty whatsoever. Hence the struggle of discrimination is unavoidable. This is one of the burdens of tolerance.

Another oversimplification lies in refusing to see that tolerance has conditions and may therefore require supporting political actions. Thus tolerance is largely pointless where the populace is destitute and uneducated. It cannot in that case further truth or community except among the privileged. Hence those who are intelligently tolerant might feel compelled, not simply to desist from repression, but to support measures of economic and social reform. Policies designed to alleviate poverty or moderate inequalities might in some circumstances be construed as steps toward a dialogic tolerance.

The burden of tolerance is partly just the burden of human nature. Significant tolerance is an opening up of interpersonal space, of a realm where persons can freely encounter one another. It is in this way an expression of respect for others, and for the truth that is sought and sometimes found in conversation. But human behavior is shaped more by pride and self-interest than by respect for others or for truth. I discover this in others and I discover it in myself. Hence, tolerance entails inner resistance. When Ortega y Gasset characterized liberalism as "acrobatic" on account of its "allowing the enemy within its gates," he saw exactly why tolerance — that is, maintaining and inhabiting interpersonal space — is difficult. It is bearing with the presence and speech of opponents (as you see them) of truth and community. The burden is light, of course, for people who care nothing for one another or for truth. Tolerance can be simple and spontaneous, the effortless outcome of attitudes that are widespread in times of cultural and spiritual decay. If we respect others and care about truth, however, it is hateful to hear people give voice to apparent error. Yet this is what real tolerance requires of us.

The very idea of tolerance is sometimes criticized as condescending. There is truth in this objection, and a defender of genuine tolerance must admit it. I would not be loyal to my own convictions if I did not in some sense look down on convictions I believe to be false. Where tolerance is genuine, however, I am not condescending toward the persons who harbor such convictions. My very willingness to listen and speak with them signalizes my respect for them. Here we see from another angle the difficulty of tolerance. It lies in the dissonance between disrespect for certain opinions and respect for those voicing them.

Tolerance is instinct with hope and would die without it. Hope watches for intimations of truth and community even though all around there is wrongheadedness and mutual animosity. And hope, at least as understood in Christianity, is not easily defeated. On the one hand it is temporal. It looks to the next year, the next week, and even the next hour, in this way enlivening every moment. But it also knows that nothing in a person's earthly life, and nothing in human history, can be perfect or lasting. Hence it looks beyond death and beyond history. Tolerance that involves such limitless hope as this anticipates, at last, the attainment of all truth in a community of all who have ever lived. It is never entirely cast down. In degenerate times it may exist only within small and scattered groups, perhaps only within solitary, listening individuals. But if we think of tolerance as a stubborn receptivity toward persons and truth, we can think of these small centers of tolerance as representatives, in troubled times, of the whole human race.

CHAPTER 9

Universality: The Public Realm

——◦(◦)◦——

Liberal Universality

Universality is, as I have tried to show, implicit in the ideal of liberty. As we start out on a set of reflections concerning the requirements of universality, it might be good to quickly recall what the idea rests on. One foundation stone is found as soon as one tries to answer the question, Why liberty? One can be rightfully in possession of liberty only if one is grounded morally in the consciousness of being, not merely a particular, distinctive individual, but a member of the human race. My own claim to liberty is based on my inner freedom, my power of choosing. Values forced upon me cannot have a real part in my life, even if those values are indubitably authentic. But the power of choice belongs to human beings universally. Hence I can legitimately claim liberty for myself only by making a like claim in behalf of all human beings. In Kantian terms, I can be legitimately in possession of liberty only by standing as a universal legislator prescribing liberty for all humankind.

Is this to trace liberal universality to its ultimate grounds? Not quite. It does not rule out the possibility that I will treat myself as belonging to a special class. And I could do this in a highly plausible way. I might argue that only those capable of choosing wisely deserve to have their power of choice recognized and protected. I might then point out that not everyone possesses that capability, although it happens that I do. Hence there is no moral logic that compels me, in willing my own liberty, to will the liberty of everyone. In fact, I might will the liberty of only a very few, of an elite. Kant often wrote as though he saw the ability to choose wisely (which for Kant meant to treat every person as an end, not a means alone) as inherent in reason and thus as possessed by everyone and as qualifying everyone for liberty. A casual glance at the state of the human race in any period of history, however, suffices to show that relatively few steadily live in accordance with the moral law. And this is what Kant's own concept of radical evil would lead us to expect. Hence one must ask how liberal universality can be defended against the possibility of a liberal elitism.

This question leads us back to the issue of human dignity. The idea that every person possesses intrinsic dignity is a way of attributing absolute value to every person even though not every person is wise or righteous. It is thus a way of attributing to people who display little capacity for freedom a right to freedom. How can such an attribution be justified? The problem is that of fully acknowledging, at one and the same time, the evil and the dignity residing in every human being. The Christian solution to this problem is, as brought out in the section on justification, that God has lifted up the fallen. More precisely, God through Christ has dignified those who have cast away their dignity. The crucifixion, meeting the claims of *justice* for every person, *justifies* every person. If I am a Christian, then, it is faith that forces me to will for everyone the liberty I will for myself.

But what if I am not a Christian? We have discussed the question, of course, in chapter 4. As I argued there, it is not manifest beyond doubt that humanist reason can provide convincing grounds for the idea of personal dignity. Saying this, however, is not tantamount to claiming that only Christians can recognize and respect human dignity. That would clearly be false, as I have acknowledged. As Christianity has faded in late modern times, the perception of human dignity has not faded in equal measure. And humanist reason, ironically, has sometimes shown a keener realization of human dignity, and more courageously pursued its practical implications, than has religious faith. If Christianity were to die out, it may be that the sense of human dignity would also eventually die out. At the beginning of the third millennium, however, this has not happened. The idea that a human being should always be treated as an end, not a means, has retained a hold on humanist and religious minds alike. It provides what may be the most significant piece of common ground on which faith and reason can meet.

Universality rests, then, on our sense of the sacredness of a human person. What does universality require? It has two major dimensions, global scope and equality. Both derive from the general principle that every person, regardless of nationality in the world at large, and regardless of social status within a nation, has a claim to respect. If this is so, then for a liberal nation questions of citizenship and legal residence are attended by a certain irrelevance. Illegal immigrants deserve careful consideration even if they must finally be expelled, and human rights violations anywhere in the world are matters of concern. And within a nation, whether a person pursues a remunerative and respected profession, belongs to the predominant race, professes allegiance to an established religion, is wealthy, is of high social standing, or is male — these things too are irrelevant. Dignity is unconditional. One way this rule is observed in constitutional democracies is in the treatment of those convicted of heinous crimes. They are not tied up in a public place to be spat upon or insulted by passersby. If prison guards mistreat them, this is understood as misconduct that must be investigated and punished. If they are executed, they nonetheless are addressed courteously and are consulted even concerning the menu of their last meal.

Some writers have criticized such universality on the grounds that it turns individuals into abstractions, separated from all marks of particular personal identity. No doubt this is true insofar as it attributes to every individual a dignity identical to what it attributes to every other individual. Abstractions can be extremely harmful to persons, and the concept of mere humanity is one of the most sweeping of all abstractions. It has been eminently useful, however, to concrete persons. It stands in the way of the moral relativism that hovers in the background whenever personal particularity is allowed to obscure universal humanity. It is a reminder that a person is not a thing.

The standard of universality, if based as it is here on the freedom universally characteristic of individuals, implies individual rights — to speak freely, to worship as one chooses, to enjoy a fair trial if charged with a crime, and so forth. Those troubled by the substitution of "mere humanity" for the concrete person often object to any emphasis on rights as obscuring duties. But if nothing can be done morally that is not done freely, then duties cannot be done as they ought to be done except by people possessing rights. Duties presuppose rights. If I am determined to fulfill my own duties, then I must take care that the rights needed for me to perform those duties are secure. If I am concerned that others be able to fulfill their duties, then I am necessarily concerned with their rights as well. This brings us back to the original liberal position. Willing liberty for all, I also will rights for all. Although I fully realize that liberty is worthless unless used for moral ends, which is to say that rights are worthless unless used for the performance of duties, first of all I must will rights. Those I can act to enforce. Duties I cannot enforce. There is no skirting the root fact that we are free. Stress on duties may be a way of resisting the idea that rights do not entail duties. But if it aims to replace the standard of rights with that of duties, it is misconceived. Duties can be fulfilled only by those who are free. Rights are prior to duties.

To avoid the aridity that critics fear in the liberal preoccupation with universal human rights, the Christian concept of neighbor has great importance. This concept suggests how the liberal stance can, without compromising its essential universality, attend to the concrete particularity of every human person. One's neighbor is at once particular and universal. He is a concrete entity, with national, sexual, racial, religious, and other characteristics, but he is also — in an ennobling sense — merely human. As someone encountered in the course of life, one's neighbor is concrete; a particular person. But as *anyone* who happens to be encountered, he is *everyone,* an embodiment of universal humanity. It may happen that one respects a neighbor for his moral, intellectual, or other qualities, and one may enjoy the company of a neighbor because his national, religious, cultural, or other characteristics render him congenial. Without fail, however, and regardless of all else, one will respect him for his humanity.

The meaning of this neighborly humanity (or, to use a rather forbidding philosophical term, "concrete universality") may be better understood if we recall the idea of serious communication as the proper use of liberty. The liberal stance is a communal stance, maintained through attentiveness and availability. According to the standard of universality, this must mean trying to hear what people everywhere are saying, whether by their words or simply by the way they carry on their lives in the sight of others. Universal communality requires first of all an attentiveness without boundaries. It means paying attention, so far

253

as the severe limits of human finitude permit, to human acts and suffering everywhere. As for speaking, very few of course can literally address the world. But all of us can try to avoid prejudgments based on nationality, race, and other such particularities. We can try to speak with an awareness of what human beings in various parts of the world are doing and undergoing. And finally, when speaking with utmost seriousness, we can try to speak in a way that would be comprehensible to everyone, if everyone was listening. Even in a state of complete isolation, as shown in accounts of solitary confinement, one can try to maintain a cosmopolitan bearing, listening and speaking as a citizen of an all-encompassing city.

Serious communication, of course, is dialogue, and the liberal stance, as we have seen, is dialogic. We have already briefly discussed whether dialogue, being essentially face-to-face, can be universal. The question is important enough to warrant further attention. Is the idea of universal dialogue a fantasy? Unless it is carefully qualified, it no doubt is. Inherent in our finitude and our dispersion in space is the impossibility of perfect communicative unity among more than a few. And inherent in our fallenness is the rarity and ephemerality of such unity even among a few. Still, the ideal of universal dialogue is not senseless. Any serious dialogue is in various ways universal. Thus, for example, all who listen in on a dialogue are participants (as is suggested in the very phrase "listening in"), and modern technology makes it possible for millions of people, in all parts of the world, to listen in on some dialogues. Further, those who listen in can inaugurate their own ancillary dialogues, and very often do. And there is a kind of universality in any dialogue inquiring into the major concerns of the human race, such as poverty and war. All authentic dialogue is situated in the midst of the world's troubles. That is why a great many may be interested in listening in. And finally, so far as participants in face-to-face dialogues address and attend to one another as neighbors, a dialogue between just two people can be implicitly universal.

Universality is a moral standard, and thus is intended for the governance of personal attitudes. Also, however, it has important bearing on society and its institutions.

The Public Realm

A nation cannot be purely and simply a community, but it can offer numerous spheres for serious communication. Nor can a nation be truly universal, although some nations, like France during and after the revolution of 1789, have claimed and aspired to universality. While the ideal of universal communality cannot be realized, however, neither is it meaningless. A nation can measure itself by this ideal and can strive to reach it. It can try to assure that its spheres of communication are open alike to all matters of serious inquiry and to all serious inquirers. In the fifth century B.C., Athens came far nearer to universal communality than did Sparta, and in the latter part of the twentieth century A.D., the nations of Western Europe were more communal and publicly open than were the Soviet Union and China. The ideal of the public realm is that of a society open, as fully as the nature of society allows, to the light.

The term "public realm" designates, not a single physical place or a single medium of communication, but a cluster of opportunities for open dialogue — open in terms of both important topics and serious interlocutors. There are always rules of entry, if only those pertaining to dress and decorum. But the rules are publicly known and in principle can be met by anyone, so that entry is not based on the personal preferences of the powerful. Thus a public realm consists of numerous public places, such as legislative and judicial chambers, classrooms and auditoriums, art galleries and bookstores, sidewalk cafés and coffeehouses. It incorporates various media of communication, such as newspapers and television studios. Even though communication occurs preeminently in words, a public realm includes places where music is heard and paintings are seen. And distinguished architecture, as expressive of personal vision, contributes significantly to the establishment of public, communicative space. To the degree that a nation offers such space, it earns the honorable, if commonplace, appellation of "free society." This of course is because searching communication is the proper use of freedom. By providing a public realm, a nation makes it possible for its members to carry on to the full the life of liberty.

The great philosopher of the public realm is a twentieth-century thinker, Hannah Arendt. While Arendt deserves to be honored for her original and elegant reflections on the concept of public liberty, her vi-

255

sion of the public realm is radically different from that being developed in this essay. In the first place, the public realm delineated in *The Human Condition,* Arendt's principal book on the subject, is primarily an arena of action. It is, to be sure, an arena of speech as well. But speech is construed primarily as a means of action rather than of inquiry for its own sake. Readers who envision her meaning with images of the ancient polis (as she encourages them to) are apt to think oftener of the Athenian Assembly debating public issues on the Pnyx than of Socrates engaged in philosophical conversation in the agora.

In the second place, and closely linked with the emphasis on action, is Arendt's aristocratic bias, as contrasted with the egalitarianism of the present essay. When Arendt discusses action, she is not thinking mainly of solving the ordinary problems of ordinary people. Indeed, she goes so far as to exclude economic questions from public debate. The final aim of action is not to solve practical problems but to achieve personal distinction on a scale that inspires lasting remembrance. The public realm is a place for doing things that bear recounting in the stories a society treasures and remembers. It is, in other words, an arena for heroes and their supporters. While it is public, it is not altogether universal.

Arendt's views are broadly similar to those of Nietzsche. For Nietzsche truth is a creative work achieved in the face of a chaotic and meaningless universe. Its aim, as one would expect, is action rather than contemplation. And any glory possessed by truth comes from the human courage and creativity that bring it forth and not from the intrinsic qualities of truth. To envision truth in this way leads almost inevitably toward aristocracy. Only a few have the strength to face the chaos at the heart of the universe and the imagination to shape representations of reality that serve human vitality and purpose. Although Nietzsche did not reflect on the idea of the public realm, had he done so he would almost certainly have conceived of it as a theater where great men could establish their identity in the sight of others. This is roughly the way Arendt conceived of it.

Emphasis on action, with its implicit pragmatism, can be attractive, suggesting qualities like resolution and courage and practical sagacity. Nonetheless, two unfortunate consequences inevitably in some form follow. The first is that truth loses its intrinsic splendor. In the thought of Plato, for example, truth is the visibility and presence of being in its glory and mystery. It does not serve any human end but is in it-self the ultimate human end. Something of the same sort can be said of the Christian idea of truth. To know God, and to know the sweep and grandeur of the destiny that occurs through Christ, is the culmination of human life. It is the "beatific vision" celebrated by Thomas Aquinas. In pragmatism all this is lost. Truth is a tool, a thing to be used. Its value lies in its utility. Hence William James's characterization of truth as the "cash value" of an idea.

The second unfortunate consequence of the emphasis on action is the loss of universality. This happens in spite of the genial and demo-cratic aura emanating from the pragmatic school of thought. That aura is due more to the personal qualities of particular pragmatists, such as William James, than to the intrinsic qualities of pragmatic philosophy. Pragmatism subordinates truth to action, action in turn requires power; and power entails the objectification of some persons by other persons. The logic is elitist. Some of the best-known pragmatists did not perceive this logic because of their insensitivity to human evil. They thought of action as arising from common agreement. Power was a neg-ligible consideration. It is not at all negligible, however, if actual hu-man nature is taken into account. A pragmatic conception of truth leads inevitably toward a conception of the polity as divided between the possessors of power and those on whom power is exercised. Granted, the line between the powerful and the powerless may be hard to draw with any precision. Nevertheless, the distinction is implicit in the pragmatic view of truth, and the consequence is that universality disappears. If a public realm of any sort remains, it is a theater for heroes, as it was for Arendt.

But doesn't the same thing happen when a contemplative, rather than pragmatic, view of truth is adopted? Plato, after all, was hardly democratic. It might be argued that the populace will be divided, if not by the requirements of action, then by the difficulties of grasping the truth, as well as the rarity of any real interest in doing so. I have already tried to show, however, that this is not necessarily so. Ordinary life and work involve ordinary people in concrete reality. In this way they pro-vide access to the truth. And if we put in place of "communication" the word "conversation," then the idea that very many who are not counted as intellectuals are capable of pursuing the truth with others, and have some interest in doing so, becomes more plausible. No doubt philosophy, theology, and the various arts are carried on by small minorities, and the majority, at least in late modern times, is distracted by the lure of entertainment and recreation. But to suppose that all in the former class are truth seekers and all in the latter class are indifferent to the truth is at the very least a great oversimplification. Plato's elitism did not follow inevitably from his reverence for truth.

The loss of full universality in Arendt's public realm, that is, the loss of equality, illustrates the chief practical problem the ideal of universality presents. It is that of maintaining the proper amplitude of the public realm. The ideal of universality sounds unobjectionable to many ears, but in fact few fully accept it. One way the evil in human beings surfaces is in the narrowness by which the public realm is continually threatened. Some of the most vulgar and destructive grounds of narrowness, such as race, class, and nationality, are so well known and so routinely condemned that little attention need be given them here. But there are more subtle and less widely recognized forms of narrowness.

There is, for instance, the assumption I have been arguing against throughout this essay: that religion should be excluded from public life. I have argued against this assumption on the plain grounds that religion and reason alike are concerned with the truth and can learn from one another and ought to do so, both for the sake of truth and for the sake of the humanity of those on both sides. The principle that government should be religiously uncommitted is valid beyond question. But that religion should not be heard in public discourse is quite a different principle. It drastically narrows the public realm, confining public dialogue to those who are committed to humanist reason. How can there be universality in a society that excludes from the public realm all who speak for as primal and ancient a human orientation as religion? The secular narrowness of modern times is of course only a reversal of the religious narrowness of earlier times. Needless to say, for the public realm to be reserved for religious faith, with humanist reason excluded, is indefensible. But so is the opposite condition.

If one kind of narrowness would confine public dialogue either to humanist reason or to religious faith, another would confine it either to culture or to politics. The cultural bias is represented by the many devotees of the arts and literature who, especially in democratic times, have disdained politics; the political bias is represented by the ancient Greeks and by the numerous writers who have drawn inspiration from the Greeks. As for the former bias, it must be granted that disdain for politics is not entirely unjustified. The human spirit rarely reaches its greatest heights in the activities of politicians and public officials. A public realm made up purely or primarily of the political would be made up largely of banal and expedient human utterances. It would be void of the highest human interests. But this does not imply that politics ought to be spurned. It implies rather that it ought to be elevated through culture. Politics is the activity through which we take on responsibility for our overall situation in history. It must therefore ask, and in words and deeds answer, questions of the good life. How and for what should we live? To deal with these questions politics needs to be enlightened, and to be enlightened it needs culture. And therefore it needs the attention and participation of the cultured. The most atrocious politics is carried on in the totalitarian states where free culture is entirely crushed.

As for the cultural bias, were the public realm exclusively cultural it would be detached from many of the daily and pressing realities in which every collectivity carries on its life. Human discourse is no doubt debased by political necessity — by the dilution of the ideal that practicality always requires, and by the vulgarity encouraged by the need for popular support. Thus politics drags culture down. But it drags it down to ground on which culture must stand if it is not to float arrogantly and blindly in imaginary heavens. What may be the most brilliant culture the world has known flourished in an era and a place in which politics likewise flourished and which has received its usual name — "Periclean Athens" — from a political leader.

One more form of narrowness must be noted, this among the most virulent. It is encouraged by an almost unavoidable anomaly of the public realm, and by an associated sentiment often called "nationalism." The anomaly is that universality must be sought and maintained within the confines of a particular society, or nation. The virulence of the sentiment, nationalism, is that the worth of the particular society is greatly exaggerated and that of surrounding societies discounted and ignored. Universality disappears. Someone might argue accordingly that the ideal of the public realm should be translated into that of a global polity. Universality must be institutional to be real. Such an argument would be logical yet less than compelling. A world state would be a very good thing if the state were perfect and its public realm also perfect —

259

at once entirely open and unerringly discriminating. But of course, states never approach perfection, and in even the best of them public life and popular culture are ordinarily unedifying. In the worst of them public life is completely stifled. Edward Gibbon noted in *The Decline and Fall of the Roman Empire* how hopeless life could be under a global despotism. There is no escape. Gibbon's observation is particularly apropos in an age that has learned the techniques of totalitarianism, and it has obvious bearing on the issue before us. It is prudent, surely, not to wager everything on the quality of one global government and one global public realm. A good public realm is so difficult an achievement, and subject to ills so diverse and numerous, that a plurality of polities seems a prime matter of practical wisdom.

A plurality of polities, however, saddles us with the virtually impossible task of attaining universality within the bounds of parochial societies. Not that the task is self-contradictory. After all, ancient Athens and Renaissance Florence, celebrated still for the breadth and depth of their humanity, were both tiny in comparison with modern nations. They were far smaller in population and area, indeed, than most modern cities. But social and political particularity is a temptation to the savage and impassioned particularity evident in twentieth-century nationalism. In its extreme form, exemplified by fascism, universality is violently repudiated.

To summarize, universality means breadth — "both-and": both culture and politics, both reason and faith, both national particularity and cosmopolitan openness. But breadth is difficult for finite and morally erring creatures. Human finitude and pride demand narrowness. Hence societies are always infected by the kind of constriction of public dialogue that results from fervent activism, one-sided secularism, consuming political passions, national arrogance, and the like. Such constriction can be resisted, however. Two kinds of resistance deserve brief comment.

One is public criticism. Communication in the public realm must be given a critical edge. Among civilized and vital people, freedom of speech always threatens, although it rarely prevents, sanctified narrowness. This is to say that dialogue can be pitted against idolatry. Behind the vicious and defiant shapes taken by human narrowness in the twentieth century there has always been an idol, a finite god, such as the Aryan race or the working class. Such idols call forth deified parties and leaders. Vital, thinking speech spontaneously resists false deities of this kind. Testifying to this is the fact that resolute idolatry is always despotic. False gods cannot allow their pretensions to be freely examined. From the Christian point of view, one distinction between a false god and God is that the former is enslaving, the latter liberating — granting that God has often been falsified (for example, by dogmatism) and thus made enslaving. Humanist reason, although not immune to narrowness of mind, has proven through people like Voltaire and Mencken its ability to bring down false gods. Thus a not insignificant piece of ground common to faith and reason is the enmity they both bear, so far as they are true to their basic principles, to idolatry. Both, so far as they are true to their essence, are on the side of the critical dialogue that makes for public openness.

Another way of resisting the narrowing of the public realm was discussed in a different context earlier in the essay. It is withdrawal into private life. Paradoxically, universality may be defended by a strong assertion of personal particularity. This may seem self-contradictory. It is noteworthy, however, that the most determined and fanatical forms of narrowness are just as bent on destroying the refuge of private life as they are on destroying free public life. As we have seen, the two realms have the same purpose — the realization of free humanity. In relation to this purpose the realms are complementary. The private realm is where you can seek community and truth by choosing your own interlocutors or by devoting yourself to solitary reflection. It is a sequestered public realm. At least this is the standard by which it is justified. If a perfect public realm could be achieved, the private realm could be abolished. As it is, the private realm is needed mainly as a place where universality may be realized in resistance to the narrowing of the public realm. A society in which that narrowing occurs, and universality is lost, alienates its most gifted and intelligent members. Often it enslaves or kills them in order to protect its idols. Safeguards of privacy are intended to assure that this does not happen.

When privacy is destroyed, universality may of course survive in hidden places. We noted this in our earlier discussion of solitude and of the possibility of a solitary communality. If some individuals with a capacity for universality are left alive, then the sequestered life of each one of them, even if carried on in prison, may constitute a kind of miniature and secret public realm. Such is exemplified by Boethius and *The Con-*

solation of Philosophy, and by Dietrich Bonhoeffer in *Letters and Papers from Prison.*

A more trying form of narrowness than parochialism may be inequality. The very ideal of public liberty does not generate parochialism, whereas it does generate inequality. And inequality, whether arising from nature or from social institutions alone, necessarily narrows the public realm. This is a circumstance that deserves further examination.

Evanescent Elites and Occasional Authorities

We have already discussed the fact that liberty naturally works against equality, even though liberty and equality are logically inseparable ideals. We now must note a closely allied fact, namely, that liberty always works against equality, not simply in one excellence or another, but in that particular excellence that consists in the will to be free. At any one time, in a liberal society, only a few will be living as reflective, responsible beings. Most people will settle down within the existing order and, without thinking of doing otherwise, will live in much the same way as those around them live. Their opinions, habits, vocations, and enjoyments will be those of their compatriots. In short, their liberty will be largely wasted. Mass society strengthens this tendency but does not create it. If liberty is an ordeal, then in any age, and in any social setting, great numbers will recoil from its demands. They will find that the social uniformities around them offer easier and pleasanter ways to live.

Perhaps the few who are living their liberty will exhibit distinguishing marks — for example, unselfishness and generosity, or creativity in the arts, or originality in their personal lives. Sometimes the few who are free will display uncommon reflectiveness or learning. They may be distinguished by professional or business success, or by strong character and dignified bearing. On the other hand, these aristocrats of liberty may be invisible to outside observers. To suppose that they are usually members of a distinctive social group or category, such as artists or intellectuals, would be greatly in error. Most members of such groups appear to be conformists, and a truly free person may be no more comfortable as an artist, or intellectual, or other exceptional type, than as a technician, a businessperson, or a civil servant. It would be in error to suppose even that a free person will stand out from society and its groups as a distinctive individual. Freedom does not necessarily issue in nonconformity. The rule of liberty is not to refuse to conform but only to think, and if possible converse, before conforming or not conforming. The free, in any liberal society, are the few who live with a constant consciousness of their untransferable responsibility for their lives, and who accordingly live reflectively and so far as they can dialogically.

The public realm must fail unless it comprises a number of these aristocrats of the spirit. In principle a regime of liberty can eventuate in futility. Everyone can refuse to be free. The very concept of freedom implies this possibility. So Hannah Arendt was not wholly wrong in delineating the public realm in aristocratic colors and forms. A public realm without "heroes" — distinctive individuals, with the courage to live their own destinies — is very nearly a contradiction in terms. And to imagine the public realm realistically we must think that some of these heroes will probably be noticeably, even dramatically, different from those around them. A convincing mark of freedom in a society is, as John Stuart Mill intensely felt (but excessively emphasized), a few striking manifestations of individuality. We know that Athens in its great age was truly a free society partly by reading of Socrates, and Pericles, and Cleon, and Alcibiades, and the other unique personalities that populate the pages of Thucydides and Plato.

Use of the term "elite" to name the free minority, in the title to this section, is half-ironical. It is not altogether ironical because going through the ordeal of liberty — living reflectively and responsibly in spite of the tragedies and failures that threaten every earthly life — is not a suitable object of irony. It deserves unambiguous respect. In that sense those who carry on the life of liberty make up a true elite. However, they are not what most of us think of as an elite.

For one thing, at least some of them would be unrecognizable. This might be the case not only when they are young and developing but also throughout their lives. They might not have written books or gained public office or accomplished anything that can be widely perceived as a mark of distinction. They might even, as judged by prevailing social standards, be apparent failures. In any liberal society, some who have achieved real freedom are sure to partake of such obscurity. This has at least one important consequence. The free cannot as a whole constitute an outwardly identifiable group. Some of them will be unrecognizable not only to the society as a whole, but also to one another. Since they are free, they are individuals, each distinct from every other individual. Scattered among the populace at large, they necessarily lack any form of inward cohesion or outward visibility.

As a group or category, moreover, the "elite" in a liberal society must be highly unstable. They are an evanescent aristocracy. This is why at the outset of this section I used the phrase "at any one time." *At any one time,* only a few will be carrying on the life of liberty. But the few who are free in one set of circumstances may, when circumstances change, lapse into thoughtlessness. In one of the greatest studies of an inwardly free person, Boris Pasternak shows Dr. Zhivago "going to seed" in the final years of his life. Indeed, most people surely at times fail to summon the courage required by their freedom. On the other hand, perhaps no one is so immersed in the world as never to be provoked, by some crisis or passing inspiration, into measuring up at least momentarily to the demands of liberty. The chance for those inwardly enslaved to free themselves possibly never passes, and remains for as long as they live. Can we deny that someone who has spent a life in thralldom to custom or prevailing opinion or a thoughtless disposition might at the end, by dying with courage and a clear mind, discover freedom? Perhaps it takes only a few years, or even a few moments, of real freedom to make one a kind of aristocrat of the spirit. Dr. Zhivago's life, as Pasternak depicts it, was not made meaningless by his final years of "going to seed," for he had once lived freely.

It deserves particular notice that the "elite" of liberty may contain many learners. The capacity for living freely may be only gradually developed, and such development may take a long time. It is striking how often the Bible indicates that even God takes time to achieve a purpose. "First the blade, then the ear, then the full grain in the ear" (Mark 4:28). The kingdom of heaven appears first, Jesus says, not as a breathtaking spectacle, but as a tiny seed, which only gradually grows into the full tree. God cannot be expected suddenly to lift one into the heavens, according to Hebrew scripture, but only to enable one to walk without fainting (Isa. 40:31). One of the principal qualities the biblical God demands of men and women, as we have seen, is simply the patience to wait. The elite of the free, all of this suggests, may consist, not only of the masterful and princely, but also of the long-suffering, the patient, the silently resolute, the dying and the dead.

Popular rhetoric often depicts "the free man" as a proud and up-right figure. Such a picture contains some truth but is also misleading. Liberty that is well understood and taken seriously is destructive of pre-tension and self-delusion. While it asks only that we be lucidly and un-failingly ourselves, we discover that so modest a demand is not easily met. Being clear-minded and responsible, among the dilemmas inher-ent in most life situations, and in spite of powerful temptations to in-dulge in comfortable or exhilarating illusions, is a task that is never per-fectly accomplished. One of the truths in the doctrine of justification by faith is recognition that few if any are justified solely by the way they live. This is to say that liberty humbles us.

The peculiar nature of the aristocracy of the free may be seen more clearly if we recall earlier discussions of suffering. I have argued that liberty brings suffering inevitably. The idea of a suffering elite may seem almost self-contradictory. Suffering casts us down. The "suffering servant" in Isaiah was "despised and rejected by men" (Isa. 53:3). And those who beheld Jesus on the cross did not see him as "lifted up," as he was said to be in the Gospel of John. On the contrary, they "wagged their heads" in scorn. And if suffering does not inspire admiration, neither does it enhance self-esteem. To suffer is to abide on the level of the low-est of the human race. Anyone can suffer. Suffering equalizes. We are no doubt unequal in intelligence, beauty, strength, and so forth, but we are equal in our ability to hang on a cross.

The idea of a suffering and despised elite is not self-contradictory but only paradoxical. At least this is the Christian view. "If any one would be first, he must be last of all and servant of all" (Mark 9:35). Those who by wealth, social status, physical health, or other advantages are spared the agonies of crucifixion are not usually thereby rendered deeper or more compassionate. They may in that sense be cast down by their good fortune. On the other hand, the afflicted may, by virtue of af-flictions they share with the vast multitudes who have lived on the earth, gain entry into the mystery of human destiny. Like Jesus, when he was nailed to the cross, they may be lifted up by misfortune.

One of the burdens often borne by the liberal elite is that of being consigned to solitude. They may have to live their liberty alone even though liberty is essentially dialogic. This is exemplified by the hypo-thetical woman on the American frontier, made wise by years of hard experience and biblical reading, but isolated from serious conversation. It is probably exemplified too by countless obscure bureaucrats, businesspeople, farmers, day laborers, and others whose conversation is confined to trivia by a distracted and unthinking society. And it is surely exemplified by many slaves in early America. As I have shown, however, in cases such as these, people may inhabit inner communities. Such inner communities may be enclaves of humanity, centers of truth-seeking inquiry, even in the midst of human and natural desolation. It is not unthinkable that those who take on the arduous labor of sustaining and inhabiting such communities are thereby in some sense ennobled.

The separateness and solitude of the free should not be overemphasized, however. Many of them will occasionally possess a degree of authority, if not over many, then over one or a few, and if not in public life, then in private life. Such authority can play a significant part in drawing people toward the truth and rendering a society a place where truth is taken seriously and now and then seen.

Authority is a formidably complex subject, partly because there are several very different types of authority, such as spiritual and political, and partly because authority has diverse sources, such as high office and personal prestige. Authority in the pure and proper sense of the word is spiritual and consists in the likelihood of being believed, not necessarily by many but by someone else. The end of such authority is a spiritual state, that of knowing the truth. The end of political authority is action, rather than a spiritual state. In a liberal society, however, the action sought by a political authority cannot for the most part simply be commanded. Others must be persuaded, and this means that political authority cannot be without a spiritual dimension. The diversity of types of authority is illustrated by scientific authority. A celebrated scientist will almost certainly be believed by almost everyone when he speaks on scientific matters. His authority differs from all other spiritual authority, however, in that very few are competent to judge whether he is right. He is believed blindly, the only check being his fellow scientists. That being the case, those who believe him cannot fully comprehend what it is they believe. Whether this quite deserves the name of authority can be fairly asked.

The main thing about spiritual authority is that it fully comports with liberty. Indeed, it depends on liberty. Authority differs from power essentially. One who possesses power is able to get others to do what he wants them to do. Those subject to power may be acutely conscious, as in obeying a hateful order, that they are so subject. Or they may be manipulated so subtly that they are unaware of their subjection. One of the central problems in political theory is how power — to which even a liberal state, needing a government, must assign a major role — can be reconciled with liberty. This problem will be taken up further on in the present essay. But spiritual authority presents no such problem. It does not exist unless it is freely assented to. If assent is contrived, as through propaganda or terror, then it is not authority that is thus exercised but power. Only in liberal societies, where assent is uncoerced, can spiritual authority exist.

If authority is fully compatible with liberty, then it is fully compatible also with equality and community. As for equality, a person is not lowered or debased by assenting to spiritual authority, for the act is thoughtful and free. It presupposes personal responsibility. And community is not destroyed by authoritative relationships. Rather, it is constituted. As the primacy of Socrates in many of Plato's dialogues illustrates, community, consisting in a common search for truth, is not compromised by the leadership of someone who is followed thoughtfully and freely.

I have paid little attention to authority. That is mainly because most authority (spiritual authority) is false. In all liberal societies there are many who know little and care little for the truth but are nonetheless voluble and widely believed. This is the case both in the political and the cultural spheres. Politicians are notoriously shallow and deceptive, and popular culture is largely sustained by writers and mass media executives who depict the world as people want to think it is and not as it is in truth. This, of course, is simply a manifestation of the radical evil in human beings. It is tempting to say that when Thomas Aquinas depicted heavenly hierarchies of authority, he depicted the only authoritative hierarchies that are valid. Earthly hierarchies are invariably infested with ambition, deceit, and thoughtlessness.

Nonetheless, true authority — authority of the kind that brings reality to light — plays a role in the creation of community. Dialogue is not always a simple interchange among equals. Although most of those who are listened to and believed in the public realm merely confirm the shallow and false sentiments already prevalent, a few among the evanescent elites may emerge onto the public scene and receive attention.

267

Those who do may be remembered and may, long after they are dead, cast light on common realities and dilemmas. Often this happens through literature. Works such as the Bible and the plays of Shakespeare are the presence on the public scene of spiritual authorities long dead. In view of the kind of speculation and debate that goes on in connection with such works, it is apparent that their authors are dialogic partners with people who live long after them. If there were not a certain number of true authorities, living and dead, in the public realm, it is difficult to see how there could be a public realm. Much of the remainder of this chapter bears on the work of authorities of one kind or another.

It is likely that authority plays an equally important role in the private realm, that is, in the multitudinous face-to-face conversations that, although less spectacular than public debates, are no less important in creating community. There are perhaps not many conversations in which there are no traces of authority — no participants whose remarks carry more weight than those of others. And perhaps there are not many of those who are truly free who do not ever in conversation open up reality for a few others. A free person is apt to be an occasional authority, consciously or not.

Even in the "idle talk" that makes up most conversation, there may be glimmerings of light due to these occasional authorities. The mark of idle talk is confinement to the familiar. It consists in gossip and in rehearsals of things long known. Placing people comfortably together in a common world, such conversations are perhaps not useless. But they are not entered upon in search of the truth. Still, the truth may break through unexpectedly. Interest in the truth is not a monopoly of academicians and their students. People without any thought of being intellectual often have the wit and penetration, even in casual remarks, to cast light on common realities. Hence, recognizing that society contains a vast mass of unexploratory talk, one ought also to recognize that running through it there may be a filigree of dialogic gold. If so, this may be due to the authority of one of those unknown, unofficial, more or less afflicted and solitary aristocrats of the spirit who are living their liberty.

Church, Culture, and Politics

Ideally, the public realm is where liberty is lived. It is where humans can speak and act on their universality. The private realm, for all its importance, is a makeshift, necessitated by the flaws in the public realm. Hence, serious reflections on liberty are bound to give attention to the institutions and structure of the public realm. Such is the purpose of this and the following section.

There can be no public realm without institutions to give it form and make it real in the social world. These institutions are of three sorts: the various churches, synagogues, mosques, and other places where people join to inquire into and worship ultimate reality, and which, for the sake of convenience, I shall call simply "churches"; the diverse organizations and groups such as universities, art museums, and film studios that sustain secular culture; and finally, the public courtrooms and legislative chambers, as well as media of mass communication, where political issues are debated. It goes without saying that these are diverse forums, governed by diverse authorities and regulations. But all are places that, under varying rules and conditions, are accessible to everyone and where, in some fashion, matters of interest to everyone can be illuminated and pondered.

It may sound odd to hear churches spoken of as an institutional form of the public realm. They are ordinarily thought of as sectarian, as places of ritual and worship, of moral exhortation, and of idiosyncratic faiths. They are all of these. But if we take the Christian churches as exemplary, they are formed in response to what they understand to be definitive truth, the Word of God, and since this is addressed to all humankind, every church is essentially universal. Their universality is manifest in the fact that normally they are open to all. They are places where anyone who wishes to can come and inquire into the truth. Ritual and worship are not unconnected with the truth; rather, they are ways of glorifying and contemplating ranges of truth that lie beyond firm rational comprehension — in other words, the mystery of being. And the cultivation of morality, also a prominent concern of churches, aims at making people fit for approaching God, that is, rendering them proper and deserving vessels of ultimate truth. And while in the eyes of all of us there are idiosyncratic faiths, none are idiosyncratic to those who pursue them. Every faith, to the faithful, is simply universal truth.

Contrary to the common disdain of secular observers, the churches have not been bad institutions. They have for the most part been innocent of crime on the scale committed by states. They have probably been less marred by personal ambition and intellectual frivolity than many university faculties. They have built a tradition that offers plausible versions of eternal truth; they have worked out liturgies that for millennia have provided form and satisfaction for the human concern for the ultimate; they have inspired exceptional righteousness in a few and have cultivated ordinary righteousness in countless generations of ordinary people. Finally, they have carried on extensive and diverse works of charity. Surely a respectable record.

Yet secular antipathies toward the churches are not baseless. Often global, they have offered positions of power and prestige, and in this way have incited both spiritual and temporal pride. Further, they have ordinarily allowed themselves to be absorbed into the world, and have exhibited the same moral mediocrity and the same intellectual shallowness that are seen everywhere around them. The upshot is in plain view. Christian clergy do not conspicuously display greater righteousness or wisdom than anyone else. As for the laity, they are referred to by Paul as "the saints," and many are truly very decent people. On the whole, however, they are not obviously more saintly than outsiders are. And while there may be great wisdom in Christian principles, efforts by the churches to make that truth known in the public realm, and even among their own members, have often involved not only dogmatism and repression, but also the confusion of eternal truth with passing prejudices and political programs.

In large measure, then, the churches have failed. They have brought forth few who are saintly or wise. Christians (and no doubt Jews, Muslims, and others with respect to their own organizations) might argue that God has nonetheless worked through them, and I believe that is so. But God apparently has also worked outside them and has left them, after two millennia of development, in a state of manifest if not glaring imperfection, a state suggesting penitence rather than triumph as their appropriate, however unaccustomed, posture.

The failure of the churches renders it singularly inappropriate for Christians to draw as sharp a line as they often do between those inside and those outside the churches. To draw such a line is to establish a dichotomy even less warranted than that between believers and unbelievers, and again to threaten the universality intrinsic to the mission of Christ. Just as the dichotomy between believers and unbelievers takes too little account of the complexities and difficulties of belief, that between people within and without the churches takes too little account of human evil and the corruptibility of every social group without exception. Both dichotomies indicate that little thought has been given by the churches either to their own moral fallibility or to the ways a merciful and sovereign God might work independently of human arrangements.

Nonetheless, the churches are essential sectors of the public realm. They offer open areas where truth can be sought and shared. The one serious question concerns their organization and operation. Should they be more decentralized and more spontaneous; less dogmatic and less hierarchical? Should they even eschew a professional clergy? Openness depends on diversity of groups, authorities, and powers. Diversity can be a confession of imperfection. It is therefore appropriate both when human beings face transcendence and when they face one another. It makes for greater public openness than does a single, centralized organization. It is surely a good thing that the Western world is no longer under the exclusive reign of the Catholic Church, even if that church be far nearer the truth than the Protestant churches. A governing principle here is simply that human evil is exacerbated when power is concentrated. Another governing principle is that wisdom cannot be reliably gained through professional training or reliably disseminated by a certified minority. Professionalism connotes the absorption of the free intellect into organized society. This can mean definite standards and habitual rigor of conduct and intellect. But it tends to suffocate spontaneity and originality, and rarely does it bring forth wisdom or sanctity. In short, professionalism means mediocrity in positions of authority.

The possibility of solitary dialogue offers one way of surmounting the failure of the churches. Just as citizens of the vitiated and strife-torn cities of ancient Greece might, according to Plato, form and inhabit their own inward cities, so Christians living amid the disorder and failure of the churches might struggle, each one alone, to establish and center their lives in their own inward churches. The capacity for doing this is a capacity for independent reflection and discernment, and for the conduct of one's life in accordance with the truth. It is a capacity for liberty. Were it lacking, institutional diversity would fail of its aim, which is the personal unity of a free man or woman.

Another way of surmounting the failure of the churches is the establishment of alternative public spaces. The fallenness of the human race, plainly to be seen in the antithesis of society and community, makes it imperative that humans not be confined within a single order of society. If the imperative is expressed in the rule of diversity among the churches, it is also expressed in the rule that there be public spaces completely outside those offered by the churches. There must be a humanist, secular culture — nonecclesiastical agencies, such as universities and newspapers, and nonclerical individuals, such as novelists, poets, and composers. Humanist realms of liberty are no less vital to believers than to unbelievers. To the benefit of believers, they may inspire and provoke the churches into greater dialogic openness. Humanist thinkers and writers may enliven ecclesiastical minds, and often have, as illustrated by Marx and Freud. And they provide unbelievers with the only public communal spaces they have. They allow creative minds to evade the constraints of established doctrines and traditional symbols. For all they increase the amplitude of public liberty.

As essential as humanist culture is to public liberty, however, its ultimate aim is not as different from that of the churches as one might suppose. Its aim is truth, and not merely any truth or some miscellaneous accumulation of truths, but a truth that is comprehensive and final. Whether any such truth can be found, or is even worth searching for, is a question certain to arise in the cultural realm and is quite legitimate. But reason by its very nature seeks to surpass every truth it possesses and to reach a truth it cannot surpass. The call of truth is the call of being in its deepest mystery — for Christians, God — and no one can ignore it. Humanist culture differs from religious faith mainly in being unconfined by any particular version of revelation. Hence its representatives can be less constrained by authorities and doctrines, and less concerned with tradition and precedent, than are their religious counterparts. It is nonetheless manifest that many philosophers, novelists, painters, and other humanist inquirers are as dedicated to the truth as are theologians and priests. Not only do they strive to enter into the mystery of being, but they imagine and reach toward a mystery that is all-encompassing and final. This is evident, if nowhere else, in the fact that they entertain visions drawn from religious traditions, as in the great requiems and oratorios, and in paintings of biblical scenes like the crucifixion. And who can deny that the lives of the great painters, poets, and novelists have the character of an unceasing search, even though it be for something that can never be assuredly grasped?

While humanist culture may be indispensable to public liberty, it is more dependent on the churches than most humanists might want to admit. As we have seen, dialogue depends on unconditional respect for persons and truth. This respect, while often found among the irreligious, depends finally on premises that are rationally undemonstrable. It depends on faith. One of the critical functions of the churches in the public realm is to articulate and encourage the requisite faith. It is an irony of history that the churches have often been enemies of dialogue, yet that a dialogic society, a society in which the search for truth is taken seriously and is open to all, may depend on the churches. Was it pure coincidence that the violently closed societies created by twentieth-century communism were always aggressively atheistic?

For many people public liberty means neither church nor culture. Rather, it means politics. The public realm is a place where political issues are debated and resolved. The main institutions of the public realm are thought to be legislatures, mass media, town meetings, and so forth. The public and the political are virtually equated. This is a serious oversimplification. Politics cannot serve the truth as single-mindedly as can religion or culture. Political authorities are responsible immediately, not for truth itself, but for the kind of liberal order in which the search for truth can be carried on. This is less a responsibility for speaking and hearing than for acting. And acting is under different imperatives than are the speaking and hearing that constitute dialogue. Even if acting takes the form of speaking and hearing, as it does when persuasion is used, it is not the same as truth-seeking dialogue. It is an instrument of power, and this radically affects its character. To act effectively government officials must sometimes hide the truth or distort it. They must mislead and deceive. Participants in the churches and humanist culture are subject to no such necessities. They can be purer, dialogically, than can political leaders.

Political institutions do, however, belong in the public realm, this for two reasons, one pertaining to the health of politics, the other to the health of culture and the churches. As for the health of politics, the conduct of political affairs is in need of the civilizing and refining influence that comes from culture. Immersion in politics does not encourage the best human qualities; it habituates its practitioners to the calculus of

273

power. It is well, therefore, that political leaders be imbued with the disciplines that make a civilized mind. It is also well for them to be compelled to share public space with writers, journalists, and others whose fidelity to the truth is free from the imperatives of action. And it may be particularly important, considering the antidialogic currents that political action sets in motion, that political leaders be shaped by the churches. Where else are they as likely to learn the respect for persons and truth that political decency depends on but political action works to weaken?

As for the health of church and culture, these need involvement with politics because they need grounding in intransigent, nonfictional reality. They need this first of all, of course, for the sake of truth itself. Unrealistic and utopian truth is not truth. And not only does it lack the inherent dignity of truth, it also endangers society's practical interests. Men and women who are intellectually distinguished but politically disengaged can have a powerful influence on the course of a society's affairs. When they are radically unrealistic, the consequences can be dire. I have already pointed to the way intellectuals in France and Russia, prior to the great revolutions in those countries, contributed through their grandiose dreams to upheavals that were wanton and murderous to a degree entirely out of proportion to any rational political purpose. In both countries, politics was the monopoly of a very few. It conduces both to the spiritual health and the worldly interests of societies, then, for its cultural and religious leaders to be kept in touch with the refractory and anti-utopian realities political leaders must deal with.

As everyone knows, however, politics and religion have scarcely been friendly partners in the public realm. The conflict between them has been virtually continuous ever since the rise of the Christian church. Both, however, have deep roots in the Western tradition, and both make strong claims on people's loyalties. The conflict between them is a troublesome, and potentially destructive, reality in public life.

Church and State

The task of harmonizing these two institutions has provoked extreme and inflamed emotions. On one side, once the Christian church had become a large, influential institution, many Christians, at least among the clergy, wanted it to rule the earth. Even late into the highly secularized twentieth century there were Christians for whom official standing, if only in some trifling form like acknowledgment of God in a grade-school flag salute, was a matter of impassioned concern. On the other side, "the wall between church and state," a useful slogan perhaps but an unworkable standard for institutions that are inevitably intermingled, was taken literally and applied obsessively. Secular minds too became impassioned about symbolic trifles. Thus adjustment of institutional relations was a source of overwrought feelings and immoderate demands.

The issue undoubtedly has profound importance — for us because of its bearing on the public realm, the main arena of liberty. Yet it has no simple solution of the sort extremists seek. This is not so much because the proper relationship of church and state is complex (although it is), but because it is ambiguous. The idea of complete separation is unrealistic because both work within the same territory and have many members in common. But the idea of simple fusion cannot, for reasons endlessly rehearsed in Western history, be seriously entertained. If there ever was an issue in which extremism was inappropriate, the relations of church and state are that issue. Let us briefly examine the main considerations on each side.

The idea of a "wall" between church and state is arguably not only impractical but also unwise. If Christianity, centered on the Logos, is — or can be for those willing to see it as such — a kind of common wisdom, then it has strong claims to a hearing in the public realm. Much of it bears directly or indirectly on matters of manifest concern to every person, such as the character of human beings, the nature and authority of the good, and the significance of death. Much of it can make sense, and even be in some form acceptable, to people believing neither in Christ or God. To this extent the churches can — for all the obscurantism that stains their history — be sources of light for a whole society.

This is a possibility not to be despised. While the state does not have to be simply an area of darkness, it does tend in that direction. Politics is always in some measure an affair of base calculation and immoral action. Therefore much that is discussed and done by political leaders is held back from the light — shielded from public knowledge and from judgment by the standards of ultimate truth. It is a matter of great moment for every polity and people that political darkness be in some degree penetrated and limited by light. People who are informed with Christian wisdom can do much to see that this happens. When supporters of a "wall" between church and state stand in the way, they side with a perilous darkness. Representatives of humanist reason are perfectly right to be wary of Christians in power. But Christians as partners in public dialogue are a different matter. They can help to illuminate the political realm.

Humanists of course are inclined to believe that reason can provide all the light needed in the public realm. But the greatness of humanists such as Plato and Kant lay partly in their keen awareness of reason's limits. When reason denies its limits, however, and dogmatically closes itself off from nonrational sources of insight, it can be either empty and futile or proud and tyrannical. In the former case it may bring forth imposing but hollow metaphysical systems. In the latter case it can do great damage to liberty. It can largely dissolve the moral ground underlying the principle of the dignity of the human person. And disdainfully spurning the doctrine of original sin, it can inspire historical projects far beyond human possibilities and leading almost inevitably to violence and failure. Illustrative is the moral abyss into which fanatically antireligious and ostensibly rational Communist leaders fell in the Soviet Union and elsewhere. And Tocqueville attributed the violent and catastrophic character of the French Revolution not only to the lack of realism among intellectuals but also to the fact that the Catholic Church had been discredited, causing Christian wisdom to be ignored by enemies of the old regime.

This is not to suggest that Christian leaders and writers are always or even usually wise. Clearly they are not. They have often, for example, embraced a conservatism with scarcely any justification in Christian wisdom. They sometimes side with repressive and militaristic political regimes that are completely at odds with Christian standards. They are adept at finding and thrusting forward scriptural fragments that sanction their own prejudices while ignoring the overall meaning of scriptural texts. There are many such examples of Christian folly and perversity. This is to say that just as reason needs to be checked by faith, so faith needs to be checked by reason. And this, in turn, is to say that the public realm is where it needs to be subjected to the rigors of dialogue with humanist reason. In sum, to bar Christians from the public realm, as humanist liberals so often urge, would be harmful not only to humanists, who need sources of wisdom beyond bare reason, but also to Christians, who need the cleansing of critical reason.

If the churches are essential participants in public dialogue, however, they also are untrustworthy rulers. This is to reiterate a maxim — separation of church and state — that is so familiar as to be hackneyed but so elemental that it has to be recognized. The main reasons for the rule have been in various ways stated and restated in the course of this essay, and indeed in the course of history. They can be largely reduced to the main theme of this essay, that human beings must as far as possible be left at liberty in their primary choices, and no choices are more primary than those put before them by religion. At the outset of this essay we noted the ironic fact that Christianity in its depths accentuates liberty, or at least the inner freedom that necessitates outer liberty, yet on its theological surface has not traditionally been strongly in favor of liberty. This anomaly is explained partly, as I argued, by the Christian sense of sin and its disruptive potentialities. It is explained also by the fact that Christians have a creed they want the whole world to believe. Can they leave the fate of the creed to wayward human impulses? They must, but the temptation not to — to promote the creed with force — is strong. Added to all this is the indisputable fact that Christian faith provides no immunity to sin. Christians in power are no less corruptible than any others in power. For all these reasons, the case against theocracy is about as strong as any case not in the area of the scientifically demonstrable can be.

Any discussion of church and state in the public realm comes inevitably upon the question of language. What sort of language can Christians involved in public affairs appropriately use — the same they might use in church, or the same their humanist interlocutors use? What sort of language should humanist reason be willing to hear? If there is any tenable rule in this matter, it is surely this, that Christians in politics recognize that some, or even most, of their interlocutors reject scriptural authority and Christian revelation, and moreover, have an unquestionable right to do so. They must ordinarily address them, therefore, in other than biblical and theological language. This is not to imply that distinctively Christian language, or candid avowals of faith, are precluded. Kant remarked, in the *Critique of Pure Reason,* that "it is perfectly permissible to employ, in the presence of reason, the language of a firmly-rooted *faith,* even after we have been obliged to renounce all pretensions to *knowledge*" (p. 426, emphasis Kant's). Christians must be allowed to stand in the public realm in their true identity, that is, as Christians. But likewise, Christians must allow non-Christians to stand before them in their true identity, which is that of free human beings who have not embraced Christianity. To do this they must seek common ground. Such ground may be found, as we have seen, in conscience, in reason, and in spiritual intuition of the kind that often visits secular minds without regard to their religious or irreligious principles. To operate on this ground Christians must usually translate convictions habitually clothed in biblical or traditional Christian language into language that is not offensive to humanist ears. Surprisingly often this can be done without spiritual loss, and sometimes, by ridding the faithful of pious clichés, with spiritual gain.

At stake in the issue of church and state are the integrity and breadth of the public realm. The rule must be polarity — neither complete separation nor complete unity. The two swords must be kept apart without creating two separate realms of discourse. To do this is a difficult and highly civilized accomplishment. It would be hard, however, to overstate its importance. The public realm being the realm of liberty, were society to fall into two mutually estranged camps, liberty would be turned into a formality without fruition in public dialogue. Were society to become a single camp, however, liberty would be unlikely to survive even as a formality.

CHAPTER 10

Universality: History

━━━◅◉▻━━━

The Question of Historical Meaning

To ask, What is the meaning of history? may be to pose the most daunting of all the questions human beings struggle with. It immediately makes us aware that we do not have history as a whole spread out before us, like a novel or a play, which we can study and reflect on. History is unfinished, and we are in the midst of it. More broadly, the question makes us aware of our profound philosophical and theological nescience. Seemingly unanswerable questions abound. Does it make sense to think of history as at some time being finished and available for inspection? How could it be? What would come afterward that would not be simply further history? What possible vantage point for observation and reflection could there be outside of history? And who would stand there? Could history have meaning if there were no one to perceive the meaning? If, for example, humans became swamped in sin and all deservedly perished, would that be meaningful? And what do we mean when we ask about meaning? Are we asking whether history makes up a single coherent story? Are we asking whether history has any worthwhile results, such as a store of wisdom or a perfectly just society? If all the evil people who ever lived ended in hell, would that make history meaningful? Or would the very existence of hell, a kind of torture chamber from which none could ever escape by dying, make history meaningless?

Such questions appear unanswerable. In spite of them, a free life leads one inescapably to ask about the meaning of history. Reflecting on the overall purport of earthly events is not the idiosyncratic preoccupation of a few sequestered intellectuals. Rather it belongs among the proper occupations of any free person, and it is not as far beyond the intellectual reach of ordinary people as one might suppose. A few answers are possible — answers that are no doubt sketchy yet are not wholly lacking in validity and value, and are not incomprehensible to a person of ordinary intelligence. The general idea of historical progress shows this. It is well to seek out these answers, and reflect on them, for false answers can do much harm. The philosophy of history may have a recondite look, but it can move not only philosophers and theologians but also human multitudes and the men of power who lead them.

It is first of all the universalism inherent in the liberal ideal that poses the question of historical meaning. Since in claiming liberty for myself I implicitly claim it for everyone, lucidly seeking or possessing liberty casts my mind in the direction of all humanity. In the preceding chapter I wrote as though "all humanity" referred simply to all those living on the earth at the moment I was writing. At that moment, however, many were dying and many were being born. And when I myself was born, countless human beings who once lived were already dead, and after I die, countless others will be born. By what logical or moral right do I confine my concept of universal humanity to those living at the particular historical moment at which I happen to be writing? Quite clearly, a truly universal concern comprises the dead and unborn as well as the living. It comprises all of history. The liberal mind, insofar as it is lucid and logical, is conscious of humanity as it extends through all time.

This is only the beginning, however, of liberal historical consciousness. That consciousness is given focus by the fact that humanity is a problematic species. It is affected by that deeply rooted disorder we have already discussed — "original sin," or "radical evil." In consequence, human history is marked by every form of estrangement, ranging from quiet uneasiness in the presence of others to violent conflict. Society is pervaded by loneliness and resentment, and history is punctuated by war and civil conflict. Furthermore, humans die — very often violently and prematurely. The passage of historical time leaves a trail of corpses. Looked upon with eyes unclouded by sentiment or ideology, the panorama of human events presents an ugly and discouraging spectacle.

We naturally try to come to terms in some way with the spectacle. We may do this by framing it as a story. This helps a little. Scattered about in the human record we can see many small stories, meaningful sequences of events, and we wonder whether there may not be a single story giving form and meaning to the whole spectacle. But the stories even of the most recent and accessible events are mere interpretations, subject to debate and change. And the stories of the entire drama (if such a phrase has any meaning) can be nothing more than surmise. Moreover, none of the stories entirely eliminates the apparent senselessness of what we see. Progress, except perhaps in technology and science, is neither clear nor unambiguous. There have been horrors in recent history that match the worst things ever to happen. And not only do these cast doubt on the reality of any apparent progress. They also force us to ask how any degree or kind of progress could redeem the sufferings human beings have endured and the crimes they have committed. What sort of story could render all the terrors and failures of human life on earth acceptable?

History looks radically antipersonal. Most persons are in some degree abused and neglected during their lives. Many die prematurely of disease or are killed, either accidentally or purposely. All without exception die and eventually are forgotten. Events ride roughshod over personal lives, and the greatest historical achievements often come only by the use and destruction of countless numbers of persons. As already noted, personalism appears to be an absurd philosophy, incongruous with basic reality. The idea of destiny seems, in the face of the mountain of suffering piled up by human history, nothing more than a desperate fancy. The life of a human being is apparently decided by fate, by occurrences that are completely indifferent to the well-being of persons. On the terms laid down in this essay, history can be meaningful only if the tide of events is somehow considerate of persons as ends in themselves. But a mere glance at history seems to show that individuals always and inevitably are treated by history as mere means — as things to be used, and eventually discarded and destroyed.

In sum, we are prompted, both by our universality as human beings — a universality we must more or less consciously recognize when we claim liberty — and by the problematic character and situation of the human species, to ask whether the whole human record will amount to anything more than "a tale full of sound and fury, signifying nothing." Are we, however, *compelled* to ask this question? Could it be that we are transgressing the limits proper to a finite and erring creature when we try to think about something so far beyond our comprehension as the meaning of history?

I submit that we are *compelled* to ask — that if we failed to ask we would be transgressing against our nature as communal and truth-seeking beings. In our universality we seek a community that encompasses all humanity. It may be impossible to imagine such a community or the means by which we could reach it. It is nonetheless in our nature to aspire to it. This is shown by the great visions of the Bible and of revolutionary humanism alike. And as truth-seeking beings we seek the truth about the entire life of the human species on earth. The truth we long for is as limitless as the community we seek. Such statements no doubt sound grandiose, but they merely recognize the nature of our communality and our reason. Both are fundamentally impatient of limits. Both seek the unsurpassable.

If history has no meaning, however, there can be no human community — no community comprising all men and women, and all eras. There would be no truth that all of us might share. Truth makes sense of things. By doing that, it tells us what our responsibilities are and guides us toward righteousness and wisdom. But if in the final analysis there is no sense in things, then there is no truth to serve as the bond of a human community. Our communality and our reason are in that case wholly unrelated to the possibilities of the human situation. We are mocked by the universe. Liberty, as a moral enterprise, is as meaningless as our history. Sartre spoke of man as "a useless passion." Such he is if his history has no meaning. And in that case liberty can be no more than a matter of whim and impulse.

Given these concerns — concerns not of overextended philosophers but of all human beings, common and uncommon — it is not surprising that ideas and declarations concerning history and its meaning are heard again and again, are given rapt attention by multitudes of human beings, and all of this in spite of the enigmatic character of history and the forbidding difficulties involved in thinking about history. It is not mainly philosophers of history who focus attention on history. It is human nature and the human situation that do this. Every political undertaking, every political concern and hope, involves more or less conscious assumptions about the meaning of history, if only the assumption that progress of certain kinds is possible and significant. Such assumptions are certain to be proclaimed in one way or another by political leaders. And ordinary busy and unreflective people care a great deal about these assumptions. Thus every nation embodies a vision of history — of the nation's origins and mission — and that vision often plays a key role in arousing nationalistic emotions and commitments. The vision will inevitably be celebrated by nationalistic politicians. It is noteworthy too that universalism does not disappear from these particularist visions. Every idea or intimation of historical meaning places my own generation, together with past and future generations, within a universal drama, however shadowy it may be. It enables me to think of myself and my fellow citizens as engaged, perhaps in behalf of the whole human race, and perhaps in opposition to some perverse but powerful segment of the human race, in a single vast and mysterious enterprise. It is the universal that makes the particular significant.

It is tempting to say that it is professors in their ivory towers, not ordinary men and women immersed in daily reality, who scorn the philosophy of history. Why was Marxism so stirring a creed for so many, and for so long, in spite of its crushing failures? In part, surely, because adherents of the creed could think of themselves as players in an all-encompassing historical drama. The savagery of events, and the hopeless estrangement of generation from generation, had seemingly in some sense been surmounted. And why has the American doctrine of progress been so tenacious in spite of events like the Civil War that seem to disprove it? Surely because it has provided, like the Marxist vision, sensations of time-spanning comradeship.

It seems, then, that we have to ask the question of historical meaning. But what answers have any claim to credence?

History and Destiny

The idea of destiny was introduced, in the chapter on personalism, as a way of thinking, not about history, but about individual persons. It was intended to show how persons might be understood as ends in themselves — possessors of dignity — in spite of the gross indignities visited on them by time. I called time, envisioned in its radically antipersonal aspects, "fate." I argued that, contrary to appearances, time might be thought of as "destiny" — as mysteriously accordant, even in its darkest moments, with the unfoldment of personal being. In Christian thought the classical instance of destiny is the crucifixion of Jesus — in appearance the humiliation and obliteration of a person, in reality (as symbolized in the resurrection) an event carrying the whole human race across the abyss of sin and death. Humanist reason may recoil, offended, from the Christian story, yet it has its own devices for breaking through the appearances of fate and picturing time with a more friendly visage. Not only is there the traditional doctrine of progress, with inspired versions such as Bergson's "creative evolution." The Hegelian and Marxist philosophies of history mark a conscious effort to transpose the dialectic of crucifixion and resurrection onto the secular plain.

Signs of destiny can be seen, as I tried to show, in every true story. Indeed, there are probably such signs in every story since there are bits of truth in every story. It does not follow that everything about which a story can be written, such as a nation or a political movement, has a destiny. The destiny intimated in stories is always that of persons. Good stories are hard to write because persons, with their destinies, are often more or less buried by events. Storytellers have to dig beneath the antipersonal surface of events to discover the persons underneath. It follows that true stories are not mere factual chronicles, which almost any observer might record. They are creative works, dependent on skill and insight. They are creative, not by inventing facts or arranging events as the narrator pleases, but rather by discerning and bringing to light the inner logic — the personalist logic — of events worthy of narration. All serious storytelling is an inquiry into destiny. Thus you look for the meaning of your life by shaping your memories as a narrative, and you come to know a friend by piecing together a picture of his past.

I pointed out that we think of meaning in a person's life as something that is discovered. Thus Michelangelo said that in carving a statue he was not imposing an image on the stone but bringing to light an image already present in the stone. Contrary to his own expectations, he discovered the criminality of Brutus in carving his bust. Dostoyevsky's notebooks show that his characters would sometimes take on independent lives, doing things he did not want them to do. It seems that a destiny is discovered, not arbitrarily chosen. Although some talk casually about creating one's destiny, the story of your own life cannot be written in advance. It cannot be created. It can only be perceived during or after its emergence. Yet freedom enters inevitably into the concept of destiny. Your destiny must be freely affirmed and freely lived, for otherwise it would not be yours. It would not be, as it is, your very selfhood. In this way it is unlike a moral norm. To ignore it would not be merely wrong. It would be a choice of nothingness over being. If you failed to affirm something required by your destiny, you would, even if you gained the whole world, lose your own soul. In this way your destiny — the life story given to you to live — has unique authority.

Can the concept of destiny be applied not merely to individual persons but also to history? To answer this question it may help to glance again at the pattern destiny exhibits in personal lives. As we have seen, Christianity holds that one story, that of sin and redemption, as told in the Gospels, is the archetype of all true and significant stories. Two great facts dominate all of human life: wrongdoing and death, our moral waywardness and our mortality. Few carry on lives that are not seriously engaged in dealing with the human bent toward doing things that ought not to be done, whether we call this bent "radical evil" or "original sin." And few carry on lives that are not shadowed by the consciousness that they must die. As understood by Christians, the first of these facts, sin, gives rise to the second, death. The main challenge to every person is to somehow face down or overcome the dominion of these facts. Destiny consists in meeting that challenge. It comes about through the forgiveness that conquers sin, and it eventuates in a life that is not snuffed out by death. Admittedly, this pattern is not conspicuous in many cases. Personal lives typically look tangled and unfinished, and novels and short stories seem to display innumerable plots. But the drama of sin and redemption can assume many forms and can be intimated in widely different events. And Christians believe that the life, death, and resurrection of Christ is the archetype of all true stories and thus is present in some form, perhaps in being partially reenacted, perhaps in being tragically defied, in all personal lives.

Sin and death are not, of course, challenges human beings can meet alone, according to the Christian story. There must be transcendental involvement. Forgiveness can come only from the author of the moral law, God, and only God can lift the curse of death. Christ, as God's "Word," or "Son," may be said to summarize the Christian understanding of God's involvement in human destiny. Christ is the event in which human destiny is revealed and given. Such a view is of course unacceptable to humanist reason. Yet almost anyone, regardless of religious or antireligious views, may feel a responsibility, not imposed merely by society or self or others, for carrying on a certain life. In that sense, it is a responsibility coming from beyond everything around us — given in that sense by transcendence. And almost anyone will sometimes feel that death is unfitting even if inevitable. And non-Christians have often displayed a composure in the face of death that suggests an awareness, if not of personal immortality, then of something in the human soul not overwhelmed by mortality. The Christian story has a plausibility that is not confined to those explicitly committed to the Christian faith.

Can the pattern of sin and redemption be seen, not just in personal lives, but in history? At first glance, it may seem that it can. Christianity asserts a close connection between history and personal life. Christ is presented in the Gospels as a historical figure. The times and places of his birth and death are carefully specified. The identity of the Roman emperor and the Roman proconsul in Jerusalem also is specified. This is striking partly because Christ is also presented as intensely personal — a matter of eternal life and death for every particular person. The Gospels seem to say, then, that history and personal life are intimately connected. And one must agree. History has an impact on every life and must therefore enter into every personal destiny. Can it be said, however, that history has the same *pattern* as every personal life — the pattern of sin and redemption?

It is hard to see how it can without obscuring the most crucial of realities, the person. History is about states, churches, classes, and various other groups; it is about collectives, that is, society and various social groups. Individual persons become historical figures only so far as they represent, act in behalf of, or color the life of collectives. But collectives do not sin, properly speaking, even though flagrant sins are committed in their name by individual persons. Nor do they die, as persons do. They eventually pass out of existence, but the existence of a society or a social group is not shadowed always by the certainty of eventual death. In short, historical entities do not have to surmount the twin challenges that give rise to personal destiny.

Moreover, the claim that collectives do have destinies, that they pass through a stage of sin and into a stage of redemption, is not only false to reality. It is also false to fundamental values. It gives to society or to a social group the same kind of reality an individual person has. Once this is done, an inevitable further step is to attribute to it the same kind of dignity an individual person has. It allows for the idea that some particular collective, such as the Nazi state or the Aryan race, is an end in itself. When that happens all grounds for liberty crumble. The primary evil in Marxism lay in the transfer of the drama of redemption from individual persons to societies.

This does not imply, however, that history is meaningless. Rather, it opens the way to a personalist interpretation of historical meaning, namely, that history derives its meaning from the contribution it makes to the realization of personal destinies. It does not exhibit the pattern of sin and redemption in itself but has a part in the fulfillment of that pattern in the lives of individuals. For Christians it does this by disclosing the ultimate truth that makes it possible for individual persons to carry out their destinies. This truth — the life and death of Christ — is not an isolated event but the key to all preceding and subsequent history. The past is preparation for, the future the working out of, the earthly consequences of, what happened on Calvary. Since it is also the key to every person's destiny, it allows all of history to be incorporated in the destiny of each person.

For humanist reason, history can take on meaning in a like way. It can be envisioned as the process through which truth comes into the world. For humanist reason, however, the key events would be such things as the lives of the great philosophers and the development of modern science. Individuals in search of the truth might look on such events in somewhat the same way as Christians look on the crucifixion. For humanist reason, as for faith, if there is such a thing as destiny, then history would have meaning by serving the destiny of individual persons.

It is particularly to be noted that the Christian and humanist visions of historical meaning as centered in the emergence of light are not mutually exclusive. They overlap. In spite of Paul's ironic dramatization of the conflict between Christian "folly" and Greek "wisdom," Christians have always been interested in, and very often respectful of, Greek philosophy. Plato has been virtually baptized. And there is every reason for Christians to be interested in and respectful of modern science, even in those forms, like Darwinism, that have been so troublesome to it. Science — even Darwinist science, one might argue — plays a part in displaying the wonders and beauties of God's creation. And humanist reason, for its part, has not been indifferent to Christian insights. As already noted, humanists long ago made their own the idea of a dignity belonging to every person. And with that idea they have accepted the universalism and egalitarianism implicit in Christianity.

Worthy of emphasis in the Christian version of historical meaning is the subordination of historical time to personal time. The drama of sin and redemption is purely personal. History partakes in that drama only by serving in the salvation, through truth, of individuals. Individuals do not give their lives significance by being actors in history. History takes on significance only by being incorporated in the lives of individuals. History may obliterate individuals and may have the look of a cosmic unfoldment. But apart from persons it is nothing. It has less significance than the least of the persons who are caught up and drowned in its currents. This is a key point in relation to liberty. Can humanist reason envision the relationship of person and history in a like fashion? Probably so. The remainder of this section may suggest to humanist minds how it might be done.

The denial of destiny to society, or to any collective entity, and correspondingly its confinement to human persons, is a move vital to any proper understanding of liberty. For reasons I have already set out, we hunger for meaning in history. We recoil against accepting fate as the final truth of the great world around us. So we look for destiny in the events that threaten us. No one can deny that we find in these events apparent hints of destiny. As early as Paul and Augustine, Christians saw a stage of sin, marked by the law, in the ancient world, and then a stage of redemption, marked by the coming of Christ. It would be easy to expand such hints into a full-fledged theory of history as a drama of sin and redemption. And also tempting. This temptation calls forth thinkers such as Hegel and Marx. If I am right, however, succumbing to the temptation is fatal to liberty. To ascribe to the lives of historical entities like states, races, and classes the redemptive drama that gives meaning to the lives of persons subverts the personalist foundations on which liberty rests. For maintaining those foundations it is crucial, instead of subordinating the person to history, to subordinate history to the person.

A human person is microhistorical. A parallel statement is often made about the order of nature, or the cosmos. A human being is said to be microcosmic. This view had an important place in the philosophy of Thomas Aquinas. It is highly important, if personalism is to be maintained, and the dignity of persons to be defended, that the same view be taken of history. A human being is an embodiment of history. It is a dangerous but natural tendency for us to be strongly impressed with things that are vast and more or less incomprehensible. Nothing is more vast, or more incomprehensible, than history. If a leader or a state can claim authority bestowed by the destiny of a nation or a class, individuals are reduced to dust, which can properly be swept out of the way. Both Nazism and Communism won their times of ascendancy by convincing multitudes of people that their authority came from an all-encompassing drama in comparison with which the drama of an individual's life amounted to less than a wisp of smoke. It is easy to see in these enormous tragedies the importance of reversing the historicist proposition (if I may so term it) and of insisting that history is within, and in this way subordinate to, persons.

Must we then abandon the idea that history has a story? Clearly it cannot have a story that conforms with the archetypal story. But it may have a story that enters into the archetypal story. This is another way of saying that history serves, and is subordinate to, the individual person. In the case of history, the main story would concern the manner of truth's entrance into the world and its subsequent development. On the hypothesis I am advancing, however, this would not be an absolute story, the same for every individual. Its form would depend on the destiny it serves. Every individual, carrying out his destiny, would have to be a kind of historian, framing his own account of history. This is a task most people would accomplish only roughly and more or less unconsciously. It would be inherent, however, simply in choosing among the truths that history makes available. There would consequently be diverse stories. Christians would frame a different account of history than rationalists, Protestants than Catholics, positivists than existentialists. Most people would largely take for granted the historical story offered by their church or their country. They would, however, if not utterly frivolous, need a rough picture of the past. Liberty would consist partly in every person being allowed and encouraged to envision history in accordance with a narrative subordinate to the narrative of his own personal life.

History, then, must be kept within the person. Still, in obvious ways the person is within history. After all, we are not gods. We are immanent in events, and do not rule them. We are finite, without firm control of history or sure comprehension either of its beginning or its end. And we are mortal and are severed thereby from both past and future generations. To refuse to be a part of history would be godly pretense. At first glance it might seem that hardly anyone could be so exorbitantly proud as to indulge in such a pretense. A second glance would show otherwise. Twentieth-century civilization was laid waste by men who considered themselves rulers of history and convinced multitudes of their fellow men that they actually were. The lesson of humility came at an exceedingly high price. It seems, then, that we face a paradox. It is important not only to keep history within the person. It is important also to keep the person within history.

The situation can be envisioned in terms of contemplation and involvement. There is a contemplative dimension, at least for Christians, to the human relationship with history. As already noted, it is widely held by Christian theologians that all earthly history is complete in the mind of God. This comprises the future. Events that from a human point of view are yet to happen, from the divine point of view lie within an eternal present. Human destiny in every detail is thus an object of divine contemplation. This suggests that it might, in eternity, be an object of human contemplation. It also suggests that, even in time and on earth, the contemplative attitude evident in a great historian like Edward Gibbon has a kind of transcendental sanction. And the secularity of a mind like Gibbon's suggests the universality of the contemplative ideal. It can attract both reason and faith. From the contemplative point of view, history is within the person.

But of course, for humans there is no eternal present. The historical scenes we contemplate are limited, fragmented, and even to a degree conjectural. Our knowledge is broken and flawed, and our view of the future largely imaginary. We do not live on a plane above history. We are not like the gods in Homer, looking down on the siege of Troy from secure and leisured habitations above. We are immanent in the tide of events. We are therefore in no position to pursue contemplation as our sole relationship with history. We must accept our situation as inhabitants of history — as parts of history — rather than as godlike spectators.

Here we encounter another of the paradoxes of personal being that have been prominent throughout this essay. Many of them were dramatically stated by Paul. We are dying, but behold we live. We are weak, yet at the same time we are strong. We rejoice in our suffering. We experience insults, infirmities, calamities, hardships, and all manner of adversity, yet we are content with these. We even glory in them. All such paradoxes arise in the mind of Paul from the supreme paradox in Christian faith, that of the crucified god (the phrase is Jürgen Moltmann's). The paradox of being part of history yet embodying history is similar to these paradoxes. In our fallenness, as perverse and evil creatures, we are reduced to being mere parts of history. In our exaltation, as recipients of grace, or (for humanist reason) simply as good persons, we are microhistorical. In our relations with history, as in all other relations, we must take into account the two fundamental dimensions of our destiny — guilt and redemption, sin and sanctification. By accepting our status as mere parts, we acknowledge our guilt and acquiesce in the conditions created by our fallenness. Through our capacity for contemplating history, at least in limited ranges, we gain intimations of a destiny that transcends history — the eschaton, a matter to be discussed in the final chapter.

Of the two basic human relationships with history, contemplation will seem to most people the nobler, for it reflects human transcendence. But willingly being a mere part is no less vital. As humbly facing our finitude and fallenness, it is essential to our truthfulness — to our efforts to free ourselves of illusions and see things as they are. It is essential also to our readiness for rising eventually above our fallenness. We must, then, take on our status as parts of history. How do we do that?

Taking Part in History

At first glance, being a mere part of history, rather than an overlord, looks problematic. It suggests subjection to sequences of mechanical causation. That cannot be a fitting relationship with history for a human being. How can it be avoided? The answer is plain: through those primal human characteristics stressed throughout this essay, that is, our freedom and our consequent moral responsibility. To be a part freely and responsibly is usually called "participation." To be within history humanly is to be, not merely a part, but a participant. As we have seen, being human is not like being a deer or a dog — being merely an unconscious and unwilled embodiment of the universal characteristics of your species. It is being consciously and deliberately a member of the human species. This brings us back to another major theme in this essay, community. To be a free and responsible member of the human species is to enter into communicative relations, so far as possible, with all humanity as extended throughout space and time. The ideal is that of universal communication. Obviously, the ideal cannot be realized — at least not by human beings, and not within history. To any one member of the human race, the overwhelming majority of humans will always be strangers. Yet the sphere of communication can be indefinitely widened, and doing that is therefore a responsibility.

Communication that is historical would presumably be with the past and with the future, with the dead and with the unborn — manifestly a daunting (some might even say absurd) project. The dispersion of the human race in time — the untraversable chasm between people of one era and people of another — is one of the most tragic, and most nearly irreparable, features of the human condition. The estrangement of generation from generation, of century from century, comes close to being an irresistible fate. We can do little about it. Yet to think no more about it, to forget the people of past and future times, would mark an elemental failure of our humanity. We know this; even ordinary, unintellectual people know it obscurely. We sense that historical research and writing are important human enterprises, and we sense that their purpose is not merely that of better understanding our present situation. Of equal or greater importance is the purpose simply of recognizing and making contact with people who have gone before us. Ancient ruins fascinate us all. Books about particular historical eras and events — the Periclean age in ancient Greece, the fall of the Roman Empire, the Reformation, the founding of the American republic — are widely read. Also testifying to our yearning for contact with past generations are our typical images of heaven. There, we imagine, we shall meet those who have died. One may think of this as mainly a common man's dream, but it was Karl Barth who remarked (not altogether jokingly) that his first act on reaching heaven would be to look up Mozart. Ancient ruins, historical accounts, and heavenly dreams: such gestures toward the past fall pitifully short of the universal human community of which our dispersion across centuries and millennia seems to deprive us conclusively. Yet they are not contemptible. They testify to our hunger for boundless community.

Moreover, the hunger is not entirely unsatisfied. We are able at some points to breach the walls that confine us to the present time. A public realm is not altogether confined to the immediate historical moment. The past is not voiceless. If great works of art and literature from the past are given attention in the course of public dialogue, we initiate a kind of conversation with people no longer living and we allow their insights to enter into present efforts to uncover the truth. And if present participants in public debate are well-informed concerning history, in that way too those who have lived but live no longer can be interlocutors in present dialogues. But what of generations yet to come?

These in some ways are more distant from us than generations of the past. No faculty, such as memory, gives us access to them. Forecasts even of coming years, to say nothing of coming decades and centuries, are notoriously flimsy. Yet in all we do and say we can be mindful that we are creating an inheritance for those who will live after us. We can try to speak in ways worthy of their attention and to act in ways they will respect and find worthy of study. We can found and strengthen institutions that will help them to live freely, and we can pass on the traditions and customs that undergird significant liberty. As acts of communication, these may be highly inadequate. They do, however, enable us to open the public realm toward the future.

Participation in history is not achieved, however, by communication alone. Communication is possible only within those protective shells we call "polities," and polities are constructed and maintained by the activity we call "politics." Hence, as participants in history we cannot confine ourselves to communication. We must also engage in action, or politics.

Politics can and ought to be historical — action not merely in the present situation but also in history. Following ancient Greek usage, the political is the comprehensive. The polis, from which the word "political" is of course derived, was the comprehensive association, comprising families and other associations lacking self-sufficiency, hence belonging within a polis. Its aim was no less comprehensive than its makeup: a good life. Participation in the polis, as small as it was in territory and population, in effect was participation in the life of universal humanity. Even though it contained only a small number of people, it provided a life fitting for all people. With the passing of the polis, this universality became an explicit ideal and in the great empires something like a reality.

In the Greek mind, however, the political was not comprehensive enough to take in very much history. Greek historical consciousness was largely undeveloped. Historiography was not a fully developed discipline, and there was no conception of history as a single, all-encompassing human drama. Hence politics was confined to the moment, even more than the pressures of practical necessity cause it ordinarily to be. Under the impact of Hebraic and Christian scripture, however, the Western mind became distinctly historical. The human realm was not only spatial but temporal as well. And comprehensiveness meant not only the whole world but also the whole of the human project, from beginning to end. This is evident in a figure like Augustine. Hence for the modern world there is sense in saying that politics can encompass our responsibilities toward humankind as extended throughout the ages. Doing this brings the historical past and future into the context of the present situation. It implies that participation in the politics of one's society is enlightened in the degree to which it is carried on with an awareness of the place of that society within, and the impact of its actions on, the course of the world's history. And it entails a sense of responsibility toward both the past and the future — a cultivated appreciation of what has been inherited from the former, and a realization of what is owed to the latter.

For the word "political" to serve its purpose in the present context, it needs to be broadened beyond its ordinary usage. Politics is not only running for office, maneuvering for partisan advantage, and the like. It comprises everything connected with the business of securing the outer safety and the inner liberty of a society. It involves both deliberation and choice, dialogue and decision. It is noteworthy that for Hannah Arendt, political action (or what she calls simply "action") is carried on mainly through speech. And for the ancient Greeks speaking and listening, especially in courts and legislative assemblies, were a large part of politics. Politics was dialogic conduct of the affairs of the polis. For modern peoples, inhabiting societies far larger than the ancient polis, and obliged often to allow multitudes of citizens a political role, it seems reasonable to think of politics as carried on not only by narrowly "political" activities, but also by varied personal and more or less private activities of a quiet and casual sort — for example, by paying attention to the situation of one's society and to the speech of those responsible for dealing with it; by conversing seriously about current issues; by taking positions in conversation and debate; and finally by voting, a quickly accomplished and infrequent act, without appreciable influence on the course of affairs (a single vote among millions of votes is necessarily inconsequential), yet an occasion for political speech, thought, and choice. In such ways as these, bearing in mind always what has gone before and what is yet to come, and our responsibilities in relation to both, we take part in history.

It hardly needs saying that the standard of historical participation gives sanction to activities of a more absorbing and dangerous kind. André Malraux was a kind of poet of heroic political action. The occasions for political action were great events, such as those generated by efforts to overthrow or defend established governments. And the actions Malraux glorified involved serious risks to one's life. Malraux's outlook is colored both by Marx and by Nietzsche. It shows a concern at once for the long-range historical results of action and for the self-sacrificial qualities that give some actions an intrinsic worth, apart from consequences. There is a degree of validity in Malraux's ethic. If participation in history is a valid standard, then political heroism is admirable. Like Hannah Arendt's ethic, however, it is inevitably aristocratic. Many who might be capable of political heroism never find themselves in circumstances in which such heroism is possible or appropriate. Moreover, it neglects the highest value, that is, communication. Everything is absorbed into the drama of action.

To summarize the view sketched above, participation in history is primarily a communicative activity. Political action is essential, yet secondary, since its primary function is founding and guarding polities in which communication can occur. Such action, moreover, is under a communicative standard. To the utmost possible extent political power must take the form of rational persuasion. Communication as historical participation means not only communicating with present interlocutors with a consciousness of the lessons to be drawn from the past, that is, assuring that all dialogue is historically well informed. It means also entering into communication with past and future generations by regarding the words and acts of earlier times as acts of communication directed into the future that we now embody and live; and by framing our words and acts so that they can be attended to and understood in coming times. To the extent that such participation is achieved, the public realm reaches beyond the present moment and encompasses all of history. Public responsibility binds one to both past and future. Furthermore, the historical consciousness that links an individual with generations past and yet to come gives a temporal dimension to solitude. The ideal of a public realm with historical amplitude, seldom realized outwardly, may occasionally be realized as an inward city, a city without temporal boundaries.

This view puts us in a position to reflect more fully on the meaning of history.

The Consummate Community

The hypothesis suggested by the preceding discussion is simply that history, in its final meaning, is the form and substance of the community toward which free and responsible human beings continually strive. It is the culmination of the drive toward all-encompassing communication that constitutes historical participation. This is to suggest that truth, fully known, will turn out to be historical truth. It will be the drama of sin and redemption — in humanist terms, of radical evil surmounted in goodness — completed, known, and eternally present. It is difficult to speak about matters we understand so little in terms with even a tinge of plausibility. But if truth, fully known and fully shared, is the highest value, and if there is a force in things (for Christians, God), or forces (for humanists, progressive tendencies in history), it is not entirely unreasonable to imagine a time when all truth will be known and unreservedly shared. Nor is it unreasonable to think that the main content of this truth would be the very drama of man's ascent from darkness into light. This, at any rate, is the hypothesis I am advancing.

This hypothesis may be saved from appearing as merely an intellectual fantasy by noting that passages in the New Testament envision all things being gathered together at the end of time in Christ. All things would presumably include all that has happened in the past, all dominions and powers, and all ventures in communication. Thus the author of the letter to the Ephesians (whether Paul or one of his followers)

296

speaks of God as having "a plan for the fulness of time." The plan is "to unite all things in him [Christ], things in heaven and things on earth" (1:10). And the author of the letter to the Colossians asserts that in Christ "all things were created, in heaven and on earth, visible and invisible, whether thrones or dominions or principalities or authorities — all things were created through him and for him. . . . in him all things hold together" (1:16-17). He asserts also that through "the blood of his cross" it pleased God to "reconcile to himself all things, whether on earth or in heaven" (1:20). These passages presumably concern a final, history-encompassing community.

Further, the hypothesis may be brought down to earth, from a heaven of excessive abstraction, by noting its relevance to the concept of neighbor, with its face-to-face implications and its associations with physical help — a concept reminding us that even though the range of human imagination and concern comprises the history of all the world, we are very limited creatures, living inside of history and not above it, and having obligations, many of them more physical than spiritual, to the particular people in our immediate vicinity. The point of interest here is that the particularity of neighborly responsibilities is not in conflict with the universality of our historical responsibilities. The neighbor, as potentially anyone, is an embodiment of universal humanity. This implies, strictly construed, that the neighbor is an embodiment of history — a microhistorical being. This suggests that one's historical responsibilities might be fulfilled, at least by those able to envision the neighbor in his full historical character and setting, through very concrete relationships. Properly understood, it calls for an imagination that envisions past and future ages in the face of a wife or friend or partner in work. This is not as impossible a task as it may at first appear to be. I do not really see a black friend unless I see him against a background of slavery and stubborn prejudice. I am not conscious of my wife unless I am conscious, continually, of the time and place in which she grew up and of the fact that she has been shaped by all the conditions, some of them historical and some physiological, inherent in being a woman and not a man. The ideal thus suggested is that of neighborly life and politics. What I know of history and the historical goals I envision should not be abstractions, floating in my imagination above the heads of the people I encounter in my daily life. They should be vivid in the faces of these people, my neighbors.

History so envisioned does have a story, a story concerning the emergence of light — for Christians, above all in the life of Christ, for humanists, in Greek philosophy, in modern science, and elsewhere. The story also concerns the ways in which human beings have apprehended and used the light. This story, however, does not constitute a destiny. There are no historical entities apart from particular persons who might have destinies. As I have emphasized, states, classes, and other collectives do not have destinies, for they do not sin, and die, and gain redemption. History does not comprise, but is comprised within, personal destinies. Hence the historical story must be envisioned as a strand within every personal destiny. An individual human being transcends and encompasses the history of the whole world. On earth this is a far-reaching (some would say "wild") abstraction. The passages quoted from Ephesians and Colossians, however, claim that it will finally be a reality.

What is humanist reason to make of these ideas? Very little, perhaps. It is hard to see how those relying on reason alone can do anything but dismiss as wayward flights of human fancy the visions of Ephesians and Colossians. In a fallen world they will usually do this with expressions of disgust and will forswear all further communication with protagonists of religious faith. If they could surmount the narrowness natural to both humanist and religious minds, however, they might indulge their religious interlocutors with a measure of good humor and remind them that, at best, they are speaking of matters no human intellect can grasp. And they might direct their attention back to that figure that both faith and reason can join in honoring, the neighbor. Doing this, they would play a fitting role in the great enterprise of universal communication.

These reflections of course open the door to great and dehumanizing illusions of the kind that gave Marxism so destructive a power in the twentieth century. The temptation to idolize races and nations and other historical entities is great, and those who generalize about history are exposed to the full force of the temptation. Further, the liberal egalitarianism that runs through the present essay invites every person to reflect on and speak about the meaning of history. This intensifies to the utmost the danger that historical idolatry in various forms will arise. But an important safeguard against this danger is simply the very liberty that gives rise to the danger. The right of every individual to construe history for himself, according to his own moral outlook and his own interpretation of historical facts, may be dangerous both for the individual and for society. But it also provides a kind of security, for it is, after all, the right of each one to live outside of and in opposition to all popular and conventional and official versions of history. So long as the right stands, every individual can contend for, and in his inner world dwell within, a true interpretation of history. The exercise of such a right, of course, will not always be uncontroversial. The ancient prophets of Israel were thrown repeatedly into great physical danger by their interpretations of the historical situation of the Israelites. To dispute reigning historical expectations is to challenge the society holding the expectations. We see again that liberty is not safe. But in this instance, at least, it provides a measure of protection against the dangers it creates.

To speak of a right to construe liberty for oneself, however, does not quite suffice. Rights trace back to responsibilities. Each person has a responsibility for paying attention to history and trying to play a part in it. Only in this way does he incorporate history into his own personal destiny. This does not necessarily mean soaring into a stratosphere of theoretical speculation. Basically, it means thoughtfully occupying one's given situation on the earth and trying to comprehend it as the human situation brought to a focus in the circumstances defining one's own time and place. The idea of accepting this responsibility, and of doing so with constancy and resolve, reflects themes that have run through the present essay.

Character and the Prophetic Stance

To stand responsibly and lucidly within one's particular and concrete situation, understanding one's personal past and future as reflections — whether by conformity or by dissidence — of one's historical past and future, and to do this with hope, both for humanity and for oneself, is to maintain what I call "the prophetic stance." The ancient prophets, whatever else one may say of them, were historically situated. We cannot think of a man like Jeremiah apart from a set of historical circumstances — that of the Jewish people, living in close relationship both with their own past and with surrounding empires and peoples — that shaped his personal circumstances, giving his whole life its form and direction. Not that he approved of Jewish attitudes and actions, or conformed with them. As everyone knows, Jeremiah and virtually all the great prophets were highly critical of their people, indeed, so much so that their lives were often imperiled by their fellow Jews.

The critical aspect of the prophetic stance is vital. Reflecting the historical situation in one's personal situation does not mean allowing one's life to be determined wholly by historical circumstances, but only being attuned to those circumstances and responding to them. Protest and nonviolent resistance are among the most honorable forms of political action and historical participation. And it is particularly fitting that these be carried on in behalf of those suffering from historical misfortunes, such as poverty and political oppression. In this respect the ancient prophets, denouncing the callousness of established society and the reigning powers, are exemplary. The prophetic stance, as one dimension of the liberal stance, presupposes personal responsibility and independence. While these may be expressed in quiet obedience — a matter to be analyzed at length in the next-to-last chapter of this essay — they are more clearly present in actions entailing personal effort and cost.

However critical (perhaps I should say "wrathful") the prophets usually were, they were never despairing. As I said, the prophetic stance is hopeful. History is taken to be meaningful. Even if every human enterprise brings irremediable disaster on itself, justice will be vindicated. And there are signs of a more ample prospect. In reading the prophets, one gathers that in some fashion God's limitless mercy and power will also be vindicated. Despite the gross and repeated offenses of the Jewish people, despite the calamities they suffer, the last word is always that God's will is to save them and not to destroy them. And that will is certain eventually to be accomplished. The prophets are often greatly distressed but are never hopeless.

The prophetic stance is an orientation not only toward history, however, but also toward transcendence. The prophets were not confined to history. Indeed, there would have been no relationship with history had there not been a relationship with God and God's law. It was by the commands of the law that the Israelites were judged. One could go further and say that it was fidelity to the unvarying and overarching law, and to the God who was the source of the law, that fixed the prophets so definitely and defiantly in their historical situations. Thus the stance of the prophets was responsive both to things above and to things below. A duality of this sort is essential to the prophetic stance. It is questionable whether human beings can inhabit history in a responsible fashion apart from a transcendental orientation. Marxists tried to, calling for and sometimes inspiring heroic action in history while relativizing the moral law. Without the moral law, however, they were swept into history and immersed in the tide of events. Revolution to liberate the masses led to enslavement of the masses. In relativizing the moral law, they relativized themselves and lost that sense of personal responsibility that impels one to stand independently of every collectivity.

These features of the prophetic stance are broadly the same as those contained in the conventional concept of character. On the one hand, we think of character as a moral condition. A person of strong character is virtually the same as someone who is reliably moral. At the same time, we would not attribute character to someone whose moral resolution had not been matured and tried by confusing and difficult circumstances. We do not think of inhabitants of paradise, whether imagined as an earthly or a heavenly kingdom, as people of strong character. Character presupposes tribulation, faced and withstood. It seems to belong on the horizon where the transcendent and earthly meet. It appears among those capable of being both moral and practical — on the one hand heeding the commands of transcendence and on the other coping with the shocks and constraints of time and history.

Particularly noteworthy is the way character calls forth hope. According to Paul's formula, in which suffering produces endurance, and endurance character, character produces hope. Why? Why should character generate hope? It seems that being morally good, being a person of strong character, cannot stand as an end in itself. A person can hold to the good, and conform with the right, in the face of adverse circumstances, only if assured that adhering to the good and right is not utterly inconsequential. For the good to be good and the right to be right is not enough. Thus the misfortunes of the just were a continual challenge to the authors of Jewish scripture. For a life of justice to bring mainly misery seemed to cast doubt on the sovereignty and goodness of God and to call into question the very concept of justice. And even so uncompromising a moralist as Kant, who insisted relentlessly that the only legitimate motive for obeying the moral law was respect for the law itself, without regard to consequences, held that moral life would be mean-

301

ingless unless it eventuated in happiness. This all suggests that the struggle to develop and sustain good character requires — and in this sense, as Paul maintained, "produces" — hope. Inhabiting one's personal situation in a way that is fully in accord with the moral law entails looking to the future with anticipation. A simpler way to put this might be to say that the very presence of a moral law implies a meaningful universe, and in a meaningful universe morality does not bring lasting misery. To be moral, therefore, is to have hope.

For a communal being, such anticipation must be prophetic, as distinguished from merely personal. Dwelling in one's personal situation with cognizance of its full historical compass entails hope for human beings universally. I indicated above that character in its constancy, in its superiority to time, is an intimation of eternal life, a foreshadowing of one's destined and lasting identity. Character is a fragmentary realization of who one really is, or is destined eternally to be. For a communal being, this realization spreads to others. Hope for a universal community anticipates the realization not only of one's own eternal identity but also of the identities of one's actual and potential neighbors.

If hope is directed to the furthest conceivable future, as it must be if it is genuine, unqualified hope, then it envisions the end of history. It is eschatological. It envisions a degree of righteousness and a depth of common discernment that would bring the sequence of earthly events to a close. Such a thing as history exists only because humans are separated from the good, by their unrighteousness and by their incomprehension. Hence the struggles that unfold in historical events. To envision a state of righteousness and wisdom is to envision the end of history. Eschatological images abound in Christian scripture, with the central theme always the coming of the risen Christ to establish a kingdom of perfect justice and truth. In Christianity, with its faith in a righteous, merciful, and all-powerful God, such a vision is inevitable. However, it may seem less than inevitable, even impossible, in any future that humanist reason can anticipate. Yet reason has a powerful dynamic toward a kingdom in which the human race is both just and happy. This is evident in figures as diverse as Kant, Condorcet, and Marx. It seems that the idea of moral constancy, or good character, whether it be understood according to Christian or humanist principles, tends to take on a prophetic cast.

The prophetic stance is double-edged. On one side it is contemplative, for the understanding of history is worthwhile in itself, and if the eschaton comprises a final and all-encompassing understanding, such as Aquinas's "beatific vision," it will be an understanding of all that has ever happened. This edge reflects the transcendental orientation of the prophetic stance. As we have already seen, however, human beings in history cannot responsibly confine themselves to contemplation. They are morally bound to come to the aid of those suffering from the endless troubles history brings on those entangled within it. These troubles lie much more harshly on some than on others. Almost all the ancient prophets directed their attention to the poor, the afflicted, and the oppressed. Hence if the prophetic stance on one side is contemplative, on the other side it is critical and engaged. It looks not only toward transcendence but also toward earthly humanity and the ordeals of earthly life.

In discussing the public realm not only in its global reach but also in its extension into the distant past and future, we have considered liberty in its widest possible range. In doing this, however, we have reached a point at which it must be recognized that liberty does not require only an extensive range, in space and in time. It requires also something more puzzling, something seemingly antithetical to liberty itself: constraint. There can be no liberty without limits.

CHAPTER 11

Limits on Liberty

——⇒•《◉》•⇐——

The Spirit and the Letter of Liberty

The spirit of liberty may, it is now apparent, be summed up in a wide variety of ways. The preceding pages have laid great emphasis on conscience and the sense of responsibility it implants in us. Conscience undeniably turns us sometimes to tragically misconceived purposes, and is sometimes silent, but when it speaks, even mistakenly, it cannot be ignored. And when it speaks rightly it leads toward liberty. Anyone who hears the true voice of conscience, I have argued, demands first of all the liberty to interpret and to heed that voice. Following on this primary demand, and in response to the sense of justice that conscience inculcates, comes the demand for liberty for all. Elementally, the ideal of liberty is a certain ideal of justice.

As it is gradually fused with experience, conscience of course leads us much further. I have described in various ways the path it takes: in terms of dialogue, of tolerance, of communality in resistance to society, of universal humanity, of submission to the ordeals inherent in liberty, and of the humility that confesses to moral failure. I have seen the spirit of liberty in the willingness to stand alone as well as in attunement to the mystery of personal being. Above all, I have been concerned with the relationship of the free human being with "transcendence" — at the very least, with the moral law in all its majesty; more broadly, with the encompassing mystery of being; and (speaking as a Christian) with God. In this connection I have characterized the proper human stance as one of receptivity. Finally, I have suggested that the quest for transcendence is in effect a quest for truth, or light — a quest that can draw both humanist reason and religious faith into the communicative inquiry that is the proper sphere of liberty.

By the letter, in contrast with the spirit, I mean all conditions of liberty, such as constitutions, laws, customs, and schools. Other components of the letter have come to the surface during the preceding discussion. The public realm is one of these. Private property, with associated rights of privacy, is another. I have emphasized such familiar prerequisites of liberty as separation of church and state, and institutions that allow for general participation in politics and hold government responsible to the people. I have repeatedly spoken of the necessity of legislation assuring that economic circumstances such as poverty do not nullify legal liberties. One of the cornerstones of this essay has been the distinction between community and society, and it is obvious that this distinction broadly corresponds to that between the spirit and the letter. If the spirit of liberty is expressed in communality — in searching dialogue, in fidelity to the truth — then the letter comes from efforts to shape society so that it is open to inquiring communication and responsive to the course and the conclusions of such communication.

There is a long-standing tendency among students of society and politics to assign priority to the letter over the spirit. For the intellect to do this is natural — although not inevitable — given the objectifying powers and proclivities of the intellect. The objective clearly belongs to the outward order, which is governed by the letter. The preoccupation of social and political scientists with the letter derives, however, not only from the nature of the intellect but also from modern intellectual biases, such as hostility to religion, confidence in the power of the human mind, and a tendency to equate the objective and the real. These culminate in the faith that human beings, now or eventually, can dominate reality and shape it to their own desires. This faith translates necessarily into stress on the letter, for the letter is extensively subject to human design and alteration. The primacy of the letter probably reached its greatest possible height in the effort to quantify all social and political knowledge, which arose in the nineteenth century and still powerfully moved the academic mind at the end of the twentieth century.

A reversal of this priority has been one of the major aims of this essay. The spirit of liberty is prior to the letter. Constitutions and laws that wisely support liberty can come only from a spirit that understands and properly values liberty. Customs and traditions favorable to liberty are products of the spirit of liberty, and if that spirit disappears, they become dead and oppressive, or simply crumble. Schools that prepare people for the life of liberty are not the foundations of liberty; the foundations lie in the spirit that creates and shapes the schools. To speak summarily, the spirit creates the letter, examines it critically, and strives to improve it. The spirit is the life of the letter. Conditions favoring liberty can exist and be effective only if the spirit of liberty lies underneath them and works through them. This premise explains why I have not focused on the conditions of liberty as such. I have wanted to deal with first things first.

This priority arises from a certain metaphysical disposition. This is a disposition to accord freedom priority over causality, moral responsibility over social conditioning, person over society, ethic over organization, personal stance over collective order. It is a disposition to grant mystery priority over objectivity. If I were asked to articulate this disposition philosophically, I would resort to Kant. Earlier in the essay I characterized Kant's concept of the freedom of the person (what many call "free will") as radical — not a sort of variability or unpredictability found within the order of nature, as it is for Thomas Aquinas, but something lying on a deeper level of reality than nature. The meaning of this may be expressed by saying that the order of nature is shaped fundamentally by human faculties, and in this shaping human faculties are freely employed. Not that we shape nature as we please, but we do shape it (the natural order as a whole is not given to us from the outside), and we do this only when and for as long as we please, that is, freely. And when we turn from intellectual work to the moral law, or to the beautiful and sublime, we do this freely too. We are primarily free. Only secondarily are we inhabitants of a causal order.

To say that liberty depends ultimately on the spirit rather than the letter is to say that it depends on things beyond our understanding and control — on transcendence. The spirit of liberty is given to us, not summoned at will. I have discussed this gift, in humanistic terms, as inspiration and, in Christian terms, as grace. On the part of humanists and Christians alike it requires a stance of receptivity. We must be receptive in our relations with the mystery that surrounds us. This is another way of speaking of that which I discuss below as "waiting." Undergirding this receptivity, Christians have what for them are compelling reasons, best summed up perhaps in the word "revelation." But receptivity depends on a humility and a faith that do not come easily to proud humans of any persuasion, whether religious or not. Thus Christians often try to capture transcendence and imprison it in dogma. The imperative of receptivity is thereby evaded. But such an effort is futile and only renders the imperative more urgent. On the other side, humanists try to bypass the imperative by denying that there is any such thing as "transcendence." But this is a device of pride, a device one can fairly claim has been cast into doubt by the crimes and disasters worked by atheistic humanism in the twentieth century. What is needed on all hands is the light that arouses and guides the spirit of liberty, and is given to us, not summoned at will. Such, at any rate, has been a major premise of this essay — a premise issuing in the ideal of the public realm as a place where Christians and humanists might demonstrate their openness toward transcendence by meeting in common discourse.

Is there really no way, however, in which humans can rise above their fundamental weakness and learn to summon the spirit on which liberty depends? Has the letter no form that can enable us to become masters of our destiny? Some of the most intelligent and resolute protagonists of liberty argue that the letter does have such a form. The spirit can be summoned. Their argument deserves respect, for it undoubtedly points toward one of the main conditions of liberty. It is a condition, however, that is easily overrated, thus subverting the openness toward transcendence, or receptivity, which is vital to liberty.

The Spirit of Liberty and Education

Good education is one of the most alluring, yet misleading, ideals in the realm of liberal thought. Enlightened schooling is supposedly the key to a stable and fruitful liberal society. The dangers of liberty can be greatly lessened, perhaps even eliminated, in lively and well-run classrooms. The power of this idea is not surprising. It seems to show how evil can be opposed, perhaps even in large measure overcome, without

307

using deceit or violence. It seems to show how the waywardness of the spirit can be tempered and access to the light assured. It is no wonder that as great a philosopher as Plato centered his political and social thought on education. And if liberty is as dangerous as I have argued, supporters of liberty will be strongly inclined to turn their minds to education. Good schools seem to be the way human evil can be uprooted without destroying liberty. Thus the greatest liberal philosophers, John Locke and John Stuart Mill, both placed great emphasis on the educational foundations of liberty.

In my judgment, however, such emphasis is false and misleading, and the sense of security it provides in the face of the risks of liberty is illusory. The grounds of this judgment are fundamental to the present essay. The purpose of liberty is to permit the mystery of personal being, which is the mystery of all being, to emerge into light. But we do not comprehend this mystery. When we encounter it in the form of an authentic human personality, such as Socrates or Lincoln, we recoil in puzzlement and scorn, and not infrequently with violence. Christians believe that the mystery of being in its personal depths is fully revealed in Christ. It must, however, be said that it is by no means revealed to every Christian. This is shown, among other ways, by the vain efforts of Christian painters over many centuries to depict the face of Christ. To speak summarily, we possess only intimations of the mystery encompassing our worldly lives and appearing from time to time in human faces, and these intimations cannot be woven into anything like comprehension. Nor can they be woven into anything like an educational program. This means that educational efforts, the further they go beyond elementary matters like reading and arithmetic, proceed in growing darkness. They never come within sight of the ultimate goal, that of the full glory and mystery of a human person and of the drama in which such a one appears.

Protagonists of education tend to ignore not only the mystery of human personality, but also the evil that resides in human beings. Thus a signal flaw in Plato's political-educational ideal is the presupposition of possible human goodness and sovereignty. It is assumed that some human beings, the educators, can rise to a height from which they can plan and bring about the re-creation of other human beings. In this respect an educational ideal as sweeping as Plato's is akin to the revolutionary ideal I have criticized in the course of this essay. It assumes a degree of human transcendence and goodness, at the outset in a few, eventually in many, which is precluded by the character of fallen humanity. Both finitude and sin are slighted if not ignored. The meaning of finitude is incomprehension before the mystery of human personality. The meaning of sin is indulgence in illusions of omniscience that render our incomprehension more crippling and dangerous. The truth is that finite and sinful creatures are little more capable of transforming flawed and finite humanity according to some model of righteousness and wisdom than they are of carrying out a swift and sweeping social and political revolution. By ignoring this fact Plato, for all his spiritual grandeur, was far more akin to Marx than is generally realized.

If self-realization comes about, and liberty flourishes, only in dialogue, then the main contribution of education to liberty would be to render people dialogic. Education is incapable, however, of this contribution. Some of the elementary prerequisites of dialogue can of course be provided through education. People can be taught to read and to speak reasonably; they can be given backgrounds in history, science, and literature. But dialogue depends on acquirements additional to these. It depends on insight and wisdom, and also on the ability to enter sympathetically into attitudes one does not share and may even despise. It depends on the "acrobatic" skills and daring required by tolerance. Qualities such as these we cannot with any assurance elicit in our schools. First of all there must be dialogic teachers, and these are as rare as is the dialogic spirit among creatures who tend spontaneously to close their minds in pride and distraction. And even dialogic teachers would not know how to call forth a dialogic spirit. We have no command, and through the schools can gain no command, of the light. Take Socrates as the model of the dialogic, hence free, personality. No one in his own time or since has been able altogether to understand him. And we have scarcely an inkling of how we might deliberately and systematically call forth personalities such as his.

The defeat of radical evil and the bringing to light of the mystery of being require something more in the nature of conversion than of education. Even Plato, living in a culture inclined to trust in the power of reason, recognized this. He maintained in the *Republic* that people needed not just to see, but to turn around and face toward, what must be seen — the idea of the Good. Hence they needed to look in a different direction from that in which they naturally and normally looked. To focus on this necessity raises immediate and immense questions concerning the powers of education. Can schools turn people around? Can they correct the moral disorientation at the root of radical evil? How? And where are the teachers who are free of radical evil to be found? What is needed, it seems, is a new spirit, and it is more than doubtful that human beings can bestow this spirit on themselves.

I hasten to say that I am not condemning all educational enterprises, or even suggesting that they are unimportant in a liberal society. Arguably, they are necessary if liberty is to endure and bear fruit. They must, however, *arise* from liberty and from liberal discoveries of the mystery of personal being. If they are thought of as *underlying* liberty, they are misconceived. They are affected by a pride not unlike the pride of revolutionaries and will fail. Good liberal education must be piecemeal and experimental, and its spirit one of humility.

The point is vital because it concerns the incalculability of the spirit of liberty, which, as Jesus said of the Holy Spirit, is like the wind. It "blows where it wills, and you hear the sound of it, but you do not know whence it comes or whither it goes" (John 3:8). This incalculability is surely one of the most fundamental facts of the human condition. And it is no less visible to humanist reason than to religious faith, as noted with respect to the dependence of art, literature, and science on inspiration. But we bridle at this dependence and therefore stubbornly deny it. The most daring of humanists do this through great revolutionary projects. Others — humanists averse to violence (such as Plato) and Christians forgetful of original sin (such as Locke) — fall back on great educational projects. In these ways we falsify our own nature. We forget the distinction between a person and a thing and assume that persons are as comprehensible as things. And we make light of the evil in us. In sum, we blind ourselves to the ordeal and the destiny inherent in liberty.

It will now be clear why I do not in this essay focus on the conditions of liberty, such as consensus, appropriate traditions, and essential institutions. For one thing, the subject is too large and complex to be adequately dealt with in an essay, such as the present one, which is on the spirit of liberty. For another thing, numerous important conditions, such as private property and constitutionalism, have been discussed in the course of the essay. But above all, I do not dwell on the conditions of liberty because prior to them is the spirit of liberty. This spirit has been our main concern throughout the essay. As already indicated, however, one crucial condition of liberty does demand our concentrated attention. This is because it is indispensable to, yet apparently contradictory of, the very standard of liberty. Liberty cannot exist unless, at certain points, it is denied.

The Fantasy of Limitless Liberty

Liberty involves the removal of restraints, but it also involves the imposition of restraints. Liberty cannot be limitless. If it were, it would destroy itself. This is implicit in the flawed nature of man. The necessity of limits makes liberalism a puzzling philosophy. The ideal of liberty implies the undesirability of restraints. Yet sensible liberals invariably advocate restraints, apparently rendering the very idea of a liberal society self-contradictory. The contradiction is particularly pronounced in the commonplace concept of liberal government, the first term implying unrestraint, the second restraint.

The most radical attempt to escape from this conundrum is represented by anarchism, which calls for the elimination of government and of all social restraints. Anarchism is simply an unqualified affirmation of human freedom. It offers a dream of social harmony flowing out of limitless liberty. It can do this, of course, only by ignoring or denying human evil. In contrast with anarchism, liberalism of the kind I am advocating in this essay takes full cognizance of human evil but affirms liberty regardless. It grants that evil must be systematically curbed and suppressed but maintains nonetheless that liberty is the supreme standard of our common life.

At the opposite extreme from anarchism is a more realistic and imaginative effort to solve the apparent contradiction in liberalism. It originated in Rousseau and was developed mainly by various philosophical idealists, thinkers inspired above all by Hegel. This theory rests on the realization that you are not free in a very meaningful way merely by doing what is dictated by momentary desires. You must do what is dictated by the good, by that which defines, perhaps not your momentary, but your strongest and most enduring, desires. This is often called the theory of "positive liberty." It contains important insights and will be discussed later in the present chapter. Suffice it here to say that the chief weakness in the theory is a tendency to neglect the absolute indispens-ability of personal choice. Such an oversight can have devastating conse-quences. It can lead to the notion that you may be free in doing some-thing you do not choose to do, even something you are forced to do.

The liberal puzzle — how to combine liberty and limits on liberty — is not merely theoretical. At the beginning of the twenty-first century it faced the industrialized countries in issues like abortion, pornography, and assisted suicide. Some things cannot be allowed, as everyone would grant. But what are those things? One cannot look at American society at the dawn of the third millennium and contemplate condi-tions such as increasing sexual license, the dissolution of marriage, widely accepted drug use, and a vulgar and often pornographic popular culture without wondering whether one is witnessing the failure of a great experiment in liberty. Finding the proper limits on liberty can have a bearing on the very survival of liberty.

Liberty and society, for all the strains between them, are not polar opposites. They can in certain ways be fused. Doing this does not consist in anything so simple and banal as "finding the right balance" between them. Speaking generally, it consists in the recognition that limits on liberty, if wisely calculated and wisely accepted, can be disciplines, in the sense given that word when we speak of academic fields, involving onerous study, as disciplines; or when we refer to the practice which mastery of a musical instrument requires as depending on discipline; or when punishment in its reformatory aspects is characterized as "disci-plinary." In such cases, although the immediate reality is limitation, the final upshot can be a purification and enlargement of the freedom that is the raison d'être of liberty. While liberty is partly negative, it is not achieved merely by removing restrictions. This is provocatively indi-cated in James Fitzjames Stephen's splendid *Liberty, Equality, Fraternity.* "The hope that people are to be rendered more vigorous by simply re-moving restrictions," Stephen writes, quoting his brother Leslie Ste-phen, "seems to be as fallacious as the hope that a bush planted in an open field would naturally develope [*sic*] into a forest tree." And elabo-rating on this point, he asserts that "restraint and coercion in one form or another is the great stimulus to exertion" (pp. 30-31).

We step here onto notoriously treacherous ground. When we speak of limits on liberty enlarging freedom, we put ourselves in peril of al-lowing totalitarian rulers to claim that their enslaved subjects are really free. Hence I call particular attention to my phraseology in the above paragraph: the final upshot of limits on liberty *can be* (is not necessarily) the enlargement of *freedom* (not liberty). As the following discussion will make apparent, limits on liberty are justifiable to the extent that they command things that a wise and righteous citizen would do without being commanded. To the extent those commands are internalized, they become a discipline that increases the wisdom and righteousness, and in that sense the freedom, of those subject to them. But liberty remains negative. It does not exist except through absence of restraint. And in no circumstances does restraint enlarge liberty. It can only enlarge the freedom that underlies liberty.

At the end of the twentieth century, however, people had for so long beheld the spectacle of liberty extinguished by tyrannical violence, and had been so affected by temptations to self-indulgence mounted by advertising, that they had come to oversimplify. In America a powerful movement, ostensibly "conservative" but in fact incorporating little of the prudence traditionally associated with conservatism, made opposition to government, and to the taxes on which government is based, axiomatic. Government was declared the main cause of society's major problems, rather than an agent that might help to solve them. This movement gained widespread popular support despite working in multitudinous ways against the manifest material interests of most of the population. Such antigovernmental attitudes are not entirely arbitrary. Government is one of the most problematic human institutions. Nonetheless, without it, and without social restraints as well, there can be no liberty. The sane alternative to tyranny is not limitless liberty but an order of carefully devised and recurrently reexamined restraints through which liberty is not only protected from its own excesses but also perhaps even stimulated and infused with moral purpose.

The necessity of limits can be clearly seen by looking at law. All but anarchists confess the need, even the dignity, of the law, and phrases like "freedom under the law" and "lawful liberty" are commonplace. The main point here is simply that law and liberty are not inversely proportional. In the first place, as already brought out elsewhere in this essay, lawful restrictions on some may widen the liberty of others. If liberty were not restricted, it would be extinguished. The principle of original sin, or radical evil, underscores this truth. The rule of liberty, as brought out by Kant and many others, is: all the liberty for each person that is compatible with equal liberty for every other person. That rule implies restrictions on everyone.

Moreover, law can contribute to the liberation even of those it restricts. For one thing, it can play an enabling role. It may be, for example, that most of the managers and owners of a particular kind of business feel some spontaneous respect for the natural world and would like to conduct their operations in ways not harmful to the environment. It may also be that they cannot afford to do this unless all their competitors, some of whom do not share their respect for nature, are compelled to observe the restrictions they are willing to observe voluntarily. In this way a law that is directly restrictive can be indirectly liberating.

A law can also signalize an important value, such as respect for property or life. The intent of major criminal statutes is not just to stop people from doing wrong but also to awaken them to the right. Here we step again onto the "treacherous ground" spoken of above. So far as law awakens people to things that are authentically good, it directly widens their inner freedom and indirectly widens their outer liberty. So I stress again that I am speaking merely of possibilities. Statutory law remains an imposition from the outside, and people are rightfully suspicious of it. So far as I do something simply because the law requires it, I am without liberty. To think of law as simply evil, however, and always and everywhere in conflict with liberty is an oversimplification, and cannot be allowed to stand. It is noteworthy in this connection that law need not take the form of absolute proscription. Without categorically prohibiting acts like abortion or gun purchase — acts that can be at the center of intense controversy — it can impose procedures that mark the gravity of such acts. It can, for example, impose time for deliberation prior to their commission. These might be called, in contrast with absolute limits, "admonitory limits." In effect, they warn citizens that conduct legally allowed may nevertheless be morally wrong.

In summary, law does not just say no. In some ways, at some times, it says yes. The same, we realize, may be true of restraints inherent in civil society, such as those of custom and tradition. By closing some doors they can open others — doors on the other side of which lie a liberty that has to do, not merely with passing desires, but with ultimate values such as truth and community. We can begin to see why James Fitzjames Stephen could speak of restraint and coercion as potentially a "great stimulus to exertion."

To say this is not to withdraw the proposition implicit in much of this essay, namely, that the life of liberty requires the utmost possible degree of personal independence from society. A free person is reflective, critical, and courageous enough to make choices different and underived from the choices of others around him. But society is indispensable. Anarchism is an entirely unreasonable ideal. While community and society are distinct and often antithetical, there is no community without society. And this means, since liberty is all it ought to be only in community, that there is no liberty without society. It is the aim of the present chapter to take this fact fully into account.

These remarks, however, are far from resolving the antithesis between liberty and its limits. This antithesis, in its full, forbidding force, appears in connection with law. Unlike traditions and customs, law is backed by the threat of violence. The state may at times be a teacher, but it is always and necessarily an enforcer. Under the threat of violence, and even death, it compels people to refrain from acts that are legally proscribed. When we face the absolute necessity of official violence, we face the liberal puzzle in its starkest form.

Liberty and Coercion: The Issue

Common sense tells us that without legal limits on liberty, upheld when necessary by force, there could be no civilized life, hence no liberty except that offered by a condition of general anarchy, a condition in which most people would be either killed or enslaved. Governmental coercion seems unavoidable. Yet when a government coerces someone, it apparently reduces that person to the status of means to the welfare of others. Locke indicated that only a majority could legitimately impose coercion. Yet it is hard to see how the moral offense seemingly intrinsic to coercion can be affected by the identity of the agent — whether it be one, a few, or a majority. Utilitarians like John Stuart Mill regarded coercion as justified by its end, the well-being of society, which for Mill meant "the greatest happiness of the greatest number." But how can it be legitimate to sacrifice the happiness of the lesser number, or even of one person, to the happiness of the greater number? To have your liberty infringed upon is on the face of it a denial of your personal dignity. That it is done by a majority of which you are not a member, or for the happiness of a multitude to which you do not belong, makes no difference at all. At least this is the case if you ascribe infinite value to the individual. Utilitarianism, of course, does not do this, which can be reasonably regarded as its signal defect. If you do ascribe such value to the individual, however, then how can coercion be justified?

Clearly, protagonists of liberty must grapple with this question. If they cannot organize and support political order without violating their own basic principles — above all, the freedom of the person and the dignity that requires such freedom — they must steadily eat away at their own moral foundations. The enduring conditions of earthly life necessitate the deliberate and organized imposition of force. This is done through the state, or through a like order, such as an empire or a feudal domain. Unless the liberal state can be justified, liberty is left morally groundless, hence ultimately doomed. Free societies will be compelled by the elemental pressures of existence to continually compromise and weaken their own moral foundations. Fully legitimate liberal government will be impossible.

Let us begin by looking at a common idea that bears on the dilemma and contains seeds of truth even though it is too broadly formulated and thus is literally false, lending itself to interpretations destructive of liberty. It is often said that governmental limits on someone's liberty are legitimate when imposed for the sake of protecting others. It is threatened harm to society that justifies coercion. The liberty of one person may be limited for the sake of the welfare of other persons. A vulgar but rather effective way of stating the formula is that your right to swing your hand stops at the point where it intersects with another person's face.

What is wrong with so apparently sensible a rule as this? It has two flaws. One is its failure to respond adequately to the issue of personal dignity. It does not tell us how coercion can be exercised without using the coerced person as a means in relation to the welfare of someone else. It may seem at first glance that it does, for it makes it obvious that coercion is practically unavoidable. If there were no coercion, liberty would be drowned in anarchy. But those coerced are nonetheless used, and their liberty abridged, to further a good enjoyed by others, the uncoerced. In Kantian terms, the imperative that the coercion of some be employed to protect the welfare of others is merely hypothetical. It turns on an "if." If the welfare of some is to be advanced, the welfare of others must be sacrificed. But the principle of personal dignity allows for no such "if." It is categorical, or unconditional. It tells us that persons must always be treated not merely as means but also as ends in themselves. The issue before us is how coercion can be carried on, that is, how a state can exist, without violating that imperative.

The other flaw in this seemingly sensible rule lies in the individualism it implies, or at least strongly suggests. It invites the assumption that each individual inhabits a sphere of life that need be of little concern to other individuals. This assumption is contrary both to facts, to our actual interdependence in society, and to norms, the moral obligations that bind us to one another. This individualism comes out in various ways.

To begin with, the rule that one person's liberty can be limited only to protect the welfare of other persons implies that a person can never be justifiably coerced for the sake of that person's own welfare. Why not? Presumably because of the individualistic assumption that harm you do yourself may do no serious harm to others and therefore is no proper concern of others. As soon as the assumption is made explicit, however, we can see how questionable it is. It is reasonable to think, in view of our physical, emotional, and spiritual interdependence, that serious harm to one person always and unavoidably involves serious harm to others. Sometimes the harm is not apparent because it consists only in benefits not bestowed. Someone who devotes himself to physical pleasures throughout his life, never marries, never begets children, never maintains serious friendships, never holds for long a constructive job, and never engages in charitable activities may not visibly hurt anyone else. But in view of all that is not done for others, it is manifest that much harm to others in fact is done. Mill called acts that have little or no impact on others "self-regarding," and argued for their immunity from state interference. The truth surely is that acts that are truly self-regarding are always trivial. Acts important to those who commit them are always important to others as well.

Moreover, even if someone could hurt himself without hurting me, does it follow that I can properly pay no attention? May I legitimately refuse any involvement in someone else's life even if I might, by intervening, help redirect a life of self-destructive choices? Affirmative answers to these questions are possible only on the premise that society is made up of individuals who are basically unconnected, not only by physical interdependence, but even by social inclinations and emotions, or by moral obligations. Such a premise is surely false. Even were it true that every individual inhabits a sphere of life scarcely touching the spheres inhabited by others, it would not follow that we can all legitimately forget about one another so long as we all stay within our individual spheres. The parable of the Good Samaritan does not suggest that the dire condition of the man lying wounded at the side of the road in any way impinged adversely on the interests of the traveler who stopped to help him. The charitable traveler simply knew that the two of them, both human beings, were not morally unconnected.

Sometimes, of course, when someone is behaving foolishly or wrongly, there is little that others can do. Failure to get a good education, irresponsibility in a job, excessive drinking, marital infidelity: such common ways of hurting yourself (and others) seem largely beyond the reach of anyone else. No doubt they often are. We cannot with assurance give even our own lives the shape they ought to have and that we want them to have; much less can we do this with the lives of others. In this respect, individualism is true. But this has to do only with practical possibilities, not with social, emotional, or moral connections. This is shown by the fact that some ways of hurting yourself can be decisively affected from the outside, and when this is so, we do not hesitate to intervene. Thus selling yourself into slavery is in civilized countries not an enforceable contract under the law, and killing yourself is generally regarded as an act that ought to be prevented when it can be. Even drug and alcohol rehabilitation, and psychological counseling, are sometimes officially mandated. But the most serious consequence of the individualism so readily read into the principle before us is that it reduces the range of assured liberty to almost nothing.

This happens by virtue of the individualistic assumption that the sphere of guaranteed liberty is the same as the sphere of acts that have no direct and important bearing on others. If that sphere were large, the sphere of liberty would be large. But if it is small, or nonexistent — as surely it is — then there is little room for liberty. True, the principle that limits on liberty are justified when imposed for the protection of others does not imply that every act bearing on the welfare of others be regulated. Only those acts bearing *adversely* on the welfare of others may legitimately be regulated. But this implies that all acts having significant impact on others are subject to governmental oversight and may as a matter of course be outlawed or curbed. What would happen to such freedoms as those of speech, assembly, and religion if such an assumption were accepted? Mill thought he was defending a wide area of liberty in arguing that all self-regarding acts should be exempt from outside interference. But if most or all such acts are trivial, he was opening the way — very much contrary to his own intentions, which arose from a profound concern with liberty — to a virtually totalitarian state. It is a great irony that in the same essay in which he laid out his distinction between self-regarding and other-regarding acts, Mill mounted what may be the most eloquent and searching affirmation of free speech ever written, for it is difficult to see that speech is in any way a self-regarding act.

The condition that invalidates any distinction such as Mill's, and any justification of coercion based thereon, is that of human solidarity. Borrowing a phrase from one of the Pauline epistles, "we are members one of another" (Eph. 4:25). We are bound together in ways that make it impossible to live except in an intricate web of physical, emotional, moral, and spiritual relationships. We are bound together by necessity and by moral law. To define the sphere of liberty in terms of acts outside of this web is implicitly to surrender liberty to power and political expediency.

It may seem that the concept of human solidarity is in conflict with the whole idea of liberty laid out in this essay, an idea according to which liberty is practiced in tension with society. Such tension is created, however, not by living outside society but by living lucidly and critically within society. The tension is inward. It arises from a critical mind, a mind as free as possible of reigning prejudice yet considerate of fellow citizens, respectful of legitimate institutions, and faithful to social responsibilities. Above all, it arises from a communal mind and disposition. A perfect example of such a life is that of Socrates, a loyal Athenian, performing all the duties of a citizen, and refusing to break the law even by escaping from prison to save his own life after an unjust judicial condemnation, yet emphatically critical and independent. And a signal element in Socrates' posture is his sociable and dialogic way of life. I have stressed throughout that liberty is communal and that community is sought necessarily in society. The keynote of authentic liberty is not dissociation but independence — an independence grounded in communality.

The commonsense rule that one person's liberty ends where harm is done to another person, then, does not resolve the issue of coercion. Rather than showing how coercion can be reconciled with recognition of those coerced as ends, not merely means, it simply appeals to expediency. It evades, rather than answering, the question. And matters are made worse when it comes to the question of what public purpose might undergird such expediency. It responds again with a stroke of common sense: society must be protected from "harm." Such an answer is plausible only on the basis of an ontological and highly unrealistic individualism. Given the reality of human solidarity, the area of assured liberty melts away.

How, then, can these issues be resolved? There are four rules to which coercion must conform in order to be justified. These rules can help us understand the possibility of so anomalous a thing as a state dedicated to liberty, that is, a coercive order that serves, and does not in the very fulfillment of its coercive functions negate, the personal dignity on which the ideal of liberty is premised. They do not, however, constitute a total theory of the kind that resolves all possible conflicts and leaves no questions unanswered. They are guides to wise and discerning government, not substitutes for the seasoned wisdom and discernment on which good government depends. The four rules concern the form of the coercive act, the purpose it is intended to serve, its fundamental justice, and the potentialities of coercion itself.

Coercion and Personal Dignity

The Rule of Universality

This rule can be concisely stated, although it invites endless reflection. It prescribes simply that every official curb on liberty be imposed not on a particular person but on a class of persons — even if there should be only one person in the class. This is a rule of fairness, or justice. If the public good requires that a particular person be in some manner coerced, then every like person must be in like manner coerced. Fairness is imposed by the very claim that coercion is required for the public good. If every person standing in a like relation to that good were not coerced, it would follow that the coerced person had been singled out arbitrarily, for example, on account of personal animosities harbored by government officials. It would demean the one who is coerced.

What the rule of universality demands, we should note, is not statutory enactment — not the rule of law — but universal formulation. This is a standard that in principle could be met entirely within the mind of the coercive agent. A single administrative act could be applied to a single person who is regarded as representative of a class of persons rather than as a particular individual. Something of this sort is done regularly in the courts. While judges decide particular cases, the rule of precedent, prescribing that all like cases be decided in like fashion, is in effect a rule of universality. The rule of universality is far more likely to prevail, however, where governments act through statutory laws. Not only are these normally cast in general terms (and in large part must be where a constitution prohibits bills of attainder). They are also made public, thus allowing their universality to be verified by independent critics and to enter into and form the public mind. In this way the rule of universality is roughly — but only roughly — equivalent to the idea of government by laws, not men.

We instinctively sense the importance of fairness. Still, it may not be immediately clear just how it saves the dignity of the one who is coerced. Even though the state coerces a class of persons, and does this for the public good, isn't it still using those coerced as means to the well-being of others? In a sense it is, and this makes plain the fact that coercion, undeniable as it is that it often serves ends that are eminently desirable, is always evil considered in itself and apart from its consequences. In human societies there is no way of avoiding completely the tragic necessity of sacrificing some for the sake of a good enjoyed by others. Nonetheless, following the rule of universality makes a fundamental difference. It does this in two ways.

First, the rule is based on the idea that all persons deserve equal consideration. This is because a person is not merely a thing. In dealing with things, I feel no compunction in using one thing in a way in which I do not use any other thing of like kind. It may be inefficient or illogical to do this, but it is not immoral. When I arbitrarily throw one piece of wood rather than another on the campfire, I hear no inward voice telling me that I am committing a wrong. In dealing with persons, however, I am conscious of the quality called "dignity." Hence I recoil from using a person like a piece of material that can be used and discarded when no longer useful. I try to recognize the dignity of the person I feel compelled to use. One way I do this is by taking care not to use one person in a way I would not use any other person similarly circumstanced. Indeed, I do not demand of the other person anything I would not demand of myself were I in the class of those coerced. I show in this way that my coercive act has been carefully considered, and is not reckless or spiteful. It reflects the necessities of the existing situation and not indifference or hostility in relation to the person coerced. And of particular importance is this, that the one coerced knows, or can know, that he is being treated with care, that is, as a person and not a thing.

But there is more to the rule of universality than this. The fairness or justice implicit in that rule is in some sense willed by every person. It follows that when I am coerced fairly, that is, in accordance with the rule of universality, I have in some sense willed my own coercion. This is the second way in which the rule of universality tends to render coercion compatible with personal dignity. The dignity of a person, as distinguished from a thing, derives from human characteristics such as conscience, reason, and the ability to love. These render all of us moral beings. Hence every person within a society, by his moral character and his consequent fitness for citizenship in a human polity, is cognizant of the rule of universality. And so far as such a person is cognizant also of the human situation and the stringencies it involves, he realizes that persons, although not mere things, must in some circumstances be sacrificed, or have their liberty limited, for the sake of the public good. It follows that when he himself falls within the class of those necessarily sacrificed, his sacrifice accords with his own mind and will. In a moral sense, a coerced person is free even while being coerced.

Here again we find ourselves on the treacherous ground spoken of above. It is the scene of many fatalities among political theorists. Most of these occur when the conclusion is drawn that coercion for the sake of the public good is not really an infringement on liberty. Thus Rousseau wrote casually of people being "forced to be free." But in practice, few governmental acts will perfectly fulfill the requirements of universality. And even when they do, those coerced will not realize that they do and will not be morally pure enough to will wholeheartedly their own sacrifice to the public good. Few will perfectly evince the capacity so powerfully articulated by Kant, that of serving as universal legislators of their own lives. To make light of these realities is a fundamental error. It permits liberty to be destroyed in the name of liberty.

Here we are brought back to the main theme of the early chapters of this essay. You do not possess liberty if you are not allowed to choose freely. I have stressed the "radical" character of freedom. It lies on an ontological level deeper than that of nature. One manifestation of this is that it cannot be fixed upon in theory. It is *act,* not outward reality. Choice is that act. To neglect this basic truth is to neglect tensions and tragedies inherent in human fallenness, and in no way fully remediable. The rules of coercion only ameliorate the evil inherent in coercion. They do not remove it. Coercion is sometimes necessary because of human fallenness. The rules of coercion cannot obviate the fact of our fallenness. They can only enable coercive agents — the state — to act with a wisdom and sense of humanity that comport with our condition.

Still, in cases of conflict between your moral will and your momentary will, forcible subjection to the former may, in some circumstances, be the lesser evil. In freely violating your own moral will, there is a sense in which you cast away your own dignity. On the other hand, in being forced to conform with your moral will, your freedom is compromised but your dignity as a moral being is not wholly lost. Moreover, you may in this way be morally awakened and become, out of your own radical freedom, a moral being. If this happens, then acting under coercion becomes a discipline and not merely a stark limitation. All of this is not as far from common sense as it may appear to be. Many of your acts in support of the public good, such as paying taxes or interrupting a satisfying career to join the armed forces, are more or less coerced. You would probably not do them voluntarily. Nonetheless, if you see everyone in your circumstances subjected to the same demands, and if you feel that these demands are based on a reasonable interpretation of the common good, you will probably submit with a certain willingness, and from your submission you may derive a certain moral satisfaction. Most people, at least in liberal democracies, do not feel that in being taxed they are simply being robbed by the government, nor do they think of a justly drafted soldier who is killed in battle as having been murdered by his country.

The rule of universality is not, however, all by itself a sufficient justification for coercion. For one thing, it provides no purpose, or motive, for action. Societies do not act in the world merely to conform with a universal law. They act to reach certain ends. Lawful governments do not engage in coercion merely to be lawful, but rather to reduce the crime rate, or to maintain full employment, or to protect the country from a foreign enemy. The concept of universality prescribes the form of action, but not the goal. This is a serious lacuna. In leaving the goal unspecified, the rule of universality falls short of fully answering the question of justification. For coercion to be justified it must not only be fairly imposed. It must also serve a reasonable end.

Furthermore, absent a reasonable end, the rule of universality opens the way to limitless government. It does, to be sure, bar governments from doing anything that cannot be cast as a universal prescription. But in principle any public act whatever might be so cast. The confinement of a particular race to concentration camps, the suppression of a particular religion, censorship of all newspapers and magazines, and like acts of government could be carried out in strict observance of the rule of universality. In short, universality severed from a liberal purpose can be totalitarian. Thus it is that the political philosophies of many of the great exponents of universality, such as Rousseau and Hegel, have a totalitarian thrust. We need a definition of the public good appropriate to a liberal order.

The Rule of Liberality

The principal end coercion must serve to be justified in a liberal state can be nothing other than liberty itself, that is, the liberty of all. Coercion must always be measured against the standard of general liberty. The goal of a liberal society is the utmost practicable liberty for each one. Coercion is justified when prevailing circumstances render it expedient, in relation to this goal. Liberty must be the standard reigning over all deliberations on public policy. Nothing must be allowed to threaten or stifle liberty. As we shall see, this does not entail a constricted sense of the public good. The rule of expediency sanctions whatever is conducive to the vitality and flourishing of liberty. Nor does it absolutely bar coercion directed to the good of the one coerced. But such coercion is justified only if it enhances the ability of the individual to make wise choices. Before pursuing these lines of thought further, however, we must reflect on the simple proposition that in a liberal state coercion can be justified only in terms of liberty.

The proposition may seem so obvious as to scarcely need saying. Strangely enough, however, it was not obvious to as intelligent a liberal as John Stuart Mill, who embraced a much broader criterion, that of harm to society. One can suspect that this criterion would seem sensible to most liberals. But it cannot be sensible if there is in human beings any such thing as radical evil. In that case men and women with liberty are apt to do a great deal of harm to society. Only by depriving them of their liberty could such harm be prevented. As one example, much of the advertising and entertainment poured so profusely into the atmosphere of modern free societies is almost certainly harmful to society. But it could not be suppressed without destroying liberty — the liberty not only of capitalists and advertisers but also of consumers, many of whom fashion their lives in response to the advertising and the proffered entertainment. The harm principle is far too broad. It would permit an ostensibly liberal state to destroy liberty in the name of some other value, such as a puritanical style of life or economic security. As the twentieth century has so starkly demonstrated, this is not merely a matter of theory. Communist totalitarianism arose from a determination to prevent certain kinds of harm to society.

Also, as we have seen, the harm principle entailed the fiction of "self-regarding" acts. If harm to society justifies limits on liberty, then the surest defense of liberty — perhaps the only defense — lies in the supposition that many acts important to the individual committing them have little or no impact on society. Since there are few if any such acts, however, the harm principle implicitly sanctions coercion of virtually totalitarian range. Defining the public good primarily in terms of liberty cuts the thread of any such logic. If the supreme end of the polity is liberty, then no other value can be allowed to get in the way.

Another end to which common sense often gives priority over liberty is order. First of all, it is said, government must guarantee order; then it can look after liberty. But the standard of order, like that of harm, is too broad. There are kinds of order that allow for little or no liberty. One of the most orderly societies in recorded history was ancient Sparta. There was order in the absolute monarchies of early modern times. Dictators sometimes win public support by guaranteeing such fundamental kinds of order as peace in the streets and dependable

325

public services. To be sure, liberty depends on order, but it is order only of a particular kind, order assuring individual rights, that gives liberty the kind of support it needs.

To assert that liberty can justifiably be limited only for the sake of liberty itself is, in effect, to define the public good in terms exclusively of liberty. Is this too narrow a definition? It may seem so. Liberty is no doubt important, one may feel, but so are other things, like available jobs, care for the destitute, and the natural environment. Don't such goods as these enter into any adequate definition of the public good and thus into the justification of coercion? I said above that the rule of expediency sanctions such coercive measures as are necessary to the utmost degree of liberty practicable for each person. One may feel this statement needs to be explained. How broad is the concept of expediency? The question is important because it opens the way to a better understanding of the liberal ethos.

First of all, while expediency does pertain immediately to things absolutely necessary to the greatest practicable degree of liberty for every person, the absolutely necessary is not a narrow category. Thus it comprises most or all of normal criminal law. For example, there can be no liberty without security of life; hence acts like personal assault and murder must be outlawed. There can be no liberty without personal property; hence acts like burglary and bank robbery also may be justifiably outlawed. And there can be no liberty unless people are protected against more subtle kinds of spoliation. It is expedient, hence justified, for the state to outlaw such acts as fraud and breach of contract. In other words, all statutes reasonably calculated to protect persons and their particular spheres of life are justified.

The range of the absolutely necessary, however, is far wider than the criminal law. Bearing in mind that the standard of liberty pertains not just to a few but to all, we see that the standard precludes slavery. Ancient Athens, with its slaves, cannot be called a free society, nor can America prior to the passage of the Thirteenth Amendment. Some of Lincoln's greatness lay in his unyielding grasp of the contradiction between liberty and slavery, and in his realization that even a civil war was justified if needed to resolve that contradiction. Closely connected with this necessity, moreover, is one concerning the economic order. A society aiming at liberty must, as already argued, outlaw economic conditions that amount to slavery for some — conditions such as twelve-hour working days and factory machinery that seriously threatens the lives and limbs of workers.

It is not, however, only things absolutely necessary to liberty — real liberty, for all — that are sanctioned by the standard of expediency. A liberal government properly takes into account, beyond bare existence, the quality — the "vitality and flourishing," to repeat the phrase I used above — of the liberty it supports. For example, liberty has its proper physical environment. This can be defined in terms of beauty. Ugliness is not merely unpleasant. It is an arbitrary check on the unfoldment of personal feelings and ideas. As Kant argued, an experience of beauty is an experience of inner freedom coming from the harmony of the intellectual and sensual faculties. Hence in a setting of stark and unrelieved ugliness, liberty is subtly weakened. For a government to act in defense of the beauty of the earth, and to further grace and harmony in the cities, comports readily with the standard of liberty. It is easy, of course, to think of conditions other than environmental beauty that contribute to liberty. Plentiful housing, good general health, clean streets, efficient public transportation, attractive and well-stocked public libraries, beautiful parks — all help people to use their freedom in imaginative and constructive ways and thus are legitimate objects of governmental support. And that is true even when such support entails, as it practically always must, some measure of coercion, if only that involved in levying taxes that some people would rather not pay.

Perhaps the most important of the coercive acts contributory to liberty are those taken in behalf of the helpless, such as the severely retarded, the very aged, the ill, the unborn. It certainly is not absolutely necessary to the existence of liberty that such people be cared for. They are themselves incapable of liberty and are usually a burden on and expense to those who are. But they present us with the issue of personal dignity. Since liberty is based on respect for persons, a liberal government that ignored persons who are helpless and infirm would be neglectful of its own moral foundations. This is why issues like euthanasia, assisted suicide, and abortion are important in a liberal society. It is arguable, of course, that the ideal of liberty implies that such practices be absolutely unrestricted. It may be argued with equal or greater plausibility that if persons who are socially useless could be eliminated at will, by themselves or by others, and if the disposition of unborn babies depended entirely on the moods and desires of their mothers, the standard of personal dignity would wither under the impact of irresponsible choices. Liberty would be doomed. Liberty depends on a moral context, and support for that context, through education, legislation, and all other possible means (all entailing various kinds of coercion), may therefore be reasonably counted as contributory, perhaps not to the flourishing of liberty, but certainly to its vitality.

We see again that liberalism is not libertarianism. It has an ample understanding of the common good. Is it, however, entirely too ample? An opponent of liberalism might charge that linking liberty with such indefinite concepts as urban beauty and care for the helpless wipes out all the boundaries on public power seemingly implicit in the proposition that the aim of a liberal society is liberty and nothing more. A liberal government might claim that almost anything it wants to do is somehow contributory to liberty. One answer to this charge is simply that while the adjective "contributory" may be indefinite, it is not meaningless. There are countless major acts that governments have carried out, like legalizing racial discrimination, censoring newspapers, and spying on private citizens, that cannot be plausibly shown to enhance liberty. But another, and equally important, answer concerns a moral quality on the part of rulers and citizens that is essential in any successful polity.

No set of principles, however sound and detailed, can eliminate the need for prudence on the part of people in power. Liberty is dependent not only on fidelity to the standard of liberty but also on a seasoned sensitivity to the social and material conditions of liberty. There is no set of criteria that can enable government officials lacking in prudence to maintain liberty simply by adhering blindly to the criteria. Every legal order is set within a wide range of tangled, complex, and often baffling circumstances. To formulate and carry out public policy in a way that renders liberty fruitful requires practical wisdom. In other words, the statecraft of liberty calls for a fusion of moral and practical discernment that is not acquired merely by mastering abstract principles. Only such statecraft allows the breadth of the liberal ideal to be understood and acted on without jeopardizing liberty itself.

Moreover, we may think that there is such a thing as *liberal* prudence. This would be a practical wisdom that in every set of circumstances repeatedly asks, "Is adequate respect being accorded every person's right to choose?" Such wisdom would be cognizant of the fact that a liberal society is one in which common life is founded ultimately on the free choices of those carrying it on. It would be a wisdom aware of the deep ontological roots of human freedom. It would realize that, if liberty is to flourish, the act of choice may occasionally be infringed upon solely to render it wiser and more righteous. It may be legitimate to prevent someone from choosing to commit suicide, from choosing to have a late-term abortion, from choosing not to receive counseling for drug or alcohol problems. This is why I spoke above, not of the utmost degree of *possible* liberty, but of the utmost degree of *practicable* liberty. Governmental agents possessing liberal prudence would ask themselves repeatedly whether their coercive acts are fundamentally respectful of the radical freedom of those subject to coercion. The act of choice would be the sentinel standing at the outermost boundaries of liberal order.

That I have not defined the rule of liberality too broadly may become even more apparent as we discuss two further rules justifying coercion. Both tend to limit the range of coercion and in that way readily accompany a definition of the public good in terms of liberty.

The Rule of Proportionality

This is a rule, one might say, that is more instinctive than theoretical. It expresses a feeling so stubborn that no process of reasoning can shake it, but so elemental in the human spirit that no process of reasoning is needed to sustain it. The feeling arises when penalties in support of coercive acts — penalties such as fines and imprisonment — are to be imposed in support of governmental coercion. The feeling is that a penalty should be proportionate to the offense committed. To cut off a man's hand for petty theft, for example, or to put someone to death for telling a lie, strikes us as unjust. Likewise, to allow someone who has broken into a house and stolen goods belonging to the owner to go unpunished also strikes us as unjust. Wrongdoers must undergo sufferings not incommensurate on either the side of severity or the side of leniency with the wrong done.

We are told these things by the law of retribution, a law requiring, in the words of the Bible, "life for life, eye for eye, tooth for tooth, hand for hand, foot for foot, burn for burn, wound for wound, stripe for stripe"

(Exod. 21:23-25). This law is often criticized on the grounds of being an expression of vengefulness and wrath. It may of course be that, and if so, it is certainly objectionable. But it need not be. Fundamentally it is an expression of our sense of justice, and justice may be administered, not from vengefulness or anger, but from a calm and settled sense of what is right. The perpetrator of an evil deed must suffer an evil proportionate to the evil he has done. Capital punishment is frequently and plausibly criticized, for it presents the spectacle of deliberate, official killing, and it is difficult to show that the spectacle does anything to inhibit crime other than doing away with one criminal. Nonetheless, there remain many decent and intelligent people who vehemently defend the death penalty. Perhaps they are wrong. Perhaps considerations such as the fallibility of human judgment and the desirability of giving a criminal all the time possible to repent and change tell decisively against the practice of capital punishment. The practice, nonetheless, will always have respectable defenders simply because of the deep-rooted human sense that the most heinous crimes must be matched by a peculiarly severe penalty.

It may seem that the Christian principle of forgiveness implies that proportionate punishment should at times not be imposed. The wrong-doer should be mercifully released from the suffering called for by the rule of proportionality. It is quite true that a serious Christian must be prepared in certain circumstances to refrain from visiting any retaliatory injury on someone who has injured him. It is highly doubtful, however, that this principle has any bearing on an official acting in his official capacity. The punishment an official brings on a criminal is always for an injury done to the public order rather than to the official personally. And the punishment is required by a law the official is responsible for administering. Within those bounds forgiveness is inappropriate. It is true that crimes sometimes are pardoned. This is not, however, because an official feels called upon by his personal faith to be merciful. It is because of considerations relating to the well-being of the polity and taken into account by the law. Hence in a liberal polity the rule of proportionality is without exception. Punishment should not be discordant with the seriousness of the crime being punished.

No more perhaps need be said about the rule of proportionality except to note its relationship with the expediency justified by the rule of liberality. By that rule coercion might be justified when it serves the cause of general liberty. The rule of proportionality enters a qualification. Some forms of coercion may be expedient, but they cannot be done if they are incommensurate with the behavior coerced. In such instances the two rules clash, with the rule of proportionality always being sovereign. The reason for its sovereignty is simply that it protects the dignity of the person coerced. To treat persons purely in ways expedient would reduce them to means rather than ends. The rule of proportionality says that even wrongdoers must be treated as persons, possessed of dignity, and not as things. This is done by treating their wrongful deeds not as mere natural events, explicable in terms of cause and effect, but as free and moral acts, calling for a public response. The importance of so treating them when the end is liberty is particularly great given the dependence of the very idea of liberty on respect for persons.

The fourth rule is likewise a limit on the range of expediency.

The Rule of Enforceability

Some acts are unenforceable because they depend, by their very nature, on the motive animating them. Charity is an example. An act of charity is in essence an act done out of a charitable spirit. It is indefinable in terms merely of outward form. Were a government to compel everyone to help the poor, then helping the poor would largely cease to be a charitable activity. It would lose its inner spirit and become merely enforced public service. Someone may of course carry out, in a spirit of charity, a compulsory act that helps others; for example, one might pay taxes in a welfare state in such a spirit. But if an act is compulsory, few will perform it as they would were it purely voluntary. Compulsion will normally change fundamentally the character of the act.

This may seem a rather obvious and colorless point. It pertains, however, to the deepest grounds of liberty. To say "unenforceable" is to say "essentially free." The ideal of liberty is based on the conviction that freedom, the ability to choose, belongs to the core of our humanity, and that an indispensable feature of a good society is the allowance, to every human being, of as much room as possible in which to choose. It follows that only those acts can be justifiably coerced that both are necessary to liberty and fulfill this function regardless of the motive from which they are done. In other words, coercion must be limited to acts that retain their value — in this case their contribution to the maintenance of liberty — even though they are done under threat. Acts that lose their value when coerced must be left in the area of personal choice. Thus the protection of private property is essential to liberty. That end is served so long as people refrain from theft and burglary, even if from fear of punishment rather than out of respect for persons. In short, observance of property rights is enforceable. An example on the other side is civility. Liberty may depend on courtesy and mutual consideration in personal relations. These qualities, however, do depend on respect for persons. They are too complex and nuanced, and too variable in varying circumstances, to be enforceable. To be civil because you might otherwise find yourself in trouble with the police is not to be civil. The rule, then, is that coercion can be justified only so far as it is heedful of the essential unenforceability of some acts.

Further examples of acts that are unenforceable, or essentially free, come readily to mind. One of the major concerns throughout this essay has been the act by which one enters into relations with transcendence, or God — the act of faith. One of my main arguments in behalf of liberty, stated in various ways, is that the act of faith is essentially free. A compulsory faith is a contradiction in terms. Christians have been partially aware of this truth, with Augustine a dramatic case in point, although it was well along in modern times before they awakened to it fully. Another example of things essentially free, one of particular interest to the humanist mind, is political activity. Participation in public life depends on a spirit of public responsibility and thus is unenforceable. A civic spirit and an intelligent assessment of common problems cannot be exacted through force. It is true that some nations compel people to vote. But mere voting does not constitute participation in politics, and even that bare requirement is dubious. If voting is compulsory, it will not ordinarily be done with the kind of care that characterizes the acts of a conscientious citizen.

Some of the most significant essentially free activities have to do with community. At least this has been my argument in the preceding pages. Freedom can be well used in many ways but is best used in seeking and knowing truth, and doing this as far as possible in communication with others. This formula is intended, as I have pointed out already, to comprise poetry and literature, the fine arts and physical sciences, refined scholarship and philosophical reflection, and theological inquiry and religious worship. It is also intended to comprise serious conversation concerning all common human interests and experiences, such as daily work, sports, and sexual relations. These things can exist and be intelligently discussed only in an atmosphere of freedom. From this vantage point it is apparent why totalitarianism is so devastating. The kind of person you are depends on the kinds of truths you care about and how you seek and follow those truths. Not merely freedom, but humanity itself, is lost when dialogue is drowned in propaganda and official creeds.

It is primarily because truth can be sought, possessed, and shared only in freedom that liberty is the supreme standard of social and political organization. Implicitly, this attributes great worth to the activities of artists, writers, philosophers, scholars, and other such intellectuals. Also, however, there can be great worth in lives devoted to the exercise of manual skills, to charitable work, to business enterprise, and to activities of other kinds that people more practical than intellectual in their inclinations can engage in, reflect on, and converse about. The glow of value in all human activities is the glow of truth, of a consciousness of existence in its depths, and this is called forth only by inner reflection and by free and spontaneous talk. A scholarly conference may for a day or two constitute a model community. But perceptive and probing conversations among friends, even among those whose interests are mainly in such matters as sports and sex, can be more common and continuing than scholarly conferences, and can be authentically communal. One of the most familiar features of modern tyranny is the dark shadow it casts over every kind of unconstrained and inquiring conversation.

The principle of separation of church and state is so often intoned and so variously and unwisely applied as to render it banal. It has great importance, however, in relation to liberty, and that is because it has become a traditional and widely accepted way of saying that certain central human concerns are beyond coercion. Spiritual matters, such as conceptions of God, are not among the proper responsibilities of the state, and this is because they are essentially free. They must be left to associations lacking in means of coercion. While this can mean different things in different historical settings, it must always mean liberty of some kind and degree. In practice, the principle cannot be pressed to an extreme of abstract purity. The state inevitably, through the examples set by its leaders, through its support for education, and in numerous other ways, exerts spiritual influence. This influence should be used with utmost respect for the spiritual preconditions and the legitimate purposes of a free society. But primary responsibility for spiritual matters belongs to individual persons and to groups and authorities with no powers except those of persuasion.

The rule of enforceability thus is centered on the fact that some acts are done either voluntarily or not at all. Charity and religious worship are perfect examples. The rule lends itself, however, to being broadened. There are acts that can be enforced, yet enforcing them involves consequences so destructive, perhaps of liberty itself, that it is prudent to leave them free. The best examples are acts of abstinence. It is possible, for example, to outlaw pornography. Indeed, it is no doubt normal for societies to do so. And there are good reasons for this, as I have already argued. Pornography is always evil, for it reduces persons to objects of lust, thus violating human dignity. Where it is outlawed, however, the liberty in which literature flourishes is seriously narrowed. This at least can be argued. Writers of exceptional merit have made it obvious that sexual candor is not necessarily pornographic. Yet to distinguish between sexual candor with an artistic purpose and that designed to appeal to prurient interests is almost always beyond the abilities of people of the sort who are willing to serve as censors. It is better to leave pornography for the most part free in order that literary creativity may also be free.

A like example concerns that tormented issue of the late twentieth century, abortion. It is possible to have a visceral distaste for abortion and to feel that abortion in most circumstances is akin to murder, hence profoundly wrong, yet to feel that it ought to be allowed, at least within limits. Laws prohibiting abortion are highly intrusive into private life, and in that way offensive to the liberal spirit. Also there are those cases of fetuses known to be severely malformed, or pregnancies endangering the health and lives of mothers. It can be argued that fetuses are persons and thus should be protected in all circumstances whatever. But to compel a woman to have a severely malformed child or to die in childbirth is compelling an act of heroism that should surely be left to personal choice. But even in the case of a normal pregnancy the sentinel of personal choice may issue a challenge. If only a free act can be a moral act, then perhaps abortions in many circumstances should be allowed simply in order that not having an abortion can remain a moral act.

The rule of enforceability can be seen as an exception attached to the rule of expediency — that coercion is justified only for acts necessary or contributory to general liberty. It takes note of the fact that some acts are essentially altered if done from fear of punishment. Such acts are outside the bounds of coercion *even if they are expedient in relation to the maintenance of liberty.* It is often argued, for example, that widespread religious faith is essential to a free society. It may be so. The rule of enforceability, however, adds a "nevertheless." However essential religious faith may be to liberty, its very essence lies in its freedom. To subject it to force would destroy it. Without the rule of enforceability, the rule of practical necessity would be susceptible to indefinite enlargement.

We can see again, from this vantage point, that the rule of enforceability goes to the heart of liberty. It expresses the conviction, no doubt implicit in moral life throughout the ages but first given philosophical form by Kant, that humanity has its core in freedom and in the responsibility freedom entails. Arising from this conviction is the liberal idea that the business of the state is above all that of securing liberty. Only in that way does it respect the essential freedom of the primary human acts. Mill, in spite of the nobility of spirit manifest in his defense of liberty, was guilty of a serious philosophical misstep when he defined the realm of liberty in terms of "self-regarding" acts. Acts essentially free are all "other-regarding." This is because the realm of liberty is that of the spiritual and moral, which is also the realm of relationships, both to ultimate reality and to persons. It is these relationships that give liberty so central a place in the whole human enterprise.

Seeing how coercion and liberty can in some measure be reconciled puts us in a position — since liberty attains its end in community — to better understand the relationship of society and community.

Society, Community, and Coercion

The idea of a liberal state, it appears, is not a contradiction in terms. Even though the state is a coercive organization, it is not locked in a fight to the death with liberty. The harshest incursion of the state into the sphere of personal freedom occurs when the state uses or threatens violence against individuals, as it does in all criminal law. Yet such violation of liberty can be in large measure reconciled with personal dignity. This happens when coercion is carried out in accordance with a universal form, in support of common liberty, and with care that punishments be proportional to deeds and that acts that are essentially free not be interfered with. Coercion of this sort ideally prescribes the actions an enlightened individual would choose if left entirely free. It may even — again ideally — draw individuals into voluntarily conforming with their own moral, or authentic, will. Of course, the actual behavior of states is always far from their ideal behavior. The point, however, is that the state in actuality can sometimes, even through its coercive actions, help individuals to become themselves, that is, to be free. The limits on liberty can in principle be a discipline.

Something like this can be said about not only the state but also society. Although state and society are distinct and are sometimes in opposition, both are organizational components of a single collective body. As Aristotle, followed by modern thinkers like T. H. Green, argued, the state is the society of societies. It assures the overall coherence of the groups making up society. This is why it has, and must have, coercive power. Hence by extension one may say that the whole web of social prescriptions, comprising not only laws but also customs and traditions, and even ephemeral fashions and expectations, is not an entirely alien order to members of society. People may find themselves partly by conforming with social prescriptions, and the selves they find may not be entirely different from their own deep, destined selves. While this is an ideal and not a fact, it is a relevant ideal, which means that it can shape the fact. Society and liberty are not always and inevitably in polar opposition.

From this it follows that society and community are not in polar opposition either, in spite of the inevitable tension between them. Community is the shared pursuit and enjoyment of true values. These values are in some degree *borne* by society, although they are *realized* only by individuals in community. They may be represented in various ways in the outward forms making up society and may be taught by society to individuals. This is why it can be said that so distinctive a personality as Socrates was typically Greek, and even that so incomparable a figure as Jesus was a representative Jew. The values at the center of community, such as truth, are often cultivated and honored by social organizations, such as universities. Of course, false ideas and meretricious values, with slavery and racial discrimination as cases in point, also are often supported by society. But hardly anyone can create new ideas and values, except of minor sorts. The ideas and values making for personal greatness are practically always taken, at least in rough form, from society. And to all this must be added the simple fact of physical proximity — essential to community and provided by society. The persons in whose company values are pursued and enjoyed are encountered in social settings such as coffeehouses, universities, and churches. Freedom is realized preeminently in dialogue, and society, if only by assuring liberty and protecting private property, is a precondition of dialogue. The concept of the public realm is implicitly an acknowledgment that community presupposes society. Community is realized in and through society.

A good society is like a theater company that provides a stage on which a drama — the drama of communication — can be enacted. And it may provide as well the words and the general form through which the drama is enacted. Nothing whatever has been achieved, of course, until the drama actually occurs. Yet the drama could not occur were it not for the theater company. The best societies are those providing for the physical proximity and spiritual resources on which communication depends.

Care should be taken, however, that the point is not overstated or misconstrued, as it often has been, even by thinkers of genius, such as Rousseau and Hegel. Man in his authentic being has been characterized as a "political animal." He has been seen as coincident in his own true will with the "general will," and as finding his life only in the life of the state. None of this is true. The truth incorporated in the title of Niebuhr's *Moral Man and Immoral Society* remains fundamental and lasting. Righteousness and truth are always personal, not collective, achievements. Societies are always highly imperfect — less principled and less sensitive than individuals. This is partly, as we have seen, because society is ruled by military and economic imperatives that absolutely require the reduction of persons to means, an act never altogether redeemed by strict adherence to the rules justifying coercion. It is partly also because reducing persons to means is a more or less congenial act to proud and callous legislators and governors, and they do it far oftener and more extensively than circumstances require. And fi-

337

nally, persons are sometimes reduced to means because those so reduced gladly forfeit the burden of personal responsibility, the burden
of setting their own ends. These are the reasons why saintly societies
are unheard of, and also why the communality, in which human beings
express unqualified respect for one another and for truth, is always a
personal, not collective, achievement.

There is perhaps no more dangerous idea in the history of political
thought than that of the general will, a will for the public good that is
identical with the moral will — the true will — of every particular person. It is dangerous partly because of the truth it contains. A general
will would be a will coming from the populace at large, enforced by the
government, and conforming perfectly with the four rules — universality, expediency, proportionality, and enforceability. There ought to be
such a will in every society. But there never is. Even in the best societies,
the popular and governmental will almost always diverges greatly from
the general will. And even if there were a general will in some society, an
individual could not achieve selfhood and freedom simply by obeying
it. As a discipline, the general will would have to be learned and absorbed into the inward being of the individual. Only thus could it be
freely affirmed. As I have said so often in the course of this essay, when
it comes to the primary things our humanity requires of us, choice is indispensable and choice is essentially reflective. Even under the governance of a general will, the individual would have to stand off from government and society and reflect on their demands and conform with
them freely. The idea of the general will jeopardizes liberty by centering
it in the social and political order rather than the free person.

Furthermore, it is vital in this context to keep in mind the primacy
of the spirit. A liberal society is not the matrix of liberty. Rather, it is the
spirit of liberty, coming only out of the depths of personal being, which
is the matrix of liberty — and of a society that upholds liberty. The spirit
precedes the letter. We tend to forget this truth because it humbles us.
As intimately personal as the spirit is, we have no control over it. The
wind blows where it wills. We arrange things deliberately — states, constitutions, laws, societies — through the letter. But we arrange them
well only through the spirit. A free society can exist and flourish only so
far as it is created, upheld, critically examined, and periodically reformed by a free spirit.

The root fact of human nature and the human condition is personal responsibility. Even if there could be a perfectly righteous set of laws and customs, these could not produce righteous persons. Righteousness is always personal, not collective. It lies in love of truth and of neighbor. It is realized in some form of dialogue — in formal discourse or casual conversation, in words or paint or stone, between persons or within persons. And whatever its form, dialogue is a highly personal activity. It presupposes freedom, the personal choices by which one attempts to walk, so far as possible in the company of others, on the path toward truth.

Coercion, accordingly, is always evil in itself, even though it sometimes is justified. It countermands personal responsibility. This is so even if it conforms exactly with the rules of universality, expediency, proportionality, and enforceability. It is impossible for the evil inherent in depriving a person of freedom to be altogether erased. And even worse than coercion are social restraints thoughtlessly accepted. A person who is coerced may at least be cognizant of his freedom and his corresponding responsibilities, whereas someone thoughtlessly conforming with customs and fashions may have completely forgotten his freedom and may thus have largely lost his humanity. The ideal human being, for Hegel and his British followers such as Green, was someone thoroughly socialized. The truth however is that human righteousness presupposes a degree of social alienation. As Camus so powerfully argued, a good human being — a communal human being — is always, in the world as it is, a rebel.

The rules justifying coercion thus show the way, not to the reconciliation of society and community, but to keeping the tension between them from becoming deadly. Rules that are more or less recognized, and occasionally and roughly heeded in practice, can make a great difference both to the person coerced and to the coercive agency, the state. For the person coerced, it is one thing to be crushed by an unapologetically malicious act of state violence, like the countless acts that created the Nazi death camps and the Soviet "Gulag." It is quite another thing to do something, although unwillingly and under threat, that can with a degree of plausibility be defended as accordant with personal dignity. As for the coercive agency, the state, by trying to conform with the rules of justification it may avoid the descent, so easy for states, into mere brutality. It is cognizant of personal dignity even if not perfectly respectful of it. Among the political lessons taught by the twenti-

339

eth century is surely this: that while there are no good states, some states are immeasurably better than others. The rules justifying coercion can help create and sustain the difference.

The most important conclusion to be drawn from these reflections concerns the individual. Even in a very good state, conformity and obedience must be critical and guarded. It is in the interest of governments, and in the nature of society and the masses, to try continually to lure individuals into unreflective compliance with all official demands and social norms. Neither lawful authorities nor society at large welcomes the presence of rebels. Nor is rebellion a small thing. For the individual, the price of social nonconformity or civil disobedience may be high. And for society, reasonable goals and sensible measures may be seriously obstructed by a rebellious minority. Rebellion is often carelessly and falsely glorified. Nonetheless, the spirit of rebellion, grounded in a sense of unsharable personal responsibility, is essential to our humanity. Persons of critical spirit may often feel constrained, whether by conscience or by fear, to protest only inwardly and privately, while acquiescing outwardly. But even that is something. It is acting, however imperfectly and uncertainly, as a free and moral being.

The overall course of these reflections reminds us of a theme central to liberty, that is, solitude. An essay on liberty necessarily deals, primarily, with the distinctive, solitary person, the primary bearer of moral responsibility. It deals with society only secondarily. The word "liberty" denotes an area more or less outside of society and the state, an area calling on the critical intelligence and wary conscience of the individual person. While freedom may be realized partly in ordinary civic and social roles, it has its roots in the solitude that is inseparable from moral responsibility. A good liberal order will provide opportunities for participation in public life, and it will try, in schools and families, to make citizens ready to respond to those opportunities. But it will also do something more basic. It will deliver its citizens into those separate and lonely spheres where, through solitary reflection and dialogic forays into the world around them, they can work out their distinctive destinies.

CHAPTER 12

Liberation: Action and Suffering

Liberty and Liberation

The enjoyment of liberty carries with it an obligation, varying in its requirements with circumstances, to engage in action in behalf of liberty. The basis for this assertion has already been laid out. I claim liberty for myself on the grounds that I am by nature free and cannot be the one I am fitted to be without the liberty that allows me to exercise my freedom. But every human being is by nature free. Hence in claiming liberty for myself, I must claim it for everyone. This is the universality inherent in liberalism. Such universality would be meaningless, however, if I recognized no obligation to help secure and widen the liberty of others when I can. To enjoy my own liberty in good conscience I must act, so far as practical opportunities and possibilities permit, in behalf of the liberty of all.

Demands on the liberal mind are commensurate with the universal range of liberal responsibilities. Over the long run, action in support of liberty can be effective only on the basis of a comprehensively critical attitude toward the established society — including, needless to say, the established government. No authorities, customs, laws, or institutions are sacrosanct. Any of them may, in some needless and preventable way, constrict liberty. This is not an uncontroversial principle, as shown in an earlier discussion. It presupposes the independent, thinking, resolutely free human being — the "disencumbered self" — which not only conservatives but also numerous liberals have held to be a fiction. No doubt it is. Nonetheless, as I have already argued, our moral nature obliges us to disencumber ourselves so far as we can. A moral principle of its very essence calls on us to rise to a vantage point from which we can critically judge the demands society places on us. Anyone who unthinkingly acquiesces in social norms and demands has given up something that defines our humanity. Hence the moral anguish and self-sacrificial acts of countless individuals in one or another of the murderous societies of the twentieth century. Disencumberment is a moral responsibility and in limited measure a practical possibility.

In their responsibility for liberating action, then, there is nothing in the social order — no authorities, customs, traditions, laws, institutions — that liberals should refrain from bringing under critical scrutiny. In this, political radicals and reformers have been in the right, conservatives in the wrong. Nonetheless, moral universalism does not justify neglect of practical possibilities, and political radicals are almost always guilty of such neglect. Even though there are scarcely any limits on the right of moral criticism, there are limits on the possibilities of fruitful action.

These limits are due, first of all, to our finitude, which entails an inability to foresee with any assurance the outcome of our actions. The "unintended consequences" so often found in the train of reformist programs occur because we are finite and only fragmentarily comprehend the realities amid which we act. This is to grant again that we are inevitably encumbered. We can never rise entirely above all the obstacles our social situations put in the way of perfect moral discernment and action. And capping our social and natural limitations is our willful blindness to those limitations — the blindness referred to earlier as "original sin," or "radical evil." We are blind to our own moral infirmities — to the deep and powerful impulse in all of us to be absolute masters of the universe we dwell in and leading us to objectify all the persons and realities around us. We are blind also to the moral distortions worked in us by our social encumberment. We fancy ourselves free of the prejudice and callousness inherent in every society.

Finally, there is this as well: not only is action always and inevitably carried on by creatures who are finite and morally flawed; action in itself — that is, social and political action, action on others — is evil. It is evil because it depends on power, and power depersonalizes those subject to it. Action entails objectification. Sometimes the objectification is obvious, as when violence is used. At other times it is so subtle as to be scarcely noticeable, as with persuasive speech. But always the aim is to induce someone to behave in a certain way, thus rendering the one so induced a means to the end envisioned in the action. It is undeniable that action can be, and often is, directed to good ends — to protecting the weak, for example, or aiding those in need. Action therefore may have beneficial consequences. But some person or class of persons — those who might harm the weak or those who resist paying taxes to help those in need — is always treated as a means, and in that way is objectified. Social action is organization, and organization is objectification, even when those organized are more or less cooperative. And since action is intrinsically evil, it normally has an adverse moral effect on those employing it. Revolutionaries, who exemplify the most radical kind of action, rarely are saints.

These chastening facts are highly disagreeable to people committed to great projects of action. Hence they are frequently ignored. This can bring disaster to any enterprise. It brings the greatest disaster, however, to the greatest of all projects of action, that of doing away with the evil in human beings. There are probably no political undertakings more delusory, or more likely to end tragically. Not only are the reformers themselves always more or less evil, and the means they employ evil, but also the very impossibility of their goal may draw them into ever more extensive uses of power. And the nobility of the goal may cause them to feel that any means they employ are justified. This is all illustrated, of course, by the sanguinary efforts of the Soviet Union to create a paradise of people liberated from capitalism and thereby liberated from sin.

Clearly, the late twentieth-century tendency to picture the good life in terms of action, a tendency reaching eloquent expression in the novels of Malraux and the essays of Arendt, should be viewed with great caution. It obscures the limits and evils inherent in action, as well as the moral infirmities of all who engage in action. And even if action were always effective, surely not every life should be absorbed in action. Can anyone feel that Descartes, or Beethoven, or Proust, or Matisse might better have devoted himself to public affairs and political causes? Would the world be better off had Plato not turned away from politics to engage in philosophy? At best, political action can offer a noble life to some people in some historical circumstances; this is illustrated by the American founders. And it deserves a degree of involvement by practically everyone. It should not, however, be glorified.

A highly useful concept for marking the limits on political action in the cause of liberty is liberation. In the twentieth century this concept took on inflammatory connotations when it came to signalize the grand ideal of a transformed human order. But there is nothing in the concept that implies transformation. And there is nothing in it that precludes recognition of practical possibilities. On the contrary, if liberty presupposes a flawed society, then liberation bespeaks caution and a concern with circumstance. Its literal, and one might say natural, meaning thus is nearer to gradualism than to transformation. Let us say, accordingly, that the aim of liberation is to establish a foothold for liberty where it does not exist and to widen it where it does. Liberation seeks greater liberty, not a perfect society. It works by exposing social and legal bonds to critical scrutiny, and loosening them where possible, but not to thoughtlessly defying them or casually casting them off.

If social transformation means revolution, liberation is a piecemeal task and prescribes no single and final social ideal. Liberation fits comfortably into the worldview underlying the present essay — that of humans as fallen, hungering for community but needing the restraints of society, and destined never in their mortal lives to be fully liberated. It proceeds by half-measures and can go on for generations. And it ends inconclusively. Its highest standard is not *total* liberty but continuing engagement in a prudently conducted campaign on the side of the utmost degree of *practicable* liberty.

The tasks of liberation are suitable for creatures who are morally flawed yet free. They are compatible with our fallenness. The idea of social transformation, on the other hand, implicitly contradicts the notion of original sin. It assumes that a few, the agents of transformation, have the moral purity, along with the practical understanding, to act on history like gods. They are able not merely to call forth and direct desired events, but also to refashion their fellow human beings, to make them gods like themselves. The dissonance between society and community will be erased. Social transformation will come about through moral transformation. Humans will become purely and wisely communal, divested of the folly and pride that render the constraints of society and state indispensable. As we have seen, when so unrealistic a goal seizes on the minds of determined men, the consequences are apt to be tragic. In a word, social transformation evinces pride, liberation humility.

In recognizing simultaneously our responsibilities and our limitations, the standard of liberation is far more effective in practice than is the standard of social transformation. This is illustrated profusely in history. In the nineteenth and twentieth centuries, reform movements, proceeding step-by-step over many decades, brought deep changes in every Western democracy. They did not bring perfect justice, as radicals rightfully insist, but they brought about societies far more egalitarian and humane — and far more liberal — than any that had ever before existed. During the same period of history in which liberation was proving its practicality, however, revolution was writing a history of tyranny and terror. Daring enterprises of social transformation, in numerous nations, shattered not only society but also all moral restraints. Death and senseless depradation stalked vast areas of the earth. Someone might claim that the feasibility of social transformation is proven by the American Revolution. That event, however, in spite of its name, was less a revolution than an overthrow of what had become a foreign occupation. One must turn to France to witness a venture in social transformation that might plausibly claim success. The events of 1789 have been hailed by many and still are hailed by some. There is no doubt that they lifted human spirits all over the West and did much to glamorize the ideals of liberty and equality. But the mass violence in the streets of Paris, the Reign of Terror, and the rule of Napoleon do not strike everyone as signs of success. And it was not until almost a century after the outbreak of the revolution that France was able to establish a relatively stable constitutional democracy.

The case for liberation as a standard of action is clearly strong. It accords with our radical moral imperfection, our moral fallenness, far better than does the standard of social transformation. And it accords far better with the intellectual and practical limitations that are inherent in our finitude. It is a relatively modest criterion. This is its virtue.

We must go beyond the concept of liberating action, however. Such action has to do with the attainment of liberty. But liberty is not an end in itself. It is an opportunity for righteousness and the wisdom in which righteousness is rooted. We must therefore ask how these ends are attained. How does liberty reach fulfillment? Trying to answer this question will lead us beyond the subject of liberty in the strict sense of the

345

term. But it would seem unfitting in a long essay on liberty to ignore altogether the end to which liberty is only a means.

The issue is one of moral and spiritual purification. It is hard to think of any writer who has shed more light on this issue than Dostoyevsky. As we have seen, Dostoyevsky's writings on one side are a polemic against the faith of revolutionaries — that political action can be redemptive. In *The Possessed* he depicts men enthralled by the illusion that they can contrive the eradication of human iniquity and thereby blaze a trail into an earthly heaven. That this illusion would lead in fact to an earthly hell was prophetically foreseen by Dostoyevsky. But he was greatly concerned with redemption, that is, with righteousness and wisdom. And in spite of his condemnation of political redeemers, he was not despairing. In figures such as Alyosha Karamazov and Prince Myshkin he provided intimations of (although he could never very vividly portray) the human grandeur that was his ultimate concern. And in Raskolnikov and Dmitri Karamazov he tried to show how this grandeur, while luring some into tragic projects of political redemption, might be attained. His answer is somewhat startling to modern secular ears. Human beings reach their full stature not through action but through suffering. They attain the full humanity for which God destines them (Dostoyevsky was a Christian) only by tasting the fury of the crucifixion. In this way he opened up a new pathway for liberal thought.

The idea of moral purification through suffering is, to say the least, not at home in the precincts of liberal political theory. For one thing, liberals typically have not thought of human beings as needing to be morally purified. They have assumed them to be more or less pure, that is, reasonable and cooperative, by nature. Further, as I have pointed out, most liberals have thought of liberty as being on the whole agreeable. So the idea that liberty might involve suffering, and that the suffering might have a role in effecting the fulfillment of liberty, was entirely outside the perimeters of their thought. Certainly such an idea never occurred to Locke, Mill, or Green. Even Tocqueville and Niebuhr, although unique among liberal thinkers in their sensitivity to the harm that can be done by free human beings, paid little or no attention to the way suffering can further the ultimate purposes of liberty.

I have not brought up the matter hitherto in this essay because it suggests that liberty is not basically an outer arrangement, having to do with observable social and political forms, but rather is an inner state. This is a view, as I have argued, that leads almost always to neglect or denial of what most of us mean by liberty — a state of not being interfered with from the outside. It leads to the ideal of an inner liberty — from sin, or radical evil — which renders outer liberty a secondary, even unimportant, consideration. One of the core ideas of this essay — that liberty entails the possibility of doing things that are wrong and thus damaging to oneself and to others — amounts to a tacit setting aside of the ideal of inner liberty. All along, however, I have argued that the purpose of liberty was righteousness and wisdom, and these constitute an inner state. This is why we are forced, as we approach the end of the essay, to consider the matter of moral and spiritual purification.

To avoid the grave confusions connected with the concept of inner liberty, I shall eschew the concept here and hold to my original definition of liberty as an outer, or institutional, arrangement. Accordingly, it seems advisable to eschew the concept of inner liberation, even though it is easy to think of moral purification as a process of inner liberation. It is essential, however, to understand that the pathways of liberating action and purifying suffering are one pathway, the end of which is righteousness and wisdom, or, in Christian terms, sanctity.

Liberty and Suffering

How does suffering do its purifying work? What reason is there for looking upon suffering with such hope as did Dostoyevsky? The best starting point for reflecting on suffering and its possible moral impact may lie in concepts already developed, those of world and worldliness. Sin, the radical evil from which we need to be liberated, consists primarily in worldliness — in the strong inclination to build and inhabit a world, a realm of things fully understood and fully under control. This inclination is often weakened and destroyed by suffering. How this happens may be better comprehended if we recall the nature of world and of worldliness.

The world is the sphere of more or less intelligible and controllable realities in which we pass our daily lives. I have tried to show that it is not the same as being in itself. We readily assume, however, that it is, thus effecting a kind of voluntary self-imprisonment. The world is seductive partly because it provides many pleasures and apparently can be understood and controlled. It is seductive also because it strikes us as "hard reality." But it isn't. It is an abstraction from the realities in normal experience. The world is made up of those aspects of things that are observable, quantifiable, calculable, and readily susceptible of generalization. Since human beings possess these worldly qualities only at one level of their existence, and God, as understood by Christians, possesses none of them, the world is an abstraction that drastically abridges humanity and leaves out God altogether.

The rise of the world is not merely accidental. For one thing, it comes about under harsh practical pressures, primarily those of physical survival. If we did not deliberately and prudently act on the realities around us, and do this cooperatively, focusing most of the time on those aspects of reality that render common and systematic action possible, the human species would quickly become extinct. We are compelled to build a world in the midst of a mysterious and threatening universe, and we are compelled in doing this to choose for our materials the fixed and impersonal. This affects fundamentally how we treat our fellow human beings. In large areas of our lives, we must weaken and circumscribe the human characteristics, like freedom and inwardness, which make human beings so incalculable. We must, to a degree, reduce persons to things. And we must do this not merely as individuals but also as societies, thus subjecting individuals through most of their daily lives to disciplines and pressures antithetical to their personal being.

It is not only the spur of practical necessity, however, that explains the rise of the world. There is also the spur of sin, that is, of the exhilaration we experience in feeling that all reality is under our control and we are virtual gods. And when reality slips from our grasp, and pride is defeated, we may fall back on the alternative form of sin already discussed, distraction. Rather than lucidly accepting our finite and mortal humanity, we may seek refuge as merely one among the multitudinous worldly realities that other human gods control. Not only does every tyranny in some measure exemplify such an occurrence, but so also does many a prosaic social or bureaucratic agency, insofar as it encourages its members to be mere functional units in its organization and operation. Sin, in short, is worldliness as a device either of self-assertion or of self-abandonment.

The sin of worldliness abounds naturally. In forming the world we necessarily form ourselves at the same time. We train and exercise our powers of worldly construction and make the use of those powers habitual. In doing this we cultivate the worldliness that gives rise to the world to begin with. We become more insensible to all but the worldly aspects of being and more strongly inclined to sequester ourselves in the world. We become ever more truncated versions of humanity. We become beings whose sole access to reality is sensual observation and whose sole satisfactions are physical pleasures. We become narrow empiricists and hedonists. This of course is not totally to falsify human nature, since some of our knowledge is basically empirical and some of our legitimate satisfactions are physical pleasures. It is, however, to diminish ourselves. Just as the world is an impoverished version of being in itself, so the empirical and hedonistic self is an impoverished version of humanity.

Worldliness banishes the mystery of being. A thoroughly organized and all-inclusive world manifests our urge to reduce the plenitude of being in itself to an aggregate of things at our disposal. The mystery inherent in the mere particularity of a being — in the particularity, say, of a rock, a tree, or a mountain — is put out of mind and forgotten, as when the physical universe is thought of as a store of raw materials. We surround ourselves with things we can use as we wish. More fateful is the fact that the mystery inherent in every human person is also put out of mind. The mystery of being, as we have already seen, is the mystery of personality. When we objectify, for purposes of comprehension and control, we depersonalize. The world is a humanly imagined and constructed universe in which there are no persons. Testifying to this are the references often made to industrial settings or bureaucratic organizations as "soulless."

All around us, however, are paths leading beyond the world — toward persons, truth, and the glories of creation. This is not conjectural. Poets and painters, architects and sculptors, philosophers and novelists repeatedly break out of the world and give us glimpses of the encompassing mystery. The world is not an irresistible fate. For Christians, however, there is the fact of original sin. While sin is not fate, it cannot easily be cast aside. It is a state from which we need deliverance, and deliverance can be brought about only by transcendence. This is to say that worldliness, our strong inclination to build and inhabit the world, has us so in its grip that, even though a few can successfully resist it, only God can set us free.

According to Christianity, the decisive act of deliverance has already taken place and now needs only to be worked out and realized. The act consisted in the suffering and death of one man. The crucifixion and resurrection of Christ was the death sentence of worldly humanity and the birth of a new humanity. It was thereby the definitive enactment of human destiny. Thus every human being, consciously or not, is involved in this event. "I have been crucified with Christ," Paul wrote; "it is no longer I who live, but Christ who lives in me" (Gal. 2:20). Every person in his worldly selfhood is marked out for suffering and death; but in his inner, or destined, selfhood he is marked out for a lasting renewal of life. And not only every person, but also the whole of creation, is thus marked out. As world, as an imperial order purporting to comprise all things, the universe is destined for extinction; all that is real in it, however, will come forth as "new heavens and a new earth" (Isa. 65:17). Christ is the passing of worldliness and the world.

This passing can be fully accomplished, however, only through suffering. First of all, the requisite suffering is undergone by Christ. But the rest of us cannot be delivered from the world and our worldliness merely by watching someone else suffer — Christ, in this case. Participation in Christ's suffering, in some degree and manner, is a universal requirement. As Jesus said, the way to eternal life is straight and narrow. Dostoyevsky's affirmation of suffering was unquestionably drawn from Christian sources. Judged by Christian standards, worldly happiness and harmony are not great goods. There is a strange sense indeed in which tribulation and discord are better. When Paul declared that "we rejoice in our sufferings," he expressed the Christian conviction that through suffering — and ordinarily in no other way — we can participate in the drama of human sanctification. A human life does not flourish naturally, like the life of a bird or a tree. It flourishes only through affliction. But why is this? How does suffering deliver us from the radical evil that consigns us to the world?

Very simply, suffering reveals the desolation of the world. Through pride and distraction we cast ourselves out of primeval reality, out of the realm of persons and radiant truth. We precipitate ourselves into a universe of our own making, a world. Here we cannot be happy. We may for a time be diverted by the exuberance of pride or by the pleasures of worldly existence. But the world is an impoverished kingdom. It is made up of objects and is comprehensively impersonal. Within it we are necessarily alienated from self, from others, and from the depths of being that Christians know as God. We are separated from every possible source of enduring joy and peace. Suffering makes this clear to us. It robs us of the pleasures and satisfactions of worldly existence, and prompts us to look beyond the world, toward transcendence.

In revealing the desolation of the world, suffering crucifies the worldly self. Suffering is always the dying of the self that builds and maintains the world. That self is either proud or distracted — the master of all objects, or merely one among the objects. If it is proud, then it is humbled by suffering. It has to know that it is not in command of reality. If it were, it would not be suffering. If it is distracted, it is awakened. If it were merely an object among objects, it would not be experiencing so profound a sense of estrangement. It is the Christian idea that dying can be a way of entering into life. If the worldly self opens itself to the mystery of being, it can be raised from the dead.

Affliction in these ways opens the doors to righteousness and wisdom. We do not, of course, necessarily pass through those doors. Suffering does not liberate us necessarily. It can lead to the disintegration of personality and to death. Whether or not it does depends on the human response. Suffering invites receptivity, that is, a readiness to accept things that cannot be called forth by our own powers — powers that in the hands of fallen creatures are inevitably used to reinforce the world. Hence the need for receptivity. For Christians the three chief virtues are faith, charity, and hope, which are all forms of receptivity — toward God (faith), toward human persons (charity), and toward all that is coming in time (hope). To be receptive is to be neither proud nor distracted but ready for participation in the glories of creation.

It is the need for receptivity that prevents devotees of action from scorning the discipline of suffering and asserting the sovereignty of the human will. This they might do through a practice that sounds benign yet is impossible due to human limitations. The practice is delineated in the reformatory theory of punishment. According to this theory, suffering can be deliberately imposed to effect a moral change. In this way action is brought back to the forefront. Suffering becomes one of the devices in the hands of proud and worldly men. Such a theory is rendered impossible, however, because while we are able deliberately to impose suffering, we are not able deliberately to elicit the receptivity that renders suffering redemptive. Faith, charity, and hope cannot be humanly contrived. For Christians they are products of grace. And humanists must grant, I suggest, that they face here a situation in which the spirit precedes the letter.

The idea that suffering can be a pathway of moral purification (and in that way a continuation of the pathway of political and social liberation) can readily be cast in non-Christian terms. Even though, out of pride and fear, we relentlessly objectify all the realities around us, objectification is a falsification of reality. It imprisons us in illusions that may for a time be diverting and absorbing but, in the long run, leave us desolate and defeated. Worldliness obscures the encompassing mystery of being and defeats the true interests of a self that is by nature a participant in that mystery. Suffering endured watchfully and without despair leads sooner or later in another direction. It leads beyond the falsities of worldly life. It brings a realization that the world is not our proper home, and that technology cannot make it such. And with this it brings a realization that our worldliness is self-defeating. In a word, it dissolves our illusions. In principle, of course, we might freely, without the goad of suffering, rise above our worldliness and abandon all worlds. But we are deeply disinclined to do this. There usually must be a compelling force. Suffering is that force.

The core issue — for humanists and Christians alike — is community. The world, as an assemblage of objects, is at the opposite pole from community. It is a realm without persons. Its charm is that it is also without the perils to which persons give rise. That is one of the sources of our worldliness. The world is a place where entertainment and organizational busyness and other forms of alluring self-forgetfulness enable us to avoid the demands of a serious life. It also provides places of power and dominion that allow us to suppress other persons and the perils inherent in their free existence. But suffering disrupts our pleasant worlds and undermines our positions of power. And it may in these ways awaken a hunger for real relationships, that is, for truth-seeking communication. Given the essential communality of the self, this is a way of saying that suffering may lead toward the authentic selfhood that is the aim of liberty.

This is an argument diverging radically from modern assumptions. Spectacular advances in science and technology, fused in America with a native practicality, have produced an assurance that most or all problems can be solved through action. The world can be perfected. Suffering therefore is not merely useless. Showing forth our incompetence, it is humiliating. In the eyes of Christians, the evils infesting society and history, although partly practical and soluble, are rooted in the mystery of sin. They cannot be eliminated, therefore, by human contrivance and action. In the eyes of science and technology, however, sin is in principle a practical problem no different from any other such problem. The sphere of potentially successful action, guided by reason, is limitless.

Such an attitude is clearly irreligious, and one might think it would unanimously capture the minds of humanists. It does not, however. Wariness of fleeing into the illusory security of the world, the sense that suffering may somehow deepen our humanity: these are not exclusive to the religious mind. Capitalism, for example, has often been extolled (whether accurately or not) as a system that can save the intelligent and enterprising from the debilitating effects of a life without risks. And the innumerable people in liberal societies who deliberately expose themselves to physical danger, as in mountain climbing or military service, testify to a natural sense that physical security and peace of mind are morally unsafe. Praise of such qualities as courage and endurance, qualities called forth only by tribulation and danger, is after all at least as common among the irreligious as among the religious. The historical figures most admired by the religious and irreligious alike are people who have gone through severe trials, like Washington in the American Revolution and Lincoln in the Civil War. And hardly anyone, regardless of metaphysical commitments and convictions, is insensitive to the imperative of maintaining dignity in the face of disaster and death. In short, many who regard the cross with indifference or disdain acknowledge that not security and comfort, but ordeals and adversities, are needed for human beings to become authentically human.

In short, the idea that suffering can be liberating is not exclusive to Christians. It is not unreasonable. Testifying to this is what might be called the "heroic" concept of liberty. Nietzsche is no doubt the preeminent philosopher of such liberty. For Nietzsche the "death of God" precipitated man into a universe void of intrinsic meaning and thus demanding the utmost in human strength and intelligence. Those able to meet that demand were truly free and embodied a glory that was more than human — as judged by conventional, and shamefully undemanding, standards of what it means to be human. For Christians the Nietzschean ideal, with its denial of God and its celebration of human strength and mastery, is unacceptable in principle. Yet even for Christians, that ideal is not lacking entirely in wisdom, or even in charm. It depicts powerfully the possible glory of a human being, and it shows this glory as accessible only to those capable, whether by inner strength or by grace, of forsaking all secure and pleasant worlds. Jesus likened the coming of the Son of Man to the lightning that "comes from the east and shines as far as the west" (Matt. 24:27). The Logos that exalts the individual human being can be glimpsed in many and surprising places.

The Unsheltered Society

The Christian understanding of the purpose of life is superficially similar to the Aristotelian concept of self-realization. Humans do not possess their humanity immediately and spontaneously but have to achieve it through the disciplines of civilized life. Selfhood is the end point, not the starting point, of human existence. But the Christian principle is far more radical. One's humanity does not just await realization; it has been lost. And the key word for Christians is not "realization," but "rebirth." The self must be re-created, so the purpose of human life, in the elemental meaning of the term, is re-creation. It is conceivable, moreover, that the self to be re-created will be in some way greater or more excellent than the self that is lost. It would not be out of character for a creative and merciful God to turn salvation into something more than the correction of a grievous error. In any case, the Christian view indicates that teleological concepts must be employed with caution. They have a biological cast and can cause us to misconstrue the qualities that render human development distinctive. They can obscure the radical character of freedom, the fact that freedom is not a natural phenomenon but the eruption into natural phenomena of another dimension of reality. They can turn the drama of sin and redemption, and of suffering and selfhood, into a merely natural unfoldment.

The re-creation of humanity is plainly a work that is more than human. It is not the task of a being who is created and not his own creator. Nor is it the task of a being who has exaggerated and misused such creative power as he has. As I have said before, the one who needs to be saved cannot be the savior. Certain modern ideologies have argued the contrary, but, as we have seen, they often make their arguments plausible by assuming that a few, such as a corps of philosopher-kings, or a party elite, are effectively sinless and are free of the dim-sightedness inherent in finitude. Not needing to be saved, they are fitted to be saviors. Or, in some cases, such ideologies have counted on a saving force, such as "nature," or the historical dialectic, that is virtually divine although not explicitly characterized as such. But to look to a finite and morally fallible (or, in the case of a nonhuman power such as nature, amoral) source for so elemental a work as the reconstitution of the human race is plainly irrational. From the perspective of humanist reason it is heedlessness of manifest facts. From the perspective of Christianity it is idolatry. Yet the human race needs to be radically changed. For Kant the task might be accomplished by reason (although Kant sometimes appeals to "nature" and occasionally to God). For Christians transcendental intervention is indispensable; humans can be re-created only by the one who created them to begin with. Humans have a part to play, but only through grace.

Grace, however, cannot always be gentle. Given the role of suffering in the realization of selfhood, likening God to a blacksmith and earthly life to a forge is not unfitting. The worldly self has to be melted down and recast. Heating and hammering are unavoidable. The archetypal act of human reshaping, in the faith of Christians, is of course the crucifixion. The cross was a divine forge. This has implications for every person. As an act of salvation, it is a gift of inestimable value. But one cannot accept the gift merely by accepting the general principle that human sins were expiated on the cross. The crucifixion must be a reality in one's life. One must be killed and made alive. The literal meaning of this event will vary among individuals. There are multitudinous ways of suffering and dying, and it is obvious that some — perhaps among God's favorites — are called on to suffer far greater woes than others. But for no one can the journey from inhumanity to humanity be altogether pleasant. The crucifixion does not spare us the journey but rather gives us assurance that the trail has been blazed and that the journey is not beyond our powers.

The basic justification for liberty lies in the spiritual necessity of suffering. Where there is equal liberty, every person is exposed to the full impact of free and finite existence, experienced in a state of alienation from the ultimate ground of being. Every person can experience the insecurities and uncertainties consequent on that alienation. Liberty is a high value, not because it makes life agreeable but for the opposite reason. It makes life more or less disagreeable and does this by exposing us more fully to the impact of the human condition than does any other kind of social order. But the ordeal of liberty can be redemptive. It can be the heating and hammering, the forging of souls, that fit humanity for seeing ultimate truth.

A liberal society is a mere worldly order, and its importance therefore should not be exaggerated. As we have seen, there are ways of evading the ordeal of liberty even within the most liberal polities. People can devote themselves to acquiring wealth and power on a scale that provides them with the illusion of having transcended the human condition. Others can waste their liberty by indulging endlessly in the pleasures and frivolities that modern industrial societies offer so abundantly. And there is always at hand the escape route of social conformity. On the other side of the coin, it has to be acknowledged that liberty is dispensable. Even in the worst tyrannies individuals can affirm their freedom if they are willing to hazard their lives. Andrei Sakharov and Dietrich Bonhoeffer simply refused to be enslaved. Indeed, from a Christian standpoint it would be blasphemous to imply that God is constrained by man's social and political arrangements.

Still, humans are obliged to ask themselves what order of life enhances to the utmost their consciousness of their freedom and their consequent awareness of their responsibilities toward the world and transcendence. And one can reasonably argue that the regime of liberty is the true answer to this question. All other regimes try to shelter people from the storms of fallen existence. They do this by enclosing them in society. They provide fixed social status, absolute material security (at however low a level), authoritative and unvarying rules of conduct, and a world outlook that is not to be questioned. Liberty means that such shelters are more or less dismantled. Everyone is set partially outside of society and invited to summon the moral sense and the rational powers that in other systems are largely closed off even to noblemen, bishops, and other dominant minorities. With liberty, every person is constrained, or at least allowed, to face everything that life can bring. The standard of liberty calls for an unsheltered society.

Some of the metaphors so far used — blacksmith and forge, storms and shelters — have one drawback. They suggest passivity — yielding to the blacksmith's hammering, submitting to the storms of unsheltered human existence. It must be remembered, then, that we are speaking of liberty, and liberty involves activity. Activity is not necessarily action, which seeks preconceived results and employs power. Activity at its best is devoted to inquiry and communication. Ideally, liberty is creative. The element of passivity, however, still is there. We touched on the paradoxical fusion of passivity and creativity in the discussion of justification by faith. Faith may seem to encourage passivity. If one is justified by faith, and not by works, then there is nothing in particular one needs to do. Yet, according to Christian doctrine, faith will naturally bear fruit in a new life, in works that are not merely in conformity with conventional morality but are unprecedented and creative. Suffering by definition involves passivity; one can only submit. But to forget that it issues in life and activity — to forget that the crucifixion is followed by the resurrection — would be to caricature Christianity.

It would therefore be better in certain ways to think of God as a teacher rather than a blacksmith. That would make clear that the cooperation of men and women, the "students," is essential to the work being carried on. Liberty, tempered with authority, is the very atmosphere of teaching and learning. Also, it would bring to the fore the principle that seeking and finding the truth, in the company of others, is the very substance of freedom well-used. And finally, to think of the central divine concern as rendering life instructive, rather than merely agreeable, might obviate some of the doubts people have had about the power and goodness of God.

We must remember, nonetheless, that God's definitive word to the human race, Jesus, did not merely speak, as does a teacher. He was crucified. Moreover, his crucifixion was not a regrettable accident, without which his mission might have been more fully accomplished. Rather, it was the heart and climax of the mission. Effecting the reconciliation of God and humankind, it was the very reason for Jesus' appearance on earth. Almost everything in the Gospels, *except the crucifixion,* is in some degree uncertain and dispensable. It was mainly in the crucifixion that God's word was uttered. In this way Christianity might well be considered a strangely severe and exacting creed. This impression should not be softened. To shift the focus of the creed away from the crucifixion would deprive Christianity of much of its force and gravity. And by cutting the connection between liberty and suffering, it would turn liberalism into a prescription for making life merely enjoyable.

Again, reference to the well-known parable of Jesus' rejection of the

357

temptations in the wilderness (Matt. 4:1-11 and Luke 4:1-13) seems fitting. Jesus was tempted to provide conditions (bread, miracles, and totalitarian rule) making life absolutely secure, hence free of suffering. These conditions would also have reduced humans to the status of well-treated animals: contented and without any power or necessity of choosing, that is, without liberty and oblivious of their freedom. In other words, Jesus was tempted to relieve men and women of their suffering, with the cost being the loss of their liberty. In rejecting the temptations, he left them with their liberty — and also with their suffering. The passages recounting this parable may be taken as the key texts of Christian liberalism.

Not all suffering, however, is dramatic as a crucifixion on a hillside by a public way. There is a kind of suffering that is so quiet and inconspicuous that it may not seem like suffering at all. It is linked with hope, with the consciousness of something desired and not possessed. It is linked also with awareness that what is needed cannot be seized or gained by action but rather must be received. In sum, it mixes hope and receptivity. Although quiet and inconspicuous, it is vital to the liberal stance and to liberal politics. The best name for it is as unassertive as the attitude itself: "waiting." Many kinds of suffering are matters more or less of fortune. Poverty, loneliness, sickness, even death afflict some more severely than others. The suffering involved in waiting, however, is inherent in our finitude and moral fallibility and is thus imposed on every free and thoughtful person. It is a universal form of suffering, and in its universality it is unique.

Character as the Capacity for Waiting

The Bible, particularly the Old Testament, contains repeated admonitions to wait — always for God or for some manifestation of God. Thus one reads in Psalm 27:14,

> Wait for the LORD;
> > be strong, and let your heart take courage;
> > yea, wait for the LORD!

and in Isaiah 40:31,

They who wait for the LORD shall renew their strength,
    they shall mount up with wings like eagles,
they shall run and not be weary,
    they shall walk and not faint.

In the New Testament the numerous injunctions, in relation to the second coming of Christ, to "watch and pray" have a similar import, and Paul in his first letter to the Thessalonians says Christians "serve a living and true God, and . . . wait for his Son from heaven" (1:9-10). As these quotations and many others like them show, waiting is understood in the Bible as a primary characteristic of the relationship of the human and divine. Waiting expresses man's deference to God. It manifests the humility that befits finite and fallen creatures before their creator and lord. Accordingly, the prophet Isaiah declares that

the LORD is a God of justice;
    blessed are all those who wait for him.   (30:18)

Waiting is a sign of trust, hope, and receptivity.

Although the waiting called for in Jewish and Christian scripture seems to be always for God, the concept of waiting is not of interest to believers alone. As already noted, it is a commonplace in literature and the arts that creativity depends on something, conventionally called "inspiration," that is given and cannot be summoned at will. Thus writers and artists may spend prolonged periods waiting for an idea or insight on which their work depends. This is true not only in painting and poetry and other such arts but also in science. Like the intuition that enables someone to write a novel or compose a symphony, the intuition that calls forth a fruitful scientific hypothesis comes unbidden, and may not come at all. Hence for serious (that is, truth-seeking) human beings of all kinds, waiting is a common state, always unwelcome, therefore always a state of suffering, yet unavoidable.

Clearly the imperative that we search for the truth needs to be qualified. Sometimes the searching must be carried on, not by doing something, but merely by waiting and watching — by doing nothing. It is noteworthy in this connection that the thinking that is indispensable to finding fundamental, or philosophical, truth almost always eventuates at first in failure. But sooner or later, after the failure, the truth being sought begins to appear. After the searching a period of waiting is imposed on us. Plato recognized this in the inconclusiveness of many of his dialogues. A long and probing conversation apparently leads only to uncertainty. We cannot apprehend the truth immediately, but must wait for it. After the field has been tilled and planted, the farmer must wait for the crops to appear. The metaphor of light is also apropos. As our dependence on inspiration, or grace, indicates, we cannot summon the light at will but have to watch for it, as watchmen in Jewish scripture wait for the morning.

Waiting is essential not only in our relations with God or (in humanist reason) the unknown source of "inspiration," but also in our relations with one another. This will be clear from earlier discussions of community. A penetrating or provocative address to another person — an address that may be a mere comment, or a speech, painting, or architectural design — must be given. Likewise, the response of the other must be given. I cannot compel anyone to attend to or understand my address. The other person, to whom I am related in an act of communication, is a gift, or else, when the gift has not yet been given, someone for whom I must wait. All good human relations, not only those between creative people and their audiences, but also those between friends and family members, unavoidably involve periods of waiting. Since waiting is suffering, these are always periods of unease and disappointment. There is no community without patience.

Here we encounter something that may at first look paradoxical but follows from preceding paragraphs and pages: one must wait even for the self. Selfhood is realized, as we have seen at various places in this essay, in relationship with other selves and not as an isolated entity. As Martin Buber argues so eloquently, the personal pronoun "I" cannot be uttered apart from the personal pronoun "Thou." Hence if the "Thou" does not appear (a possibility Buber somewhat neglects), the "I" will not appear either. I must, then, while waiting for the other, wait for myself as well. I may do this in solitude, as well as in society. As I have argued in earlier pages, solitude can be communal. It can be an inward relationship, constituted of attentiveness and availability, with those — among them the self — for whom one is waiting.

Since the present chapter is entitled "Action and Suffering," it is noteworthy that wise action is unlikely to occur without waiting. Wise action depends on an insight or inspiration analogous to that which is needed in the arts and sciences, and indeed, in all serious discourse and conversation. A good political leader must be someone who is patient in the midst of crisis, who can watch and reflect, willing to let evolving circumstances disclose the necessities of the hour. Great leaders, such as Pericles in the first years of the Peloponnesian War or George Washington during the American revolution and founding, are often notably patient, capable of waiting. And the man accounted by many historians as the wisest of American presidents, Abraham Lincoln, seemed to many observers at the time of the Civil War a dangerously passive executive. If wise action is patient, unwise action is apt to be heedless and proud, carried out under the illusion that we depend, in our actions, on nothing but our own initiative and imagination.

There would be sense in saying that wise suffering, no less than wise action, depends on waiting. We do not usually speak of wise suffering. As we have seen, however, suffering can, by freeing one of worldliness, lead toward truth, community, and selfhood. In this way suffering can be creative. But it is not necessarily so; it can be corrosive. Everything depends on whether it is undergone in a spirit of receptivity, which entails a willingness to wait. Suffering in despair is suffering with a closed mind, unready for the unbidden insight. Suffering in hope, on the other hand, is maintaining a ready mind during an experience that is working personal change. Suffering of that kind opens the way to the self, the other, and the spirit that moves the whole human enterprise. A Christian might be defined as someone who lives under the authority of the crucified Christ and is ready, accordingly, to undergo crucifixion — which may come in any of a vast variety of forms — in a receptive spirit. Such a spirit is expressed in waiting for a destined resurrection, and this, like a crucifixion, may come in any one of many forms, but must always amount to the appearance of the self, the other, and unsurpassable truth, or God.

The need for waiting is not occasional but rather is unremitting. A human life is never finished even though it eventually ends. There is always something as yet unattained. The most successful action and the most fruitful suffering do not round out our destinies; they do not bring us to the selfhood in shared truth for which we were born. When that which one is waiting for appears, there always appears with it a need for waiting longer. Hence a capacity for waiting, as not merely an ephemeral trait but also an enduring aspect of character, must underlie every serious life. It is a capacity for living a destiny.

It is manifest that the ethos of waiting is particularly at home in liberal regimes, and that the posture of waiting has a significant place in the liberal stance. Liberty has to do with openings and possibilities, not with assured results. While the purpose of liberty is community, there is no knowing what its actual result will be. The primary impact of liberty is negative. When I live in a liberal society, I am placed under restraint. I must give others room in which they can live their own lives. This means that I cannot exact any particular response, or any response whatever, to my communications. One meaning of original sin is simply that people often respond to others in inappropriate ways or do not respond at all. Inattention and irresponsibility are among the possibilities opened up by liberty. It is because waiting is trying that the capacity for waiting is a necessary component of liberal character.

It is clear that readiness for waiting is a major imperative of liberal politics. Unwillingness to wait, on the part of leaders of genius and determination, lay at the source of modern totalitarianism. We are not able collectively, any more than individually, to bear ourselves wisely through our own resources alone. We are not sole authors of the historical and personal dramas through which we live. We are dependent on something from beyond — from God, Christians believe, or from the source of the unbidden insights without which human life would fall into drudgery and frivolity, if not utter ruin. Our destinies are given us. Willingness to wait is recognition of this primal feature of our condition. When that willingness vanishes, the consequences can be deadly for nations and for the whole earth. When Ivan Karamazov declares that he must have justice now, on earth — in other words, that he cannot wait — he prophetically voices the impatience that can, as the twentieth century shows, lay waste to nations in the name of progress.

CHAPTER 13

Liberty and the Last Things

———=◦(◉)◦=———

Liberty, Righteousness, and the End of History

Liberty can be fully understood only — to use a forbidding but exact term — as an eschatological concept. Eschatology, which I briefly touched upon earlier in the essay, is usually defined as the doctrine of the last things, or the end of history. I will try to elucidate the term further in the course of the discussion. Suffice it here to say that liberty has to do with living within history toward the end of history. History is not all there is; it is relativized by transcendence. It is not, however, rendered meaningless by the fact that it is destined to end. What is beyond history renders life within history tolerable, and it does this not by providing an escape from history but by giving history a final purpose and conclusion. It is a story with a fitting climax. In the Christian view, God did not call human beings out of history, but met them within history. And God will meet them again at the end of history. The purpose of this chapter is to clarify these statements.

I have emphasized throughout the preceding pages that liberty is not justified by the immediate happiness it brings. Rather, I have spoken of the ordeal of liberty. Were it an ordeal and nothing more, however, there would be nothing to recommend it. An ordeal is tolerable partly because it is a test or trial and therefore has an issue. It does not go on forever. One is carried through an ordeal by hope. Liberty, then, can provide life and joy in the degree to which it is lived with hope. Hope for what?

To speak plainly about matters that lend themselves to grandiose terminology, we are carried through the ordeal of liberty by the hope that finally all will be well — that all misunderstanding, within our own minds, and between ourselves and others, will be ended. We will find ourselves in a boundless community. None will be dead or unborn, and none strangers. No truth will be unknown. The idea of such an end, I suggest, must glimmer at least faintly in the minds of all who take on the responsibilities of liberty. It is not an esoteric sentiment, confined to a few, or difficult to attain. Yet, if fully defined, it is obviously not a modest hope. It presupposes a conquest of the moral flaws that bedevil all human striving toward truth and mutual understanding, and also an end of time in all its destructive aspects. Spokesmen for humanist reason have referred to a community thus freed of sin, time, and death with terms like "kingdom of ends" and "communist society." Augustine called it the "city of God," Jesus the "kingdom of God."

The burdens of liberty are bearable, I believe, insofar as we are able through imagination, faith, and fragmentary experience to anticipate such a community. We can inhabit a ravaged and ephemeral city with a certain serenity if we also inhabit, through hope, a better city. The key to Jesus' life and mission lay in the proclamation that the better city, the kingdom of God, is at hand. Paraphrasing Nicolas Berdyaev, historical time is always on the verge of eternity. If the significance of Jesus for Christians can be summed up in a phrase, we might say he was an eschatological figure. He dwelt at once in an earthly kingdom and in the kingdom of God, and he made it possible for all human beings in one fashion or another to do this.

Morality, as I have already argued, does not look only toward righteous actions. With near inevitability it looks toward a world in which such actions are carried out always and by everyone. It looks toward a righteous society, that is, a true community. Thus arose, with Kant, the concept of the kingdom of ends. Kant was as intensely concerned as a thinker could be with the moral law and with the obligation of every person to adhere to that law. He began, therefore, with an examination of the nature of the moral law, and with questions concerning the rectitude of particular actions and the righteousness of individuals. But this quickly led him to invoke a society in which every person is, so to speak, a moral legislator. Every person, in Kant's vision, wills, and lives in perfect accordance with, the moral law. This creates a society in which all play the role of persons, not things, and thus are not even potentially means to another end. They are ends in themselves. Kant's kingdom of ends was a forerunner of well-known ideals, such as the Hegelian state and Marxist communism. And it was a humanist version of Jesus' kingdom of God.

This is to say that moral philosophy tends to become eschatology. It looks toward the end of history. This is because there would be no history if everyone, at all times, were perfectly righteous. History presupposes human evil, and accordingly it also presupposes the absence of community. I have dealt at length with the ideal of community and with the ways we seek community. In effect, I have defined liberty as a communal — that is, moral — opportunity. Such an opportunity leads ideally to a perfect community, and this in turn brings history as we know it — involving sin, decay, and death — to an end. This is the sense in which liberty is eschatological. Well used, it calls forth the idea and vision of all-encompassing communication, uninterrupted and unending, as the culmination of earthly events. And it provides this idea and vision as a refuge and hope for free men and women living, not in the eschaton, but amid the shocks and uncertainties of history.

What does eschatology, the idea of the *end* of history, say about the nature of history in itself? That depends, of course, on the relationship of the historical end to the historical process. If the end is accidental, particularly if it comes suddenly as a catastrophic irruption into the historical process, it renders the historical process meaningless. The fear of an all-consuming nuclear catastrophe envisages such a finale. But the idea that history will sooner or later be disrupted and ended in a way that is totally unconnected with the historical process goes very much against the human grain. For humanist reason, it places worldly life under the shadow of absurdity; life governed by reason would be impossible. For faith, it suggests that human affairs are outside the control and concern of God. Reason and faith alike look for meaning in human events and circumstances. Hence thinkers of different persuasions have tried to see in history a comprehensible relationship with the purpose and final outcome of history. There are two fundamental ways of doing this.

The most direct and understandable way lies in the doctrine of progress, so widely held during the Enlightenment. History moves either directly, or through the indirection of a dialectic like Hegel's or

Marx's, toward its own end, that is, toward a perfect community. History merges gradually into its own transhistorical culmination. Here again Kant provides a ready example. Even while his main energies were absorbed in the development of his critical philosophy, he was drawn into speculation about history. Very broadly, he envisioned history as a gradual course of moral improvement reaching finally a perfect moral kingdom, a community.

The idea of progress appears at first glance to be a natural and sensible idea. Humans are reasonable and will surely learn by their mistakes and gradually bring harmony into their lives. The idea is gravely flawed, however, at least for those whose standards are moral rather than, say, technological. The righteousness of mothers and fathers is not inherited, nor can it be reliably transmitted to daughters and sons. Hence, from a moral standpoint, every generation is a fresh and formidable challenge. To put this in terms of the present essay, even if a generation of perfectly dialogic men and women could somehow come into being, thus constituting a true community, universal and egalitarian, there would be no way of assuring that the next generation would match this achievement. In short, history would not end.

Someone may object that moral progress nevertheless does occur. Laws and customs gradually become more humane. Slavery is outlawed, and racial discrimination is gradually erased from statutes and customs. There are countless instances in Western history that show society gradually becoming more humane. This must be admitted. But do human beings in themselves become more humane? Perhaps they do, for a time. But not irreversibly. There is no security in the letter. The spirit is capable of shocking lapses. It may inexplicably depart from and attack the most humane laws and customs. This is shown in the instance of Nazi Germany, a savage regime arising suddenly from a highly civilized society. The priority of the spirit over the letter again becomes evident. A people that grows more humane will produce more humane laws and customs. But the sequence cannot be reversed. Humane laws and customs do not necessarily produce humane people.

Moreover, progress is of limited significance unless it lifts from humanity the burden not only of sin but also of death. It must not only bring about perfect communality among human beings but also somehow guide them into a realm in which life is no longer overshadowed by inevitable oblivion. While human beings can enhance their longevity, however, they cannot eliminate death. That would require an ontological transfiguration we cannot even imagine. The idea of eternal life is not that of temporal life prolonged throughout endless millennia and aeons. This would be a daunting, even dismaying, prospect. It is the idea of a life qualitatively — not merely quantitatively — different from the kind we live on earth. The word "eternity" says more about value than about duration. Yet it is difficult to be clear about the nature of this value. We cannot define eternal life. Nor can we specify its relationship with temporal life on earth. How, then, can we think reasonably about the gradual merging of time into eternity, which would be the fulfillment of historical progress?

We cannot. But we cannot think about a sudden, rather than gradual, merging of time and eternity either. We cannot imagine the end of history as either a protracted or an abrupt occurrence. If this is so, then we cannot categorically reject the doctrine of progress. Since we do not understand the relations of time and eternity, we cannot know how one might pass into the other. And there is another aspect to this whole matter that makes it impossible to rule out unconditionally the doctrine of progress. I have been speaking of progress as proponents of progress usually do — as a human work — and I have pointed to the human inability to bring about gradually the end either of sin or of death. But for Christians, it is a question not of human powers but of divine powers, and who can say that God may not work gradually? In many things he obviously (for Christians) does. Typically, the doctrine of progress is a humanist idea and eschatology a religious idea. It is their very religious presuppositions, however, that bar Christians from rejecting the idea of progress conclusively.

Still, a prominent warning sign may prudently be attached to that idea. In the first place, it is apt to obscure the incomprehensibly great distance between the sinful and mortal life we live on earth, and the undefiled and immortal life human beings have always imagined. Further, progressivism is apt to call forth idolatry. If history is a process of the sort that can gradually take on the proportions of eternity, it is tempting to imagine a power on the historical plane that is more than merely human. Hegel in effect depicted the state as a divine kingdom created by earthly statesmen, and followers of Marx of course made mortal gods of the working class and the Communist Party. A final warning sign — and for some Christians this decides the matter — is that Christian scripture, at least symbolically, rejects progressivism. It depicts the end of history as a sudden and catastrophic occurrence. This does not quite settle the matter, even for Christians, for there remains the question of how literally the Gospel accounts should be taken. Few Christians by the end of the twentieth century took literally the story of God's creation of the heavens and the earth. They readily construed the six-day miracle of Genesis 1 as a mythical account of a very gradual earthly process. Obviously they might construe the eschatological miracle of the Synoptic Gospels in the same fashion. Nonetheless, for Christians and for anyone respectful of Christian wisdom, New Testament eschatology accentuates the doubts I have raised. It comes near to precluding progressivist eschatology and prescribing the alternative form.

The alternative form turns on what is sometimes called the "eschatological break." There will be a fissure between the course of history and the climax of history. Following this break there is established the kingdom of God, a perfect community. The fissure is obviously a response to the difficulties and dangers of envisioning a perfect community — a human gathering unaffected by sin and death — as a gradual development. It dramatizes the chasm between time and eternity. And because a fissure points toward intervention from without, it is seen as God's doing rather than man's. In sum, the eschatological break asserts at once a radical discontinuity between historical and eternal life and the infirmity of human beings in the face of this condition. It comports far better with the extremity of the human plight than does the gradualist and humanist vision.

It does not follow from the fissure, I must emphasize, that all preceding events are meaningless. That would imply a powerless or inattentive God, one who allowed life on earth to unfold haphazardly and aimlessly. Christian eschatology holds that history has an end that follows from, even though it is discontinuous with, the developments leading up to it. History is progressive, to be sure, and thus has meaning, but its meaning lies beyond history and depends on a transcendental agency. History leads toward and into eternal life. And while it is carried on by men and women, it is governed and completed by God. Even though not all Christian writers construe history in precisely this way, it nevertheless is very much in accord with basic Christian concepts. It is foreshadowed in Augustine and clearly articulated in the works of Reinhold Niebuhr.

Here, in the antithesis between progressivism and the eschatological break, we seem to confront an issue dividing reason and faith irreparably. It must be carefully noted that this is not mainly because of the question of social reform. It is true that eschatological images like Christ's descent to earth in clouds of glory are offensive to humanist reason and that this is partly because they seem to pronounce a sentence of irrelevance over all human efforts to reach justice and community on earth. They dramatize the "pie in the sky" so despised by secular progressives and radicals. It is true, also, that secular suspicions are partially justified by the behavior of professed Christians on earth. There is little doubt that many of them have used the supposed coming of the kingdom of God as a cover for neglecting the plight of the poor and oppressed on earth. On eschatological premises, however, such neglect is thoroughly illogical. As I have said elsewhere in this essay, those who are indifferent to community here on earth — community from which none are excluded — cannot have much genuine concern with the coming of an eternal community. It may be said that social reform, or liberation, is a matter of eschatological integrity. Conservatism finds little support in the eschatological break, which affirms the instability of all earthly things and the sovereignty of justice and community.

Nor is the issue opened up by the eschatological break owing to the total otherworldliness that concept seems to imply. A suspicious humanist will imagine someone living in hope of eternal life as living without any hope at all for temporal life. But such a suspicion is unwarranted. I have based much of my defense of liberty in this essay on the argument that liberty is necessary if values are to be freely chosen. An unavoidable premise of this argument is that authentic values are at hand to be chosen. And these values are in no way negated by eternal values. They are the same values; worldly values are glimmerings of eternal values. Taking dialogue as a standard of value, a good conversation in a coffeehouse is a presentiment of the kingdom of God. To say this does not drain the conversation in the coffeehouse of value. If anything, it brightens its value and enhances its significance.

It is not social reform, or otherworldliness, but the inescapably religious character of the eschatological break that divides faith and reason so deeply at this point. The eschatological break must clearly be of God's making, not man's. We can conceive of prolonged historical progress as a human work, and perhaps can think that millennia upon millennia of progress will so enhance human powers and bring the human race so close to the verge of perfection that the culmination of history can be a human work. But the eschatological break throws in our faces, so to speak, the vision of an event that only God could contrive. It is an uncompromising affirmation of the impenetrable mystery and the absolute finality of God's dealings with the human race. It is not immediately apparent how humanist reason can do anything but reject it.

In rejecting the eschatological break, however, reason puts itself in a difficult position. As we have seen, the bent toward eschatology — as the vision, not necessarily of an eschatological break, but of history culminating in a true community — is present, in varying degrees and ways, in all serious people. It is difficult even for skeptics to avoid at least occasional thoughts of humanity somehow eventually getting free of the endless accidents and tragedies that make up much of our earthly story. The doctrine of progress is one response. But that doctrine, aside from the flaws discussed above, puts impossible demands on patience. We must, it implies, wait during an inconceivable span of ages for the final conquest over history to be accomplished. Hence the imminent utopias and the paradisiacal fantasies that have infested the modern humanist mind. Yet these tend to either evaporate into irrelevance, as have so many socialist utopias, or be taken up in earnest and produce historical atrocities. Radically falsifying human nature and the human condition, they eventuate practically always in violence and dictatorship. This, then, is the dilemma that faces humanist reason: how to respond to the compelling urge toward an end of history without affirming an ideal that is either a historical irrelevance or an invitation to violence and chaos.

A possible answer to this dilemma — the only one visible to the author of the present essay — might be termed "the satisfied conscience." There are people whose moral convictions are strong but whose religious convictions are weak or nonexistent. They apparently find rest in the assurance simply that they have done what they ought to have done. They feel deeply the majesty of the moral law and seemingly feel that by conforming with that law they give themselves and their lives a kind of eternal validity. A Christian would be apt to respect those feelings but to argue that they are implicitly religious. They presuppose inchoate concepts of eternity and salvation. For many intelligent people, however, they are altogether secular. For such people, it might be said, history reaches a culmination in every instance of human rectitude. A good man or a good woman is a kind of earthly, inner-historical eschaton. Much of this attitude was expressed in the writings of Kant, although it did not represent his final position.

One may be reminded of the concept of personal dignity. I argued earlier in the essay that the idea of every person, however ruined in body and mind, as a possessor of absolute worth — of "dignity" — is implicitly religious. I granted, however, that irreligious people often seemed to sense this dignity just as keenly as religious people. Can we think that the perception of human dignity is in some sense eschatological, even in a secular mind — a perception of what every person ought to be, or even will be, when the whole human enterprise has ended? And if it is that, is it virtually identical with the sense on the part of a satisfied conscience that a moral person is a kind of inner-historical eschaton? It is noteworthy that the idea of personal dignity is often translated into the proposition that every person ought to be treated as an end and not merely a means. Through that proposition every person is set beyond historical calculations and thus beyond the whole network of causal connections that constitute history. This suggests that the perception of human dignity arises from the sense that a person is not properly among the means that go into the production of historical results but is, in some rationally inexplicable way, the end or purpose of history.

In any case, the chief point is simply the one already made. Liberty is eschatological. It is an opening for community, and community is a product of righteousness — of love of truth and respect for persons. The drive toward community is toward final truth, perfectly shared, and is thus a drive (whether consciously or not) beyond all earthly circumstances and beyond history. It is toward the end of history. Liberty is an ordeal because it subjects those who fully accept its conditions and obligations to all the anguish of worldly existence. It is an ordeal also in the sense of having an issue — the awareness (perhaps through Christian faith, perhaps through a satisfied conscience) of dwelling in a community more perfect and lasting than any earthly community. In this awareness is the life of liberty.

This is one of the central themes of this whole essay, and the main arguments of the essay take on full meaning only when seen in its light. For example, the essay has dealt at many points with dualities — of society and community, of faith and reason, of religion and philosophy, of church and state, of public and private. All such dualities spell inconclusiveness. They call out for some kind of resolution. But history is replete with dualities, and we cannot conceive of history without them. Hence the dualities set up an impulse toward the end of history, toward the kind of full resolution that is achieved in community. They bespeak the provisional character of all earthly arrangements and the nonfinality of every group and authority. In a word, they are proleptic, pointing beyond themselves and beyond the world.

Given its prominence in this essay, the duality of faith and reason deserves particular comment. I have stressed both the possibility and the importance of communication between faith and reason. I have also noted the frequent bigotry on both sides and the consequent failure of communication to occur. And this situation will no doubt endure. Some, as long as history continues, will seek the ultimate ground of things through faith alone, while scorning reason. Others will be inspired by powers and possibilities that are merely human, and therefore neglectful of human finitude and sin, and unconcerned with transcendence. Such is the normal state of affairs in the world. Even if normal, however, it is a moral scandal, a failure on the side both of faith and of reason to foster the universality that each professes. It propels us toward an eschatological future. It cries out for community of a kind that cannot exist in history and therefore would bring history to an end.

Similar comments are invited by the duality of community and society. It is community we seek, at least insofar as we care about truth and persons. But under the pressure of physical needs, and of our own proclivity toward objectification and domination, we continually find ourselves living in and building groups and societies. Community is not thus foreclosed. Through communication we create enclaves of community, and where there is liberty these can be indefinitely deepened and widened. If all were community, however, and society had passed out of existence, history would have ended. We can hardly avoid having an impulse toward such an eventuality even though, since it is not a practical human project, we may think little about it.

A great deal has been said about equality and universality. Both are commanded by the principle of personal dignity and by the ideal of community. For reasons already extensively discussed, however, they are beyond our reach. So long as we are living in history, we find ourselves confined within particular classes and within parochial societies. For over two thousand years the human race has repudiated such a state of things. This is why the standards of equality and universality have gained such wide currency in spite of the impossibility of their realization. We can sense here the force and tenacity of the eschatological impulse. Only beyond history might the duality of the ideal and the actual — of community and class, of cosmopolis and nation — be fully overcome.

It is now apparent why eschatology is implicit in the very idea of liberty. Liberty is our primary political need because we are aliens within earthly societies. We are aliens, in turn, because the societies we inhabit are not communities. At their best, they provide conditions — above all, liberty — that allow communication to occur. Within history, however, communication is always constricted. Historical communities are invariably fragmentary and ephemeral. Hence the dualities we have discussed. Every social group and social principle is flawed or incomplete, and thus is dialectical, giving rise to a contending group or principle. Faith and reason, community and society, state and church are not chance phenomena. They testify to the enduringly inconclusive and unsatisfactory state of man on earth. We can be lucidly free, therefore, and our minds in some measure at rest, only if we are able through faith, fugitive intuitions, and imagination to look beyond history. Free lives can involve a degree of serenity and happiness, as I suggested at the outset of this section, only if they have an eschatological cast.

It is not easy to give our lives such a cast. The end of history is literally inconceivable, for an event that brings history to an end cannot be a historical event. We can think about the extinction of the human race, but not about its passage from time into eternity. As for what follows the event, eternal life, efforts to imagine it usually tell us far more about the constricted character of human life and imagination than about eternal life. Yet, as the preceding pages have shown, thinking about the end of history is unavoidable. The tragedies of history and our thirst for values that do not melt away in the course of time render the task incumbent on us. All we can do, then, is address the task but, by leaving our images tentative and unfinished, acknowledge that the task is quixotic. It exceeds the measure of our minds.

Where can we start on so precarious a venture? Values may offer an opening. If worldly values are enhanced in eternity, not simply negated, then it seems that reflecting on those values might provide a glimpse of something we are incapable of understanding. One value has been central in this essay, that is, truth — or, speaking metaphorically, light. Liberty has been construed as primarily an opportunity to search for the light and to live in its circle. Faith and reason are for humans the two main passageways toward the light. Community is primarily a sharing in the light and in the struggle to reach it. This is because persons, so far as they are united in community, are bound together by love, and love is the perception of light. And this love sparks a further striving toward the light because the light we have in the world is never enough. It reminds us, as Christians see it, of the supreme light in which the universe has its origin and its purpose. This light is mysteriously the same as the author of the eschatological drama, and the one who at the end of the drama is at the center of the eschatological community. Accordingly, to reflect briefly on this light may provide eschatological insights of a kind.

Thomas Aquinas, for whom God is light, is a convenient vehicle for such reflection. While I am not a Thomist, Thomas's idea of truth as having value of a kind and degree that renders it divine, is of great interest in connection not only with the topic at hand but also with the whole thrust of the present essay. This, of course, is to offer a Christian version of the value of truth. It might be said, however, that if for a Christian like Thomas God is truth, for a great many people on the humanist side truth is a kind of god, the ultimate human end. Also, Thomas's Christian theology was infused with a humanist philosophy, Aristotle's. Thomas's ideas, accordingly, can be illuminating both for faith and for reason.

"God Is Light"

In one of the most familiar passages in the New Testament, John proclaims that "God is light and in him is no darkness at all" (1 John 1:5). This famous aphorism may tell us something of note about liberty. If God is light, then light — or truth — is not just an inert state of affairs waiting to be discovered. It is a kind of radiance. Its nature, to use words from John's Gospel, is to shine in the darkness. God can be thought of as generous, self-imparting light. At the same time, however, God can be thought of as free, as possessing the greatest possible measure of liberty — liberty flowing from sovereign power, hence limitless. It follows that the light of God does not emanate naturally from the divine being, as does light from the sun. It is freely given (and sometimes withheld). This is not unrelated to human nature and thus not unrelated to liberty. As everyone knows, the Bible asserts that men and women are created in "the image and likeness" of God. This suggests that the innermost nature, or the ultimate destiny, of a human being — in the eyes of faith, at least — is to receive and impart light.

The idea of God as light is the key to Thomas Aquinas's theology and philosophy. God is light first of all in the sense of possessing perfect knowledge of all reality. In God's case, however, this knowledge is a peculiar possession; it is identical with his own being. God is not a substance with certain accidental qualities, any of which might be abstracted, leaving the divine nature in essence the same. God is altogether simple — one of the propositions in Thomas's theology that humans cannot fully grasp. Hence we should say, not that God is all-knowing, or omniscient, but rather that he *is* omniscience. God *is* light. The very essence of God is a supreme resplendence, a shining — in perfect freedom — in comparison with which all else is darkness. Plato apparently had an intuition of the same kind when he likened "the idea of the Good" to the sun.

This may seem to make God a mere onlooker — contrary to the biblical picture of God as highly active, a figure of power and enterprise, and not a mere knower. But God is far from passive in Aquinas's vision. God is the single unqualifiedly real entity in existence, and whatever is real, in Aquinas's metaphysic, is act in contrast with mere potentiality. Reality does not connote passivity. Reality is the act that turns potentiality into actuality. The root of every reality is its act of being. For finite beings, that act is dependent on God, who is the primal, or supreme, act of being. Every being but God, as evident in its finitude, is less than fully actual, a mixture of actuality and potentiality. God alone is pure actuality — pure act — and thus the ultimate source of actuality for all other entities. It follows, if God's very identity lies in knowing all things, that his act of being is an act of knowing. In other words, as pure act, God is truth. But doesn't this still suggest that God is by nature a spectator?

Here we can only "see in a mirror dimly" (1 Cor. 13:12). We assume almost unavoidably that if God knows all things, that is because they are there to be known, there before he knows them. If that were the

375

case, however, God would be as humans are, dependent on observing reality in order to understand it. God would be mere potentiality, and finite. We must therefore reverse the proposition and say not that God knows things because they are there, but that they are there because God knows them. In knowing the universe, God calls the universe into existence. The light, in God's case, is creative. All things in the universe, it might be said, arise from truth. Again, Plato anticipated Aquinas with his analogy between the sun and the idea of the Good. The sun not only illuminates all things, but with its light and warmth it also enables living things to grow and flourish.

God spreads the light he is, then, by calling forth a universe of creatures, some of them living. Not only does the divine light call forth living creatures, however. It also calls forth *knowing* creatures, who possess intellects analogous to the intellect of God. These are angels and human beings. Unlike God, both confront realities that are there before they know them. Both are finite, both know only in part. Both are called, however, above all else to be faithful to the truth. Both are assigned the vocation of knowing God. Between the two, however, there is a great difference. This must be taken into account if the human state is to be understood.

Angels apprehend reality spontaneously and immediately. Human beings do so laboriously. Humans must go through a difficult process of observation and discursive reasoning to acquire such truth as they are capable of. And they are capable of relatively little. Their knowledge of particular beings and of being as a whole is always limited in scope and filtered through concepts. Still, a human being, by virtue of intellect, is "the image and likeness" of God. Intellect defines human nature and the human vocation. And while human knowledge is always on earth limited and imperfect, it is the destiny of men and women to partake finally in the fullness of divine light that Aquinas calls "the beatific vision."

This is to say that men and women are destined finally to know God. The statement that God is truth means that God is not only all-knowing but can also be fully known. The supreme intelligence is exhaustively intelligible. "Whatever can be," Aquinas writes, "can be known" (*Summa contra gentiles* 2.332). To be is to be knowable, and God is fully knowable because he is the fullness of being. While religious people often speak casually of "knowing God," it is not easy to understand what this means. How can one know a being who is not a thing in the world, like a rock, but who is an act of knowing, indeed of perfect knowing? Assuming that knowing God is possible, it cannot be like knowing a rock. It must be more like sharing in the knowledge of a highly intelligent friend, who knows far more, far better, than you do. It must be a very mysterious — "mystical" — state. What is important here, however, is not speculating about what it means to know God, but rather realizing the nature of the Christian universe, as Aquinas sees it. It is filled with light. The supreme reality is a God who is truth — in the sense of knowing all things perfectly, of being himself perfectly knowable, and of calling forth creatures with the capacity and vocation of taking in this light.

Even the most assiduous dedication to careful observation and careful reasoning, however, does not enable man to follow to its end the pathway from human darkness to divine light. Why this is so will be clear to anyone who recalls the concept of original sin. Human sinfulness does not, as we have seen, consist in a localized flaw, which might be objectively identified and then eradicated. It infects every faculty and every power. It undermines the very possibility of careful observation and reasoning. For man to seek the light, the light must shine in the darkness, and for that to happen the light must enter into the darkness. There must be a pillar of fire, like that which guided the Israelites at night during their years in the wilderness, to empower and lead the human intellect. It is the main article of Christian faith that the pillar of fire for the whole human race, and for all of human history, is Christ. In traditional Christian language, Christ is the Word of God.

For this to be comprehensible, it is necessary to note that Aquinas thinks of ideas in a different way than do most of us. The range of ideas varies, so to speak, with the metaphysical rank of those holding them. Among humans, ideas are relatively narrow, so that a broad range of knowledge requires a multitude of ideas. The ideas of angels (who can be interesting in the context of Thomist thought even to those doubtful that they exist) are broader than are those of humans. Angels not only can comprehend more than humans can; they can do this with fewer ideas. Towering over human beings and angels, God understands all reality within the scope of a single idea. This one infinite idea comprehends everything in time — past, present, and yet to come — and everything beyond time. When expressed, this idea is God's Word.

None of this implies that the ideas of angels and God are more abstract than those of human beings. On the contrary, they are more concrete. Angels know particular beings as well as universals, and God knows perfectly not only every particular being in existence but also every such being that has been or ever will be. One may gain an inkling of Aquinas's insight here by recalling the struggle we have all gone through to say a great deal without taking too much time or space, that is, in a few words. This is a struggle, it may be said, to achieve a perfect generalization, synthesizing a great deal in one or a few propositions. With God, no propositions are needed. All realities are synthesized through a more intensive and all-encompassing concentration of truth than humans can imagine. All is compressed into one idea, one "Word."

That Christ is the Word of God, the fullness of God's imparted truth, is the core of Christian faith. In one particular human being, Jesus, "the Word became flesh," that is, the whole truth became visible and present among human beings. But if God is that truth, then Christ was God incarnate. He was, and is, as John put it, the light shining in the darkness of the world. Such assertions, while assented to by most Christians, are more or less mystifying to everyone, Christians and non-Christians alike. The truth is veiled, as Karl Barth insisted, at the same time it is revealed. This is particularly evident in Jesus' crucifixion, which, as construed by Christians, presents the very strange spectacle of God as a criminal, tried in court, and put to death. And for Christians, the crucifixion was not just one final incident among many in Jesus' life. It was the core of all that Jesus had to say. The truth about human fallenness and destiny, and about divine justice and forgiveness, is all mysteriously concentrated and put before humankind in that one event.

Christians do not claim that human beings are capable all on their own of deciphering these mysteries. God must light the fire in their minds, so to speak, and he does this in the form of the Holy Spirit, which is God as the bringer of light. The Holy Spirit, it might be said, is the generosity of the transcendent light. It is inherent in this generosity that, just as light streams outward from the sun, the Word is not simply uttered and left, as it were, to float in space in case anyone notices it. It is made comprehensible by the one who utters it. It accomplishes that which God intends. Entering into human thoughts and emotions, into the human spirit, God keeps the Word alive, assuring that the darkness does not overcome it.

Everything in Christianity, it can be fittingly said, is about truth, or light. Cannot something of the same sort be said about the ideals of humanist reason? In both camps there is allegiance to truth and to the human intellect as having a crucial part in the attainment of truth. This indicates that my aim in these pages — to say something that is both distinctively Christian and universally human — is not absurd. I do not mean to deny the obvious: that faith and reason must often be in contention. As I have already granted, Christians are bound to draw apart and form circles of communication based on belief in Christ as the Word of God. Protagonists of humanist reason are bound to seek truths independent of any particular revelatory claims. But the word "enlightenment" should have resonance everywhere. Both sides see truth as an ultimate value; both sides respect reason. Where there is so much common ground, there can and ought to be communication even though there cannot be complete agreement.

Still, as we have already noted, in addition to the word "enlightenment" there is another word: "faith." Human light, as envisioned by a Christian such as Aquinas, is weak and flickering. This is a way of characterizing human fallenness. It is evident not only in the dependence of humans on sensuous observation and discursive reasoning, and on the light of revelation. It is evident also in the fact that the most important things for us to know — about the eschaton, for example — we do not know, in any strict sense of the term, and can never know in our earthly lives. Hence our dependence on faith. To be sure, through intellect much can be known. Even God, in a rudimentary way, can be intellectually known. And we can expect in the course of our lives to approach ever nearer to the truth. But knowledge adequate for guiding not only the quest for truth but also the conduct of our lives depends on divine self-disclosure. It is by faith that such disclosure is recognized and affirmed. Without revelation and faith, the human orientation toward truth would be a kind of curse, a consignment to ultimate frustration, and our lives would be carried on in a darkness far deeper than that enshrouding the children of Israel in the wilderness. So, at least, Thomas maintained, as do Christians generally.

Faith thus is a gift of inestimable worth. Yet it is only, for Thomas, a makeshift. It is far from the same as knowledge. When knowledge is gained, faith will disappear. Its function is to serve as a kind of beacon, enabling men and women to steer a course toward truth, and to carry on their lives, while still far away from the truth. Moreover, steering this course depends on human faculties, in particular on intellect. Faith does not crush human faculties but makes it possible for them to flourish. There is no conflict, therefore, between the absolute necessity of faith and the primacy of intellect. It is intellect that distinguishes human beings from animals and marks their likeness to God. It is intellect too that defines human destiny — that of becoming finite centers of light. Thomas believed that all creatures strive to be, in their own way, similar to God. Humans strive toward divine similarity by using and trying to perfect their intellectual powers. This is to say that they measure themselves by the example set by Christ, who, as the Word of God, realized the perfect unity of the human, as physically embedded intellect, and the divine, as perfect truth. Christ, the "God-man," was light made manifest.

There is obviously a strong note in Thomas of humanism. And in this connection the term "enlightenment" again comes to mind. The human vocation is to inquire into the truth and to approach as closely as possible to complete and absolute truth. The good life, for Thomas, is an intellectual life, a life devoted to thinking and cultivating insight, so far as possible in the company of others. It would be disingenuous to obscure the fact that the good life, for Thomas, is also something less universally acceptable. It is religious and is carried on in the church. Intellectual life can be what it ought to be only if it is centered on faith. But faith affirms human nature and calls forth the full use of human faculties. Followers of humanist reason clearly cannot side with Thomas in all ways. But neither can they view him as a total stranger.

Throughout this discussion, it may be said, we have been dealing with liberty. Thomas did not ordinarily use this term, but Paul, who laid the foundations of Thomas's thought, did, as when he wrote of "the glorious liberty of the children of God" (Rom. 8:21). It would have been in the spirit of the *Summa theologiae* for the name of "liberty" to be given to the search for light and to the full enjoyment of light that lies in "the beatific vision." True liberty, I have argued, lies in choosing what is supremely valuable. That, for Thomas, was the light that in its fullness is God. If intellect is the faculty of light, then humans will find liberty in the use of intellect and the pursuit of intellectual goals. "Ultimate felicity," Thomas wrote, "is to be sought in nothing other than an operation of the intellect, since no desire carries one to such sublime heights as the desire to understand the truth." This desire, he goes on to say, "does not rest until it reaches God" (*Summa contra gentiles* 3.50).

I have scarcely mentioned eschatology. Thomas did not have a strong historical consciousness. He tended to look on all reality as natural order, inwardly dynamic yet invariable in its overall structure. God was primarily the creator and governor of this order, not the overlord of history. Hence Thomas paid little attention to the idea of humanity as engaged in a great historical drama with a final end. In short, Thomas's vision is not in its overall form eschatological. Nonetheless, I believe that the picture of his thought I have presented can readily be cast in eschatological terms. The meaning of history would lie in the deepening of truth and the spread of truth over all the earth. The culmination of history would come as a burst of light. All humankind (except for those cast into the nescience of hell) would partake in the beatific vision. Granted, there would be degrees of vision. As already noted, Thomas regarded human inequality as perdurable. But even a slight share of the vision of God, to be enjoyed eternally, would be paradisiacal.

In discussing what might be summarily called the "eschatology of light," we are implicitly discussing the human situation. This is a situation illuminated by the light that is God but also overshadowed by the darkness that is sin. We must take a final glance at this situation — the setting of liberty — before concluding this essay. Christian scripture provides a convenient way of doing this. In the Gospel of John, Jesus, wearing a crown of thorns and a purple robe, and mocked by the Roman soldiers as "King of the Jews," is brought by Pilate before the Jewish priests and the crowd attracted by Jesus' arrest. Pilate pronounces him innocent of the crimes charged against him, and then exclaims, "Behold the man." The story may of course be apocryphal. In any case, Pilate's words point to Christ as a paradigm simultaneously of life carried on within the darkness of history yet illuminated and guided by the pillar of fire that is the end of history. This paradigm can help us to understand man in his eschatological existence.

"Ecce Homo"

Jesus lived, as it were, on the crest of the wave of history, and as though world events were breaking finally onto the shores of eternity. He was an eschatological figure. Jesus' orientation toward the end of history is reflected in moral proscriptions that are at once absolute and, in history, impossible: resist not one who is evil, never turn away a borrower, take no thought for tomorrow's food and lodging. Jesus' gaze seemed fixed on life of a kind that cannot be carried on in history. At the same time, his own life was shaped by a historical setting. He lived at a particular time, in a particular place, under particular rulers. And his crucifixion, at the end, was a historical event. His gaze may have been transhistorical; his life and death were historical. Such a life is necessarily paradoxical — for Jesus first of all, in turn for every human being observant in any way of the Logos. The end imposes one set of standards and experiences, history another. This can be illustrated in a variety of ways.

Estrangement and community. Jesus was, so far as we can judge, the most thoroughly communal figure in history. In the sweep and purity of his attachment to others he surpassed even Socrates. And being attached to others meant speaking with them about ultimate truth. He evidently felt bound to other human beings by a love that refused even the qualifications dictated by common sense, such as resisting an enemy. At the same time, he was, like Isaiah's suffering servant, "despised and rejected by men" (Isa. 53:3), and at the violent end of his life was forsaken and alone. The cross is a symbol of extreme personal isolation.

Tribulation and joy. To be oriented toward the end of history is to fit only uncomfortably, or even not at all, into the roles offered by one's society and time. It is consequently to be exposed to scorn, threat, and assault. We can only think of Jesus as vulnerable and afflicted. Yet to suffer from historical conditions, while anticipating a paradisiacal culmination of history, is to be glad in the midst of tribulations. Thus Paul, as a greatly afflicted follower of Jesus, writes of rejoicing in his sufferings, of glorying in his infirmities, and of being strong when he is weak. At the source of such self-contradictory experiences there was manifestly Paul's absolute certainty of the eternal life that had, in Christ, come upon him and upon all the world.

Death and life. A reader of any of the Gospels is conscious of Jesus as a doomed man. Everyone knows that his life was carried on under the shadow of the coming crucifixion, and Jesus apparently was keenly aware of this all the time. But everyone knows too that Jesus was destined not only for crucifixion but also — at least in the Christian creed — for resurrection. And these were not disconnected or contradictory phenomena. Only through dying could Jesus live. Jesus was not purely and simply immortal, in the Christian understanding. He was destined to die and only by dying to gain everlasting life. Everyone of course lives, like Jesus, under the shadow of death, for awareness that one must die is constant in the life of every mature person. In Christian faith, however, such awareness need not be morbid, for by passing through the valley of death one can emerge into life. Thus Paul described his own state, and that of his followers, when he spoke of them as "dying, and behold we live" (2 Cor. 6:9).

Guilt and innocence. This paradox is necessarily manifest in a different way in the life of Jesus, the savior, than in the lives of the saved. Jesus was not guilty, as presented in the New Testament, and did not need to be forgiven. He did, however, voluntarily bear the guilt of the human race. He took on the sins of all other human beings and was punished as though he himself had committed those sins. He was, it might be said, although actually innocent, voluntarily guilty. What made him the savior of the world was that by his voluntary guilt he made his own innocence available to all humanity. Just as Jesus became voluntarily guilty, human beings at large, while actually guilty, could through faith become voluntarily innocent.

We gain some sense of how guilt in all its squalor and anguish may be extinguished by grace when we note again that guilt is sometimes seen in the Bible as a stepping-stone to something better than pure, never-defiled innocence. Just as life, gained through death, might have a luster that a life unvaryingly eternal would not have, so innocence entered into through guilt has a glory that, inborn, enduring innocence would lack. Hence the Old Testament blessing on anyone "whose transgression is forgiven, whose sin is covered," and the New Testament exultation over the sheep lost and then found.

Darkness and light. This — the master paradox, so to speak — relates to all the main evils we have discussed. To be deprived of community is to dwell in darkness; to suffer is to be oppressed by darkness; to die is to enter into seemingly total darkness; to be guilty is to embrace the darkness. In all of these is the darkness of history. But the destined end of history casts light into the darkness. Thus a person standing eschatologically is a singular figure — someone singled out, as it were, by light (which, as Saint John of the Cross asserted, is often seen by those habituated to the world as darkness). Ordinary Christians are here in a different position than Jesus was. According to the Gospel of Matthew, they are, unlike Jesus, "poor in spirit" (Matt. 5:3), at times mistaking light for darkness. Jesus, as understood by Christians, far from being poor in spirit, was the light of the world. But Jesus too inhabited a paradox, that of seeing the light — even being the light — in the midst of darkness. Such ways of speaking are redolent of Christian experience. But they do not pertain just to Christians. As I have said so often, Christ was the Logos, hence not entirely outside the range of reason. People of varying religious and philosophical persuasions may perceive that life within history is by its very nature dark and incomplete, yet in some measure illuminated and meaningful.

All such paradoxes dictate a dialectical course of personal and historical development — from estrangement to community, from tribulation to joy, from death to life, from guilt to innocence, from darkness to light. We can see the nature of the dialectic by contrasting it with the teleological view of human development. In the latter, the self is concealed in the infant but will gradually emerge in the mature man or woman. The embryo of a coming utopia — for example, Marx's proletariat — is confined, yet destined to grow, within the womb of an oppressive society. The determining force is natural growth, aided by human educational or political efforts. While teleology can be construed dialectically (for example, adolescence in some sense "contradicts" childhood), the process of development is relatively continuous. Christianity does not altogether preclude teleology, as is illustrated by as great and influential a Christian philosopher as Aquinas. It holds, however, that self and community are confined not only by natural immaturity but also by sin, and that owing to sin the worldly self and the established society are doomed. This view renders the discontinuities of personal and social growth sharper, and the dialectic thus more conspicuous, than is usual in teleology. And the saving of the self and the emergence of community depend not only on natural growth but also on grace. Such grace comes, as Christians see it, through the crucifixion and resurrection of Jesus, and imposes a dialectical pattern on the lives of all who live their liberty by looking for the light.

All of us in one degree or another resist that pattern and fight to remain in the darkness of the world. We may be acutely conscious of our estrangement, our vulnerability, our mortality, and other such conditions. But few are steadily confident of being destined to inhabit an eternal community. It is difficult for us to imagine a life free of the limits and perils of historical circumstances. On the whole, moreover, we do not want such a life. We do not want to abandon the world and time. That is what it means to be fallen. We are far more at home among things than among persons. Our reason is habituated to dealing with things and our natural desires amount to a lust for things. As the Gospels so often and in so many ways assert, human beings on earth love the darkness and hate the light. How, then, can the journey to the light ever be accomplished? Only with the dissolution and re-creation of the natural self.

Christianity holds, of course, that this comes about in Christ's crucifixion and resurrection. But this event profits us only if it engages us. Grace does not grant us the luxury of being saved merely by looking on. The Christ story has to be lived, not just told. "He who finds his life will lose it," Jesus declares in the Gospel of Matthew, "and he who loses his life for my sake [that is, for the sake of the life offered by Christ] will find it" (Matt. 10:39). And in the Gospel of John, Jesus says that "unless a grain of wheat falls into the earth and dies, it remains alone; but if it dies, it bears much fruit." And in a particularly pungent declaration he adds, "He who loves his life loses it, and he who hates his life in this world will keep it for eternal life" (John 12:24-25). Particularly to be noted is the order of events. Prior to the resurrection is the crucifixion. Professed Christians often claim to have been "born again." But they take little notice sometimes of the fact that being born again means, in a Christian context, being raised from the dead, and for that to happen you have to die. They aspire to share in the resurrection but not in the crucifixion. Both the Gospels and the letters of Paul say, in various ways, that this cannot be done. Humans can, to be sure, pass beyond the mortality and guilt inherent in historical existence — but not altogether easily and pleasantly. The only passageway through history and into eternity is the one symbolized by the cross.

Our one consolation, a large one, is that ordinary humans do not have to endure the terror and agony of the primeval experience, the experience endured by Jesus. He was, so to speak, the first one through the straight and narrow way. He was starkly alone, abandoned not only by his disciples but even by God. But he suffered his ordeal as "the son of man" — humanity incarnate. The rest of us can therefore face the ordeal in the confidence that in some sense it is already behind us. "It is finished" are Jesus' dying words in the Gospel of John (19:30). Something like this is conveyed also by Paul's exclamation that he has been crucified with Christ but still lives (Gal. 2:20). And finally, the author of Colossians declares that "you have died, and your life is hid with Christ in God" (Col. 3:3).

The eschatological paradigm, while delineated with unique authority and clarity in the life and death of Christ, is not confined to Christian sources. I have already referred to the same paradigm as found in the "suffering servant" passages of Jewish scripture. And in the Greek world there was an actual human being, Socrates, whose life and death can readily be construed according to an eschatological pattern.

Socrates was a thoroughly historical figure. We know when and where he lived, we know how he dressed and what he looked like, and we know the places he frequented and the people he talked with. We know him too as a participant in the events of his time. He fought in the Peloponnesian War and engaged in more than one life-threatening altercation with the authorities of his native city. He was both incurably sociable and unremittingly serious. He was an inveterate conversationalist, being found daily in the marketplace and gymnasium. But he turned conversation invariably into philosophic and moral inquiry. He lived the life his situation as a fifth-century Athenian gave him to live, yet he did this far from casually. His life was a mission. He lived and died for the sake of the philosophical conversations — each one a foray in a lifelong quest for truth — that he carried on in public places.

It was those conversations, and the death to which they led, that gave Socrates' life its eschatological accent. Not that Socrates thought in terms of history or the end of history. But the road to truth was a road into eternity. Socrates pursued his conversations knowing that they might cost him his life, as they eventually did. His final afternoon was filled with what can be readily seen as eschatological light. He devoted it, while waiting for sunset, when the executioner with the hemlock would appear, to a long and searching discussion of the immortality of the soul. Socrates showed forth clearly the singularity and the imperturbability of one standing on the thin line between history and eternity. He showed that an eschatological stance, or something very much like it, can be sustained by protagonists of humanist reason.

Eschatology is a forbidding and difficult topic. This is why so many, even among those skilled in abstract thought, refuse to entangle themselves in it. Yet liberty is one of the most common and least esoteric of all ideals, and if thought through to the end, as I have tried to show, it is eschatological. Liberty is demanded by personal responsibility, which is a kind of fidelity to ultimate values. The highest of these values is truth, or light, universally shared. This is a vision beckoning men and women into community and thence to a place where there are no shadows, a place beyond history. As forbidding as the topic of eschatology may be, reflection on liberty leads to it inexorably. The idea of the end of history is no less implicit in the sense of personal responsibility than is the idea of liberty itself.

Still, it may be that the eschatological stance, or something rather like it, can be described in terms less recondite, and closer to common sentiments, than some of those used in the preceding paragraphs. Eschatology is largely a matter of hope.

Liberty and Hope

To enter fully into the life of liberty is to forswear all worldly security and certainty — that which comes from an ostensibly infallible leader, for example; or from a great and unfailing association, like a nation or a party; or from a doctrine or philosophy taken to be unquestionably true; or from past deeds seen as so manifestly and thoroughly good that they provide assurance of justification. To be free is to be, in a sense, out in space, without visible support. It is, to take a phrase from earlier discussions, to live an unsheltered life. Hence the ordeal of liberty.

Christians who laud "God and country," and speak of a stable, integrated family as the one proper setting for a righteous life, are wrong. They are prescribing a sheltered life. Jesus did not. His fidelity to Israel was distant from idolatrous nationalism. As for family, he forecast that his ministry would fracture families and he ruthlessly bade his followers to be ready to abandon sons and daughters, and mates and parents, for his sake. And the temptations besetting him in the wilderness all had to do with outward, visible things — power, miracles, bread — that might provide illusions of shelter, thus inducing people to evade the ordeal of liberty. Jesus was aware that he could relieve people of the burden of having to think, of having to choose and freely sustain their faith, and of having to be responsible for the course of their own lives. This he might do by telling them with dictatorial finality what to believe and how to live; by numbing their rational powers with spectacular miracles; and by providing them with a stultifying degree of material security. Jesus was tempted to do these things, but refused. In his refusal he called on all of his authentic followers, and indirectly the whole of the human race, to enter into the ordeal of liberty.

No one can endure this ordeal without hope. Hope is the key liberal virtue. No doubt faith of some sort is prior to hope. The kind of transcendental assurance exemplified by Paul (and manifest often in the lives of non-Christians, and apparently missing sometimes from the lives of Christians) is at the ground of every free life. Such assurance may be given the name of faith. But when it enables one to face the anxieties and disappointments inevitable in the course of an unsheltered life, and to live in time, it is known as hope. Hope is confidence in the ultimate outcome of personal and historical events. It does not say "probably," but rather "assuredly." It is expectancy — based on faith. This is why, in defiance of probabilities, it can be "hope against hope." Love also is in some sense prior to hope. Paul said this unequivocally in his great hymn to charity in his first letter to the Corinthians. But love envisions a person not only as the one he is at the moment but also as the one he is destined to be eternally, at the end of time. In short, love is an eschatological vision, and in that sense hope is prior to love.

Hope enables human beings to live with purpose and with good spirits in spite of worldly uncertainty and insecurity. This is to say that it enables people to live without idols — without ostensibly infallible and omnipotent leaders, outside of deified parties, races, and nations, independently of philosophies and doctrines claiming exemption from criticism or question. When Jesus resisted the temptation to issue absolute commands, perform miracles, and supply bread, he refused to open up an exit from the human situation. In this way he impelled human beings to learn how to live with hope. Hope is assurance that even though our state in the world is unsheltered, in the universe as a whole we are engaged in a destiny. We should therefore not lose heart.

Today the exploitation of human weaknesses for the sake of riches and fame cultivates a trait at the opposite pole from hope, that is, absorption in the present moment. People are lured into devoting themselves to pleasure, entertainment, and recreation. In none of these is there concern with the future, hence in none is there hope. To be lacking in hope, however, is to be in despair, although despair can for a time be quiet and scarcely recognized. It can easily cohabit with worldly pleasures. It is likely that many Americans at the beginning of the third millennium, immersed in a variety of pleasures and distractions, are living in a state of inconspicuous despair. As shown by the fate of the Weimar Republic, however, the inconspicuous despair of a democratic populace may suddenly become very conspicuous. If hope is the key liberal virtue, despair is the most dangerous liberal failing. To bear the responsibility of living a life unsheltered by bread, miracles, or absolute authority, there must be assurance concerning distant prospects, both one's own and the world's. There must, in a word, be hope.

Hope is usually for something that may happen in a day, or a month, or a year. It is temporal. However, it is delusory — quiet despair disguised as hope — unless it envisions something eternal as well. Unless it looks beyond temporal satisfactions, it cannot help asking a question fatal to hope. I have noted the question earlier in this essay: After what I hope for has been attained, and has passed away, then what? If that question is fully faced, within the confines of temporal hope, what had seemed to be hope melts away. It is suddenly obvious that every historical achievement, however satisfying and impressive, is doomed by time. Hence the situation of a creature without eternal hope, yet able and inclined to ask relentlessly, "Then what?" is patently hopeless. This is to say that anyone with a clear mind, but no hope for anything beyond the world and history, must live in despair. Since the ability to look beyond everything finite is inherent in human nature, anyone may at any time suddenly face the excruciating little question, "Then what?" and thus come suddenly face-to-face with the issue of eternity.

Humanist reason has long scoffed at such ideas. However, insofar as the humanist critique of religious hope is aimed at our very concern for eternal life, it is radically false to human nature. It mocks the transcendental powers that belong to the essence of our humanity. The abject failure of Marxism in practice is not unrelated to its falsification of human nature and its consequent falsification of human hope. In spite of its ostentatious "materialism" — supposedly a stern way of seeing reality as it is — it was oblivious of real human beings. And the hope it offered its followers was in reality a form of despair.

Often, moreover, humanist reason has been oblivious not only of human nature, but also of the way an eternal hope can arise, without any conscious religious faith, from certain temporal realities. Various common experiences convey an impression of things imperishable. Perhaps no one encounters a work of great beauty, such as the Parthenon, or the Ninth Symphony of Beethoven, or a painting by Matisse, without sensing something outside the stream of time. And despite the casual professions of moral relativism that were so common in the twentieth century, there may be no one who denies that some deeds are admirable, that some are vile, and that the difference is mysteriously significant — not to be effaced by the ultimate oblivion into which they are supposedly passing. Most important of all, perhaps, is the way love bestows, or discovers, immortality. There are few, if any, who have not loved another person and have not, at least in their subterranean minds, regarded the loved person as something more than a passing temporal phenomenon.

Needless to say, temporal hope must be guarded. While there is meaning in temporal life, there is no fulfillment. Yet even the most guarded temporal hope, illuminated by eternal hope, can be vital to the life of liberty. This is evident in the way it can be focused on every coming moment. Time, both in personal lives and in the history of nations, is punctuated by disclosures of meaning. Every value — every manifest truth, every intuition of beauty, every beloved countenance — can be a foreshadowing of eternity. True hope, even though focused on eternity, is attentive to time. It is watchful of passing moments. Intimations of eternity are momentary possibilities. Thus the eschatological character of hope should not mislead us into thinking that a hopeful person surveys the ages and meditates on ultimate things but ignores present realities and responsibilities. Every day is a day that the Lord has made, according to one of the most moving of the Psalms, and ought to be an occasion of rejoicing and gladness (Ps. 118:24).

Hope, as Christians see it, is the power, given by grace, of living in response to the destiny that gives meaning and glory to every life. Through this power the discontents and torments that plague the life of liberty can be kept in bounds. To sense that one's life conforms with a transcendental story is to taste what Paul called "the peace of God, which passes all understanding" (Phil. 4:7). As an orientation toward eternity, hope is indefeasible. Temporal disappointments can always be surpassed and hope renewed. Hope can recover even from happenings so traumatic that one's life is engulfed momentarily in darkness. In the Christian mind, indeed, the greatest evils may call forth the greatest hope. The wellspring of hope, in the Christian vision, is the crucifixion. That event, at the moment, marked an ultimate abyss of suffering and hopelessness. Yet it was transfigured in the resurrection and became the decisive event in the destiny of the entire human race. Given that destiny — which is accessible not to Christians alone but to all human beings — life can be without fear, and where there is no fear, there can be freedom.

Index

Abortion, 334

Action: as evil, 342-43; liberation as a standard of, 344-45; limits on the possibilities of, 342-44; obligation to engage in, 341-45; and social transformation, 344-45; and unintended consequences, 342; and waiting, 360-61

Alexander of Macedon, 116

American Revolution, 39, 345, 361

Anarchism, 50, 132, 311, 315

Angels, 376-78

Antinomies: Christian, 203-5; Kantian, 201-3

Aquinas, Thomas, 3, 5, 8, 208, 306; and authority, 267; "beatific vision," 257, 303, 376, 380; and courage/fear, 183-84; and eschatology, 381; and God as light/truth, 374-81; and the human being as microcosmic, 289; and mystery of personal dignity, 143; and ontological grounds of inequality, 192; and value of truth, 71

Arendt, Hannah, 255-56, 258, 263, 294, 295, 343

Aristotle, 1; case against final withdrawal, 154-55; and character, 182; idealization of citizen life in the polis, 45, 154-55; and inequality, 59; and personal dignity, 109, 117; the state and society, 336; and the value of truth, 71-72

Atheism, 6, 16, 24, 35, 119, 145, 157, 211, 236, 273, 307

Atomization of society, 38-45, 166-67; ambiguity of, 43; and the disconnected individual, 38-45; and group loyalty/political activity, 44-45; industrial capitalism and evil, 42, 43; and moral/cultural relativism, 40-41; and pride, 43, 45; and radical individualism, 38-40

Augustine, Saint, 8, 288; and dialogue, 198; and eschatology, 364, 368; and freedom, 65, 242; and human damnation, 11, 12, 13, 15; and liberty, 3, 29; and original sin, 31; and personalism, 101-2; and tolerance/love of neighbor, 242; two cities, 12, 98, 364; and value of truth, 71; on whether non-Christians can be good people, 17

Authority: and the creation of com-

tal, 315-16, 321, 328, 339-40; and
personal dignity, 320-35, 339-40;
and rebellion, 339, 340; the rule of
enforceability, 331-35; the rule of
expediency, 320, 324, 326-27, 330-
31, 335; the rule of liberality, 324-
29; the rule of proportionality, 329-
31; the rule of universality, 320-24;
and "self-regarding" acts, 317-19,
325, 335; and society/community,
335-40; and standards of order,
325-26

Communality/the communal stance:
and charity/assistance to others,
165, 167; as civil stance, 169; and
communication, 27, 81-82, 153-54,
162-66, 167-68, 240, 253-54; and
critics of liberalism, 166-67; and
history, 282; and human uniqueness, 164; and Jesus' concept of
neighbor, 170, 176-77; liberal ideal
and communal ideal, 167; and the
liberal stance, 162-71; as paradoxical, 170-71; past economic obstacles to, 168; popular culture and
sin as obstacles to, 168; and universality, 169-70, 253-54

Communication: and action, 165-66,
295; attentiveness/listening, 167;
and authentic community, 163;
and charity/assistance, 165, 167;
and communality/the communal
stance, 27, 81-82, 153-54, 162-66,
167-68, 240, 253-54; and community, 188-89, 194; and creativity,
163-64; and justice, 165; and participation in history, 292-96, 373;
and personal dignity, 165;
personhood and the capacity for
speaking/listening, 101; and pornography, 248; and tolerance, 223-
24, 229, 239-40. See also Dialogue/
the dialogic ideal

Communism, 36, 139, 143, 144, 147,
159, 227, 273, 276, 289, 325, 367
Community: and communication,
188-89, 194; distinction between
society and, 81-82, 173-74, 336-37;
history and the consummate, 296-
99; and light, 374; and rule of
enforceability, 332-33; and society,
372; and tolerance, 226, 228, 235,
240. See also Communality/the
communal stance
Confessions (Augustine), 102
Conformity, 50-55. See also Freedom,
flight from
Conservatism, 59, 142, 159, 313, 369
The Consolations of Philosophy
(Boethius), 261-62
Constitutionalism, 131-32
Courage, 183-84
Creativity, 163-64, 234
Critique of Pure Reason (Kant), 201,
216, 277-78
Crucifixion of Christ, 385-86; and
Christ as the Word of God, 378;
and destiny, 284; and eschatology,
382-83, 385-86; and forgiveness,
93-94, 151; and hope, 391; and justification, 93-94; and paradoxes of
historical/transhistorical in Jesus,
382-83; and personal dignity, 251;
and rebirth/re-creation of humanity, 355, 357; and redemption, 217;
and suffering, 93-94, 186, 350

Darwin, Charles, and Darwinism, 8-9,
288
Declaration of Independence, 39, 110
The Decline and Fall of the Roman Em-
pire (Gibbon), 260
Democracy: and the dialogic ideal,
220-21; and liberty, 39; Plato's cri-
tique of, 50
Descartes, René, 102
Destiny, 120-28; and Christian subor-